Homemade Money

Bringing in the Bucks

Also By Barbara Brabec

HOMEMADE MONEY
How to Select, Start, Manage, Market & Multiply
the Profits of a Business at Home

CREATIVE CASH
How to Profit from Your Special Artistry, Creativity,
Hand Skills, and Related Know-how

THE CRAFTS BUSINESS
ANSWER BOOK & RESOURCE GUIDE
Answers to Hundreds of Troublesome Questions About
Starting, Marketing & Managing aHomebased Business
Efficiently, Legally & Profitably

HANDMADE FOR PROFIT
Hundreds of Secrets to Success
in Selling Arts & Crafts

MAKE IT PROFITABLE
How to Make Your Art, Craft, Design, Writing or
Publishing Business More Efficient, More Satisfying,
and More Profitable

Homemade Money
Bringing in the Bucks

A Business Management and Marketing Bible for Home-Business Owners, Self-Employed Individuals and Web Entrepreneurs Working from Home Base

By Barbara Brabec

Featuring low-cost marketing success tips from nearly a hundred business pros, an encyclopedia A-to-Z "Crash Course" in Home-Business Management, and hundreds of print and online resources to help your business grow

M. Evans and Company, Inc.

New York

M. Evans and Company, Inc.
216 East 49th Street
New York, New York 10017

Library of Congress Cataloging-in-Publication Data

Brabec Barbara.
  Homemade Money: Bringing in the Bucks / Barbara Brabec
    p. cm.
  The new edition of Homemade money separated into two books: Homemade money : starting smart and Homemade money : bringing in the bucks. The later picks up where the earlier left off.
  "A business management and marketing bible for home-business owners, self-employed individuals and web entrepeneurs working from home base"—Added t.p.
  ISBN 1-59077-001-3
  I. Home-based business--Management. 2. Handicraft—Marketing. I. Title.
  HD62.7.B6839 2003
  658'.041--dc21

Printed in the United States of America

Designed and typeset by Evan Johnston

10   9   8   7   6   5   4   3   2   1

Dedicated to the Memory of
William J. Schaumburg

Unlike his children, my father did not have the benefit of a good education. Yet he was smart enough to teach himself what he needed to know to make a living, first as a farmer and, later, as an auto mechanic and repairman who never met anything mechanical he couldn't figure out.

With little more than talent, determination, and a belief in himself, he built his own home and garage business in the small farming community of Buckley, Illinois, where he lived until he died in 1982.

As children, my two sisters and I did not realize that our father, by example, was quietly instilling in each of us his work ethic and entrepreneurial spirit, but as three entrepreneurial women, we certainly know it now.

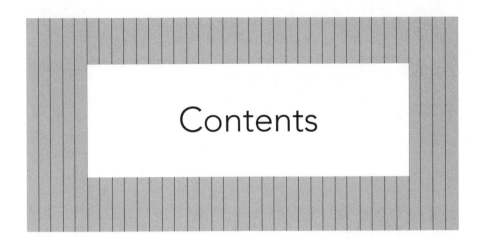

Contents

Section I

1

Dreams Versus Reality   7

Coping with Interruptions • Home-Business Perks • Positive Workaholism • Honing Your Sense of Humor

2

Time, Space, and Help Concerns   17

Solutions for the Lack-of-Time Problem • Addressing Lack-of-Space Problems • Getting the Help You Need • Alternatives to Hiring Help • Using Lists to Stay in Control

3

Financial Considerations   37

Balancing Management and Marketing Tasks • Doing Regular Business Analyses • Understanding the Break-Even Point • Reconsidering Your Pricing Strategies • Coping with Ever-Increasing Costs of Doing Business • Handling Lack-of-Money Problems • Collection Strategies

Section II

Acknowledgments

I am indebted to the many business professionals who, through the years, have made special contributions to earlier editions of *Homemade Money* and this new book as well. In particular, I wish to thank attorney Mary Helen Sears, specialist in copyrights, patents, and trademarks for her help in ensuring that all my information on these topics has always been accurate and up to date. I also owe special thanks to CPA Bernard Kamoroff for his help in checking the accuracy of my information on tax deductions, accounting, and other related business content. The time and talent of these professionals, so generously contributed, has benefited all of us.

My thanks, too, to the countless home-business owners and other business professionals in my network who have been sharing their experiences and expertise with me through the years so I could pass the information along to my readers.

Finally, a special nod of gratitude to my husband, Harry (last on the list, as usual). Now retired, his help with my business for more than twenty years made all the difference in my ability to find extra time for writing books. Today, his support for my work and his sense of humor continue to make the difference between a good day and a bad one.

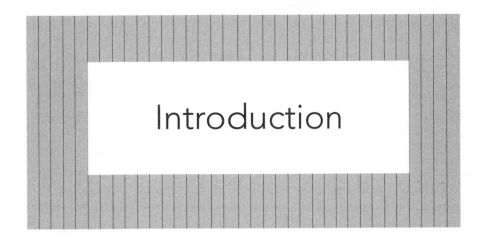

Introduction

Millions of Americans are generating income—I call it "homemade money"—from an incredible variety of homebased activities. This book is one of two Homemade Money guides that explain how to get in on the action and maximize profits from a business at home.

These two books—a dynamic duo!—are actually the second generation of my home-business bible, *Homemade Money*, published in 1984. Between 1984 and 1997, I updated or completely rewrote this book five times to ensure that readers had the best information possible, each time adding additional content until the book was practically bulging at the seams. (Weighing in at nearly two and a half pounds, the last edition was the heftiest home-business bible ever published, with more than 120,000 copies sold.)

By 2001, after my first intense year of writing for the Web and launching my own Web site, I finally understood how the Internet was dramatically changing both the home-business industry and the lives of those involved in it. Once again, I was ready to write a totally new edition of *Homemade Money*, but—surprise!—the publisher was no longer interested in the book. Frankly, I was stunned by this lack of interest at a time when people were losing jobs every day for one reason or another. The failure of so many dot-com businesses in 2000, followed by the September 11 terrorist attack and the 2001 recession convinced me and another publisher, M. Evans, that thousands of people needed a new edition of my home-business bible. Because of all the new Internet/Web-related content I now needed to add to the book, however, it was necessary to turn my old home-business bible into two new *Homemade Money* guides.

Whereas *HOMEMADE MONEY: Starting Smart* is aimed at home-business beginners (see page 393 for detailed content information), *HOMEMADE MONEY: Bringing in the Bucks*, picks up where book one left off. It's directed to established business owners who need help to grow their business and improve profitability. Its focus is on how to find and keep customers or clients through better marketing and PR strategies; how to expand a product line, add new services, or diversify into new business areas; how to do business on the Web, improve business management skills, handle employee/independent contractor issues, maximize profits, and much more.

Both books are a reflection of my lifetime of business experience coupled with that of thousands of other professionals who have shared information with me through the years. Trial-and-error experience is a great way to learn, but it can be quite expensive in terms of both time and money. Fortunately, there is no need for you to learn everything the hard way, because so many people are willing to share the benefit of their experience with you. This book is but one example. In both of my *Homemade Money* guides you'll find inspiration and ideas from many business owners, authors and other experts in my network who have "been there, done that." Something that makes these books especially valuable is the fact that many of the business owners and experts quoted or featured in them are people whose businesses I have been tracking for twenty years or more. In fact, many of them launched their businesses with an early edition of *Homemade Money* or one of my other books, then went on to share information I added to later editions. How they grew and overcame obstacles, generated new business, changed directions, or went on to do other things entirely is the kind of real home-business history you won't find in other books in this field.

An added feature of both *Homemade Money* books is the inclusion of the Web site addresses (URLs) for most business owners quoted. (For the sake of simplicity, in all cases the "www" has been omitted from contributors' addresses in the text.) In generating my list of interview prospects, I was pleasantly surprised to find that nearly everyone had one or more Web sites now—something that wouldn't have been true a couple of years ago. As you identify with different business owners featured in the book, you can go

Preface

directly to their Web sites to get a visual example of their business and see exactly how they're operating. (If you e-mail them, tell them you read about them in *Homemade Money*—but please don't ask any of these busy professionals to give you free advice by e-mail.)

Don't tackle this book with the idea that you need to absorb all of it in one sitting; rather, think of it as an idea stimulator and answer book you can turn to for help as you continue to develop or diversify your homebased business or other self-employment venture. For additional information and support, visit my Web site at BarbaraBrabec.com and join my network by adding your e-mail address to my subscription list for *The Brabec Bulletin*.

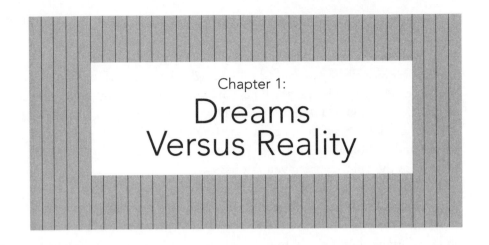

Chapter 1:
Dreams
Versus Reality

Always expect calamity. Then when a mere misfortune arrives,
it's good news.
— from *Timothy's Game* by Lawrence Sanders

To be able to work at home . . . oh, how idyllic it sounds! At last you'll able to get up in the morning when you feel like it, instead of being forced out of bed by a nagging alarm clock. You'll don your most comfortable robe, fix breakfast, and leisurely peruse the morning paper over a second cup of coffee. You might even work in your pajamas for awhile, just for the heck of it. You'll stroll down the hall to your beautifully appointed home office or studio, turn on your state-of-the-art computer to download your e-mail, and settle in for another satisfying day of doing what you love most and do best. Oh, how you pity those friends of yours who are stuck in their going-nowhere-nine-to-five jobs, still trying to find the right day care center for their kids and struggling to keep their blood pressure under control as they commute to and from work each day.

Is this how you imagined things when you started your business? Yes, it truly *is* a blessing to be able to work at home, but does this make for an idyllic life? Not exactly. I'm sure you enjoy the luxury of being able to get up when you feel like it, especially if you worked till midnight the night before to meet a pressing deadline. But how many times have you settled for only a few hours of sleep because you had so much to do? How often do you grab a high protein bar or skip breakfast altogether, getting by on three cups of coffee instead and grabbing a peanut butter sandwich or cup of yogurt for lunch because it's the quickest thing you can fix?

You've probably decided that pajamas are okay for late-night work, but you really feel better if you get dressed for work during the day in comfy jeans, T-shirt, and tennis shoes. You've spent time making your workplace attractive and comfortable, but if it's like mine, it's often so messy with work-in-progress and files strewn everywhere that you can hardly appreciate the artwork you've hung. And those lovely bookshelves that used to hold only books are now a catchall for whatever doesn't fit anywhere else. What you probably need is another room twice the size of your present workplace, but you're stuck in your present home, so you know you must get organized and learn how to better use the space you've got. (More on this topic in the next chapter.)

Coping with Interruptions

If you've been in business even for a few months, you've already learned that just because you're at home, you're subject to constant interruptions all day long—from the phone; the doorbell; your children, friends, or relatives; the demands of pets; even your home appliances and office equipment. Because you're the one who's at home, you get to walk the dog, entertain repairmen, run errands, and do the weekly grocery shopping. Often, when you're totally involved in work, a friend or relative who doesn't have to work and thinks there is something wrong with you because you're not working a job like everyone else decides to phone or, worse, pops in for a "quick cup of coffee" that steals an hour of your precious time. Sure, you needed to discuss a couple of things, but couldn't it have waited until Saturday? You decide you're going to have to get tough with your family and friends and make them realize that your time is not your own just because you work at home. But how can you do this without getting everyone upset?

Dreams Versus Reality

It's ironic how often your best-laid plans for work are ruined. You may turn on your computer, preparing to print out a report you need today only to discover that your ink cartridge has run dry, and you forgot to buy a spare last week when you were at the office supply store. Now you'll have to run out and pick up a cartridge before you can do anything. It's unbelievable how bad the traffic is this time of morning. *Stress!* Just what you're trying to avoid. You decide to start ordering supplies from a company that will deliver them to your door.

Although every interruption breaks your intense concentration and work stride, you've learned how to "go with the flow." You have noted, though, that you're getting up and down a lot as you move from one work center to another during the day. This may be good exercise, but it could also be a great time waster. Maybe you'd be more efficient if you rearranged your work centers so the things you use more are closer at hand. Hmmm . . .

After a five-minute break over that lunch you practically inhaled, you wash it down with another cup of coffee, dash downstairs to throw in a load of laundry, and quickly return to work, hardly missing a beat. But when you go down later to toss the first load into the dryer, you discover the drain sink has overflowed because it was full of lint. What the basement drain didn't catch has soaked a couple of rugs and boxes that need emptying, and there goes another hour of your precious time. But, hey, this is a piece of cake when you remember that, a few months earlier, you had to mop water for seventeen hours straight as it poured in around the foundation during what would later be called one of those "hundred year" floods. That cost you a week's worth of time and threw your back out to boot, but it would have cost even more if you hadn't been there in your home office with a shop vac nearby when the problem began. At least the whole basement didn't flood. No question about it . . . working at home can be a real blessing!

> You know you're moving up in the world when you move your home office from the basement to a bedroom on the first floor.

Home-Business Perks

You're well aware of all the special perks associated with running your own business at home. Being your own boss has certainly increased your self-esteem, confidence, and feelings of self-worth. You're home all day, so you're there for your family when they need you, whether it's the kids, a sick or disabled spouse, or aging parents. You may have interruptions, but you're still in control of your own time and working hours and your chances of being burglarized are nil. You're especially grateful that you no longer have to face other commuters on trains or buses, or fight for a seat in the restaurant at lunchtime. You're happy to be able to work in the most comfortable clothes and know that the office is just a few steps away. You love being able to spend more time with your dog or cat (even if it is a constant struggle to keep the cat off your computer keyboard). You can choose your own kind of background music or work in silence if you prefer. Best of all, by working at home you're saving a fortune on clothes, lunches out, transportation expenses, and day care costs.

Gee, five o'clock already? Where did the time go? Funny how time used to drag when you worked a day job, but in your own business, the time seems to evaporate. Your nine-to-five counterparts are now on their way home, but you haven't begun to accomplish half the things on your to-do list today and you hate to stop work . . . but "life" beckons.

As you go to bed with your latest business idea or problem still perking in your brain, you set your internal alarm clock to go off early. When you awaken at 4 A.M., your brain literally exploding with ideas, you sneak out of bed to avoid getting the "all-you-think-about-is-business" lecture from your loved one. You make a cup of coffee and accomplish a great deal of work before the rest of the household comes alive. Today is another day and, as always, in spite of all the interruptions and the stress that normally accompanies your work-at-home lifestyle, you remain excited about your work.

Although working at home isn't quite as idyllic as you once imagined, you're not complaining. In fact, you'd gladly work sixteen hours a day on your business (and often do) to avoid working eight hours for someone else. You may not have it all together yet, and the money could be better than it is, but Rome wasn't built in a day. All you need is more time to plan your work, work your plan, and bring in the bucks!

Ah, there's the rub. *More time.* The challenge is to find more of it, save it, stretch it, and, as Kipling put it, "fill every unforgiving minute with 60 seconds' worth of distance run." (See the next chapter for some great tips on how to do this!)

De Plan, De Plan!

Organizational specialist Pat Katz reports on a scenario that she says her seminar attendees have painted for her again and again:

Just 15 minutes into your work day, your list of things to do today is dust. A whole new set of problems has hijacked your attention. At day's end 'the list' floats to the surface again. Though you've been taking care of business all day long, you've accomplished few, if any, of the tasks that seemed so important at the beginning of the day. You feel like a failure. It's a tribute to the spirit of optimism that even though we have the same experience over and over again, we continue to believe that if we create a plan, the day will unfold exactly according to that plan. We need to think again. Days like that are rare. When your list of accomplishments at day's end doesn't equate with your list of intentions from day's start, you can still consider it a success if you tackled the tasks that really mattered, made sound choices on the fly, and invested a few moments in learning from your experience of the day.

—from *Pause—The Voice of Sanity in a Speed Crazed World,* an ezine published by Patricia Katz (PatKatz.com)

Positive Workaholism

In a survey of 450 entrepreneurs, a Boston University professor learned that most of them believed that total immersion in their work is necessary for success, and that personal and family sacrifices are almost universal. Although most of the entrepreneurs in this particular survey could afford to take vacations, few of them did, preferring instead to work.

That prompts the question, "Is working hard on your business harmful to your health?" A lot of people believe that so-called A-type personalities like the entrepreneurs mentioned above are prone to heart attacks, high blood pressure, ulcers, and a number of other health problems. Some of them—those who cannot deal with stress—probably are. But a lot of hard-working people, myself included, agree with Dennis Hensley, who claims that it isn't stress that kills, but boredom. Dennis, author of several books and hundreds of articles, believes the answer to all problems is hard work that a person enjoys. He urges ambitious entrepreneurs to work as hard as they want, because the satisfaction they realize from productive work probably will do more to combat the ordinary stresses of life than anything else.

There must be something to this theory. I have felt stressed all my adult life, yet I have never been unhappy or unhealthy. My attitude is positive, I've never had ulcers, and my blood pressure has stayed in the normal range (until recently when I added caregiving duties to my daily workload). I have always suffered from insomnia, however, sometimes from stress but more often because I just can't shut down my mind at 10 o'clock. I often go to bed thinking about what I'm going to do the next day and then spend half the night making plans, writing copy in my mind, or exploring new ideas. It's as though I'm trying to steal time by not sleeping or, as John Steinbeck wrote in *Journal of a Novel*, "Last night I hardly slept at all. It was one of those good thinking nights."

Dennis Hensley coined the term "positive workaholic" in 1976, and he is living testament of his own positive workaholic systems. He says he never sleeps more than six hours a night, and is at his most productive from 10 P.M. to 2 A.M., the time when he does most of his writing. He always has a new book in the works, and one you may wish to read is *Positive Workaholism for the 21st Century* (Possibility Press, 2003). Although Dennis has always been active as a lecturer, teacher, publicist, businessman, church deacon, husband, and father, this did not kept him from realizing his dream of becoming a professional writer. His philosophy is that success is obtainable to everyone who desires it and is willing to work for it, and he cites four common denominators among positive workaholics: a winning attitude, high levels of energy, fierce independence, and a "mystical sense of destiny."

In summary, don't fret if you find you're always having to defend your work habits to others who keep telling you you're going to kill yourself by working so hard. It could be that working hard on your own business is the most healthful thing you could be doing.

This doesn't means that you don't have to develop a good stress management plan, however, because extra stress comes with the territory when you're in business. You'll find some special tips on this topic in Chapter 12.

Honing Your Sense of Humor

There's no question about it: laughter is both healthy and healing for people of all ages. Humor is a proven therapeutic tool, a valuable business tool that can diffuse potentially explosive situations, and a helpful tool for facilitating camaraderie. If you don't have a sense of humor at the time you start your business, you'll acquire it quickly or you won't survive long as a homebased entrepreneur.

Working at home naturally presents certain home-related problems, from dealing with the attitude of friends and family who don't understand what you're doing, to just doing business with children underfoot. In one of Erma Bombeck's columns, titled "Trying to Separate Home From Office," she said that she had been working at home for twenty years and it was no day at the beach. "If I had any advice about home offices," she said, "it would be to never locate them outside a bathroom door. We're talking freeway traffic here, plus outbursts of steam, singing and gargling." Clearly this kind of background noise isn't what prospective clients expect to hear. (It must be hard to deal professionally with a client when your child has answered the phone loudly proclaiming, "Mommy can't come to the phone now, she's in the bathroom!")

Some women have solved their children problems by using incubator facilities. I'll never forget the mother I met at a home-business conference who explained how she handled client meetings. At that time she was renting an office in an incubator facility one hour at a time as needed. And she had this interesting little box that contained a couple of pictures for the wall, a calendar, and desk accessories—all those little office touches a client would expect to see. She set everything in place just before the client walked in the door and, at the end of her meeting, she packed her little box and went home.

And then there was the entrepreneurial mother who told me she threw her kid a jelly bean to keep him quiet every time the phone rang. But my favorite story is from speaker and author Silvana Clark, who once took a business call in the kitchen when she was in the middle of baking cookies. As her two-year-old toddled into the room, mouth open, all set to vocalize, she grabbed a handful of chocolate chips and threw them on the floor. Entranced, her daughter picked them up, eating them one at a time. "And I kept throwing handfuls of chips until I was able to complete the important contractual agreement I was then negotiating," she said.

Sometimes when working at home, we try to sound professional on the phone, but it's hard because of some crazy scene that's playing itself out around us at the moment. One of my publisher friends told me about the time she had put a pot of fresh green beans on the stove with the burner turned to high. The phone rang across the room—an important prospective client—and my friend couldn't bring herself to interrupt while she watched the beans dry up and begin to burn. Finally, just as she was bringing the conversation to an end—now resigned to ruined beans—the smoke alarm went off, totally shattering the office illusion she had been trying so hard to maintain.

Home-business owners use a variety of tricks and devices in their home office routine. For example, I've encountered people who say they feel more professional when they wear a dress-up outfit for work and change into something casual at day's end. To mentally mark the end of a working day, one woman told me she carried her purse into her office every morning and then carried it out at night. One fellow I read about signals to the family that he's through for the day by leaving the house, then coming back in, slamming the door and hollering, "Hi, honey, I'm home!"

The demands of a homebased business often place a strain on family or spousal relationships, and sometimes the oven is not the only thing that heats up. Speaking of ovens . . . Harry and I once had quite a heated go-round about one. Prior to leaving on one of my speaking engagements, I had prepared a meatloaf dinner for Harry—one of his favorite meals—telling him to put it in the oven at 350 degrees about 4:30. When I called him about 10:30 that night, asking how he liked his dinner, he was furious with me. "I don't know," he said through gritted teeth, "*because it's still in the oven!*" What he did when he put it in the oven was close the door and *also pull the oven cleaning handle.* Of course, this slide-handle only releases hours later after the oven has completely cooled down. This was one time when my husband's sense of humor failed him. Instead of laughing at himself for being so dumb, he got mad at me because I didn't tell him *not* to pull the handle.

> *Laughter is instantaneous and brief, yet its effects can be positive and lasting. It is far from frivolous if it can reduce stress, enhance communication and improve the quality of your life. And that's why there's no business that isn't funny business. Humor is accessible. It adds zest to life, and it is absolutely free.*
> —Esther Blumenfeld and Lynne Alpern, *Humor at Work* (Peachtree Publishers)

Dreams Versus Reality

Having a machine answer your phone is the ideal way to avoid conflict with a spouse who likes to sleep late or retire early. It's also a good idea to turn on the answering machine before you engage in a "serious" discussion with your spouse. Have you ever been in the middle of a really heated argument with a loved one, only to be interrupted by the phone . . . and you answer so sweetly and professionally, do your business thing, hang up, and immediately pick up the argument right where you left off? That's what I call flexibility. Reminds me of a joke in *Reader's Digest:* "Marriage is nature's way of keeping people from fighting with strangers."

Because you work at home, your schedule is susceptible to all of life's little interruptions, from things already discussed above to situations totally out of your control. Beverly Williams had planned to spend her time quite differently the day she returned home to find that her house had been struck by lightning. It had totally destroyed a corner of her living room and all the electronic equipment in her home office, and it took two weeks to get her business back in order. As soon as Beverly finished crying—her way of accepting the tragedy—she tried to find something to laugh about. She said her husband's two machines upstairs, which belonged to IBM, were not damaged, so she figured this was God's way of telling her it was time to upgrade her equipment. "Besides," she said, "although we had just redecorated the living room, I really wasn't happy with the color of the paint."

When the worst actually does happen, call on humor to help you survive. When you feel overly stressed, take time to reset your funny bone. As one fellow put it, "If you don't learn to laugh at trouble, you won't have anything to laugh at when you're old."

Smart Tip

Whenever you find yourself in water over your head, keep afloat by latching on to the lifesaver raft of laughter and take a tip from society columnist Elsa Maxwell, who once advised, "Laugh at yourself first before anyone else can!"

Chapter 2:
Time, Space, and Help Concerns

We don't run our business out of our home; we run our home out of our business.
—a diversified home-business owner

Many business pros in my network contributed information, ideas, and practical tips to this book and its companion guide, *Starting Smart!* But not every business pro has answers to *every* question or problem posed in this book, even though they may have been in business for years and achieved a considerable degree of success in their field or industry. When I asked my contributors to tell me how they had solved problems related to lack of time, lack of help, lack of space in which to work, lack of capital for business expansion, and the ever-increasing costs of doing business, a sculptor with a good sense of humor quipped, "If I had solved all of these problems, maybe I'd be making more money than I am now!"

Clearly, the degree to which you are able to deal with or solve these five problems will have much to do with the amount of gross income you can generate from your entrepreneurial endeavor. *Profit* is another matter entirely. As many entrepreneurs have learned, a huge gross income that entails higher overhead, equipment, or employee costs does not necessarily translate into higher profits for the business owner. As quilting expert and diversified business owner Kaye Wood once quipped, "Does a million-dollar business mean one million *gross*, one million *net*, or one million *owed*?"

Solutions for the Lack-of-Time Problem

Too much work and too little time has long been the cry of the self-employed individual working at or from home base, but time isn't everything. Even if you had all the time you needed, success in business would ultimately depend on your ability to successfully finance and manage your growing business while continuously bringing in the bucks through savvy marketing and promotional efforts. The sooner you get a grip on managing your time, the sooner you'll be on your way to successfully managing and marketing your business. You may not always be able to get rid of things that cause interruptions in your work, but there are a number of things you can do to cope with them.

Like money management, time management requires an awareness of how much you have to spend. Although it takes time to plan how to spend time, such planning generally saves more time than it takes. You need to know not only how much time it's going to take to do various tasks related to your work or business, but also how you're going to find more time later on when things heat up. *And they will.* As a popular poster proclaims, "I try to take one day at a time, but lately several days have attacked me at once."

Doing a Time Study

People who have learned to control time, instead of letting time control them, are generally organized, self-disciplined workers. You can't begin to save time if you don't know how you're spending (wasting) it, so for awhile at least, keep a written record of how you spend your time. (It's the same principle as noting everything you eat when you are on a diet, to see where all those extra calories and pounds are coming from.)

Time, Space, and Help Concerns

This exercise first proved beneficial to me back in 1985 when I began to wonder whether I was wasting my time by performing certain routine tasks or doing other jobs that ought to be farmed out. I didn't have a computer at that time, so I also needed to know exactly how much time I was spending on the development and maintenance of my mailing list. It took a great deal of discipline, but I kept a faithful log for an entire year, logging a total of 2,235 hours on the business, not counting five full workshop days out of town. At year's end, I felt as though I had worked around the clock all year long. In truth, I found that time not devoted to the business totaled the equivalent of 93 days—including normal days off plus lost time of all kinds.

The average employed person who works a 40-hour week puts in 2,000 work hours a year (allowing for two weeks' vacation). When one works at home, however, work hours may run from early A.M. to late P.M., yet with normal home and family interruptions, one is lucky to end up with eight hours a day in which to work a full-time business. Unlike employed workers, home-business owners must work irregular hours, and because we have to squeeze in work time whenever we can, we get the feeling that we're working *all the time*. Therefore, you may feel better about your business if you keep a true record of the time devoted to it. You may find that, for the hours you're expending, you're earning a better hourly wage than you thought. Or, you may find you're wasting time on one facet of your business that isn't profitable. You can then take whatever steps are necessary to correct the situation.

In studying how I'd used my time in that first year of record keeping, I began to see what I had to do to become more efficient. This was when I knew I could not long delay the purchase of a computer, for I found that management of my mail list was eating up 12 percent of my time, and handling my mail (including processing of subscriptions, renewals, and routine address changes) was occupying another 20 percent. Two months after getting my computer (while continuing my time log), I saw a dramatic savings of time and an overall increase in productivity in both my writing time and management of my ever-growing mail list.

The feeling that there is never enough time weighs heavily on everyone who works at home, and this automatically makes time management problems a big contributor to stress. Whether you're working part or full time on your business, strive to establish regular starting and stopping hours and try to adhere to them. Every interruption in your workday by family or friends costs more than just the minutes or hours lost. It's also a drain on your energy because it's difficult to keep shifting mentally from "business" to "personal." Although it's hard to do, you must communicate to friends and relatives that you're running a business at home and you need certain uninterrupted blocks of time to do your work. But try not to overdo it. My research confirms that many business owners flog themselves relentlessly, working as many as 80 to 100 hours a week, not only in the beginning of a business but often for up to five years or more afterwards.

Most of us tend to overdo it at times, exhausting ourselves until we feel totally washed out. I've often related to a comment my grandma once made after a particularly hard day's work on the farm. Picking up the edge of her apron to wipe her brow, she sighed and said, "I feel like an old rag that has been wrung out in greasy dishwater."

Smart Tip

In setting priorities on the things to be done, note that the Pareto Principle, or 80/20 rule, will apply. In business, this rule relates to the fact that 20 percent of your customers generally account for 80 percent of your business. In matters of time, it means that 20 percent of what you do will probably yield 80 percent of the results. So be sure you identify and place uppermost on your list the 20 percent of the work that's the most important to your business or personal life.

Coping with Deadlines

"I love deadlines. I love the whooshing sound they make as they fly by." This humorous observation, attributed to Daniel Adams, hit home with me because I've had to meet one writing or publishing deadline after another for more than thirty years. Although deadlines are a common part of doing business, I've learned they were made to be broken. We need deadline dates to spur us onward, but the very fact that we work at home sometimes makes it impossible to meet them. When this happens, we must ask for (or give ourselves) an extension, or pay the consequences of what too much stress can do to us.

I feel as though I've spent my entire life rushing to finish one project so I could get started on yet another, but in most cases, I was the only one doing the pushing. I think I was born with the knowledge that life is short, because I can't ever recall a time when I didn't feel I had something special to do, and I'd better not waste time getting to it. While it's a blessing to feel you have a mission in life, it's a curse to be so propelled that it's almost impossible to ever slow down, let alone stop. Everyone I know is always rushing, including my two success-oriented sisters, suggesting that this syndrome runs in families.

Lynette M. Smith calls it "hectivity," her coined word for "hective activity." And what a perfect word this is to describe our fast-paced home-business activities and daily lives! I don't know if it's like this for everyone past the age of 55, but when I hit that particular "lifemark," I suddenly woke up to the fact that I was never going to get it all done before I died, and it was high time I took a sharper look at what I was doing and where I was going. Now that I'm in my mid-sixties, I continue to review and narrow down my list of goals so I can focus on those things most important to me at this stage of life. Whatever your age, it's always a good idea to review your life and consider how you might change some of the things and circumstances that have always stressed you in the past.

Smart Tip

Try to look differently at things that may be causing problems in your home-business life and think how you might react to them in a more positive way.

Addressing Lack-of-Space Problems

What do you do when you find you have insufficient space in which to work? Sometimes it's merely a matter of reorganizing your office or workshop or finding new places to store additional supplies and materials.

If you do office work of any kind, you need to "get centered," says organizational expert Patricia Katz. She suggests grouping working materials and equipment around your most critical centers of operation, which may include communications, mail handling, computer work, printing and copying, finance, planning and reference work. "Some of the centers develop naturally as a business grows and as responsibilities are divided and delegated," she says. "Others need to be deliberately masterminded. As you consider the placement of various work centers, take a second look at your furnishings. Trading in a tall

How Busy Women Find More Time for Business

"I'm a night owl. I answer e-mail during the mornings, as time and children permit, but when the sun goes down and the kids are in bed, I can be found working the night away! The smartest thing I've done to make this happen is to make the whole family take a nap every single day. Every afternoon we turn off all the phones and whoever is home has to lie down and at least rest so Mom can nap. This is a real mind-rester for me, and it gives the kids some relaxation time, too."
   —*Tammy Harrison*

• • •

"The smartest thing I've done to give myself more time is get my oldest son a car. I was chauffeuring him more than I realized. Also, a cell phone has helped a bunch."
   —*Velda Solomon*

• • •

"The best thing I ever did was to invest in Franklin-Covey courses (FClearningCenter.com). They are far from cheap but worth every penny, as is their planner (FranklinPlanner.com). There are many other planners on the market, but none of them will help unless you are taught to use them and you follow their system."
   —*Michelle Winterhalter*

• • •

"I've learned to set schedules, especially for the amount of time I spend on the Internet. With scheduling, I also do better at completing things I *need* to do (like working on the books) instead of things I *want* to do (like planning new soap scents for the upcoming season)."
   —*Karen White*

four-drawer file cabinet for two shorter cabinets will create a spare desk height working surface. Consider grouping desk and tables in L-squares or U-shapes to bring frequently used centers closer to hand. Grouping your working materials and equipment according to function and setting aside enough space for each aspect of your operation will make you and your business that much more efficient." (On her Web site at PatKatz.com, Patricia offers a good collection of articles on time management, organization, encouragement, motivation, and getting your life in balance. She also publishes a free ezine titled *Pause–The Voice of Sanity in a Speed Crazed World.*)

"The best thing I did to open more workspace and be more efficient with my time was to separate the paperwork/office work from my sewing room," says Terrie Kralik, MooseCountryQuilts.com. "With both in the same place, I was always being distracted by one thing or another and couldn't focus fully on either the design end of things or the business end, but now I try to keep the papers out of the sewing room and the fabric out of the office."

Product makers must have not only office space, but studio or workshop space in which to manufacture goods for sale. When the space originally allotted to the business turns out to be too small, the only answer is to steal additional square footage from one's living space. Commonly, cars are moved out of the garage, basements are emptied, back porches are enclosed, attics are finished, a room is added onto the house, or an outbuilding is set up on the property (zoning laws permitting).

"My sister recently told me my basement looks like a factory," says clothing manufacturer Pamela Burns, Injeanious.org. "Except for a work table in the center, there is no furniture and all the walls have floor-to-ceiling storage shelves. My real 'factory,' however, is my dining room where I do all my sewing and store all my bolts of fabric. If my business continues to grow, we may have to move soon."

Other Ideas to Try

If your business actually takes over your home or begins to stress you beyond your ability to handle it, you will have some serious thinking to do. (I've discussed this topic at greater length in Chapter Twelve, along with how to manage the stress that comes from having to make major decisions such as this.) Following are examples of how some business owners have responded to growth and the need for additional workspace at home.

- **Find Outside Storage Areas.** As a mail order and exhibit-booth seller, Martha Oskvig has always had to work in a tight home space. At various times, her space-getting strategies have included using a cabinet plus underbed and closet containers to store inventory, converting a basement area with storage shelves and a desk, taking over a section of the garage, and renting a storage unit to keep boxes from overwhelming family space. However, Martha really showed her ingenuity the day she came up with the idea of renting storage and workspace from businesses in her area.

  "When I needed to store more bulky inventory in a climate-controlled space (low humidity, constant temperature), a storage unit wasn't the answer," she says. "So I went to a block of downtown business owners and asked each if they could rent to me a nonpublic storage area on street level (not basement). I was surprised to find three different places had appropriate space and were very willing, and all were accessed from back entrances not used by the public. All three provided me with a key so I could work in my area after their store hours (two sites even had large tables they let me use when they weren't open for their own retail customers). I eventually used each of the three sites: one for two years (the owner even provided shelves for me), one for one year, and the other for three years. This meant some travel time for me, but it was worth the rental fee so my family didn't see my business overwhelming our home space. Plus it was handy for mail orders to work with tables and have all my mailing supplies nearby. I took all orders from my home phone line, and I could go day or night to pack the orders, updating my inventory count daily on a master sheet I kept with me. In one location, I had poor lighting so was limited to daytime hours, which is why I only used this space for one year."

- **Build Your Own Workshop.** Dodie Eisenhauer, VillageDesigns.com, lives in a small town in Missouri. "I started in my basement, grew to the garage, expanded to working in the driveway, and expanded again to take over the old house next door," she says. "Frustrated with small rooms and no indoor plumbing, I made the decision to build a workshop. With several thousand dollars' worth of orders in hand, my husband and I made a trip to the bank to borrow money to build it. We put the shop on a separate piece of land next door to our house so we would have the option of selling it if things didn't work out. Looking back, I see this was a big financial risk, but the building is now paid for and it will always be an asset."

- **Buy a Larger House.** "Jerry and I have always worked out of our home," says Sharon Richwine, JerryAnthonyPhoto.com. "First we used one room, then we used the entire upstairs, then we needed to move. We looked at commercial space, but after a couple of years we found the perfect solution for us: a U-shaped house that offered us two separate areas for business and personal use. It has worked great! We had separate phone lines installed for the business part and we don't answer them after hours or on weekends. We can go back to work in the evening if we want to catch up, or we can just relax in our personal quarters with no worry about our possessions being in a commercial space. We still need to take more time off, but it's nice to be able to throw a load of laundry in between calls and it certainly saves on the cost of lunch."

Organization versus Perfectionism

It's easy to confuse perfectionism with organization. Perfectionists stuff papers, supplies and anything else that would otherwise clutter a desk into drawers to be dealt with later. They want to give the appearance of being organized, yet when it's time to work, they spend extra time taking everything out again. Being organized means setting up your office to be functional, so that you don't have to rearrange your desk when you are ready to work.

—a tip from *Organizing Your Home Business* (Made E-Z, 2002) by Lisa Kanarek, HomeOfficeLife.com

Getting the Help You Need

What do you do when you've tried all the time-management strategies above and still have more work to do than time to do it in? You either seek help from family members, outside services, independent contractors, or employees, or you cut back on your marketing, deliberately limiting the number of customers or clients you will serve.

Although all business owners want to increase business profits, this doesn't mean they want to increase the *size* of their business to the point where it totally disrupts their personal or family life. Often, financial growth is impossible without hiring extra help, but not all home-business owners want to grow their business to this extent. Whether or not to hire help is always a tough decision. Although there are many full-time businesses based at home, there are probably as many (if not more) part-time businesses being operated by women with growing children or job-holders who can only work a business in the evenings or on weekends. For the growing full-time business at home, the too-much-work-not-enough-hands problem is ever present.

"My biggest problem is how do I grow the business while still doing the work I enjoy and providing high quality service to my clients?" muses consultant Judy Schramm. "I think this is a huge problem for most consultants. At some point you reach the limits of your own time. At that point you either keep your business to a small enough scale that you can do all the work yourself or hire other people to do it. But if you expand that takes you out of doing what you love and puts you into managing people who are doing what you love. And it's very easy to grow your business to a size where all you are doing is managing, your stress level is higher, and you're not making any more money. (The business is, but you're not keeping any more of it.) What's the point in that? This is a real dilemma, and the answer is probably different for everyone."

"Sometimes in the past year I've gotten so busy I thought I could not handle everything myself," says Karen White, NaturalImpulse.com. "But I'm not yet to the point where I want to hire employees. One thing I have done to try to alleviate the problem is to cut back on items that were rarely ordered or had a low profit margin. When I found I had a few items that required a large investment of time for a small profit, they had to go! (This helped reduce my stress level as well.)"

Hiring Independent Contractors

We all want our business to be financially successful, but few of us want employees coming into our home. Even if this were legal from a zoning standpoint, it would be an unwelcome invasion of privacy to most of us. We may also lack the necessary space for even one part-time worker. While hiring independent contractors seems a logical solution for many, this is a touchy legal area that has gotten a lot of homebased entrepreneurs into trouble. (See the tips and cautionary notes on hiring employees and independent contractors in the A-Z business management area of Section II.)

Where independent contractors are concerned, the legal danger comes when you hire someone who works for no one else but you. One way to safely employ independent contractors is to hire entrepreneurs or small business owners who serve other clients. "I have a number of independent contractors and other small businesses who work for me part-time," says Judy Schramm. "This works better for me because I have a lot of different types of work that needs to be done. There's not enough of any one type to justify a full-time person, and this way I can better handle the ebb and flow. This also allows me to have people who specialize in different types of work, which means I can provide better quality results to my clients; for example, graphic design for print, graphic design for the Web, Web integration, Web site management. Sometimes when I need additional assistance, however, the problem is trying to find someone I can trust to outsource some projects to who has both the experience to do the job and the time to do it on my schedule."

Finding Help in Your Community

BeautiControl consultant Martha Oskvig (Beautipage.com/here4u) solved her help problem by identifying easy activities others could do for her. "Sometimes they were my own children," she says, "but most of the time they were unemployed customers or church friends. For example, I helped a woman start a secretarial service in her home by contracting with her to do my photocopies, format and print my newsletters, update my mailing labels and create greeting cards. She made a rate sheet which she then offered to other business owners in the community. Eventually she had several regular clients each month because she offered pickup and delivery service. All of my literature, postcards and envelopes for monthly newsletters, annual catalog and promotional mailings were labeled and stuffed by a different person—an elderly woman in her home. I paid her the predetermined lump sum with my business check and had her sign a receipt at pickup. Although I haven't tried this, I've heard that other businesses in a nearby town are hiring residents at a special-needs care center to label and stuff during the day."

Hiring Your Children

Putting your own kids on the company payroll is both a smart tax move and a real help to many homebased business owners, particularly those involved in the production and sale of products. "It's a beautiful solution for working parents," says Michelle Winterhalter, a network marketer of At Home America products (on the Web at AtHome.com/shelle). "Currently, you can employ children that live at home and pay them up to $4,600 per year tax-free. There is a form you must submit with your taxes for each child, but they are not taxed on that income and neither are you! I pay my children minimum wage to do things such as data entry, folding and stamping mailers, stamping my name on catalogs and literature, walking PR stuff door-to-door, working at fairs and events with me, filing, etc. They are able to do many menial tasks freeing me up to do those things only I can do." (See also "Hiring Your Children" in Section II.)

If you decide to involve your children in your business, don't take advantage of a good thing. Sue, the owner of a sewing business, once told me about her youngest child, Jason, then five, who had been brought into the business as a "runner." Her business was spread all over the house, on different levels from the garage to the attic, and Jason's job was to carry work in progress from one location to another or "gofer" things other family members needed as they worked. One day when I was speaking to Sue, she told me Jason wasn't happy at the moment. On that day, he had literally stomped his foot and said he was tired of doing all this "home business stuff," tired of running all those errands! Hiding her amusement, Sue simply gave her youngest some time off—plus a special reward for being such a big help to the business.

Alternatives to Hiring Help

Not everyone has a spouse, partner or child they can employ in their business, and even when they do, help from others is not always the solution. In fact, anyone who builds a business around their own skills and talents—such as artists, craft designers, Web designers, writers, and consultants—will have a hard time farming out enough work to make a difference. In my experience, I found it always took more time for me to explain to someone how to do a menial office job than it did for me to do it myself. First, they couldn't do it as fast as I could, and second, they were not only underfoot, but had to be constantly managed (lots of questions that interrupted my concentration). My husband, Harry, was a great spousal employee for many years (best little tax deduction I ever had!), but after 2000 when he was no longer able to help me with the business due to health problems, I found myself back where I started, with too much to do and not enough time to do it in.

In the recent past, I've hired people to help me get my Web site up and running, and I have computer experts I can call if I run into a technical problem I can't handle myself. But the only way I have consistently found the extra time needed for work is to either work longer hours or *not* do numerous home-related jobs my Bohemian husband has always thought a good wife should do, even if she is working full time. (I may be a good business woman and a great cook, but my house hasn't had a spring cleaning in forty years.) I think Annie Lang, Annie Things Possible, has the perfect solution to my current problem (if only I can convince Harry to go along with it). Instead of hiring help with her *business*, she hired *housekeeping* help (easier to find and cheaper than an office worker). "This is the smartest thing I've done lately," she told me. "This saves me six hours a week—the equivalent of three eight-hour work days per month."

Unless they're blessed with a fellow who likes to cook, most women running businesses at home have to devise clever ways to cut down on the time spent on shopping and meal preparation each day. With no children and just me and Harry to cook for, my solution has been to shop one morning a week and prepare six servings of meals that take a long time to prepare. I then freeze a portion and serve a repeat or variation of that meal a couple of days later. Martha Oskvig's strategy is to cook an oven full of meat in one day, then debone it (with hubby's help) and freeze it in the evening so she's ready for a variety of quick meals all month long.

Smart Tip

Take a look at all the routine home-related work you do that is stealing time from your business and figure out what it would cost to hire others to do this work. For example, if you're mowing the lawn, raking leaves, washing windows, or shoveling snow to save money, consider how much income you might be able to generate if you worked in your office or workshop while someone else did this menial work at a much lower hourly rate of pay.

If you can gain more time, you may never need an employee. If you have a family, this may be easier to do than you think. "I didn't fully realize how much time I was spending on ironing, matching socks and folding underwear for my family of six until I quit doing it," says Martha Oskvig. "I delegated most laundry duties to my children years ago, giving each a personal basket for carrying dirty linens to the laundry room and carrying them back when removed from the dryer. I put a shoebox into drawers for my youngest children to hold their unfolded underwear, and they made a game of matching socks. Today, I fold no laundry except for my husband's T-shirts and our bathroom towels, and I iron only a few special shirts and dresses."

Martha has also managed to get her family to agree to her having one night out a week for business activity—something that's really important to a network marketer. "My family knows not to count on my presence at home from 5 P.M. to 10 P.M. on Mondays," she says. "I don't have any concerns about cooking or childcare on this one evening so I can fully concentrate on my business. (If my husband decides not to be home that night, he has to arrange child care.) This means I don't have to recheck schedules while I attempt to book evening classes or meetings with my prospects for that night. If I don't have appointments prescheduled, I still usually use at least two hours away from the house that night for business—sometimes for business research in the library but more often for a meeting with a good customer or prospective business partner who appreciated my personalized service."

Using Outside Services

When you need to free up some of your time for more important work, consider using the services of outside business professionals or companies or try different methods of product distribution.

Time, Space, and Help Concerns

● **Work with a Virtual Assistant (VA).** To some, a "virtual assistant" is just another name for "secretarial service," but the work they do usually involves more high-tech skills than a secretary might provide. "Virtual assistance is the art of helping people organize the details of their business and personal lives without being physically present," says Donna L. Gunter, SohoBizSolutions.com. "A VA will provide a collaborative partnership or another set of eyes and ears for the business owner, rather than simply completing piecemeal tasks."

Donna typically performs such jobs as answering e-mail, returning phone calls, sending/receiving faxes, doing research, updating Web sites, making travel arrangements, doing newsletters or desktop publishing jobs, establishing vendor relationships, and creating office systems. If you believe you could move ahead in business if you could find someone to handle business details that do not need your personal attention, then a VA should be perfect for you. (A search of the Internet for "virtual assistant" will lead you to many other individuals who provide such services.)

● **Hire a Fulfillment or Packaging Service.** If you've been selling products to individuals by mail and find that order fulfillment is eating too much of your time, hire an order fulfillment service to do this work for you. For years, Harry was my shipping clerk, which involved his dragging cases of books into the house and down to the basement for packaging and stamping, then hauling packages of books back upstairs, into the car, and to the post office. In time, he could no longer do this kind of physical labor, and I certainly didn't have the time to do it, so hiring a fulfillment service was the perfect solution for us. From that point on, all we had to do was paperwork, and the cost of the service was small compared to the benefits we derived from it.

Many product makers hire out work related to the packaging of products, but sometimes quality suffers in the process. "Although many soap-makers contract out their wrapping, labeling, and shipping, I'm reluctant to do this," says Karen White. "You must be careful to exercise quality control, especially if the service ships the product without you seeing it. A colleague was losing wholesale accounts and couldn't figure out why, until one store told her that the products were arriving looking as though someone had used their feet to wrap them!"

● **Use Sales Reps or Distributors.** If you're a product maker with a growing wholesale line, consider working with sales reps who can get your products into the right kind of shops, take your products to trade shows, and get them into gift marts. The additional business a good sales rep team can generate for you should more than offset the cost of their service. (For more information on this topic, see Chapter 8.)

When Terrie Kralik (MooseCountryQuilts.com) found herself spending too much time on marketing to individual quilt shops (with little success), she focused on getting distributors to carry her patterns and get them into shops. "They have a network of representatives that cover a lot more territory than I can, and they have their own contacts and know what their previous purchases are and can target them better than I can," she says. "This strategy has both increased dollar sales and decreased sales and marketing time on my part."

● **Deliver Products Electronically.** Self-publishers quickly figured out how to save time and money by publishing their books electronically, but pattern sellers on the Internet have also embraced this technology. Instead of wholesaling her print patterns to shops or selling them one at a time to individuals, Debbie Spaulding now delivers 90 percent of her patterns electronically from PuppetPatterns.com, saving not only printing, packaging, and postage costs, but tons of time she can more profitably spend on designing new products. "My customers just love my e-patterns because they are immediately available without their having to wait for them to arrive in the mail," she says. "I do think people are becoming more comfortable with ordering online and with eBooks in general. It takes awhile for everyone to become more comfortable with any change, but once people see how easy it is they are more willing to try it."

Using Lists to Stay in Control

Time management experts always advise, "make lists," and busy, organized people do tend to be list-makers. Often, without a list, you may feel there is so much to do you can't possibly handle it all. Yet, once a list is made, it seems less impossible. In addition to being time-efficient, lists of things to

Office Hours of Small Business Owners
(Author Unknown)

Open most days about 9 or 10,
    occasionally as early as 7,
    but some days as late as 12 or 1.
We close about 5:30 or 6,
    sometimes as late as 11 or 12.
    Some days or afternoons we aren't here at all.
Lately I've been here just about all the time,
    except when I'm someplace else,
    but I should be here then, too.

be done are great spirit-lifters. The very act of scratching off each task as it is completed gives one the sense of accomplishing yet another small goal. It's little things like this that keep us going when the pressures of business tend to pull us down.

Once, after Harry and I had relocated to Missouri, I received a timely letter from a friend. "The trouble with moving," said Sarah, "is that it realigns your priorities whether you want it to or not. Getting your house/life in order takes precedence over a lot of things that you need to be doing to keep your business running. If you should feel an anxiety attack coming on, and you feel guilty and inadequate because you can't do everything fast and efficiently, just remember that you are demanding too much of yourself. Say to yourself, 'I am one person. What needs to be done . . . will get done. Now, what needs to be done *today?*'"

Sarah's letter arrived shortly after the moving van. As I read it, half of me was concerned about where I had put the frying pan so I could get a quick meal on the table and the other half was trying to figure out how to set up a temporary office to handle the mail that had piled up since we had packed the office. Sarah's advice brought a smile to my face: "Ask yourself what needs to be done before Friday of this week, then make a list. Go through this process and set reachable goals for the month, three months, and one year. Just making the list will relieve a lot of pressure."

She was right, of course. I had made just such a list before leaving our old residence, and although it took a whole day to plan my last month's work in that area, it was as if a giant weight had been lifted from my shoulders when my day-to-day schedule was completed. I knew then that I had to worry only about what was on each day's list of things to do. Try it. You will be amazed at how much it helps when you feel you can't cope with all the work ahead of you.

Smart Tip

The trouble with making lists is that you will rarely get to the bottom of any list you make. Don't fret about it, however. Just keep putting the most important things at the top, and as time goes on, the jobs at the bottom that you never have time for will seem less important or will automatically take care of themselves, much like leftovers in the refrigerator. We keep them because we'd feel guilty if we threw them out, but after a respectable holding period, it's easy to justify dumping them.

Making lists of the work to be done is one good way to stay in control of things even when you don't feel overwhelmed by the weight of your responsibilities. But, no matter how many lists I make, something unexpected always seems to happen to upset my work schedule. Like the morning I went to the freezer to take out meat for dinner. To my dismay, I discovered the door I had last opened the morning before had not closed because a package had shifted and jammed against it. Now the ice cream was dripping through the shelves, berry juice was streaming down the inside of the door, and all the green beans and peppers I had worked so hard to freeze the month before had thawed, along with about thirty pounds of meat and a lot of specialty foods we had brought from Chicago on our last shopping trip.

At first, I was close to tears. Then I got angry at myself for being so careless. The office work I had planned to do that day clearly was second on my list of priorities. After I spent another five minutes feeling sorry for myself, the part of me that always welcomes a challenge came to life. An unsympathetic Harry helped me carry everything to the kitchen, where I made a list of the thawed ingredients, got out my recipe box, and went to work. While stewing about the fine mess I'd gotten myself into, I cooked, baked, and boiled my way out of it. Eight hours later, I had more meals in the freezer than I could count. All in all, it wasn't a bad experience. In fact, those prepared meals turned out to be a great time saver in the busy weeks that followed, and the experience was good for at least one laugh. One evening when Harry complimented me on one of the stews resulting from this fiasco and asked me how I made it, I said, "Well, first you let the freezer thaw. . . ."

• • •

As you go about your business in the months and years ahead, hang on to your sense of humor and remain optimistic about your future. "The power of a positive mental attitude isn't just a bunch of hooey from the motivational speaker circuit," says author Jeff Zbar, ChiefHomeOfficer.com. "True optimism drowns out the unfounded fears and voices that can lead us astray. Moreover, it helps keep those around us buoyant. Many of us could use a shot of positive thinking. It's infectious."

Chapter 3:
Financial Considerations

There is no such thing as easy money. Setting objectives, committing to a realistic business plan, budgeting, and follow through are an absolute must if one truly wants to reach an objective. Most people fall short when it comes to the follow-through stage, thinking "stuff happens" overnight.
—Annie Lang, AnnieThingsPossible.com

Statistics from the U.S. Small Business Administration tell us that between 45 and 48 percent of all businesses fail within the first five years, and about 95 percent of these failures are attributable to poor management. Although you have to be a smart marketer to bring in the bucks, *managing your business efficiently is even more important than mastering the principles of marketing.* You might be a whiz at advertising, getting publicity, networking, and running a Web site, but if you don't know how to run an efficient office, finance growth, manage time, and handle a heavy workload or an unexpected surge of business, you could find yourself in hot water.

A story from Eileen Heifner, CreateAnHeirloom.com, illustrates my point. "When our doll business was at its height, I decided to participate in an advertising program that I believed might bring in about a thousand requests for our catalog," she said. "I told the nice man on the other end of the phone that we were not equipped to be bombarded with catalog requests and he told me I didn't have to worry about it because only Victoria's Secret ever got more than 5,000 requests."

Surprise! Eileen got *17,000* requests for her catalog, and if she hadn't been a smart business manager, this kind of response could have put her out of business. "We were up to our ears dealing with inventory management, shipping issues such as lost packages, broken parts and missing items, plus every odd-and-end problem imaginable," she recalls. "It was a very stressful time, but we got through it because we were experienced in taking care of problems like that on a smaller scale."

Balancing Management and Marketing Tasks

Eileen's story illustrates how good business management and marketing automatically becomes a fine balancing act. Too much emphasis on marketing and too little on business management—or vice versa—and you'll upset your apple cart. The goal of this book is to help you solve common business problems and keep your balance as your business continues to grow, but that's easier said than done. From over three decades of experience as a home-business owner, I've learned that nothing is as simple as it seems, everything takes longer than expected, and unexpected happenings will always force us to change our well-laid plans.

Smart Tip

Whatever you plan to do, hope for the best, prepare for the worst, and *always leave yourself an escape route*. Whether you're in a plane, a public building, or in a new business endeavor, it's always comforting to know where the Exit is.

Making Written Business Plans

As emphasized in *Starting Smart!* (this book's companion guide for home-business beginners), good business management involves constant planning. Throughout the life of your business and even at its end, there will be a need for a variety of plans at one time or another, including comprehensive business plans; time plans (short- medium-, and long-range planning); creative, routine, and problem-solving plans; production and marketing plans. All plans must be changed regularly based on the records of past experience, but the longer you're in business, the easier all this planning becomes. Without a plan, even the most experienced business owner will have difficulty managing time, money, or stress, staying organized, expanding a business, or planning a new marketing campaign.

Plans must be in writing, of course. Although a plan can be something as simple as a list of things to do, you need more than this if you want to analyze certain aspects of your business and learn how to:

- Measure the annual growth of your business

- See how it's changing from year to year

- Calculate true overhead costs

- Identify your most profitable products or product lines

- Spot sales trends that signal a need for new products or services

- Stay focused on your various goals.

Although nothing stays the same in business, we continue to do the same things over and over each month and each year, so part of our planning needs to be directed to how we're going to handle all of our repetitive jobs, from financial tasks such as cash flow projections, financial reports and year-end tax work, to record keeping, mail list development and maintenance, and routine Web site updates. We also need plans for monitoring overhead and supplier costs, tracking time spent on one job or another, and routine analyses of how our business is doing as a whole.

Judy Delapa, author and publisher of *High-Impact Business Strategies*, calls them *reality checks*. "Show me a business that takes time out for a mid-year reality check, and I'll show you a business that's on course and ahead of the pack at year's end," she says. "Every business team starts the year with good intentions to make this year better than last. But then as the weeks and months roll by, unexpected problems distract the team from their goals."

Ask these tough questions, challenges Judy: "Are sales and profits on target? Are you staying within your budget? How many new accounts have you gained? Or lost? What are you doing to build and solidify relationships with new and existing customers? Are you making progress on each of your goals? What can you do—what *must* you do, starting today—to get back on track?"

Nine Causes of Serious Financial Trouble

"Of the nearly one million new small businesses established every year, nearly 63 percent will fail after six years," says bankruptcy attorney and author John Ventura. "But many business failures could be avoided if their owners had the right information and advice."

Why do small businesses have such a tough time surviving? In his now out-of-print book, *The Small Business Survival Kit: 134 Troubleshooting Tips for Success*, Ventura explained it is because many do not have the skills or knowledge needed to run a successful business. Others become so enamored with a business idea that they plunge forward with little or no thought given to its viability, much less to what needs to be done to reduce the risks of being in business and to maximize opportunities for success. Based on his experience in working with small business owners, Ventura identified these nine fundamental causes of serious financial trouble:

1 Lack of up-front planning

2 Poor or nonexistent management skills

3 Lack of attention to day-to-day details

4 Inadequate financial resources and too little cash

5 Insufficient knowledge of low-cost/no-cost sources of business management advice and assistance

6 An inappropriate business legal structure

7 Troubles with the IRS

8 Failure to keep up with important market, economic, or technological changes and trends

9 A tendency to avoid acknowledging the seriousness of a problem and, therefore, failure to deal with it.

"Every small business owner must become familiar with the signs of financial trouble and take appropriate action," Ventura stresses. "It is painful to acknowledge that the undertaking you've poured your heart and soul into—not to mention your money—may be in serious trouble and that you may not know what to do about it. However, avoiding reality can be very costly since most problems only grow worse with time."

Doing Regular Business Analyses

For an example of the kind of things you might do to prevent problems in the future, consider how Marc Choyt and his wife, Helen Chantler, have grown their business and manage it today. Helen started designing jewelry in 1990 for James Reid, Ltd., a Santa Fe company known for its southwestern style gold and silver belt buckles. She had no formal art school training, but apprenticed with other jewelers in Santa Fe. In 1995, she started her own company, Reflective Images. Marc joined the company in 1996 and began to take Helen's first designs on the road, doing cold calls in various cities around the country. A year later, Helen took on an apprentice so she could have more time for designing. As the business grew, it became necessary to hire employees.

With increased wholesale orders from galleries and the opening of two Web sites, CelticJewelry.com and EarthCharms.com, sales exploded.

"In the early days of our business, we were so busy scrambling we didn't take time to plan," says Marc. "But Helen and I are long beyond *planning*; for some time now we've been into *making strategic decisions* based on a continuing analysis of our business." In addition to doing monthly (sometimes weekly) analyses of what's happening in their business, Marc says their year-end decisions are now based on a detailed study of their

- "Resource conversion" (building, equipment, tools, employees, and business consultants);

- Product development (new products they might bring into market and how they will be delivered);

- Overall marketing efforts (retail, direct mail, wholesale, catalogs).

"We have a brainstorming session with our employees based on the Holistic Management business model (HolisticManagement.com)," Marc explains. "What we always look for at year's end are weak links in the above categories. Once identified, we allocate our budget to address them. For example, in 1999 we saw that our resource conversion base was the strongest area of our business, but we also saw that if we kept growing at the same rate, we would have to move the business out of our home (which we ultimately had to do when the Web sites and wholesale business took off). At that time, however, we were handling a lot of our growth by subcontracting menial work (such as carding jewelry) so our two employees could keep doing what they were doing best."

In previous years, Marc admits to making business and marketing mistakes that cost him thousands of dollars. "Initially, we didn't know how to target our market or keep the kind of books that are now making it possible for us to grow. Now we've learned the importance of studying our computerized financial records and responding to what we see there each year, and the dollar volume of our business has grown accordingly." (Like many other craft businesses, Marc uses *QuickBooks* software for their accounting. "It's not the most powerful program available," he says, "but it's easy to use, and each new upgrade has given us more options for pulling reports and analyses.")

Financial Considerations

When I checked back with Marc in 1999, he was developing a budget based on that year's income and trying to predict what his 2000 expenses would be so he would know how much money he had to strengthen his weakest business link. "At that time, our weak link was in the marketing area," he recalls. "Not enough people knew about us. We saw that a lot of our growth had been the result of big orders from one large company, and if that company were to change its ordering pattern in the next year, our sales would be greatly impacted. To strengthen that weak link, we planned a grass roots marketing campaign the following year with the goal of selling to hundreds of smaller companies that would reorder on a continual basis."

As it turned out, instead of wholesaling to hundreds of smaller companies, Marc built a hugely successful Web-based mail order retail business by developing a broad-based marketing scheme to drive sales to the Web site. This change of direction was prompted both from a study of their records and the remark of a SCORE representative who challenged, "Why aren't you focusing on what's most profitable—which is retail sales?"

"That's when we began to do $300 to $400 spot ads in Irish and Scottish magazines throughout the country," says Marc. "This totally changed our company's focus and dramatically increased annual sales and profits. We're still getting business from that one large company, but now their orders are only 15 percent of our total sales (instead of 35 percent), and every year, that percentage decreases as our overall sales increase."

Marc and Helen's success story illustrates how a small homebased business can grow when proper attention is given to both management and marketing concerns. They now employ eight full-time employees who receive generous salaries, a health insurance plan, three-week paid vacations, and an annual bonus. And each year, they continue to spend a full day brainstorming with their employees and looking at their weakest links in terms of marketing, production, and resources.

Analyzing Sales versus Profits

Since profit is so closely tied to both sales and costs, you must consider both of them whenever you are looking for ways to increase business profits. Selling more goods or services won't mean much if your costs also increase to any degree. On the other hand, if you can lower your costs, your profits will increase even when you don't make additional sales. In addition to doing the kind of annual analysis described above, you should also analyze the income and expenses related to each income-generating activity of your business.

An accountant once told me it was a lot easier to increase profits by decreasing costs than by increasing sales because of the high cost of marketing and obtaining each new customer. I saw the wisdom of that remark the first time I did a serious study of my own business records. I worked at my publishing and mail order business for almost two years before I found the time to get serious about my record books and the information in them. What I finally learned came as a real surprise.

At that time, I was writing articles and trade books, publishing a couple of my own books, reports and a newsletter, speaking, and doing some consulting. Each of those activities took a certain amount of my time, a factor that was fairly easy to estimate on an annual basis. Although I had always kept track of the income each of my business activities was generating each month and year, it was not until my third year in business that I decided to break down all the business expenses and overhead costs relating to each of those income categories. Suddenly I could see what really was happening with the business. Then I knew the direction I had to take to realize greater profits in the years ahead.

At the same time, I began to analyze the income and expenses related to each item in my product line. Then I could see that some products that seemed to be making money (based on gross sales) really were not profitable at all in terms of their material and handling costs. As a result, I dropped some of them.

Study of a Fictional Business

A thorough analysis of your books after a year or so will no doubt surprise you, too, particularly if you make and sell a variety of products, or if you are involved in a diversified business involving both products and services. Perhaps the fictionalized account below of a business that involves the sale of both products and services will give you a better idea of what I'm talking about. Let's assume that this business grosses $120,000 one year—$100,000 of which is from the sale of products, the balance from some service—let's say teaching. Here's how the figures might look on the Schedule C tax report:

Gross receipts or sales	$100,000	
Cost of goods (labor + materials)	− 25,000	(25% of gross sales)

Financial Considerations

Gross profit	$75,000 (75% of gross sales)
Other income (services)	+20,000
Gross income	$95,000
Less business deductions	−40,000 (42.1% of gross income)
Net profit before taxes	$55,000 (57.9% of gross sales)

There are many costs related to a product business, but the costs related to the service portion of this fictional business are nominal (a few materials and overhead expenses) because all direct expenses are paid in addition to the teacher's fee. That means the profit margin is going to be very high on the service side of this business, as the following illustration shows:

Product Portion of Business

$100,000	gross receipts
− 24,500 (24.5%)	labor + materials
$ 75,500 (75.5%)	gross profit
− 38,400 (38.4%)	deductions
$ 37,100 (37.1%)	net profit before taxes

Service Portion of Business

$ 20,000	gross receipts
− 500 (2.5%)	labor + materials
$ 19,500 (97.5%)	gross profit
− 1,600 (.08%)	deductions
$ 17,900 (89.5%)	net profit before taxes

In total, this fictional business has $65,000 in expenses. Although the bottom line is still the same—$55,000—the service portion of the business is clearly the most profitable in terms of labor, materials, and other expenses. But, to really understand what's happening here, one would need to continue the analysis by separating all the income and cost figures *for each individual product or service*. Although there might be ten or twelve products in a line, such an exercise might show that one of them was generating 50 percent of the income, and one or more were, in truth, costing more to inventory and ship than they were worth.

Whether this business owner decides to expand the service area or the product area would have much to do with the particular business and the market for the products or services it offers. If it is a one-person manufacturing company, and no plans are being made to hire employees to increase productivity, then perhaps it would pay to drop part or all of the product line and concentrate on providing additional services. Choosing the right direction for this business may not be a simple matter, but with figures to work with, at least the owner will not be making plans in the dark.

At least annually, do an income-versus-cost analysis for each product and service you offer. The answers you get will help you evaluate the correctness of all your prices and give you the comfortable feeling that you know where you're going and why, even when the profit picture is not as rosy as you would like it to be.

Understanding the Break-Even Point

Sometimes the price decision on a product or service can be made as a result of a break-even analysis. The "break-even point" is the point at which your annual income from sales covers your costs. The income received after this point is profit. Let's suppose that you've created a new product you think will sell for $25 at retail. You estimate you can sell 1,000 of these items in one year. You know your direct costs per item (materials; labor) will be $10, and you estimate your annual fixed expenses for the business (overhead) to be about $6,000. Here's how to find out how many items you would have to sell to break even:

1 The difference between the selling price of $25, and the direct costs of the item ($10) is $15, which is your "contribution to fixed costs per item." Until you reach your break-even point, every penny of this amount has to go toward covering your fixed expenses.

Dropping Unprofitable Products or Services

The only way to ensure continued profits for any business is through constant analysis of what's happening in that business. Whether you are selling products or services, it's important to periodically study sales and costs figures relating to your business. In them you will discover clues to what you must do to increase profits each year. Sometimes this means cutting expenses or increasing the price of certain products or services; sometimes it means adding something else to your line (which, incidentally, may have little effect on your overhead costs); and sometimes it means dropping a product or activity that clearly is proving to be unprofitable.

"We regularly try to analyze what is making us money and what isn't, and what is taking us too much time to do," says Sharon Richwine, JerryAnthonyPhoto.com. "Then we drop what isn't—including the occasional client who takes too much of our time. (This must be done tactfully of course—but sometimes it is best to tell them it is in both of your interests to find someone else to work with.")

"It's essential to have your customer names, history and record of purchases on computer," says Dodie Eisenhauer, VillageDesigns.com, who uses *QuickBooks* software for her business. "I pull reports regularly to learn how many of each item I've sold. I know what percentage of my income is generated by a particular item, what products to drop, and which ones to focus marketing attention on. By studying sales figures, I can tell how my business is changing from one year to the next. By doing annual comparisons, I can see how last year's gross sales compare to current sales. More specifically, I can study the buying habits of all my shops, looking at last year's sales versus sales to date and see the difference between the two."

2 Now apply the following formula to find out how many items you have to sell to break even:

$$\frac{\$6{,}000 \text{ total fixed costs}}{\$15 \text{ contribution to fixed costs}} = \begin{array}{c} 400 \text{ items, or number of sales} \\ \text{needed to break even} \end{array}$$
$$\text{per item}$$

3 To prove the calculation:

$$400 \text{ items} \times \$10 \text{ direct costs} = \$\ 4{,}000 \text{ direct costs}$$
$$+ \ \underline{\$\ 6{,}000 \text{ overhead}}$$
$$10{,}000 \text{ total costs}$$
$$\text{or } 400 \text{ items} \times \$25 = \$10{,}000 \text{ total sales}$$

Thus, if you have built in all your direct costs and other expenses related to this particular item, you would break even for the year when you had produced and sold 400 items.

By keeping careful records, you can determine the break-even point on a service-oriented project, too. My literary agent, Barbara Doyen, shares this tip on how her husband, Bob, helps her track the break-even point on the seminars they run together: "Bob maintains a project spreadsheet in his computer so we know when we've recouped our expenses on each seminar series. By keeping the bookkeeping current, we know whether we can afford more advertising, and whether we can fly instead of driving, etc. I do the same thing, only I tally our 'time expenses,' and by comparing our figures, we can determine if the results of our project were worth the investment in terms of both time and money."

Setting a Cost-Competitive Price

"No matter which method is used to monitor costs, costs alone are insufficient to fix a price," says the U.S. Department of Labor in one of its booklets. "Expenses must tell the entrepreneur one important fact: the price below which he is losing money. Costs only set a floor. Consumer demand will set the ceiling. In between, the business person must fix a cost-competitive price. In the last analysis, your price must lie somewhere between a product's cost and the ability of the buyer to get it somewhere else."

Reconsidering Your Pricing Strategies

The most expensive marketing mistakes are often those made as a result of hasty decisions based on inadequate market research or knowledge about one's industry. Such business ignorance, coupled with a lack of self-confidence or a fear of losing sales (or not getting customers at all) may also cause novice business owners to charge much less than the market will actually bear, making business survival almost impossible. (If you still need help with basic pricing problems, see the pricing chapter in *HOMEMADE MONEY: Starting Smart!*)

If you've been in business for awhile, it's probably time to check your pricing again and consider how it might affect the way buyers are positioning you or your business in their minds. (You'll learn more about repositioning strategies in the next chapter.) If you entered the marketplace with prices that were too low to begin with (as is so often the case with new businesses), your customers or clients may think you less worthy than your competition, being naturally suspicious of anyone who would offer good products or services at too-low prices. On the other hand, prices that are too high can just as easily position you in prospects' minds as being totally out of their financial reach when these may be the very people you're counting on to build your business. Thus, pricing becomes an important part of your overall marketing strategy, and you can't set the right prices without a thorough understanding of your costs, your industry, the economy, and a dozen other factors, not the least of which is your reputation as a business owner, entrepreneur, or expert in your field.

There comes a time, I've learned from experience, when it's necessary to raise prices not merely because they are justified by increased inflation or the cost of doing business, but simply as a matter of principle. During my years as a professional speaker, I gradually raised the fee I charged for seminars and keynote addresses not out of greed, but because the program directors I was dealing with naturally expected someone with my credentials to charge accordingly. I would have lost credibility as a business authority if I hadn't demanded prices similar to those of other professionals in my field.

Now relate this logic to your own business. I firmly believe that, as water always seeks its own level, so, too, will a business find its own level (market) by the way it prices its products and services.

Smart Tip

If you do something better than someone else, don't be afraid to say so, and charge accordingly. Be prepared to lose a few customers, clients or prospects when you raise your prices, but don't fret about it because you will automatically attract a whole new audience of buyers who can finally relate to you because your pricing fits their preconceived notion of what a business like yours ought to be charging.

Think Twice Before Lowering Price

When business is sluggish, and particularly in recessionary times, many sellers lower their prices in hopes of selling more products or services. Before you do this, stop and consider that a lowering of prices by 20 percent will mean that you have to bring in more than a 20 percent increase in sales just to offset your loss of revenue. It's tough to increase sales by 20 percent in a good year; in recessionary times, it's likely to be impossible. Perhaps a better strategy is to keep your prices the same, but introduce new and less expensive variations of your stand-by products and services. For example, I learned during one recession that, while fewer people purchased my books, more of them purchased my inexpensive line of special reports. And they often spent more on several reports than they would have spent on a book, indicating that lack of dollars was not the issue here. In recessionary times, people simply become more careful about how they spend the dollars they have. Perhaps buyers perceive special reports to be worth more to them when money is tight because they zero in on specific topics of interest to them at the moment.

An even better solution to lowering prices is to increase them—even double them. I've been giving this advice to product sellers for years, and many have told me how well it works. I've found it works even when done accidentally. In one of my monthly magazine columns, I once offered one of my books at $11.45 ppd, but due to a typographical error the price appeared as $22.45. Nevertheless, I received almost as many mail orders for the book as I'd received when it had been offered earlier at the correct price (and had to send a lot of refund checks as a result). Clearly a certain percentage of my column's readers felt this book was worth twice what I was then charging for it, proving once again that you can double your present prices and still find a market willing to pay for what you offer. Think about it.

Pricing Psychology

If you can't sell something at a certain price, try reverse psychology. Don't lower the price—raise it! Yes, you may lose some customers, but your higher price will automatically attract a totally new audience of buyers.

Once there was a woman who started a teddy bear repair service. When she eventually decided to do something else, she thought she had an excellent strategy for killing her bear business: she would simply double her prices to discourage customers. To her amazement, business increased. As one customer explained, "I was reluctant to bring my antique teddy to you before because your prices seemed suspiciously low. Now I'm confident you can be trusted to do the job."

Coping with Ever-Increasing Costs of Doing Business

"What is the smartest thing you've done recently to lower your overhead costs or increase your net profits at year's end?" I asked my book contributors. Some said they had simply raised their product prices or rates for services, while others sent these interesting responses:

- "I have diversified my business," says marketing consultant Tammy Harrison. "Instead of selling one thing at a time (such as advertising), I do a lot of things. It's kind of like your retirement plan—the experts tell you to make sure you have real estate if the stock market is soft, and vice versa. I have created some additional business opportunities for when the ad market isn't going so great."

- "I've encouraged clients to send larger loads of sharpening instead of nickling-and-diming me to pick up stuff at their businesses," says Velda Solomon, who owns a sharpening business. "I guess you can call this 'consolidating trips,' which I do anyhow for everything. Also, I bought an ultrasonic cleaning tank. It cost a bunch, but it saves a ton of cleaning time on equipment, thus speeding up our turnaround time and enabling us to do more sharpening jobs in an evening."

- "I use only black-and-white ink in my computer printer and print fewer items," says network marketer Martha Oskvig. "I look at every drive in my car and every expenditure for our home with my business deductibles in mind, recording odometer readings and a description of the business activity on every eligible trip. I also keep a folder for all grocery household expense receipts. (In case I later decide to use an item for customer refreshments or in my business, I can locate the receipt to mark and file with my tax records.)"

- "I self-publish my own quilt patterns, and have to be constantly aware of changes in cost to print and copy, both black-and-white and in color," says Terrie Kralik, MooseCountryQuilts.com. "My first few patterns were designed to fit paper sized 18" × 24" or 24" × 24" paper, which costs a lot to print and only a few print shops have this capability. I have since rewritten those pages to fit on standard paper sizes like 8$^1/_2$ × 11", 8$^1/_2$" × 14," or 11" × 17", making copying simple and inexpensive. The tradeoff is that it's easier for consumers to photocopy and share among friends."

Raise Profits by Cutting Costs

One of the smartest things I ever did was to become "unit price conscious." See the card below? At the end of my third year of business, I took the time to set up a three-year cost history of previous printing jobs, office supplies, and other materials used in the business. I continue to use these cards today. Now, each time I order supplies or printing, I have a handy record of where I last got them, and at what price. By checking invoices against these cards, I can quickly spot any billing errors that might occur, and what I see on the card may also prompt me to look for a new source of supply, or perhaps increase the size of certain orders to get a better discount. (I don't include shipping costs in my per-unit figures because I want to compare apples to apples when comparing suppliers. Freight costs mount up, and you may get not only lower unit prices from new suppliers, but cut shipping costs if they're nearer to you.)

Becoming unit-conscious in your business can result in increased profits at the end of the year. Whenever you see your suppliers increasing their prices, consider whether it's necessary for you to increase prices as well. Small business owners cannot afford to waste any of their profits, and attention to small details like this can often make a big difference.

ARTICLE				
71629				
Date	Quantity	Price	Per	Purchased From

Handling Lack-of-Money Problems

Unless you're a rare bird, you're going to have occasional (if not continual) cash flow problems that necessitate the need for occasional bank loans, a line of credit or, failing either, a credit card you can max out for awhile. In chapters that follow, you'll find tips on how to successfully bring in the bucks through marketing strategies that cost little or nothing at all, and in the business management area of Section II, you'll find additional tips on how to get loans or extra cash for business operation or expansion. Meanwhile, here are examples of how some business owners have dealt with their need for additional capital for day-to-day operation or business expansion.

Bank Loans

Russ Schultz, author of *Back to the Basics—Running Your Homebased Business for Profit* (an eBook available on WriteandReap.com) advises home-business owners never to pledge collateral to obtain a business loan or to take out a second mortgatge on their home. "If the business fails, you can lose your home or other valuable assets," he warns. "Although it may take longer to realize financial success when you use business revenue to pay for your expenses month to month, the struggle is worth it especially when you don't have to worry about paying a large loan back over several years."

A safer way is to build a good credit history as soon as you begin your business. "When I first started out on my own, a friend told me to go to my bank and borrow a few thousand bucks for thirty days," says copywriter Bob Westenberg. "If you have a good credit rating, you won't need any major collateral for that. Pay back the loan a few days early, wait sixty days or so, and borrow an amount a bit higher. Pay it back a few days early. Then, when you go to borrow something more substantial, you have an excellent history that will help get approval for your quest for capital. Costs a bit of interest, but not much. (If you put the borrowed $2,000 in an account and get 5 percent or more on it and it costs you 10 or 15 percent interest on the loan, it's peanuts").

Smart Tip

When your money just won't stretch far enough, certain bills should be paid first to keep your credit history clean. Banks, finance companies, and major credit card companies generally report to credit agencies right away, so pay them first. Gas credit charges and American Express may not report late payments until an account is several months overdue. The same is true of doctor and dentist bills, utilities, rent or mortgage payments. If you can't make a business loan payment, or the full mortgage payment, ask the bank if you can pay just the interest for one month.

Line of Credit

"Business loans for homebased businesses are tough to obtain because the banking industry is generally suspicious of the viability of homebased business activity, especially when it is in the start-up phase," says Russ Schultz. "However, my wife, Karen, was able to get an $8,000 line of credit for her new Interior Redesign business at home based on her excellent personal credit history (and the fact that she had a checking account with this particular banking institution). She was able to write checks to cover expenses without worry of bouncing them. Six months later, when she had used over $5000 of the credit line, the bank offered to raise the limit to $12,000. She declined because her business flourished. After one year, she paid off the credit line and now has an $8,000 line of credit as a back-up."

Credit Card Loans

"Before I had a line of credit, I put a lot of charges on my business credit card to get ready for the fall and holiday season of 2001," says clothing manufacturer Pamela Burns, Injeanious.org. "Based on my previous sales I felt I was not taking a risk to be able to pay it back in full by the end of the year. Unfortunately business suffered after the 9-11 terrorist attack and I was left with a lot of inventory and didn't have the sales to pay back the credit card debt. When I finally went to my bank about this problem, the manager told me that all businesses should have a line of credit just waiting for this type of thing, even if it is never actually used. Since I had a business account there and good credit, I was able to get a line of credit at the current prime rate and pay off the credit card debt. Luckily, I have not had to increase what I owe, and am paying it down while keeping up with current expenses. I would highly recommend getting a business line of credit right away."

Many small business owners handle temporary cash flow problems with credit card loans, but if you're going to do this, try Russ Schultz's strategy. "A financing tool I have used has been the zero percent interest credit card," he says. "Of course, you have to have good credit to get one of these cards. For example, I just received an offer for a Platinum Visa card offering a zero percent fixed introductory APR on balance transfers for a year (after which time the normal interest rate would kick in). I could simply write a check for what I needed (this sometimes requires a small advance fee), paying off the interest-charging card and transferring my credit card debt to the zero-interest card. I can usually get up to $5,000 interest free for one year doing this. During the next year, I put a major portion of my earned revenue from the home business into a savings account and at the end of the year, I pay back the 'loan' with no interest."

Getting Cash in a Flash

If you cannot (or simply prefer not to) borrow money, it's important to hone your marketing skills to the point where you can bring in a flood of extra cash in a flash. For example, gift wholesaler Dodie Eisenhauer encounters cash flow problems during periods when she is building inventory for holiday selling seasons. In addition to the line of credit she maintains, she often generates quick cash by entering a few retail craft shows. "Such interaction with customers always boosts my morale while giving me cash in a hurry," she says.

Rubber stamp manufacturer Sue Krei, WoodCellarGraphics.com, uses eBay to keep cash flowing into her business. "The main part of our business is now retail, with orders coming from our Web site and rubber stamps that we auction on eBay," she explains. "These auctions work great for us as it keeps cash coming in regularly and also sends people to our Web site. Each auction that we list on eBay has a direct link to our site. Also, when I send out notices to the winning bidders, there is information on the notice about current sales on our site, so we get a lot of add-on orders as a direct result of eBay auctions."

In my publishing/mail order days, I could always generate two or three thousand dollars in a couple of weeks' time simply by mailing a follow-up postcard or promotional newsletter to one of my best prospect or customer mailing lists. Here are some additional quick tips on how to get some business (money!) in a hurry:

- Telephone some of your best customers or clients to see if they need one of your products or services at this time.

- Also make telephone calls to a selected list of "hot prospects."

- Contact the rest of your prospect and customer bases with postcard mailings promoting specific products or services likely to be of interest. (Turnaround time: two weeks.)

- Check your business competitors to see if they could use your help in handling overflow work.

- If you sell a service, look closely at prospects in your community to identify a few who clearly need your business. Depending on what you do, a quick, observant walk around the neighborhood might do the trick.

Collection Strategies

Coping with ever-increasing costs is one thing—making sure you get all the money that's due you from customers or clients is another. We've all been stiffed somewhere along the line, and when it's money we've really been counting on, it's hard to accept the financial loss. Here is how some business owners deal with this problem.

- **Set Established Payment Guidelines.** To avoid problems in the first place, establish ground rules for how payment must be made and stick to them. (See "Terms of Sale" in the A-to-Z section of this book.) Also have set guidelines for how you will handle checks and credit cards (a topic discussed at greater length in *HOMEMADE MONEY: Starting Smart!*). For example, Martha Oskvig makes it a point to obtain authorization on credit card purchases before delivering products. She also handles any bank paperwork on such charges within a day of the transaction.

- **Get It in Writing.** "Be sure your agreement/contract or memo of understanding states what the payment expectations are and the consequences for non-payment," advises Donna Snow, SnowWrite.com. "When you go over the contract with your client, be sure they initial the payment policy section. This way they can't say, 'you didn't tell me' or 'I didn't understand,' and this can be used later if the event escalates to small claims."

  "It is always helpful to have something in writing that explicitly states what the terms and conditions are," agrees copywriter Gary Maxwell, GaryMaxwell.com. "This gives you more leverage in the actions you take."

  "I limit amounts due to me from new accounts by requiring monthly (or phased) payments for my contracted and writing services," says Martha Oskvig. "Even if a project is ongoing, this is prearranged as part of the contract agreement. It is part of my professionalism: if (after their legal counsel says the agreement is fine) they won't sign it, I don't work for them. I submit itemized bills on the month's work (or regarding completion of the phase of a project). If payment is not received within seven days, I do no more work for them. To make this work, I must create phases of the work with an accountability aspect to which both of us can agree before the project is done. I specifically chart my time and progress on a daily basis for the grant-proposal writing and consultant work I do for different clients. Each billing includes a brief progress report, projections, and recommendations."

- **Send a Series of Reminders.** "What has worked for me so far is just being nice, polite, and persistent—calling on a regular basis and always asking nicely," says consultant Judy Schramm.

"When you work virtually, it is very difficult to handle collections," says Tammy Harrison, TheQueenofPizzazz.com. "I have an advertiser owing me money at this time, and it is very inconvenient. It's not a lot of money, but I will not let it be until I have resolved it, or until I decide to write off the expense. Thus far, it's only a couple of months late, so I am still pursuing it with e-mails. Should it become much more delinquent, I will start telephone calls (daily) to get the issue resolved. I used to work for attorneys, so if it becomes necessary, I will follow through with a 'lawyer letter' as well as pursue legal action. I performed the duties I was to be paid for, and I do not take non-payment lightly."

"Only customers you trust should have more than one outstanding invoice at a time," says designer Terrie Kralik. "And don't tell them until *after* they've paid that they've now become a COD or credit card-only customer."

When Leila Peltosaari, Tikkabooks.com, needs to collect overdue accounts, she lets her husband make the call. "That is his strength," she says, adding that she's too sweet. However, with a large company like Baker & Taylor, who would pay eventually but might take months to do it, Leila found that sweetness worked just fine. "I called and explained that I was just a little guy trying to survive, so could they please help me by paying their bills on time. The woman who answered the phone said she would put a note in my file, and since then I have been paid promptly."

- **Evaluate the Situation, Present Options.** "My strategy for deadbeats is to first evaluate the integrity of the client," says Gary Maxwell. "This is not always easy to do but experience says to give the client the benefit of the doubt. If the client is overdue by a small margin (say a week) give them some time (again, the benefit of the doubt). But as the days turn into weeks and then months, I suggest starting with a friendly phone call or e-mail to follow up and let them know that payment is overdue. Next, I would send a registered letter. This has the effect of getting your point across in a weighty manner without your having to confront them verbally or in person. After all else fails, let them know that all other avenues have been exhausted and that you are either (1) turning the matter over to your lawyer or a collection agency, or (2) taking them to small claims court. Keep in mind that if you ever want to work with this client again in the future, you will use these collection methods wisely."

"A while back, I had a large insurance company not pay me for services they'd asked me to provide," recalls medical-legal nurse consultant Susan Kilpatrick. "The amount was huge—many thousands. I first sent the 'perhaps you've overlooked the bill' letters, then called, then had my attorney call, and finally sued in Small Claims Court. But I ended up receiving only a percentage of the money owed me. Of course, I'll never do business with this client again, and I have told my closest colleagues about their unethical behavior. This was a huge eye-opener for me. Now I've learned to stop a project as quickly as a client stops paying. I tell them *why* the project has been stopped and explain that I'll resume upon receiving payment due."

● **Be Persistent in Trying to Collect.** "Persistence is the best way to collect," says author Jeff Zbar, ChiefHomeOfficer.com. "Many companies become delinquent because of laziness, not necessarily a desire to stiff someone. Weekly phone calls or e-mail often result in the client or accounts payable person just wanting to get you off their back."

"The hard part is sticking to your guns and demanding payment," adds Donna Snow. "Hard luck stories and our natural tendency to rescue others puts us in a quandary as to how to deal with non-payment. When selling a service, we tend to do the work first and bill later, which often leads to problems collecting. It's hard for clients who don't pay to conceptualize what it is you as a service provider are losing when they do not follow through with their end of the deal."

● **Be Willing to Sue.** "You have to be willing to sue, or even threaten suit, to show that you mean business," adds Jeff Zbar. "Often, as small business owners, we're perceived as weak-willed and unwilling to go to the mat for what's ours. Until we demand professional attention—whether that's getting paid on time or being given a chance to compete with larger organizations— we're always going to be relegated to second-class status. Sometimes a few well-chosen words in the business community can let others know the potential downside of working with a slow-paying customer. If they value their reputation, they may pay up to get you to shut up. For those who refuse to pay, keeping an attorney on hand to write the occasional letter can help."

● **Know When to Quit.** "If you can't collect, don't let it get to you," advises Bernard Kamoroff, author of *Small Time Operator*. "Try to collect if you have the time and ambition to do so, but if not, just write it off to experience. Forget the money—it's not worth the aggravation."

Judy Schramm agrees. "So far everyone has paid, although some have paid very late and one client is still paying off a project I did seven years ago. If I did get stuck, I would probably just write it off. Unless it was a very large debt, I would lose more money taking the time to pursue it than I would gain."

For more information on using collection agencies and small claims court, as well as specific how-to collection tips and an example of how to use humor in your reminder letters, see "Collection Techniques" in the A-to-Z Section of this book.

He Invented a Fictitious Credit/Collections Manager

Copywriter Bob Westenberg didn't like writing collection letters, so he decided to invent a credit and collections manager to write them for him. He picked the manager's name the day he looked out his office window and saw Kentucky Fried Chicken across the street. Thus Mr. K. F. Chin was born!

"I found I could be tough when writing as Mr. Chin," Bob says. "When anyone called and asked for him, I knew it was about a credit problem and I could play good guy/bad guy on it. (K. F. was always out of the office.)"

Believe it or not . . . K. F. even got into *Who's Who in the Midwest*. Just for fun, Bob—ever the copywriter—filled out a biography for him and submitted it. K. F. Chin thus became Kenneth Fu Chin, son of Wang and Su Li Chin. He had an interesting background, all made up. "The publisher wrote back, and I figured I had

(Continued on Next Page)

been caught," Bob recalls. "Nope. They just wanted to know his date of naturalization. They never did notice that he served two years in the U.S. Air Force while he was living in Hong Kong! When I sold my advertising card deck to a Fortune 500 company, an executive in the company called about the details of the sale. 'You don't get K. F. Chin with this sale,' I told him, laughingly explaining that Mr. Chin was a fictitious character who was actually listed in *Who's Who*. There was a long, uncomfortable, icy silence, and then he said, *'That happens to be one of our publications!'*

"Oops. The deal went through in spite of this mini confrontation, and I still use K. F. Chin when writing to someone in arrears. He's been with me about 28 years now. I can hardly get rid of the guy! Whenever someone brags to me that they're in *Who's Who*, I love to tell them the story of the fictitious character who is also in there. Deflates 'em rapidly! Mr. Chin attended Hong Kong U. (no such school), was credit officer of Hong Kong Export Intl. (no such firm), taught a credit and collections course at Coconino County College (no such college), member of the Society of Credit/Collection Management (no such organization), inventor of 'nail-hold' (no such product), and writes for National Credit Exchange (no such publication). Other than that, Ken is just your average entry in *Who's Who*. (You can see they check info carefully. Their main goal is to get you to buy the book. Of course, Ken didn't buy it.)"

P.S. Have you ever noticed on business letters how the typist always includes her initials down at the bottom of a letter to show it wasn't typed by the sender, but by a secretary? Well, Bob also invented "es," initials for Effie, who has been his fictitious typist for 29 years. "We one-man bands have to look like we have others in the office and don't have to type our own letters," he says. "I like to tell people that a one-man-band has to play all the instruments, but on payday he also gets to keep all the checks. I wouldn't have it any other way."

Chapter 4:
Developing a Marketing Strategy

Link what you stand for (your values) to what you are seeking to accomplish (your vision). Then build on this synergy, creating a mission statement that outlines precisely where you want to go and what you'll do to get there. Given this powerful linkage between values, vision and mission, two plus two equals five. In this context, you have extraordinary motivation to achieve your goals.

> —Dan Stamp, founder, Priority Management Systems, Bellevue, WA

Some people with a college education in business and marketing don't understand some of the basic marketing principles discussed in this chapter. As a marketing major once told me: "The nuts-and-bolts rules of business are not mentioned in business school. It's assumed 100 percent of graduates will go to work for someone else who's already figured it out. A marketing major is trained to be a salesperson. I was taught to sell but learned nothing about the channels of distribution, advertising, or sources of supply for businesses outside of the Fortune 500. It is expected you will learn these things on your way up the corporate ladder in your chosen industry."

Don't let the word "marketing" intimidate you. It is just a cumulative word that describes a company's total promotion, advertising, and sales activities. There is a difference between sales and marketing, and you should know it since you probably will have to do both for awhile, if not forever. A *salesperson* is concerned with what products or services he or she has to offer, and which of their features can be emphasized to make the sale. The *person in marketing*, on the other hand, needs to be concerned with what customers want, how many different kinds of customers there are (called the "universe"), and how they can be located and then convinced of the benefits of the company's products.

Focusing on Benefits

What you need to concentrate on is not your product or service, per se, but its *benefits to users*. "Run a perception check," advises super-salesman Tom Stoyan, CanadasSalesCoach.com. "Ask your present clients why they decided to buy from you. You may be surprised by their answers. We want different things from different people, and prospects are the same. They may want price, quality, a problem-solver, a friendly ear, an intelligent discussion. Your job is to discover needs you are able to fulfill. Then convince the prospect you can."

More important to customers than the quality of your product or the swiftness of your service is how well it's going to satisfy their needs or desires. Or, as one writer said in a marketing article, "People buy drills because they want holes." I've always liked the mousetrap illustration Leonard Felder once used in an article for *Publishers Weekly* on how marketing concepts had changed over the years. In the old days, he explained, all you had to do was build a better mousetrap, then go out and sell it. "Now, any old mousetrap can catch mice," he said. "But consumers want a silent unseen trap that leaves no mess and won't hurt domestic animals; they want, in other words, not only relief from mice, but also safety, cleanliness, convenience, and peace of mind."

In short, Felder emphasized, the goal of selling mousetraps has now been replaced by the goal of marketing a service to customers who need safe, clean, and convenient protection from mice. If you are going to bring in the bucks from a business today, you need to apply this kind of thinking to every product or service you sell.

Home business novices typically begin with little money and a strong belief that if they deliver a quality product or service and work very hard, they'll succeed in business. While this is important, it's only part of the picture. More than likely, the difference between financial success or failure will depend on management and marketing skills—one's clever approach to the marketplace . . . the way the business idea is publicized or advertised . . . the way a product is packaged, presented or delivered . . . or the pizazz with which a service is performed. Most entrepreneurs learn about marketing the hard way, by making expensive mistakes that teach them what not to do the next time around—like placing display ads in the wrong publications, exhibiting in trade shows without a knowledge of industry pricing structures or channels of distribution, or offering the right product or service to the wrong audience and vice versa. Like Alice in Wonderland, many business beginners lack a sense of direction:

Alice asks the cat, *"Can you tell me, please, which way I should walk from here?"*
The cat replies, *"That depends on which way you want to go."*

So it is in marketing. Once you have determined your most likely market, you need a plan—some kind of roadmap—to get your products from here to there. It begins with market research that enables you to identify, describe, and categorize the current and future market for a particular product or service. Although sophisticated marketers use demographics available from government sources (such as the Census Bureau), and statistical information compiled by trade associations, publications, and private research firms, small businesses rarely need to go to such lengths to learn about their market. Many simply talk to potential buyers to see if there's any interest; network with other business professionals at conferences or trade shows; or browse shops, stores, and mail order catalogs to see what's selling at what price.

Your research will be concerned with the customer, the product or service, the competition, and outside forces (like the economy) that might affect one's business. It is interesting detective work and a critical part of your marketing plan. It's not enough to know that a market exists for what you offer. *What is important is that you know—in advance—exactly how you're going to connect with it, promote to it, and sell to it.* (See sidebar, "Market Research Checklist.")

Remember to Listen!

"My number one commandment for selling a service is *Listen!*," says Robert Bly, author of *Selling Your Services* (Henry Holt). "Most people who sell do it absolutely wrong. They go in and tell the prospect what they want to say, reciting a memorized list of product features and benefits. But what prospects care about is what is important to them—their needs, their problems, their concerns, their fears, their desires, their goals, their dreams. Successful salespeople tailor their presentations to show how the features of their products or service can give every client what he or she desires most or needs to solve his or her problem."

Niche Marketing

Any time is a good time to look for market niches—little "pockets of riches" your competition may be overlooking. Many businesses that have failed during hard economic times might have succeeded if they had simply concentrated on selling not to the masses, but to niche markets. Others might have survived if they had taken steps earlier to diversify their business. Niche marketing and diversification are closely connected since the discovery of a niche market often requires one to create, or at least vary, an existing product or service. (You'll find a wealth of diversification ideas in Chapter 11.)

Niche market ideas often open up when you begin to think in terms of how your products will benefit specific buyers or solve a particular problem. Also ask yourself what you can do to stand out in the crowd. Is there a niche your competition has failed to fill? Can you, perhaps, become a specialist in an area where there are many generalists? The most successful niche marketers will always be those with special expertise in a particular area. In some cases, their knowledge and experience enable them to speak to their market as a friend who knows and understands what they're going through. (I'm a perfect example of this kind of marketer.) In other cases, an individual's special skills

Developing a Marketing Strategy

or techniques command total control of a particular niche market. One example that comes to mind is the Celtic jewelry being created by Helen Chantler. (You'll recall husband Marc Choyt's comments in the previous chapter about the incredible growth of their business.) "Our design line is contemporary Celtic, but we use southwest jewelry techniques and Etruscan chain to create an original 3D look that has been highly successful," says Marc. "No one else in the world is doing what we're doing."

Susan Kilpatrick provides another interesting example. "As an RN, I worked in case management coordinating the diagnoses and treatment of those who were injured on the job," she explains. "Here, I began to see a rather large segment of people who had more than simple injuries and rapid returns to work. I saw malpractice, insurance company fraud, and injured worker fraud. Putting two and two together, I decided I wanted to be on the ethically correct side, so I began to tell attorneys what I could do for them as a medical-legal consultant. My services are expensive, but when an attorney wants a real answer about a client's situation, it's much less expensive to hire my expertise than it is to hire a physician's opinion."

Like Marc and Helen with their unique jewelry, Susan doesn't have much competition. "It's unusual for an RN to make as much money as I do and others are trying to replicate what I do," she says. "I wasn't the first to do this, but I am one of few in Oklahoma and I have a reputation for telling it how it is. I welcome competition because there is ample work to go around. As more nurses enter into my area, it serves to further educate the public as to what my expertise can do for them."

In looking for niche markets, you've got to narrow your thinking and remember that different segments of the marketplace will require different copywriting and advertising approaches. For example, if you have a product or service for mothers, are you really trying to reach every mother in the country, or only young working executives with preschool children and discretionary income? If you offer something for gardeners, are you trying to reach every gardener in the country, or only those who are interested in growing herbs or roses? If you're a business specialist, are you planning to help everyone in business, or will you target specific groups, such as retailers, small manufacturers, Web entrepreneurs, or other business professionals such as doctors, lawyers, and accountants?

Smart Tip

To find new niches for your products and services, begin by dividing your market into logical segments. Then take a closer look at each of the products and services you currently offer, and relate them to the market segments you've just identified. Now consider which of your products or services can be modified to serve a different segment of your market. Have the needs of one or more segments changed because of the economy, technology, or other factors? If so, start brainstorming for new products and services you can add to your business mix. Each group of people or businesses with similar needs or demands adds up to another market niche just waiting to be filled.

Repositioning Your Business

You've surely heard the old adage about how stupid it is to expect different results while continuing to do the same things in the same old way. Yet this is just what many unsuccessful business owners are doing. They keep placing the same kind of ineffective ad or sending the same kind of direct mailer, or attending the same kind of shows, hoping each time for a different response than they received the last time around, when what they really need to do is try a different marketing strategy.

One of the things you may need to change now is the way you've positioned your business. *Positioning* is something you do to the minds of your prospects to make them perceive you in a particular way. You automatically position your business by your choice of a business name; the title you use to describe yourself; and the way you design your Web site, business cards, and stationery. Your choice of words when you communicate with people, your business motto or logo, the positioning statement you may use in your advertising and promotional material, and the special names you give to your products or services also work to position you badly or beautifully in the minds of buyers.

Every time we turn around today, we find that something that used to be called one thing is now called another, and these changes are generally made for marketing purposes or because someone has decided that the

Market Research Checklist

To take the mystery out of marketing, look for clues to who your customers or clients might be, where they are located, and how you might reach them with publicity, advertising, or sales calls. The following questions will help you define the market for any new product or service:

- What, *exactly*, am I trying to sell? (If you can't define your product or service in 50 words or less, you will have a hard time trying to publicize or advertise it.)

- Why do I think my product or service will sell?

- Is my product or service something people want, or need? What are its benefits to buyers?

- If it's something people do not need, why might they want to buy it anyway? (As a gift? For leisure time enjoyment? Business convenience? To save time, money, aggravation? To beautify their home, enrich their life, or satisfy a nostalgic desire?)

- Who is my ideal customer or client? (Male? Female? Young, middle-aged, older? A white-collar worker? Blue-collar worker? Corporate executive? Homebased business person? Professional or technical worker, homemaker, consumer . . . who, exactly?)

- Where do my clients or customers live or work? (In the community, my county, my state, a specific geographic region, or nationwide? Worldwide, perhaps?)

- How can I connect with these people? What trade or consumer periodicals, ezines, organizations, trade shows, directories, or mailing lists are available? What established networks exist for my clients or customers?

- Is my product or service available elsewhere in stores or by mail? At retail or wholesale prices? Can I compete pricewise?

(Continued on Next Page)

- Is there currently a strong demand for my product or service? Why? Is it related to the economy? Is demand likely to increase, or decrease, with a change in the economy? Is the current demand a fad, or is it likely to endure for a long time? If a fad, can I move quickly to capitalize on it before it dies?

- Is the market for my product or service likely to expand slowly, quickly, or not at all? Is my product or service closely tied to some other, similar product or service for which the market could expand—or collapse—very quickly?

- Is my entry into the marketplace more dependent on price than on quality? If so, can I successfully compete in this type of market?

- What kind of competition will I/do I have . . . locally, regionally, nationally?

- Is my product or service newer, better, different from that of my competition? Does it offer higher quality? Longer life? More speed or efficiency? (The very fact that competition exists proves a demand, or at least a *need* for what you offer. In the end, your competition may become your marketing strength, provided you work with it and not against it.)

- How does my competition publicize and sell? Will the same techniques work for me? What can I offer, say, and do that they can't?

- Is the competition overlooking a segment of the market I can reach? (Larger companies often ignore smaller markets because they are not worth their time and trouble, but such markets may be perfect niche markets for homebased entrepreneurs.)

- If there is no competition, why? (Maybe the need for your product or service is being satisfied in some other way, or maybe it simply is not a profitable idea to begin with; or maybe your idea is so new and unique, no one has thought of it yet.)

—an excerpt from *HOMEMADE MONEY: Starting Smart!* (M. Evans) public's preconceived image of someone or something needs to be changed. For example, when management of a local hospital started getting flack from its patients about the $16 charge being made for an ice pack, they neatly repositioned that ordinary item in the minds of patients by giving it a more expensive-sounding name: a "Thermal Therapy Kit." When the traditional cedar chest (often called the "Hope" chest) fell out of favor with young brides, the Lane Company began to call its products "love chests," thus positioning itself as "the company that makes furniture for lovers." A candymaker who began with a mailing to 75 friends on his Christmas card list went on to generate candy sales of more than a million dollars a year after repositioning his product in the marketplace. Instead of selling candy in food and gourmet shops, where it was *expensive* in relation to other items being sold, he sold it in fine gift shops, where it was *inexpensive* when compared to other items being sold. (In addition, it was often the only edible in the shop.)

Smart Tip

If you didn't create a positioning statement when you started your business, take time to do this now. Look carefully at who you are and what you do; then try to write a brief core concept statement that summarizes your positioning statement (see related sidebar).

The Game of the Name

Novice business owners rarely realize how important the use of words and names can be to the success of a business, but long-time pros will tell you it is possible to attract a totally new market for your products or services merely by changing the words you use to describe yourself or your business and the products and services you sell. In fact, there is quite a game to this business of a name, and it can greatly affect your ability to command higher prices for both products and services. Here are some examples to get you thinking about changes you may need to make to increase sales and profits.

Creating Your Positioning and Core Concept Statements

In creating a "positioning statement," you need to consider what business you're in, your primary goal, what you feel your strengths and weaknesses are compared to those of your competition, and how you see the need for your product or service in today's marketplace. In short, you need to be able to state *why your product or service has value, and why it should be purchased.* No product or service can be all things to all people, so you must deliberately position your products, services, and your business itself or you may find they have been positioned by circumstances you do not control, and not always to your advantage.

Once you've written a positioning statement, try to create a "core concept statement" as well—a tight seven-word summarization of your positioning statement. Remember that what you do isn't exactly what you *do.* Consider, for example, this positioning statement of a homebased beauty shop owner who doesn't just "do women's hair."

"No," she says, "I satisfy the need for physical enhancement among working women in my town who don't have much time." To translate this positioning statement into a seven-word "core concept statement," she might say, "I make busy working women look good!"

—excerpt from *HOMEMADE MONEY: Starting Smart!* (M. Evans)

Picking the Right Product Names

What you call a product you make or manufacture has a lot to do with how well it's going to sell in both the retail and wholesale marketplaces. Changing the name of a product or product line or giving it a different identity is a great way to quickly reposition it in the minds of buyers. For example, a catalog seller found a charming brass doll bed he wanted to offer, but he was concerned that its high price would discourage sales. After all, one will pay only so much for a doll bed. Solution: He added a colorful mattress and a doggie bone and offered the item as a Deluxe Dog Bed, which, not surprisingly, became a hot seller.

A common complaint from many product makers—particularly those who make handcrafts—is that they can't find the right market, or worse, they have the right market in mind, but their pricing structure will not allow for wholesaling to it. If this is your problem, one solution might be to change the name of whatever you're selling (i.e., reposition the product), double or triple its price, add a fancy designer label and hang tag, and offer it to a more affluent market.

For example, if you were to offer an originally designed vest and call it a "handmade patchwork vest," you'd likely appeal to the type of buyer who might pay from $25 to $45 for the item at a crafts fair or in a small shop. On the other hand, if you were to take this same item, create half a dozen other unique vest designs and call the line "InVESTments," you might be able to sell the garments for up to $500 or more in the right outlets. (The "InVESTments" word came to me out of the blue—I don't know if it's original or merely remembered. Do not use it without a thorough trademark search.)

Merely by changing the name of a product or giving it a unique identification, while adding other professional touches—the fabric labels required by law, a "designer label" (in this case, an InVESTments logo on a fancy hang tag that proclaims each vest to be "One-of-a-Kind Wearable Art")—you would be in a position to sell to exclusive shops in major cities. Here, you could reach a whole new audience of women who are used to spending hundreds or thousands of dollars on designer clothing because they know they're not going to meet themselves coming down the street. In a word, they are paying for the benefit called *prestige*.

Back in the 1960s when I was selling handpainted boxes and other crafts, I had an interesting shop experience that taught me a valuable lesson. I took several of my boxes to an exclusive shop on the north shore of Chicago and was amazed when the manager opened them and said, "But there's nothing in them." Of course not, I said; people buy empty boxes because they have things they want to put in them. But she just wasn't interested. I thought about her strange attitude and came up with an idea. When I went back a few weeks later, I presented the same line of boxes, with one difference: This time, each one had a musical movement in it. "Ah!" she exclaimed. "What lovely *music boxes* these are." Voila! The same boxes I could not sell empty were now attractive to her at three times the price. Yet my only extra cost was an inexpensive movement and fifteen minutes' labor to insert it.

You don't have to make boxes to apply this kind of thinking to your product line. Just look at everything you make and ask yourself what changes or additions you could make that might enable you to call things by a different and more expensive-sounding name. (For more ideas, see sidebar, "Naming Handcrafted Products.") There's quite a game to this business of the name, and don't you forget it.

Your Title and What You Do

The title you use for yourself—the words you use to describe what you do— is also a powerful positioning tool that has much to do with the kind of customers and clients you will attract. For example, are you a "legal typist," or a professional whose motto is "The Lawyer's Best Friend"? Are you the fellow down the street who fixes old furniture, or are you an "Old World Artisan" who offers expert refinishing of antiques?

When I began my business, I called myself a "crafts marketing authority" because I began as a crafts seller, then went on to write a book and publish a crafts marketing newsletter. Initially, I attracted creative people only. With the publication of the first edition of *Homemade Money*, however, I had a product with a market much broader than the crafts industry. To tap it, I had to reposition myself and my business in the eyes of book buyers, and I did this by (1) changing the name of my business from "Artisan Crafts" to "Barbara Brabec Productions," (2) changing the name of the newsletter I was then publishing from *Sharing Barbara's Mail* to *National Home Business Report*, and (3) changing what I called myself. (I was the first one in the United States to use the title of "Home Business Development Specialist," but many others soon picked up on it.) In total, this repositioning move greatly broadened my market, increased my sales, enhanced my reputation as an expert, and enabled me to command higher speaking fees—not bad for just changing a few words here and there.

In describing what you do, remember that what you do isn't necessarily what you *do*. For example, in the years when I was writing and publishing books, producing a newsletter, speaking at conferences and presenting home-business seminars, what I was actually *doing* (my "core concept statement") was "helping people succeed in a homebased business." Today, even though my activities are different, I'm still doing the same thing. Marketing consultant Daryl Ochs, StreetSmartBusiness.com, offers another example. He helps people build business success but, as he explains, "What I do doesn't describe the result—it describes the *cause*. When speaking to a prospect, I need to focus on the result, not the cause. In my case, my core marketing message is *'I help business owners and professionals attract more customers and clients.'* Immediately you know the result. If you are interested in attracting more business, this message demands close attention. If it doesn't interest you, then you're not a prospect for me. See the connection?"

Using a Motto or Slogan

A motto (a short expression of a guiding principle) is a good positioning tool, particularly when it points to an unfilled niche in the market or emphasizes something that is lacking in a competitor's product, as in "the only soap that floats." For her SnowWrite.com site (a clever play on words), Donna Snow promises "Charming company . . . princely productions."

Many businesses use slogans as well. A slogan is a word or phrase used to express a characteristic position, stand, or goal of endeavor. Like a motto, it is generally included in advertising to make a point. On her BusinessCardDesign.com site, Diana Ratliff asks, "Shouldn't your business cards work as hard as YOU do?" She also uses a variation of this slogan on her Web design site because it so clearly conveys what she does and usually leads to a YES response. Cathryn Peters, WickerWoman.com, reminds people that she is "Preserving a Slice of American Wicker Furniture History, One Piece at a Time!"

Slogans often "play on words" or add a touch of humor that customers appreciate and long remember. Bunny DeLorie's business name, Fe Fi Faux Finish (also her dot-com name) prompted the humorous slogan she uses: "Proving quality and service—Faux Sure!" Other examples include a window cleaning service that uses "Your Pane is Our Pleasure" and a lawn service that claims "We're Easy to Get a Lawn With." My all-time favorite, however, is Art's Electric in Pullman, Washington, which coaxes, "Let Us Remove Your Shorts."

Smart Tip

Since your motto or slogan is a valuable sales tool, always include it on your printed materials and make it part of your business e-mail signature. (For information on copyrighting or trademarking a slogan, see "Slogans" in Section II.)

Changing Your Business Name or Logo

Although it's difficult to do if you're already established in business, changing your business name can make a dramatic difference in your ability to sell the same (or similar) products or services. When Phillippa K. Lack found that people didn't want to pay for the custom bridal wear she was offering under the name of Custom Couture, she moved into silk painting and changed her business name to PKL Designs and began to offer products that were perceived as works of art—painted silk scarves, wall hangings, and embroidered items using hand-dyed silk ribbon. She now markets from PKLdesigns.com.

Puppeteer Tim Selberg has twice repositioned his business and each time attracted a new market for his products merely by changing his logo. For years, he sold his handmade puppets exclusively to professional ventriloquists. In 1993, after gaining a reputation as an artist in his field, Tim decided to launch a new line under the name of "Tim Selberg's Living Wood Puppets," appealing primarily to collectors. At that time, he updated his logo to give it a more contemporary look, making the puppet artwork (formerly a ventriloquist's dummy) look less old-fashioned and more contemporary (a collectible puppet). While this change didn't affect his sales to ventriloquists, it did open up a whole new collectors' market. When he opened SelbergStudios.com in 2000, he further expanded his market by modernizing his logo once again to appeal to a younger contemporary audience of collectors than he had been able to reach before.

Giving Yourself a Whole New Image

Here are three examples of how a higher class of clients or customers can result from changing a combination of things, including your business name, title, slogan, and printed materials. In each case below, the repositioning move was absolutely essential if the business was to grow and be all it could be. Of course, this is not something the average business owner is likely to know at the beginning of a business. Such knowledge comes only with time and experience, and financial success will often depend on whether the business owner is savvy enough (and brave enough) to make changes like these:

Developing a Marketing Strategy

• Sherry Huff Carnahan used to do business under the name of Gal Friday (Your Paperwork Professional). She found a much more profitable client base when she renamed the business, Total Office, Inc. (A New Way to Get Things Done). "The new name reflected my broad-range capabilities in office and Web site administration, as well as the bigger vision I had for my company," she says. "My old tag line made people think I was a temporary service, not a virtual administrative service. The new tag line created curiosity and the opportunity for me to explain what I do. My clients used to be construction workers who worked out of their trucks. Now I serve multimillion-dollar financial advisors throughout the United States. Changing my company's business name and image was the smartest thing I've ever done." (On the Web, Sherry operates under the name of SherryCarnahan.com.)

• When the "country" hype of the 1970s faded, Cathryn Peters knew it was time to change the name she was using for her chair caning business. "Cathryn's Country Stuff" was no longer appropriate for a business that was moving in the direction of specializing in the sale and restoration of antique wicker furniture, seat weaving repair service, and marketing of her contemporary antler baskets. By renaming her business "The Wicker Woman," Cathryn not only made it easy for people to remember her, but she positioned herself for greater financial success and attention from the media (who always love to interview "experts"). This change of name also involved a change in Cathryn's business logo and the colors she was using on her printed materials. Blue lettering on white was replaced with brown lettering on cream to show off the deer antler baskets and antique furniture that were now her specialty.

"My business name has alliteration, is easy to remember, and encompasses all that I do," says Cathryn. "It has stood the test of time while still leaving room for possible changes in the business as far as product or services go. I recently closed my wicker repair shop after 26 years in business and no longer sell my wicker restoration services or antique wicker furniture. Although I've changed the focus of my business, I'm still profiting from my lifetime of expertise in this field." (On her Web site, WickerWoman.com, Cathryn advertises herself as a "Wicker Furniture Restoration and Seat Weaving Expert, Basketmaker, Teacher, Lecturer, Pattern Author & Writer.")

● Susan Kilpatrick began business operation under the name of Case Management and Rehabilitation Enterprises, Inc. "I called it CARE and I loved the acronym," she says, "but when my business expanded to include not only case management but also life care plans and consultation to attorneys, I knew I had to change the name. I selected M. Susan Kilpatrick & Associates, Inc. because this name seemed more like the names of firms I'd be marketing to (familiarity helps!). At that time, I also redesigned my business letterhead to include a three-phrase description of the work I do, which includes Medical-Legal Consulting, Life Care Plans and Medical Case Management—three phrases that now appear on my business letterhead along with my complete contact information. I placed this content at the *bottom* of the page because the majority of my clients use my reports in files that have a clasp at the *top*. When flipping through the pages, my info is always readily available." (*Note:* Susan's easy-to-remember e-mail address, MedLeglRN@aol.com, also helps position her in the minds of clients.)

Marketing in the "Age of Skepticism"

A new reader once said of my newsletter, "You may be a hoax and you're really a grumpy gremlin raking in money in a cave—but your publication comes across as being written by a warm and caring person, so I shall picture you that way." While this letter gave me a chuckle, it also reminded me that we were then living in what *Direct Marketing* magazine called "The Age of Skepticism" or, "the age in which nobody believes anybody, in which claims of superiority are challenged just because they're claims, in which consumers express surprise when something they buy actually performs the way it was advertised to perform." Are we still living in the "age of skepticism"? And if so, how should we market to today's skeptics? I asked businesses in my network to comment on this subject.

"I tend to agree that our whole society is living in an age of skepticism," says Web designer Richard Tuttle, CalliDesign.com. "After September 11, it just seemed to escalate and the situation has been intensified because of the growing number of con artists out there today. I'm not doing anything unusual to have people trust me and believe in our product/services except to give the best

Naming Handcrafted Products

Consider the following list of common handcrafted items now being made for sale in countless homes across North America. Merely by changing the names of such items—and thus suggesting greater consumer benefits—higher retail prices can often be commanded. Examples:

- *Candles* can be sold at higher prices when their image is not merely functional, but decorative, as in *Wax Sculptures.*
- *Folk paintings* may seem more valuable to buyers if they are called *Early American Folk Art.*
- *Crude wood carvings* attract a more affluent buyer when they are called *Primitives* and sold in art galleries instead of craft or souvenir shops.
- *Large cloth dolls* can command higher prices when they become *life-size sculptures or manikins* for use in fine shops and stores.
- *Found-art jewelry*, made from pieces of wood, bone, shell, etc. might bring higher prices if given a fancy name such as *Nature's Treasures.*
- *Sewing machine embroidery* takes on a new image when it is called *Machine Artistry.*
- *Quilts* will sell for more when they are offered as *fine art collectibles.*
- *Replicas of antiques* may be worth more in buyers' minds if they are called *Authentic Period Reproductions.*
- *Knick-knacks* of all kinds will be worth more to buyers if they are identified as *collectibles.*

service possible. Since we rely on referrals and word-of-mouth advertising, this is essential for success."

"I agree people are skeptical," says medical-legal consultant Susan Kilpatrick. "I'm skeptical, too; however, I'm a strong believer in consistency and open communication. When I promise to have a project completed by a certain date, I do it. In the rare instance that the date becomes an impossibility, I communicate with my client. Truth and honesty are old-fashioned virtues that should (though often do not) apply to today's world. I base my business on my Christian values. God is the CEO of my company, and I do nothing without His 'green light.' Without a doubt, I could earn more money altering my reports to fit a certain situation, but the bottom line in business is serve your client well, keep in touch, charge a fair fee for your services, and tell the truth."

"I have found that word-of-mouth will put someone in or out of business faster than any marketing plan," says artist and product designer Bunny DeLorie. "In my thirteen years of business, I have never paid for advertising, yet I have always been busy because of word-of-mouth or repeat customers. I have always provided the best service and on-time, reliable quality work at prices that are not the cheapest, but are reasonable. I truly listen to my customers and always give them a little extra on the job. Of course, it is important to point out what extra you have provided at no charge, both verbally or on the written invoice. *Example:* On a large mural job of an English countryside, I added at no charge a couple of handpainted butterflies. This might have taken me twenty minutes to do and was well worth the time in customer satisfaction. I think it's often the little things like this that prompt word-of-mouth advertising and repeat business."

"I'm not doing anything differently," says writer and accessories designer Patricia Kutza. "I still include a handwritten card with every purchase because I think folks miss the personal touch and this gesture is my way of fulfilling it. I also think there is a bit of 'shock value' to this approach as letter writing seems to be a lost art. On another front, sites like eBay have become 'service cops' for the sales industry. They do that by providing a rating system for both buyers and sellers. I am assuming that this type of audit has been rather successful at weaning out a lot of would-be crooks. I have made several eBay purchases and have been satisfied with the quality every time."

You'll notice a common thread running through the above remarks, which is the importance of doing everything possible to get the good word-of-mouth advertising that is so critical to the success of a self-employed individual or homebased business. You must be sincere when promoting yourself, your products, your services; you must give good service and offer "little extras" your customers or clients don't expect, and always offer a guarantee of satisfaction or money back.

Ultimately, the degree of success you achieve in business will have much to do with how credible you are perceived to be. In their book, *Credibility: How Leaders Gain and Lose It, Why People Demand It,* coauthors James M. Kouzes and Barry Z. Posner offer this simple method for strengthening credibility: DWYSYWD—*do what you say you will do.*

"Credibility is mostly about consistency between words and deeds," they say. "People listen to the words and look at the deeds. Then they measure the congruence. A judgment of 'credible' is handed down when the two are consonant."

Working with the Competition

One of the smartest marketing moves you can make is to work with your competitors, not against them. I've never forgotten the advice I once received from Donald Moore, a publisher in England. "Your competitor as an enemy will give you nothing but competition," he said. "As a friend, he will give you information you can obtain in no other way. Everyone running a business should be keen to meet as many men and women in the same field of endeavor as can possibly be managed."

I agree. As a leader in the home-business industry, I have always worked very closely with my competitors and, in fact, credit much of my success to their support of my work. There is a feeling of family among home-business owners that enables many of them to work cooperatively, even when one might imagine the businesses would be natural competitors. One example that comes to mind is two word processing businesses in the same small community who work together passing job referrals back and forth. Because each specializes in a particular area and doesn't want the kind of work the other does, they are happy to trade business. They also use one another as independent contractors when the press of business becomes too heavy for them to handle alone.

Nina Feldman (NinaFeldman.com) took this idea a step further by offering her clients referrals to computer and office support services at no cost. In addition to offering her own services, she has been brokering to other word processing/desktop publishing/computer support services since 1981. She markets through a regular column ad in the Yellow Pages and places classifieds in local free papers where people frequently look for word processors.

"Some entrepreneurs believe that all competition is harmful to them," say one marketing guru. "But there are others who believe that competition is the best thing that can happen to them because the combined effect of everyone's advertising and sales promotion creates a much larger market than anyone can create through his or her own efforts alone." As Nina Feldman confirms, "One of the benefits of coordinating such a large, diverse network of word processing businesses is that their marketing and advertising works for me."

Business-to-Business Networking

Business-to-business networking has become one of the most successful marketing strategies of homebased entrepreneurs. A *network* is a system of supportive people who are interested in one another and willing to help each other succeed. Your involvement in even one established home-business network could make the difference between success or failure in your particular endeavor. An involvement in several could double, triple, or quadruple your chances for success.

If talking to strangers doesn't come easy to you, read a book on the topic to gain confidence and learn how the game is played. Remember that networking should not be abused by always asking people to give something to you. True networking requires that you give back to others—not necessarily at the time the original networking is going on, but somewhere along the line. While the obvious benefits of networking include industry contacts, a source of "inside information," and client referrals, many see networking as the ultimate advertising tool: through networking you "get the word out" about your business without an outlay of cash. Networking offers other benefits as well, says an artists' representative and consultant. "It not only generates business leads but is a source of support and sharing of ideas and expertise between business owners. It also alleviates the loneliness and isolation of a homebased business."

Futurist Joanne Pratt (see Chapter 10) says the biggest help to her business was joining a MasterMind group available to members of NAWBO, the National Association of Women Business Owners (1-800-55-NAWBO; **www.NAWBO.org**). "Eight or nine business owners with non-competing firms meet as a board of directors, usually about once a month. The meeting agendas come from the group and may include topics such as how to get business, fire partners, make a presentation and so on. Sometimes a member just needs hugs (literally!)."

Networking is not something that must be done in person, of course. Some of your best networking opportunities today will be found on the Internet. Many business owners participate in newsgroups and chat rooms so they can pick the brains of industry experts. And, although it is very time-consuming to participate in mailing list discussions, this is often the best way to network with your competition, connect with people who can advance your business, and get answers to nagging questions.

Smart Tip

You can get a lot of publicity for yourself or your products by sharing helpful information on electronic bulletin boards in response to questions posted by others. Including your e-mail address on bulletin boards is a great way to get it on the list of spammers, however, so never use your personal e-mail address for this purpose since you may later want to discard it to stop the extra spam it will generate.

Join an Organization. Membership in an organization is a wonderful way to make networking contacts. My younger sister, Mollie Wakeman, ran a busy music teaching studio in her home in California for twenty years. Thanks to networking, she never found it necessary to advertise for students. In fact, she always had a lengthy waiting list. After joining a music teachers association, she quickly learned the benefits of networking with the competition. Once she acquainted them with her special skills and background, teachers with too-busy schedules or a lack of expertise in a certain area began to refer students to her. As a skilled teacher and performer, word-of-mouth advertising did the rest.

It was my other entrepreneurial sister, Mary Kaufmann, who taught me the importance of networking with chamber of commerce members. When she was actively engaged in her own insurance business in Colorado, her regular attendance at chamber meetings enabled her to get to know virtually everyone who was anyone in the Denver area—including many attorneys, bankers, doctors and other professionals who sent her a steady stream of referrals while also serving as an information pipeline to business happenings in the area.

When book publisher Leila Peltosaari joined an association for English-language publishers in Quebec, she wasn't sure anything would come of it, but membership has since connected Leila to editors in England and Finland, resulting in articles about her. "I don't know where this publicity may lead," says Leila, "but I've learned that visibility of any kind often gives us potential gates to directions we would never think about otherwise."

Myrna Giesbrecht, Press4Success.com, produces textile art of high quality with a matching price tag. She has sold pieces in Canada, the United States, New Zealand, Germany, and Malaysia. To further build name recognition, she has joined guilds in her field. One of them, the Association of Pacific Northwest Quilters, sponsors an invitational traveling show in which Myrna has participated. She is also a member of FAN (Fibre Art Network), a group of professional textile artists in western Canada. "I joined to network with other artists and support the growth of the industry in the particular area in which I live," she says. "I have a piece in an invitational show with them right now touring parts of Canada."

Start Your Own Network. New home-business owners quickly recognize the need for organized networks that will enable them to trade information and ideas on a regular basis while also gaining encouragement and motivation. If a network doesn't already exist in your area, consider starting one. Two or three people can meet for lunch, or announce a meeting in the local library or chamber of commerce with a news release to the local paper. Although it's fairly easy to bring a local group together for the first few meetings, it's often difficult to hold it together. The demands of business tend to prevent attendance at meetings, and the one or two individuals who start a network may eventually pull back when they can't get any help from others. While such networks exist, however, they can be invaluable to beginners and pros alike, and they are always worth joining or starting.

You've heard the old saying, "If you can't lick 'em, join 'em." Soapmaker Karen White explains how gathering all the "competition" together can be beneficial to all. "When I started NaturalImpulse.com in 1997, there weren't many other soapmakers around," she says. "Now they are everywhere. But instead of worrying over this situation, several of us in Alabama have banded together to share ideas and pool our resources. We meet at least twice a year, and we do co-op buys on supplies to save money. (At a recent meeting we saved from 25 to 50 percent on the price of several of our basic supplies because we were able to pool our money and buy in larger amounts.) We also contacted several manufacturers and suppliers who donated samples and door prizes to our meeting. Everyone who attended the meeting came away with a bag full of samples and at least two door prizes. At our main meeting in the summer, we also have demonstrations and classes by our members, and we are now discussing pooling money for advertising. Beginning with five members, we have sixty in the group now, and we invite soapmakers in Alabama (or those with ties to Alabama) to join us."

Developing a Marketing Strategy

Turn Your Competition into Lifelong Friends. Nowhere else is this strategy more widely used than in the field of art or crafts. Sculptor Robert Houghtaling (Frogart.com) offers a wonderful example. "Most of my fellow sculptors and I have always helped each other," he says. "Sure, some folks think they have a particular technique or process they want to guard because that makes their stuff unique, but for the most part I have found they will bend over backwards to help out a fellow artist. For example, when I was doing cast aluminum sculptures I had a friend who did similar stuff. We both did our own casting. If for some reason one of us couldn't cast we would share the other's foundry or even cast the pieces for him. When I was doing commercial figurines, much of my work was sub work for other sculptors. If one of us got too many jobs at one time or maybe a type of job that we didn't care to do, we would either sub it to a friend/competitor or just refer the customer to him. Now that I am doing more fine art again I still do this. If I am going to the foundry I check with a friend who does bronze sculpture to see when he is going to go so we can either take/pick up the other's pieces or, better yet, make the trip together and have a nice lunch. I've been at this a long time and as I look back over the years I can't remember who outsold who. I can't remember how much I sold a sculpture for, or what I bought with the money. What I *do* remember are the friends I have made, the good times we've had, and the adversity we worked through together. That's the stuff no amount of sales could purchase. 'As a man soweth, so shall he reap,' it says in the Bible. I've had a good harvest so I'm going to continue to sow the good stuff."

Don't Discuss Prices!

It's great to network with the competition. . . but are you aware that you cannot legally meet with your competition to discuss the prices you are charging? You *can* keep tabs on what your competitors are charging, then adjust your prices accordingly, but it's a violation of the Sherman Antitrust Act to *discuss* this action with the competition. Each year, many small businesses who mistakenly believe that this law applies only to "big business" find themselves facing lawsuits, so be careful here.

The Illusion of Success

While you're waiting for success to happen to you, remember the importance of maintaining the *illusion of success*, especially in those darkest hours when even you begin to have serious doubts about what you're doing. Make your business look financially successful even when it isn't by having classy stationery, cards, brochures, catalogs, or a well-designed Web site.

When dealing with business contacts, it's important to speak with confidence because people in the business world like to deal with confident, successful people. "Your voice and the words you choose combine to convey a message that speaks volumes about you," says June Johnson, VoicePowerOnline.com. "How you hear yourself is not necessarily how others hear you. To speak with the voice of authority and be successful in the business world, it's important to present yourself as a person of power and let that power reflect in your voice. But don't confuse power with speaking louder or faster. You communicate your power when you speak with confidence and conviction with a voice that sends a message that expresses your thoughts clearly and precisely. There is a definite connection between the language you choose and the power you convey. Choose action verbs that make a strong statement and energize your speech. Focus on the message using short, crisp active sentences that deliver positive statements."

Since nothing sells like success itself, even the illusion of success may be enough to convince a prospective buyer that your products or services ought to be seriously considered for purchase. (Half of all big business is one big bluff, and you might as well play the game.) Nowhere is it written that you have to be honest to the point of saying, "You're my first client" or "I have only a few accounts right now." Instead, you could say, "My new service is generating tremendous interest" or "You wouldn't believe the response I've received." You won't be lying, but you'll certainly be giving the impression that business is better than it is.

It's rather like the story of the egotistical violinist who was looking for compliments after a bad performance. "How did I play tonight?" he asked a friend. Not wanting to hurt the violinist's feelings, the friend said, "I've never heard anything like it."

After publishing my "illusion of success" remarks in my newsletter, a reader responded: "You cleared up a point I had accepted in theory—maintain the illusion of success—but which I had not really been practicing. Sometimes we have an idea firmly in mind, but only in mind, and need a comment from a different angle to see how it can really be put into practice for us."

Another reader saw it quite differently, however, saying that what I was suggesting was borderline dishonesty. "My business acquaintances are friends," she said, "and therefore my business relationships have to be built on trust and honor, just like my personal relationships." I agree, but my early years of experience in the "hard, cold business world" taught me that it's not good business sense to tell all you know when you're negotiating a business deal or trying to close a sale. You can be honest and loyal while still "playing your hand close to your vest."

It's natural for different people to have different opinions on a topic like this, and in the end, we must all do what we believe to be right for us. A crafts producer agrees: "I try to base my life on the Golden Rule," she says, "and I don't see any conflict with that if I tell a shop owner, 'This is my most popular item.' It doesn't matter whether you've sold three dozen or three hundred; if you've sold more of them than anything else, it's your most popular item. It also sounds more positive to say, 'This is a new design,' instead of, 'I haven't sold any of these yet,' though both statements are true. We've all found ourselves in a strange town at mealtime, and nearly all of us will choose to eat at the restaurant with the larger crowd. That's reacting to the 'illusion of success,' so if we really want to be successful, looking as if we already are is a good way to start."

I'm reminded of a job my husband got shortly after we were married. He was a freelance drummer in Chicago at the time, and there was a great deal of competition for each job in town. When a contractor called and asked Harry if he had four kettle drums, he said yes. "But you don't have *one* drum, let alone *four*," I said worriedly. "Yeah," he replied with a grin, "but I know where to *get* them. If I'd been totally honest, I'd have lost the job."

"Star Quality"

In an interview, comedian Tim Conway once said he didn't think of himself as a "star," but that he had learned early on the importance of surrounding himself with people who were stars. He said that the very fact that he was always in their company made others think of him as a star, too.

It works that way in business, too. To become a professional in any endeavor, it's a good idea to surround yourself with professionals. That old saying, "You're known by the company you keep," makes a lot of sense in this light, and Conway's remarks also add weight to the illusion-of-success comments in this chapter.

Chapter 5

Marketing Without Money

You must be positively consistent in what you say, think and do. That sends a clear picture to people of who you are. People believe you and want you to succeed and will do what they can to assist.

—Wally "Famous" Amos

There will always be a demand for worthy products, and getting the first few customers to buy isn't hard. What's *hard* is coming up with a steady stream of new prospective buyers month after month. What's *harder* is getting enough of them to buy to turn your little money machine into a year-round income producer. And once you have a good customer list going for you, what's *even harder* is keeping them interested by always coming up with new products, new promotions, and new offers that will entice them to buy again and again.

Self-employment is wonderful when there's enough business to pay the bills, but what happens when extenuating circumstances cause business to drop off? First there's concern and maybe the thought that you've "got to watch it" because you don't like the way things are going. If things do get worse, panic begins to set in as you ponder all the problems you're going to have if you can't pay your supplier bills, business overhead costs, or living expenses. You may find yourself thinking, *I've got to do something to bring in some business RIGHT NOW, or I'll never be able to pay these bills. But what can I do without money for advertising?*

From experience, and from observation of hundreds of businesses in my network, I've concluded that entrepreneurs and self-employed people in general (not all of whom consider themselves "entrepreneurs," by the way) are at their most creative in hard times. Instinctively, we know we must do something *right away* to bring in business, or we're going to be in mighty hot water. We don't have the luxury of sitting around and waiting for things to get better. But if we have no money for bills, we certainly have none for advertising, which is something of a Catch-22. So what's the solution? We need to explore all of our no-cost/low-cost marketing options, just as we did when we first started our business.

In this chapter you'll find a handy checklist of the various advertising, promotion, and marketing options available to you, divided into categories according to cost. As you can see, there are many free or inexpensive ways to bring in the bucks without spending more than a few dollars up front, and that's the focus of both this chapter and the one on publicity that follows. (The various topics on this checklist are discussed in chapters 6 through 10. Check the index to locate all discussions of any specific topic.)

One Shot at a Time

While many of us are naturally creative (else we wouldn't have chosen self-employment in the first place), we still need "idea stimulators" to get our creative-thinking process moving. That's one reason why we subscribe to magazines and newsletters. We're open to suggestions, and it's very helpful to learn how other small business owners are generating new business. Of course, we don't have to be in the same business as the person who's shared a valuable idea. An idea that works for one business is likely to work for another, and with that thought in mind, I asked a number of business pros in my network to share their most profitable, low-cost marketing experiences with me. All you have to do is translate their practical ideas to your own business situation. A minor change here . . . a subtle variation there . . . something new from you . . . voila! An immediate solution to a specific marketing problem.

As a small business owner, you have a special edge over major concerns with large advertising budgets. Unlike large corporations that get locked into high-cost marketing plans and advertising programs, if you make a mistake or see a turn in the market coming, you can immediately stop and turn around. While large corporations must use the shotgun method of blasting the mass market with an expensive television or radio commercial, you have the luxury of "rifle marketing" (also known as "guerrilla marketing"), which is going after one customer or client at a time. And in many small businesses, one new customer, client, contract, or shot of publicity is all it takes to get a new business going, or a failing business back on track.

For example, a speaker could go after a high-paying job that might yield an immediate $1,000–$5,000 fee. A word processing business might land a contract with a corporation that wants an in-house newsletter published each month. A mail order seller could mail a thousand first-class postcards promoting one special item, and generate enough business within two weeks to yield a tidy profit. A craftsperson could build up inventory, enter a prestigious show, and bring in cash immediately.

Business is business . . . and the same idea used by the smallest homebased business may be viable for the retailer down the street or the aggressive entrepreneur who's building a new plant. Before you spend any of your hard-earned profits on traditional advertising, take a lesson from the folks who find these mediums either unnecessary or useless. Give some of their no-cost/low-cost promotional ideas a try. You may be astonished by how well they work, and you will have saved precious dollars in the bargain.

Smart Tip

Good customer service is sadly lacking in many retail and corporate businesses today, and that gives you an important "home-business edge." Always emphasize that you can offer something that's mighty rare these days: personal service, attention to detail, affordable prices, and a guarantee of satisfaction.

Advertising, Promotion and Marketing Checklist
**(The following topics are discussed in
Chapters Six through Ten—see also Index)**

FREE
(No up-front costs of any kind, beyond your time and effort)

- [ ] Word-of-mouth advertising
- [ ] Referrals from business associates
- [ ] News releases sent by e-mail
- [ ] Promotional articles e-mailed to ezines or Web sites
- [ ] Radio interviews that may promote your toll-free number or Web site
- [ ] Guest appearances on television
- [ ] Listings in annual directories
- [ ] A display you create locally (bank, library, etc.)
- [ ] Per Order (PO) advertising
- [ ] Sales made in conjunction with speaking/teaching jobs

INEXPENSIVE
(Low cost of printing, postage, telephone, samples, sales aids, ad costs, labor)

- [ ] Printed signs or announcements on bulletin boards
- [ ] Distribution of flyers at meetings, workshops, conferences, etc.
- [ ] News releases mailed or faxed to media contacts
- [ ] Promotional articles distributed to print publications (print and Web-based)
- [ ] Telemarketing (cold calls to get prospects or follow-up calls to get additional business)
- [ ] Direct mail promotions to your own prospect and customer/client lists
- [ ] Selling to dealers or distributors (you may need to supply camera-ready artwork for ads or flyers)
- [ ] Drop-ship arrangements
- [ ] Free product samples to prospective buyers or reviewers

(Continued on Next Page)

Marketing Without Money

- [ ] Free sampling of your service to people in a position to refer other clients to you
- [ ] Donation of your product or service to a community event, conference, or meeting
- [ ] Two-step classified ads or small display ads in small circulation periodicals
- [ ] Classified ads in ezines

MODERATE COST
(Moderately high ad rates, sales commissions, printing/postage costs, Web site expenses)

- [ ] Two-step classified ads in large circulation magazines
- [ ] Display ads in small-circulation magazines or trade publications
- [ ] Yellow Pages listing or small display ad
- [ ] Presentation packages or media kits to selected clients or media contacts
- [ ] Per Inquiry (PI) advertisements
- [ ] Selling products through sales reps (commissions, samples, color flyers)
- [ ] Working with an agent (commission)
- [ ] Selling through your own Web site (merchant account provider costs, Web site maintenance)

EXPENSIVE
(Higher ad rates, postage/printing costs, booth or space rental fees and travel expenses)

- [ ] Display ads in large circulation magazines
- [ ] Direct mail promotions to a rented mailing list
- [ ] Package inserts
- [ ] Advertising through special point-of-purchase displays for retailers
- [ ] Trade show exhibits
- [ ] Exhibiting in Merchandise Marts
- [ ] Advertising specialties imprinted with your name and address

Building Word-of-Mouth Advertising

Word-of-mouth advertising is the best advertising there is, not only because it's free, but because it often is the only advertising you may need once your business gets rolling. When Pam Hunter launched her Creative Office Services business in 1989, she sent out a direct mailing of about a hundred letters and landed three attorneys as clients. "Those three attorneys led to three more law firms and then word-of-mouth kicked in," she says. "Since then I have done a few postcard mailings here and there, but because I found a profitable niche (legal administrative support), I have not had to do any other kind of promotion to date." (Like many others who don't have to advertise to get business, Pam has a Web site, CreativeOfficeService.com, because it enhances her professional image.)

The best way to assure word-of-mouth advertising is to offer products and services that give people real value for their money. Satisfied customers will always be quick to tell others about good books they've read, handy products they've discovered, and helpful services they have used—particularly those that have saved them time, money, or aggravation. If you're good at what you do, your business peers will also give you valuable referrals from time to time, so long as it doesn't cut into their own business profits to do so. Some people just naturally like to help others, and will want nothing in return for their kind words on your behalf. Others will talk about you even more if you offer them a small incentive for spreading the word—a discount, perhaps, on purchases of your product or service each time one of their friends contacts you and mentions their name.

To keep the word-of-mouth advertising flowing, find a way to thank those who are helping you. When Judy Schramm owned a maternity clothing rental shop, she sent a thank-you note folded over a lottery ticket to everyone who gave her the name of a specific person or company that might be interested in her service. With this idea, Judy not only found a way to capitalize on the goodwill she had created during her several years in business, but also got a terrific wave of publicity in the small business press when she sent out press releases titled "Maternity Rental Shop Rewards Referrals with Lottery Tickets."

 Smart Tip

Once you begin hearing from satisfied customers, don't hesitate to ask them for testimonial copy you can use in your promotional material. (See sidebar, "Customer Testimonials.") If written testimonials don't come automatically, jot down verbal comments you receive from customers (wording remarks to your advantage), then send them a copy asking permission to quote them by name in your printed materials, ezine, or on your Web site. Many will be flattered by this request.

Using Printed Materials Effectively

Make it easy for people to give you word-of-mouth advertising by having good printed materials on hand. (If you need help in creating professional printed materials, see this book's companion guide, *HOMEMADE MONEY: Starting Smart!*) When customers or clients compliment you on your product or service, ask if they would like a few of your business cards or brochures for friends or business associates, but don't load them down with an excess of printed materials that will only be thrown away.

"When you know you're going to have a captive audience somewhere, be prepared to back up your chatter with the appropriate selling tools," advises accessories designer Patricia Kutza. "Every time I appear at a convention, either as a speaker or a vendor, I truly work at working it. This means I will have at hand (or visible on a table) press releases, a mailing list book, postcards with pictures of my products on one side and a schedule of speaking engagements and shows on the other side, a resume, fabric samples, sample catalogs, and photos and/or drawings showing ways to use my accessories. I also furnish my business card upon request. If I can't make an immediate sale to a customer, I want to make sure they walk away with something related to my line of WHATKNOT™ products. I keep remembering that Andy Warhol remark about having fifteen minutes of fame in a lifetime. If you can't give me two minutes of your time now, perhaps later on in the day I will get twenty minutes of it if I give you something to carry away."

● **Brochures.** In creating a brochure, ask what you want it to accomplish. Are you trying to get orders from individuals by return mail with check enclosed? Are you trying to sell wholesale to shops, who may request shipment with invoicing? Are you trying to get the recipient to return an enclosed postage-paid reply card or other vehicle that says, "Yes, send me detailed information by mail?" Or are you mostly interested in getting an expression of interest so you can follow up with a personal sales call?

The primary goal of a brochure should be to show recipients how your product or service can solve some particular problem or need they may have at the moment. Stress the benefits of what you're selling in terms your particular market can relate to. The inclusion of testimonial copy will show that others value your products or services and help persuade many people to buy. Make it easier for the recipient to respond by providing a convenient order form or reply vehicle of some kind. (It need not be prepaid to be effective.)

Some business owners make a habit of carrying brochures with them everywhere they go because they never know when they might stumble across a prospect while chatting with someone in the supermarket, a doctor's office, a Laundromat, or a checkout line. If you have a brochure that "tells it all," this can be a marvelous sales tool.

● **Business Cards.** "Everyone you meet knows 250 other people," says Stephan Schiffman, president of a sales training and consulting company in New York and author of several books. "Thus, every time you meet someone, you are, in essence, meeting many more—some of whom may be interested in your product or service."

You need to get your business card into the hands of people who might use your products or services, but going to a networking event and handing out your business card to everyone in sight is likely to be a waste of time. Instead, you need to make an impression on people by first using small talk to discover a reason to exchange cards. For example, you might say, "I'll send you a copy of that article," or "I'll check on that for you and give you a call. May I have your card?" Then write on the back of it what action you need to take when you return to your office and hand your card to your new networking friend as you part company.

Marketing Without Money

"Take notice of what people do with your business card once you hand it to them," advises Diane Welch, Watermark Printing. "Do they put it immediately in their pocket, or do they give it a second glance? If they look at your card, chances are you've made a positive first impression." Diane recommends changing your business card every five years to keep up with the times. A new logo or a change in paper stock or typeface may be all that's necessary to boost your image and draw in more companies. Besides the standard $3^{1}/_{2} \times 2"$ format, a business card can be cut into different shapes to fit into a Rolodex or be folded in half to hold much more information. Photographs, illustrations, and head shots can also make a business card stand out, as do different colors, foils, card stocks, and textures.

 Smart Tip

Think how you might turn your business card into a promotional item. One artist uses a small yearly calendar as her business card. She prints them in October when she prints her annual calendar with sketches, then tucks them into all the bags during Christmas sales and gives them away afterward. "People like them because they are handy to stick on the refrigerator," she says.

"I don't go anywhere without my business cards," says Donna Snow, SnowWrite.com. "I have a stack of Thank-you/Nice-to-meet-you cards sitting next to my computer and when I exchange cards or information with a potential lead I *always* send a thank-you card or a note following up with them on a particular topic. I try to find out what they do and what their concerns are and offer to research or connect them with someone who may have the information they seek. *This is the follow-up.* They are open to being contacted again knowing that I have something to offer them other than a sales pitch. Find something in common, share that commonality, and develop a relationship."

Look for places locally that might take a stack of your business cards. Velda Solomon, who owns a scissors sharpening business, leaves stacks of business cards at a local fabric store that she sharpens for on a regular business. "We get business every month from that," she says, "People often ask where to get their sewing scissors sharpened, and the store hands them one of our cards." If you give a local printer your business and have a service of interest to their customers, ask if they will accept a stack of cards for their countertop. Many hardware stores have a binder that includes a collection of business cards of people who provide home maintenance or repair services, and so on.

Customer Testimonials
by Jeffrey Lant, CEO, WorldProfit.com

"In my continuing informal review of hundreds of marketing documents, I find that only one in ten offers even the most cursory testimonial, even though testimonials, properly used, constitute a superb means of expediting sales. Moreover, those who do use testimonials are not attempting to get and use endorsements that do them much good. A good testimonial must confirm the precise benefits a satisfied customer has gotten from the product or service you are now offering while also identifying the person giving the testimonial as someone your prospects can relate to.

"Ever notice how many testimonials end with 'Mrs. J.D., Sioux City'? My cynical mind immediately assumes there is no Mrs. J.D., that in fact she has been invented by the seller who actually doesn't have anyone who will stand up publicly and endorse his product or service. Don't be sheepish about prompting your customers for testimonials. Ask them about particular aspects of your product or service, write down what they say, and then ask for their permission (which you must always have) to use it. Once you have obtained good testimonials, use them in your ads and every marketing document you produce. Every time you make a major claim for what you're selling, provide a satisfied-buyer testimonial for that claim and use the person's full name and city/state location."

Packaging with Flair

I'm not talking about wrapping things here, but packaging as it relates to the marketing of products and services. I encourage you to offer a little pizzazz and *charge* for it. For example, instead of trying to market all your handcrafted products on an individual basis, take a look at what you have to sell and see if you can't combine several items (some handmade, some commercial) and market them as a:

- Holiday Gift Pak

- Gourmet Selection

- Beauty Care Kit

- Designer Bathroom Ensemble

- Mother's Sanity Kit

- A Bundle for the Baby

- Gift Basket (basket ideas are endless)

Not only would you sell more product this way, but you would surely increase profits as well. People are always willing to pay more for a complete package if they perceive it as something that will save them time, stress, or merely aggravation (i.e., shopping for a gift when there's no time).

The same concept also works for service sellers. Businesspeople speak in terms of the "business package" they offer, and maybe you should be offering a business package, too. It can be presented either in a plain brown wrapper for a plain brown price—or you can add some glitter and command whatever the traffic will bear.

To sell the glitter, you must identify and promote your true customer benefits. Why should people use your service instead of that of your competitors? Do you have more experience, or a better business reputation? Do you offer special guarantees of satisfaction, faster service, more attention to detail, glamour . . . what? Remember, buyers often will pay extra for intangible benefits like these. (How many times have you heard yourself saying things like, "Well, you only get what you pay for" or "This is important to me, so I want the best I can find—price is no object.")

A savvy party planner, for example, would not limit her service to merely planning a party, but would offer a wide variety of separate services that included every little detail, from sending invitations to planning the menu and decorations, to finding just the right entertainment. And perhaps she will also diversify into the sale of products related to parties, from nut cups and decorations to gift wrap, hand-printed announcement cards, even a photography service that provides framed mementos or novelty items (cups or plates with photos on them, for example).

Smart Tip

If you offer a wide variety of services and products, you need to give yourself a special title, your business a special name and professional image, and your complete "package" a title that will make prospects beat a path to your door. When you successfully play "the game of the name" and professionally package your products and services, you may advance to "GO," collect the money, and wave bye-bye to the competition.

Developing and Maintaining Your Mailing Lists

As soon as you begin your marketing efforts, you'll begin to build your all-important prospect and customer/client mailing lists. If you are just getting started on your prospect list, here are some suggestions on how to get more names:

- Contact all friends and business associates with a possible interest in using your products and services

- Ask everyone you know to give you names of friends who might be interested in what you offer

- Collect business cards at any meeting you attend

- Add any names you get from regular publicity, ads, and other promotional efforts

- Donate something that requires people to write their full name, address, and phone number on a card for a drawing

- If you want to collect only e-mail addresses, offer something free on your Web site (ezine, eBook, free report)

- Obtain exhibitor lists from trade shows or attendee lists from conferences and meetings

- Order membership directories from organizations serving your targeted market (often—but not always—available)

- Compile targeted neighborhood lists using criss-cross directories available in your library (see sidebar)

- Glean small business publications for addresses of individuals and other business owners for networking or business-to-business marketing purposes

- Solicit publicity (see Chapter 6) or place advertisements to build your prospect list (see Chapter Nine)

Note: The time may come when you are approached by another home-business owner who offers a list for rent or trade. In some instances this can be profitable, particularly when it's a business associate you know and trust. But always ask when the list was last mailed and whether address corrections were requested at that time since lists go out of date very quickly.

 *Smart Tip*

Never clean someone else's mailing list. If it is suggested that you will get twice the number of fresh names for every address correction you send back to the person who offers the list, pass on this "opportunity." This is a clear signal that the list is one of those worthless mail order opportunity lists—names of individuals who have responded to get-rich-quick programs, work-at-home ads, and so on. These individuals are not likely to buy your high-quality products and services.

Mailing List Programs

If you don't have your mailing list under control yet, there are literally hundreds of software programs that can be used to manage lists. If all you want are address labels so you can send postcards or brochures to prospects or customers, any database or mailing list program will do the job, including shareware you can get off the Internet. John Schulte, Chairman of the National Mail Order

Association (NMOA.org), says the simplest database program he has found is *Microsoft Access*, which is usually bundled with *Microsoft Word* under the name of *Microsoft Office*. "Some people have this software and don't know its capabilities, but it's easy to learn," he says. "It includes a Database Wizard that does all the work for you. Just click here and there to build an address book, order entry files or a dozen other types of database files."

If you need only labels, *Microsoft Access* is all you need, but if you want to send personalized letters to your customers, then you'll also want *Microsoft Word*. Other programs with capabilities (and price) similar to *Microsoft Office* include *Lotus Smart Suite* and *Corel Office Suite*. Less costly programs include *FileMaker* (ClarisWorks) and *My Advanced Brochure and Mailer* (MySoftware Company). The latter program will also do a mail merge of addresses into correspondence for sellers who want to send personalized mailings. *Office Access* is another program you might want to investigate. This is a "relational database" software program, which means that you put in your point of contact once, and then assign different relationships to that contact (i.e., client, subscriber, prospect, media, friend, etc.). Switching from one software program to another should be easy, since most allow for the exportation of files in ASCII format that can then be imported into a different program. (For example, I could easily take names and addresses from my old dBASE files on my DOS computer and import them into my *Outlook 2000* e-mail software program on my Windows-based computer, or vice versa.)

Since you may not know initially how you will later wish to communicate with people on your various mailing lists, always capture as much contact information as possible, including personal and business name, mail and e-mail addresses, telephone and fax numbers, and Web site URL. Also include in the notes section of your mailing list program as much information about the contact as possible, such as names of family members, special interests, community involvements, and topics you've discussed in previous e-mails or phone conversations. Having this kind of information will enable you to later communicate with people on a more personal basis and develop not only profitable business relationships but long-term friendships.

"A trend I see," says Diana Ratliff, BusinessCardDesign.com, "is the increasing value of making personal connections. We're surrounded by impersonal means of communication—the Internet, pagers, faxes, e-mail. Consequently, those times and means by which we can directly connect with customers and prospects have added importance. I believe that entre-preneurs who foster personal relationships will prosper (which is one reason why business cards will never be replaced)."

Smart Tip

When new business comes in "over the transom," always ask people how they heard of you. By keeping track of where most of your prospects are coming from, you'll know where to place advertising or promotional emphasis in the future.

Criss-Cross Directories

If time allows, you can use "criss-cross directories" or "cross reference directories" to build a mailing list of potential customers in a specific market area. Call the chamber of commerce or the reference librarian at your city library to find out which publisher serves the market area you want to reach. These directories can be leased, or used free of charge in a library. With a local criss-cross directory in hand, you can establish a mailing list of apartments and homes within specific areas. You cannot get individual family names, but you can address your mailing to "Occupant," at each address on your list.

Marketing Miscellany

Here are a few miscellaneous low-cost marketing and promotional ideas that have worked for business owners in my network:

- **Join Organizations to Open New Marketing Doors.** Membership in a professional or trade organization is a great way to make networking contacts and open new marketing doors. Many organizations also sponsor annual trade shows or conferences where members may showcase their work or present workshops that promote their products and services.

Network marketer Martha Oskvig has found membership in her chamber of commerce invaluable. "I've participated in their packet distribution program for newcomers to the community, and I help the chamber by donating my products for civic-festival prizes. At chamber events, I help in their booths, always wearing my corporate-approved name badge so my own business is visible. Annually, our chamber sponsors a pre-Christmas Parade of Trees at our civic center with holiday decorating tips for the public, and my entry always includes new products for use either as tree ornaments or as presents under a theme-decorated tree. I place a 'FREE—Take One!' literature rack by my tree's guardrail for viewers to take more information with them." (For other business/marketing benefits of membership in your local chamber of commerce, see discussion under this heading in Section II of this book.)

- **Create a Contest.** "For consultants, experts and speakers, creating events to wrap around ourselves is an ideal way to gain positive exposure and attract sponsors," says journalist and author Jeff Zbar. "With sponsors come additional fees, prizes to give away, and exposure through their promotional machines." To promote his book, *Safe@Home: Seven Keys to Home Office Security*, and Website, ChiefHomeOfficer.com, Jeff created a contest built around a national day he created himself—a PR strategy used by many businesses and organizations today. (See Chapter 6 for more information on this topic.) "I made the second Sunday in January National Home Office Safety & Security Week and parlayed the contest off that," he explains. "It was easy to get companies to pony up product, especially after I hit them up (and they subsequently turned me down) for thousands in sponsor fees. The money would have been nice, but getting their products *and* permission to use their names in my materials lent an aire of authenticity and authority to the contest."

Although it's difficult to measure the marketing value of this kind of event, Jeff figures at the very least, he has built valuable new marketer relationships and further established himself as an expert in the home-office community. "I've also gotten valuable media exposure that may result in greater sales of my products, bookings for speaking engagements, and other additional revenues," he adds.

● **Do a Survey.** Consider doing a survey to learn what your customers like about your products or services (which may give you clues as to why some people aren't buying). Surveys can be done by phone, by mail (with SASE enclosed for reply), on your Web site, or directly to your e-mail lists. On the Web, it's easy to create an online survey to gather customer demographics or get input on the types of products customers want to see offered on your site. You could also ask questions to help you learn what your visitors think of your site, its functionality, its shopping cart, or its linking system. You could do this with a pop-up page or use a free online survey system such as **www.CoolSurvey.com**. Here, you can cut-and-paste HTML code for your site, making it easy to create your own interactive survey to encourage visitor participation in your site. Also check out **www.CreateSurvey.com** and **www.Zommerang.com**. More sophisticated survey tools, such as **www.SurveyMonkey.com**, are available at a fee. You can turn up others by doing a search using the words "survey tools" or "conduct online surveys."

E-mail surveys of your ezine subscriber list or prospect and customer databases can be very effective. Organizational expert Patricia Katz (PatKatz.com) publishes weekly issues of *PAUSE—The Voice of Sanity In A Speed Crazed World*. As her subscriber list neared 1,000, Patricia announced that she would award her 1,000th subscriber a "Pause Pak," including a complete set of her books and other useful items. To all others who responded to the survey, she offered a new article unpublished elsewhere. Subscribers were asked for comments on what they liked or disliked about her ezine and the kind of information they'd like to see in future issues. "The net result was a collection of great testimonials, specific examples of impact, and a host of suggestions for topics for future issues," says Pat. "I also learned that quality writing (personal, anecdotal, punchy) is important, and readers want their ezine copy to be 'short and simple.'"

Surveys can also provide valuable market research information. Prior to manufacturing a special product for sewers, a designer in Canada first sent a postcard announcement to everyone on her large mailing list, briefly describing the product and asking her customers if they'd be interested in buying it if she manufactured it. The tremendous response she received gave her valuable market research information, confidence that the new product would sell, and a list of ready-and-waiting customers.

- **Donate Something.** To gain recognition for your business in your community, get involved in community affairs. Whenever possible, donate items for raffles, asking that your business be mentioned as the contributor. Such activities often lead to local newspaper publicity and extra sales.

  "Little things are often links to larger things," says Dodie Eisenhauer, VillageDesigns.com. "I can't bring myself to write a press release, but I do give talks to any group that asks and I donate products to many auctions and organizations. I also have three five-foot angels and several smaller ones in stock that I offer to area churches each year during the Christmas season (on a first-come, first-served basis). I do this because I love to see people enjoy my work, but it often comes back to me in orders, customers to my shop, or publicity. After seeing my angels in a church, a visiting writer from Phoenix came to my shop, picked up my literature and interviewed me for a feature article in the December 2002 issue of *Missouri Life*."

- **Set Up a Library Exhibit.** Consider creating an educational display about your craft, industry, or profession that would be appropriate for the library or a bank's lobby during a holiday season or special community event. Include historical information, samples of your work (if appropriate), and a small sign that promotes your business. When book publisher Leila Peltosaari got an opportunity to display her books at a library, one of the visitors had a mom with an online mail order company who immediately ordered 500 copies of one of her books.

- **Design a "Car Window Cling."** Martha M. Oskvig, owner of Martha Oskvig & Associates, lives on a busy street at the edge of town near the high school parking lot. One way she advertises her business is to use a "car window cling" on the window of her garage door that everyone can see as they drive past. (On higher-traffic game nights, she keeps an outside light glowing.)

  A "car window cling" is similar to a bumper sticker in size and shape but clear plastic in the background of the colored logos or words. It sticks to glass with no sticky adhesive. "Car window clings are offered by many direct-sales companies now as a promotional item for use by their sales consultants," Martha explains. "They generally feature the company's corporate logo so sales representatives can promote the business while simply driving or in a parking lot. However, they do not include a phone number or the representative's own address, like the magnetic signs some agents place on their automobile doors. My own door window's cling simply has the corporate logo and name on it." Independent business owners who are not affiliated with a larger corporation are not likely to use this kind of promotional item; however, ad specialty catalogs do sell "cling materials" for bulk personalization orders, so you could create your own (at some expense) if you wanted to promote your business this way. (Or maybe this is something you could create and sell to local businesses?)

● **Get Listed in Directories.** There are more than 15,500 directories published worldwide, and they are described in a two-volume reference called *Directories in Print* (published by Gale Research, **www.GaleGroup.com**, available in many libraries). It will take some time to search out directories that might be useful to you, but such listings are generally free and worth the effort.

● **Create a Great E-mail Signature.** If you do business by e-mail (and especially if you have a Web site), be sure to add a professional e-mail signature to the end of all your messages. (Check your e-mail program to learn how to get this signature to appear automatically at the bottom of every new message you send.) What you include in your signature is entirely up to you, but the idea is to make the signature do some advertising or selling for you, answer questions people may have, and link them directly to your Web site or a specific page you happen to be promoting at the time.

"Savvy marketers tend to change their signature contents frequently," says Jeff Zbar. "Some people include pithy sayings or quotes, changing them every few days or weeks to increase the message's memorability among the recipients. As a business owner with new products and services debuting on a regular basis, my inspirational messages have given way to marketing-oriented content (see sample below). Each new book I write earns a mention in my signature, as have the publications I write for and the awards and memberships I have earned in recent years. These help build my persona as an award-winning and respected author in the SOHO marketplace."

Note: While your e-mail signature can be as long as you wish on messages to friends and business associates, some discussion boards and public forums discourage or forbid use of signatures or blatant marketing or promotional messages in their chats.

Some who sell products prefer not to make their personal name part of their e-mail signature, but I think this is a mistake since everyone likes to know they're dealing with a person and not just a "company." Inclusion of a telephone number depends on whether you invite calls or not. Some people include their full address (especially if it's a P.O. box address), but inclusion of your home address should be avoided unless you normally invite customers or clients to your door.

Some sellers include their motto or slogan while others add a tag line that describes their products or services. Inclusion of your e-mail address is optional (since it appears automatically at the top of your message), but be sure to include your complete Web site URL (with the http://) as this will turn the address into a "clickable hyperlink" that many e-mail recipients can use (the exception being AOL users). Here are some examples of e-mail signatures that do a good selling job:

Jeff Zbar, Author of: Teleworking & Telecommuting:
Strategies for Remote Workers & Their Managers
($14.95, Made E-Z Products, September 2002)
The www.ChiefHomeOfficer.com
U.S. SBA 2001 Small Business Journalist of the Year
Member: American Society of Journalists & Authors
jeff@chiefhomeofficer.com | 954-346-4393 | Coral Springs, FL

GlamKitty, LLC: Home of Tabby Chic—Beauty for Busy Women With 9 lives
Cosmetics & Skin Care That Delivers Results—Backed by our 110% Guarantee
http://eglamkitty.com Email for your FREE Consultation Today!
GlamKittyConsult@sendfree.com

Karen Wylie, Owner—The Blue Ridge Soap Shed
(828)765-6001
http://www.soapshed.com
See Soap Made the Old Fashioned Way at The Blue Ridge Soap Shed
Soapmaking Daily May-October * 100 Varieties * Tour Groups Welcome

Located .06 miles off Blue Ridge Parkway Milepost 331
in the gem mining district of Spruce Pine, North Carolina

Steve Maurer
<mailto:steve@maurer.net>
Steve Maurer Publications <http://www.steve.maurer.net>
Check out our tips and tutorials section!
On the net for over a year, downloaded all over the world,
check out my FREE Email Primer—From @ to Zip.
Now also available in PDF format with illustrations -
<http://www.steve.maurer.net/email_primer.htm>

Marketing in Tough Times
Robert Bly, Author/Copywriter, Bly.com

"In tough economic times, prospects want their vendors to advise them on how to get maximum results at minimal cost," says copywriter and author Robert Bly. "This means you should sell the product or service that best meets their needs, even if it's not your most expensive item and doesn't give you a big profit right now. You should be seeking to make *customers*, not sales. Build the long-term relationship by doing it right by the client. It will pay off handsomely. Also stress the low cost of acquiring your product or service. Today's consumer wants to spend smaller sums, so your marketing campaign should make your service or product appear as inexpensive as possible."

Creativity and the Idea-Generating Process

When I first met Reg Rygus a few years ago, I was impressed by his self-published book, *The Idea Generator*. Although his book is currently out of print, the thoughts he originally shared with me for publication in an earlier edition of *Homemade Money* remain valuable to a new generation of readers.

"Every business begins with an idea, grows, and is sustained because of ideas, and will die for the lack of them," he said. "Everyone has the potential to be an idea generator and to profit from their ideas, but many people let others' expectations of them govern their lives and they stifle their own dreams in the process. Life is too short to live it wishing you were doing something else. Regret for what we didn't do often looms larger in old age than regret for what we did do."

Reg explained the correlation between intelligence, creativity, idea generating, and innovation like this: "*Intelligence* is a storehouse or womb for knowledge. *Creativity* is the process by which ideas are generated, formulated and birthed. *Innovation* is the process by which these ideas are transformed and implemented into real, practical and useful products or services. People who don't exercise their creativity forfeit their independence and security. They are captive to outdated means of thinking and problem solving and outmoded methods of doing things. They are bound to a job because of the money, and the failure to develop their creative ability locks them into mediocrity."

"Creativity is just doing what other people don't do," says Hal Riney, creator of the Bartles and Jaymes television ads. Adds Alan Ashley Pitt, "You have two choices in life: you can dissolve into the main stream, or you can be distinct. To be distinct, you must be different; you must strive to be what no one else but you can be."

Emulate, But Don't Copy

"You must always steal, but only from the best people," says actor Michael Caine.

Everyone in business studies the work of others for ideas and inspiration (particularly the competition), and to some extent we all borrow ideas and techniques from others. But we must be careful not to directly copy anyone else's material since this has dangerous legal implications. This book contains hundreds of ideas and techniques being used by others. While you may borrow their concepts, you must never take their words. Use a similar format, but add a new twist. Lift an idea, but improve it with your own creative touch.

In Summary

Don't be discouraged if you lack money for advertising, because this may turn out to be a blessing in disguise. Without money, you'll find yourself using creativity instead of dollars or, as one marketer puts it, "substituting brains for bucks." The less money you have, the more creative you're likely to become in your marketing efforts; the less money you have to invest in paid advertising, the less you'll stand to lose if your ads fail to pull results. This book is based on the assumption that you may have only "pennies for promotion" and lack skill in bringing in the business you need. Here's a recap of what I believe to be the six most important, low-cost marketing steps you can take, not only at the beginning of your business but throughout its life:

1 Establish a word-of-mouth advertising base to limit your need for paid advertisements.

2 Use inexpensive "two-step" advertising techniques to build a large prospect list.

3 Develop a variety of mailing lists for marketing and publicity purposes.

4 Consistently mine both your prospect and customer lists with follow-up promotions.

5 Become an expert at getting publicity.

6 Keep looking for new ways to diversify and expand.

Except for word-of-mouth advertising discussed in this chapter, all topics on the above list are discussed in detail in chapters 6 through 11.

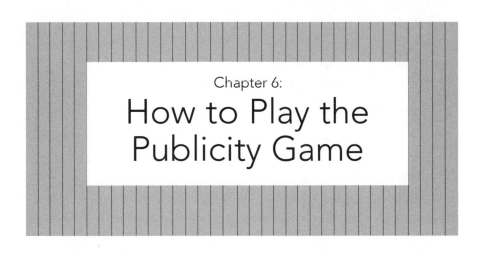

Chapter 6:

How to Play the Publicity Game

The game of publicity is really not a game at all. People's lives, careers, and businesses depend on it. A publicity campaign can make or break a good idea. Today, every business or professional needs continuous publicity. It is a vital factor for growth. Failure to recognize publicity's significance is business suicide.

—R. J. Garis, Master publicist, from *Sharing Ideas*

This chapter is all about publicity—what it is, what it can do for you, and how to get some of it. Publicity is literally *free advertising*. Your only costs in getting it (besides time) will be for the printing of press releases and the stamps and envelopes to mail them. If you plan to e-mail releases, your direct costs drop to *zero* unless you opt to use one of the special PR distribution services on the Web or hire a PR consultant to write or refine your release.

Some people refer to publicity as "tooting your own horn," but I prefer to think of it in terms of "getting the word out." Whatever you call it, there is a *lot* of publicity to be had and homebased entrepreneurs don't try nearly hard enough to get it. This little ditty makes a powerful point:

He who has a thing to sell,
and goes and whispers in a well,
is not so apt to get the dollars,
as he who climbs a tree and hollers!

I've been using publicity as a marketing tool (hollering for attention) throughout my entire business life, and I can tell you *it really pays to master PR techniques*. Except for a few ads when I first started, I've never spent a dime on traditional advertising. Instead, I built my book selling/publishing business by first drawing thousands of interested prospects through publicity mentions and then selling them on my products by using a variety of direct mail packages (see next chapter). On several occasions, I struck it rich and pulled in thousands of dollars' worth of business with the right kind of press release sent at the right time to the right person.

This chapter shares some of the things I and other publicity hounds have learned about getting publicity, and its information should convince you of publicity's value to your business and the fact that you can get it if you try. Space does not allow for detailed information on how to write good PR copy, but there are numerous books wholly devoted to this topic.

Why Some Businesses Don't Seek Publicity

When I asked my book contributors why so few of them had sought publicity in the past, many said they didn't *need* publicity because they had all the business they wanted or could handle. Others said they didn't feel they were doing anything "newsworthy." Some home-business owners fail to try for publicity because this is just one more thing to learn, and they don't have the time for it. And if they do try it once and get no action, they just never try again.

"Publicity is much misunderstood, and generally under-utilized," confirms marketing consultant Daryl Ochs, StreetSmartBusiness.com. "This is largely due to the assumption that it takes a lot of experience to get it right, so many people simply shy away from even attempting it. Or, they make one or two efforts that don't work out well, and give up in frustration."

How to Play the Publicity Game

Some entrepreneurs are simply so busy managing their successful businesses that publicity plans end up on the back burner. "When we first started our business, I would always do press releases for shows," says Marc Choyt, CelticJewelry.com. "I got good results, too. Several magazines wrote about us and this was fantastic guerilla marketing. But as we got busy, I stopped doing this, though always in the back of my mind I knew I ought to get back to sending releases. I'm hoping time will open up a little for me to start focusing on this again. It is stupid not to."

The response I got from copywriter Bob Westenberg (whose *IMP Newsletter* is featured in chapter 9), suggests that many small business owners fail to seek publicity because they either have the wrong conception about what publicity might do for them, or they limit their thinking to getting publicity locally. "Local publicity doesn't do me much good because none of my business is local," Bob told me. "A one-man band doesn't have many newsworthy events in the organization."

But Bob is missing the boat by narrowing his thinking this way. If I find his clever marketing strategies interesting enough to include in a book, isn't it logical that other business writers and editors across the country would also find them interesting? Bob needs to write press releases focusing on how successful postcard marketing has been for his copywriting business (an excellent guerrilla marketing tactic), and how other businesses (both locally and nationally) could use his strategy to promote their own products and services, either doing it themselves from the tips offered in his release, or *getting assistance from Bob*. The trick here is to have a great "for more information" line at the end of the release that offers something free and includes contact information.

Smart Tip

Do not seek local publicity if you are operating an unregistered homebased business or operating in violation of local zoning ordinances as this will only invite trouble from local authorities or neighbors who may be best "left in the dark" about what you're doing. Also, if you use independent contractors in your business, *never* discuss this in an interview since it might draw unwanted attention from Labor Department officials.

The Special Benefits of Publicity

You might be more interested in seeking publicity if you understood its special benefits, which include:

● **Free image advertising**. Although image advertising won't put a jingle in your jeans, it will enhance your professional image in your community or industry and may help you in ways you cannot imagine. *Example:* A crafts couple in a small town in Illinois, population 350, wrote to say that everyone in town soon knew about the national publicity they had received. Having come from a town of only 500 myself, I was amused to hear that the banker had hung a copy of their article in the lobby, and now called the couple by their first names. Who knows how this publicity might have affected the bank's decision when the couple asked for a business loan later that year?

Remember that people who never get their names in print tend to be impressed by those who do. Or, as my music teacher/sister Mollie Wakeman put it after I'd gotten her spot of publicity in *Entrepreneur* magazine, "I know I won't get any new students from this mention, but if I put a copy of this article where my students' parents can see it, they'll be so impressed I can raise my rates!"

● **An ego boost**. Any publicity you can get will always give you an ego boost. This can be especially important to business owners who lack support and encouragement from family or friends. "The goal of publicity is not always to sell something," says veteran publicity-getter Leila Peltosaari, TikkaBooks.com. "It's important to keep your name, product, service or business visible because we all need some kind of recognition merely to survive in business. Making constant small efforts in getting publicity will help you stay motivated and pay dividends later."

● **Increased credibility.** As one who has received a steady stream of publicity for over three decades, I can tell you that each national mention I've received has added to my credibility as an expert in my field while also increasing the degree of confidence people have in my advice. Likewise, your prospective customers and clients will be more interested in ordering from you or hiring your services if they perceive your business to be successful—and that's precisely what publicity does best.

How to Play the Publicity Game

● **Promotional clippings.** Another major benefit of publicity on any level—local, regional, or national—is that it gives you a great promotional clipping you may be able to use for marketing purposes or to get publicity in other places. Permission to reprint an article is no longer a 'given,' however. These days, to avoid copyright problems, you must always seek reprint permission before using publicity in this way. (See related sidebar, "Recycling Your Publicity With Reprints," as well as the collage illustration of article reprints in this chapter.)

● **Additional business.** Last but not least, additional sales or business is always a goal of publicity, and when contact information is included in the article (phone number, address, e-mail, or Web site), this can be quite profitable.

Smart Tip

Ask yourself what you want your publicity to accomplish. Identify the problems you are in business to solve and how your products or services solve them. This translates to the benefits your customers or clients are seeking.

How Publicity Rolls

Getting publicity is a lot like shooting pool, a game I have a fondness for because it was one of the first games my husband taught me after we were married. I like the delicious clicking sound the pool balls make as I break them with that first thrust of the stick. It's rather like the "good vibes" I used to get whenever I put a few hundred press releases into the mail. "Click, click, click," they went as they landed on editors' desks across the country.

In pool, if you're good, your first shot will knock a few balls into pockets and position the rest near other holes for easy tapping in later. The same kind of thing can happen with a press release after it's mailed. For a moment, think of yourself as the pool stick, and the white cue ball as the press release. Imagine you have just mailed a couple of hundred copies of a printed news release to your publicity list, which may include local papers, a few major newspapers, regional and national magazines, special-interest publications, radio stations, organizations, and so on.

One of your releases—let's relate it to the number three ball that just rolled into the center pocket—has landed on the local newspaper editor's desk. He decides that what you are doing is worth at least a short article. On publication, it brings you to the attention of the president of a local organization (the number four ball), who asks you to speak at the next meeting. This will be an excellent publicity break for you. Hard to tell what opportunities await you here.

Meanwhile, you have other balls on the table—or, a lot of press releases still circulating—just waiting to be knocked into pockets. In pool, you often have to shoot two or three times to pocket a ball. The same thing is true when you shoot for publicity. Your first release may work beautifully, resulting in publicity in several publications, or it may just fizzle out. Or so you may think. What you may not realize is that your "publicity push," like those pool balls on the table, is in a state of limbo, waiting for yet another push from you. Maybe it's a follow-up telephone call, another press release, or some additional visibility you are able to get for yourself. Often, these things work together to trigger other publicity you could not have received if the first publicity effort had not been made.

For example, good articles in larger newspapers may be picked up by smaller papers through a newspaper's syndicated network. Publicity in one consumer magazine may also lead to additional publicity since some magazines sell material to other publications. (One example is *Freebies*, a consumer magazine that regularly syndicates columns in magazines such as *Family Circle*.)

Leila Peltosaari, a master at getting PR, understands the need for patience when you launch a PR campaign. "I regard publicity efforts like fishing," she says. "I throw out the baits and move on, forgetting yesterday's efforts (except for some follow-ups of the best), and results start popping up here and there. And the only way to get more results is to throw out more baits. Even if only a percentage of my efforts bear fruit, that is worth my while. And the beauty and drama, of course, is that I never know which one might bear fruit so I just keep on trying with a positive attitude, learning and hoping and stopping once in a while to assess the situation. There are no guarantees ever in publicity, or life itself, but without trying there is not much hope either."

How to Play the Publicity Game

Always hope for publicity but never expect it. Publicity is a gift that people in the media give to newsworthy individuals, businesses, or organizations. Even if you were to hire an expensive PR agency to write and mail releases, publicity could not be guaranteed.

How to Handle "Wannabe" Calls

The minute you get publicity, the "wannabes" start calling, hoping you'll give them all your trade secrets so they can start a similar business with no effort on their part. It's probably your nature to be helpful, but unless you can afford to work for nothing, your first responsibility is to your own business. Decide now how you will handle such calls when they come, and accept the fact that you will often be wasting your time when you give free advice to such callers. To ease the guilt you may feel at saying no to someone who sincerely asks for help, try these suggestions:

1 Get your "help me!" callers off your back by referring them to a book that answers their questions (this one, perhaps).

2 Offer to consult with them on the telephone for a fee.

3 Write a special report, booklet, or how-to guide you can sell that contains helpful information but doesn't make it too easy for someone to start a competing business in your backyard.

4 If you have a Web site, post a page of FAQs or offer a free eBook that offers helpful information while promoting your products and services.

In my experience, people will go away happy if you simply take a minute to acknowledge their call, letter, or e-mail and offer them one of the four options above.

How to Get on Radio or TV

"There are four ways to profit from radio/TV publicity: increase sales, gain credibility, expand distribution, and build a mailing list," says Steve Harrison, co-owner of Bradley Communications Corp. and publisher of *Radio-TV Interview Report*. This trade publication is the world's largest database of authors and experts who are available (free of charge) for live and telephone interviews on a wide range of subjects. Published three times a month, each issue of *RTIR* features 100–150 authors and other spokespeople and reaches over 4,000 radio/TV producers across the United States and Canada. (For ad rates, call 1-800-989-1400 or check the Web at **www.RTIR.com**.)

"Most radio shows will let you give an address or phone number out over the air so the audience can order your product or request more info," says Harrison. "TV shows will often put your ordering info on the screen, but be sure to ask about these arrangements before agreeing to do the interview. Also, consider having a toll-free number you can give out on the air."

If you're shooting for major television talk shows, read some publicity how-to books for inside tips on how to crack this market. Unless you happen to be in the right place at the right time, it will take some PR savvy and extra effort to get on such programs. My most exciting TV experience—a weeklong appearance on ABC-TV's *Home Show*—came not because I was savvy at the time, but because one of my magazine columns was spotted by the TV producer. As the guest expert on a daily seven-minute "Homemade Money" segment named after my book, I had about two minutes of talk time each day, and at the beginning of each segment, my book was flashed on screen for about five seconds. A few months later I learned the value of such publicity. As near as my publisher and I could determine, more than 10,000 books were purchased in bookstores as a direct result of this exposure.

While waiting for your big break on national television, don't overlook your opportunities on local TV and radio programs. During my travels as a speaker at home-business conferences, I was often interviewed by local media, but you don't have to travel to get attention. In fact, getting print publicity is one of the best ways to be found by program directors. That's how I got started doing radio interviews years ago. After being briefly quoted in *Money* magazine as the author of *Homemade Money*, the magazine's publicity director called to ask if I would like her to arrange a few live radio interviews for me. "Sure," I said, trying to sound confident while shaking in my boots. As it turned out, each interview was easy and fun, just like talking to an interesting friend on the phone. Like everything else in business, doing this kind of thing just takes a little getting used to. Experience breeds confidence.

Collecting Your Clippings

When you reach the point where you have a collection of PR clippings, avoid copyright problems by creating an "art collage" like this one. With more than 300 PR clips in file, Leila Peltosaari created this first clippings collage as a matter of convenience because she had too many write-ups and couldn't send all those photocopies to editors.

"I decided that what was important was to show which publications had featured one of my books previously, and show just glimpses of text," she reasoned. "I now have a collage for each of my books, and it's a history of what I have done so far. I send these to radio stations and editors who want to know more about me. When I have a new title with no previous write-ups, the collages of my previous books are useful to show editors that I have been featured several times over the years and consequently have earned a certain reputation. Somehow my collage seems to impress and intrigue editors even more than a thick stack of complete write-ups. I also use the collage to get advance mail orders for new books yet to be published. My mass of clippings validates me in my readers' eyes and makes them trust me. And it never fails to inspire me to remember what I have accomplished over the years."

Recycling Your Publicity with Reprints
Tips from Joan Stewart, PublicityHound.com

Reprints are a valuable marketing tool and one of the very best ways to recycle your publicity. They can be used in dozens of ways—tucked into your media kit, handed out at trade shows, included in your handouts if you do public speaking, mailed to existing clients and hot prospects, handed out during sales calls, and sent to editors at larger publications along with a pitch letter. The only problem is getting permission to reprint your PR mentions.

The "no reprint" rule is cropping up more frequently these days. Newspapers and magazines are trying to generate more revenue by denying reprint rights and, instead, offering their own expensive reprint services. Others, like the giant Gannett chain of newspapers, simply refuse to allow anyone to make reprints—period.

If a story appears about you or your company, call the publication immediately and ask for permission to reprint. If they say no, buy as many back issues as you can afford because you never know when you'll need them. Don't wait a month or two after publication and then call, or the back issues might be gone.

When you visit **www.PublicityHound.com** to sign up for *The Publicity Hound's Tips of the Week*, you'll receive free by autoresponder a handy list of "89 Reasons to Send a News Release."

How to Write an Interesting Press Release

A press release (or "news release" as you prefer—both are correct) does not have to be filled with actual news to be newsworthy, but it must be worth publishing as news because it cannot be published as advertising. What editors want, more than anything else, is a "news peg" on which your story can be hung. Actually, the key word here is "new," not "news."

Anything that's new is likely to be newsworthy, such as a new business just starting, a new product that offers some special benefit to consumers or business owners, a new achievement of some individual in a community, locality, or industry, a new twist to an old idea, and so forth. The news peg or "hook" for a story can be almost anything. Sometimes it is the very thing that makes you, your business, or your product stand out from the rest. Often, it's the benefit offered to consumers in your news release.

All businesses have characteristics or qualities that lend themselves to a news release, but not all releases are appropriate for all media. In fact, it may take several different releases to get all the publicity that's available to you. If you shoot a shotgun loaded with buckshot, you will get an interesting scatter effect; aim a rifle, however, and you hit one target dead center. In thinking about publicity, you need to consider both approaches. An example of the rifle technique would be to target a specific magazine or TV talk show and send a sensational media kit (see below). Another option is to send a release headed *Exclusive to (name of publication)*, a technique I once used to get publicity in *Family Circle*, which always loves to get an edge on its competitor, *Woman's Day*. (I received 10,000 letters from a one-paragraph mention in this magazine, each with a dollar enclosed for my "home business information package." The catalog I included in this package generated a 30 percent order response with $7,000 in book/subscription sales.)

Different products and businesses require different approaches, and you should be prepared to adjust your thinking and strategy at any time. Information that is *not* news to one editor may be news—or at least human interest material—to another. A release designed to attract attention from local media—newspapers, radio, or television—probably will not work for a national publication or station because the news impact is not the same. Curiously, small businesses that may be taken for granted in their own community often find it easier to get publicity in national media, especially if the release shares tips or information other business owners can use. If you do get this kind of publicity, be sure to send a release about it to your local newspaper since it could then lead to a feature article about you along the lines of "local business recognized nationally." *That*, you see, is *newsworthy*. (Being quoted or featured in a book like this is also newsworthy, and should be the basis of a release sent to local papers, organizations, and trade periodicals.)

Holiday E-mails Generate Publicity and New Business

"I haven't sent an 'official' press release since 1999," says Sherry Huff Carnahan, SherryCarnahan.com. "It was written by a professional publicist who got it in the paper, but it didn't bring in much business. However, what does bring in business are simple e-mails I send to clients, prospects, and people on my PR list. For example, an e-mail announcing my Christmas holiday hours generated two magazine interviews, a second radio spot on a syndicated show, hundreds of e-mail responses, and three new clients. I now make it a point to send simple e-mails to these people whenever something new is happening in my business or I take a holiday."

How could such a simple e-mail be so effective? In this case, it obviously gave editors story ideas on how a professional can serve clients over an extended holiday vacation. It also jolted prospects to act before the two-week holiday period began and reminded current clients that Sherry would respond to their urgent client needs during this period. (Sherry's Christmas holiday policy is to check phone and e-mail messages every Tuesday and Thursday and return only the most urgent calls. More home-based businesses should follow her lead.)

Key Elements of a Printed Press Release

● **Source Information.** This information, which should be placed near the top of the release either to the left or right side of the page, gives the name and contact information for the individual who can supply more information if needed. (Omission of this information will make it impossible for writers or editors to double-check points of interest or verify that a release is still timely.)

● **Release Date.** Most news releases carry the line, "FOR IMMEDIATE RELEASE" (always typed in capital letters and usually underlined) on the right-hand side of the page, positioned just above the headline. But I also have seen this line positioned to the left, and sometimes it's not there at all. The release dateline tells the media that the release can be used immediately upon receipt, or at their earliest convenience. If news is of a particularly timely nature, a specific date may be given for release. Press releases bearing the line "USE AT WILL" may have a longer life, held in reference files until space is available, or the copy fits into an issue with a special theme.

- **Headline.** The headline, also typed in capital letters, should be neatly centered on the page. It should summarize the content of your press release. Although most editors will write their own headline, the one you put on your release may have a lot to do with whether it's read or not. (See also "Finding a PR Hook" below.)

- **Basic Facts.** The most effective product releases concentrate on one product or service at a time. The first paragraph of your release should include the most important facts the media should know—the who/what/when/where/why and how of your story. If you can't get all of them into the first paragraph, get them into the second one.

- **Important Details.** In addition to the basic facts of your press release (the news peg and vital news), a good release will include other details as well—the kind that might suggest a feature story instead of just a short announcement.

- **Supplementary Information.** Any colorful background information you can include will add to the important details mentioned above.

- **"For More Information" Line.** Always include a last, short paragraph that serves a particular marketing purpose. If you seek a direct response, make some kind of promotional offer and include a short and simple way for people to get in touch with you. Although this is certainly free advertising, editors may include this kind of information if it benefits their readers. Examples:

A free (brochure or catalog) is available from (business name and address) or (your toll-free phone number). [Careful: this one can cost you dearly if you get hundreds of responses from the wrong audience.]

(Name of product) is available in (kind of retail outlets), or for (your postage-paid price) from (address or toll-free number).

To receive (special information package), send ($1 to $6) to: (address). [Use a coded "Dept. No." address so you can monitor results from this type of promotion.]

For more information about (products, service, business, etc.) visit the company's Web site at www.(URL).

Finding a "PR Hook"

You can't catch fish without a fishing hook . . . or publicity without a "PR hook."' The juicier the worm on that hook, the better your chances for getting a bite. (Once you've gotten the hook, it will be easier to create a catchy headline for your release.) There are many angles you can play here. See if one of the following fits your business:

● **Do your products promote your community or state or a certain group of people?** Do you sell products made by people in your city or state? Are you helping people survive job layoffs by helping them start their own businesses? Teaching them useful skills? Does your service benefit a particular group, such as seniors, single moms, dads at home, children with learning disabilities, etc.?

● **Is your business unusual or rare?** Craftspeople who are practicing a lost art or craft may find it easy to get publicity. (Examples: Native American crafts, carousel pony carving, or ethnic crafts such as English wheat weaving, Polish paper cutting, German woodcarving.) Service providers and Web entrepreneurs who are carving out their own market niches will also be appealing to the media if they have information to share that is hard to get anywhere else.

● **Is there a human interest angle to your start-up story or amazing success?** Did you, perhaps, launch your business because you lost your job? Do you have an amazing dot-com story that counters all those failed dot-com stories we've heard? Are you a senior who has enriched your life with a part-time business? Do you work full time in another field and consider your part-time homebased business a stress-relieving avocation? Are you a mother who started a business to be at home with your kids? Stories about such people are in the news every day. Pay attention! Follow their lead.

● **Can you tie your publicity to an event or anniversary?** Releases are often hung on national holidays or other proclaimed events found in *Chase's Calendar of Annual Events* (Contemporary Books). "Anniversaries of major events and days or weeks established to commemorate certain causes are a publicity seeker's dream," says Kate Kelly, author and publisher of *The Publicity Manual* (KateKelly.com). "If you can tie your business in with one of these occasions, then you will likely have a good chance for additional press coverage."

These sample days/weeks/months will give you ideas: National Small Business Week, National Bookkeeper's Day, National Business Women's Week, Fun Mail Week, Pets Are Wonderful Month, National Homesewing Month, Week of the Young Child, and Clean Off Your Desk Day. If you don't like any of the events you find, create your own without charge. (See sidebar "Pick a Day—Make It Yours!")

● **Are you an expert?** It has been said that anyone can become an authority on anything, given about three months' intensive study and concentration on a topic. After acquiring certain skills and knowledge, I became an expert simply by telling media people I was an "authority" on my topic. Before long, I was being quoted as a "home-business expert," and because my credentials and books backed up my claims, I naturally evolved into being recognized as one of the country's most trusted home-business advisers.

You may not feel like an expert now, but you may wake up one morning and find you are one. If so, don't be afraid to let others know because media folks *love* experts. "Experts 'happen' quickly," said Art Spikol in one of his *Writer's Digest* columns. "One day you're an ordinary person who knows a lot of big things about something little or a lot of little things about something big. The next day you're quoted somewhere. Before the next 24 hours go by, you're an expert."

Pick a Day—Make It Yours!
by Jeff Zbar, Chief Home Officer.com

Did you know that the second Sunday in January every year marks *National Home Office Safety & Security Week* and *America's Safest Home Office Contest*? Or that the Friday before Father's Day is *National Work@Home Father's Day* and the *Why I Work@Home: A Dad's View Contest*?

Before 2001, none of these existed. But in each case, I realized how ignored—and potentially lucrative—the market was. So I created the dates to promote my books (including *Safe@Home: Seven Keys to Home Office Security*) and I market the heck out of them. It's really as simple as that. Here's how to create a date of your own:

Find a niche. What expertise do you have that consumers and marketers would find interesting? Work@Home Father's Day and Home Office Safety Week are unique takes on emerging trends in the home office arena. Both provide interested companies compelling and newsworthy topics to which to attach their names and brands. Be sure to give your event or contest a catchy name so it grabs journalists'—and readers'—attention.

Pick a date. Peruse *Chase's Calendar of Events* at your library's reference desk, and register your date for free. The book lists more than 14,000 local, regional, and national milestones or annual events. Entries range from the birth (or death) dates of celebrities and historical luminaries to such obscure events as Sinkie Day (annually the day after Thanksgiving), which was created by the Association of People Who Dine Over the Kitchen Sink to celebrate people who do so. Obscure? Sure. Interesting to the news media? You bet. Just make sure your date is a logical fit (since January begins the year, I figured it was a good time to put a safety bug in people's minds), and that it doesn't conflict with a larger event that could overshadow your own.

Printed Press Releases

When sending printed releases, appearance counts because you will be competing for attention with many other pieces of mail. Strive for a "crisp" look, which means using quality paper, legible typefaces, and ample margins. PR expert Alan Caruba, author of *Getting Famous—How to Write a Successful News Release*, says the old rule about double-spacing a release is no longer applicable, but I think many editors prefer it because it makes it easier to edit a release (which will seldom appear as you've written it). However, many businesses do print single-spaced releases on their business letterhead or specially designed NEWS letterheads, so use your own judgment here. (Caruba's Web site, **www.Caruba.com**, contains several articles with tips on how to write more effective news releases.)

Try to keep releases to one page if possible unless you're sending a release written in a style that lends itself for use as an article. In this case, two pages are fine. Just write "MORE . . ." at the bottom of each continued page. (The old rule said "never print on the back side of a release," but no one pays much attention to this anymore. In the interest of conserving trees, I vote for printing on the back side, which also saves stapling time. Paper size can be standard 8 1/2" × 11" or legal-size, depending on your copy needs.)

PR Copywriting Tips

- Use simple English and short sentences. To avoid embarrassing errors, ask a knowledgeable friend to read your copy. (Grammar checkers and spell checkers help, but they're not perfect.) See also sidebar, "Words the Media Hate."

- Avoid "me-centered" releases. Unless you're a notable personality, don't begin a release with your name, which will only generate a yawn from editors. You can talk about yourself in a press release, but always write copy in the third person, as though someone else has written it about you. This makes it easy to quote yourself, which is important. Since publicity legitimizes information, you can make strong statements about your business or yourself through quotes in a press release, and people will believe them simply because they have appeared in print. If you said the same thing in a sales brochure, it would be suspect, simply because *you* said it. Example:

Brochure copy: *I believe my service is the only one of its kind. Give it a try. I'm sure you'll benefit from it because I get thank-you letters from satisfied customers every week.*

Press Release copy: *To his knowledge, the service offered by Bob Jones is the only one of its kind. "I know it helps people, too," says Jones as he shuffles through the week's stack of thank-you letters. "I get mail like this every week."*

● In promoting a service, your best bet for attention is to offer free advice others in your field can use. This immediately positions you as an expert who has answers people need. Although your advice will enable some people to do for themselves what you might have done for them as a service provider, it will also emphasize to many others that you're *there* and ready to do the job they may not have the time or inclination to do themselves. (This is when having a Web site could make all the difference in whether publicity works for you or not.)

● In describing handcrafted products in a release, omit detailed information about all the colors, sizes, or styles available and don't go on about different payment options you will accept or the fact that sales tax should be added if you live in such-and-so state. This kind of information belongs in a brochure or catalog, not a press release. Pay the sales tax yourself on any orders you get from publicity, and count yourself lucky to have this extra business.

● When writing releases to be e-mailed *never* use an attachment to provide text. "Attachments are an invitation to delete the e-mail because they can spread computer viruses," warns Alan Caruba. He also stresses the importance of qualifying an e-mail address by sending an inquiry asking whether the media contact wants to receive news via e-mail. "Some do," he says. "Some do *not!*"

Creating a Media Kit

In addition to the press release itself about whatever you're trying to promote, start planning a complete media kit, looking forward to the day when you have a really big opportunity to impress someone, like the editor of a

Words the Media Hate
Tips from Joan Stewart, PublicityHound.com

If I had to choose one word or phrase that really gets under the skin of media people, I'd choose the word "unique." It is overused in bios, news releases, and pitch letters. Even worse are the phrases "somewhat unique" or "very unique" which don't make sense, because unique means the only one of its kind.

You should also avoid phrases like "the only one of its kind," "the first to," or any other description that you are not absolutely sure is accurate. During my days as a newspaper editor, we'd often print stories about someone who claimed to be the first person to do something. Then, the day after the story appeared, we'd get three phone calls from people claiming *they* were the first to do it. Then we'd have to print a correction. The source we quoted looked silly. So did the newspaper.

If you're not sure, it's better to use the phrase "believed to be." Or bypass that angle altogether and find a better hook. For the record, the media also hate "cutting edge," "thinking outside the box," "the information superhighway," and any other trite phrases. Ditto for self-promotional words like "fantastic," "amazing," or "remarkable."

major consumer magazine, or the producer of a network television show. Here is what you might put in your kit:

● **Bio**. If a separate biographical release and a photograph accompanies a news release, you will greatly increase your chances of getting a feature article in newspapers and magazines. Basically, the bio tells who you are and why your business is interesting. It generally reads exactly like an article, the idea being that a busy editor can simply run it as is, or a lazy reporter can submit it under his or her byline. Many writers, of course, use bios to form the basis of their own lengthy feature articles. (You'll find several examples of good bio releases by checking the Web sites of the various business owners quoted in this book.)

- **Promotional Clippings.** As soon as you get any print publicity at all, start a clippings file and follow the guidelines in this chapter for using them legally.

- **Q&A Backgrounder.** If you've done something a lot of people might like how-to information on, create a question-and-answer sheet (or FAQ page) that answers questions reporters might ask about how you got started, how you do one thing or another, facts about your industry, etc.

- **Photographs**. (See special tips on next page.)

- **Additional Releases.** You may wish to include more than one release, each with a different headline and copy slanted a bit differently.

- **Printed Materials.** Include your brochure or catalog—whatever best describes your products or services.

- **Business Card.** Often placed in a media folder that has slots cut to hold a card.

- **Promotional or Novelty Item.** Some businesses also include some kind of promotional or novelty item, but don't waste money on this until you have a track record in getting publicity and can afford this kind of "extra." (See sidebar, "PANIC Button Package Triggers Call to Bomb Squad.")

Photo Tips: What Editors Want

Being able to offer professional photographs or transparencies of you or your products can make the difference between a brief mention and a feature story in a major consumer magazine. When I met folk artists Clark and Ronnie Pearson a few years ago, they were carving and painting primitive Santas and other country items and getting publicity in several of the best country magazines. Ronnie then shared their secrets of success.

"We began by first writing detailed descriptions of each of our products, along with a background story about our business and how it evolved," she said. "Then we gave this information to business friends skilled in photography, graphic design, copywriting, and publicity. They developed a color catalog, professional background article, press release, and presentation folder suitable for mailing to magazine editors. Each press kit included photographs and color transparencies designed to make it easy for editors to create a story with little effort on their part." Granted, the Clarks spent some money to develop their promotional materials, but the resulting publicity brought them thousands of dollars' worth of business.

While major business magazines (and most newspapers) will send a photographer to your home or office if a picture is needed, entrepreneurial magazines on tighter budgets will probably ask you to provide pictures for consideration—either black and white glossies, or color slides. Once, when I offered to refer a writer to specific businesses in my network she might interview, she said she wanted only successful businesses in cities where it would be easy to dispatch a photographer to get a picture for the article. This is just one reason why some businesses get publicity and others don't. It also suggests that the inclusion of a professional photo with a press release might sometimes make the difference in whether you get a PR mention or not.

Another time, when *Entrepreneur* magazine asked me to provide the names of five unusual homebased business owners they might profile in an upcoming issue, I later heard from some of them about how their pictures got into the magazine. One woman quickly "hired" her husband to take a picture of her in her office. One couple rushed to have pictures taken, and when they weren't acceptable to the magazine, a photographer was sent to their workshop where he spent hours doing the shoot. Years ago when I was interviewed for a home-office article in *Time* magazine, they asked if they might send a photographer to my office and I said yes, providing I could have a day to "organize my chaos." A top professional in the Chicago area came in with four cameras and over a period of four hours shot four rolls of film, taking snaps from every possible angle and even rearranging my office. I could not have afforded this professional's shooting fee, but he did agree to sell me four color slides (of his choice) for $200, and I got a lot of mileage from them. By having a color slide to send when other magazines asked for a picture, I got several nice color spots in articles.

In one of his photography columns for *The Crafts Report*, Steve Meltzer indicated that newspapers and magazines need 5" × 7" or 8" × 10" black-and-white prints for reproduction. "Bigger prints have more impact and are likely to be printed larger," he said. "Newspapers love visually striking, human-interest photos."

"It pays to take good photos of your products," adds Patricia Kutza. "Digital photos should be at least 1,000 dpi or better if you want to publish in a traditional magazine. No one knows better than you what tone you want to set, what audience you wish to reach. With today's digital cameras, it is possible to photograph with that type of quality and then compress the image for Web use, where 'dumbed down' images (about 200–600K or so) are still acceptable."

Writing Promotional Articles

If you don't like writing press releases, write promotional articles instead that include your special tips, advice, or know-how. This is one of the best ways to get publicity both on the Web and in special-interest consumer magazines and business periodicals, and it's a strategy that will work for any type of business.

When I was publishing a print newsletter and selling my books by mail, I didn't have money for magazine advertising, so I started offering free articles and book excerpts to selected editors. This publicity drove thousands of people into bookstores to buy my books and also gave me thousands of prospects to whom I could market directly. I continue to use this strategy to drive traffic to my Web site and encourage the sale of my books in bookstores or on the Web.

The benefit of writing promotional articles is that you can insist they be published exactly as written, which means you can write your own how-to-order information at the end of each article—what master marketer Jeffrey Lant calls "the resource box." Prior to getting on the Web, Lant regularly mailed print editors a lengthy list of articles currently available, a strategy that soon made him the most widely read small business expert in the industry. Today he publishes several ezines and regularly sends promotional articles by e-mail to sell the Web marketing services offered at WorldProfit.com. "You must produce articles at regular intervals to continue to keep your name and services before the proper public and underscore the fact of your indispensability," he states in his book, *The Unabashed Self-Promoter's Guide.*

How to Play the Publicity Game

Getting More Publicity on the Web

Here's how one entrepreneur used a series of promotional articles to build his ezine base and recycle ezine articles to other publishers on the Web. (See Chapter 10 for more about autoresponders.)

When Jim Turner started YourProfitStation.com in late 1998, he produced a dozen short articles related to doing business on the Internet as a part-timer or moonlighter. At the end of each of these messages, he offered readers more up-to-date information if they would join his newsletter group, and that's how he got his ezine off the ground.

"The twelve messages were sent using a sequential autoresponder," he explained. "Over the next few months I continued to advertise in other ezines by trading ads. My ad would be asking people to sign up for my Internet marketing tutorial. (Trading or swapping ads is an excellent way to get free advertising in other ezines.) I wrote most of the articles for my ezine. After publishing them there, I circulated them to other publishers to insert in their ezines. This gave me more publicity because I always included a signature file that asked people to sign up for my ezine, enticing them with a freebie such as an eBook or special report.

"Using these tactics drove my list up to over 22,000. Now, everything that I sell is done through my ezine. I never purchase advertising anymore. It's all done via trades and swaps with other publishers whose target market is the same as mine. The key is trading with the right audience."

Following is an example of how to write and format a news release to be sent by e-mail. Its content includes valuable tips on how to multiply your chances for getting publicity. (Type size shown here is smaller than the 11 point size you should normally use.)

For: Creative Ways, P.O. Box 1310, Boston, MA 02117
Contact: Marcia Yudkin, marcia@yudkin.com, 1-617-266-1613.

FOR IMMEDIATE RELEASE
Internet Publicity Expert Spills the Secrets of Press Release Optimization, Techniques that Multiply Chances That Company News Reaches the Target Market

Homemade Money

Boston, MA, July 16, 2001 - In crafting a news release, PR practitioners have always rightfully paid disproportionate attention to the headline, the angle and the who/what/when/where/why in the first paragraph. Now that releases generally become part of the World Wide Web, through a wire service or the company's own site or both, specific keyword phrases used in a release take on greater importance, according to Boston-based publicity consultant Marcia Yudkin. (http://www.yudkin.com/printernet.htm)

"When I went looking for techniques to make releases more likely to turn up when potential buyers are searching the Web, the phrase 'press release optimization' itself turned up a big fat nothing on the search engines," says Yudkin, who recently compiled a manual called PR in the Internet Age detailing what she then learned in her own intensive self-education campaign.

Yudkin recommends that Internet Age publicity seekers begin by analyzing the phrases that potential customers or clients will use to look for something in the arena of the product or service being publicized. "When distributing a release about a new service, a bed and breakfast in Truro, Massachusetts, might be better off using the phrase 'Cape Cod' repeatedly than 'Truro,' for instance. Similarly, if travelers think in terms of 'country inn' rather than 'B&B,' that's what should be in the release." The selected phrases then need to be repeated a few times in the release, for instance by replacing pronouns with nouns, even if that sounds a bit stilted, she says.

To increase the chances of the release getting found by searchers, a company releasing a new product should deemphasize the name of the product (because no one will be searching for it) and instead emphasize the generic label — for example, "child safety tag" rather than "SafEze." "There's a completely new audience for company news in Internet searchers, who can now use search engines to find products, services and companies even if no third-party media coverage results from a release," says Yudkin.

Besides discussing press release optimization techniques, Yudkin's report on Internet publicity techniques offers 101 sites that welcome free posting of news releases, 40+ sites that invite free submission of articles for posting, instructions for using free directory listings and case studies for publicity, and more.

Marcia Yudkin is the author of Six Steps to Free Publicity (Career Press, 2nd ed.) and Internet Marketing for Less than $500/Year (Maximum Press), moderator of Adventive.com's I-Content discussion forum and a syndicated columnist on marketing. For more information about PR for the Internet Age, visit www.yudkin.com/printernet.htm.

How to Develop a Good PR List

Media lists can be rented from a variety of sources or you can meticulously compile your own, picking up contacts as you read various publications, surf the Net, or research directories at your library (see "Other Resources"). You should have your own PR list even if you also plan occasionally to rent special media lists or use distribution services to print and mail or fax/e-mail releases for you. Only with your own list can you be sure your message is reaching the individual editors and other individuals most likely to respond to your press releases or media kits. Developing and maintaining your own PR list will be a never-ending job, however, because new opportunities for publicity are always presenting themselves and editors tend to move around a lot.

Here are some specific directories and Web links that will be helpful to you in building a PR list of your own:

- *Writer's Market*, **www.WritersMarket.com.** This directory lists periodicals in dozens of categories in consumer, trade, technical, and professional areas. Online, you can subscribe to an update service (a good idea, since as many as 300 listings may go out of date in a month).

- *Gebbie Press All-in-One Directory*, **www.GebbieInc.com.** On this site, you can link directly to specific radio stations, magazines, newspapers, etc. that are on the Web. Gebbie publishes three print directories (currently $120 each) listing daily and weekly newspapers, AM-FM radio stations, television stations, general consumer magazines, business papers, trade press, black press, farm publications, and news syndicates. (Syndicates, by the way are often interested in material related to "living and lifestyle," which includes everything from cooking to car care, from contemporary living to coping with old age, from growing plants to raising a family. Health, food, nutrition, and money topics also are of interest.)

- *Bacon's Publicity Checker,* **www.Bacon.com.** Similar to Gebbie's directory, but different in that you can create your own PR list using Bacon's MediaLists Online service. Here, you can select from a variety of PR categories (print magazines, radio stations, E-Mail Media, etc.) and pay only for the names you decide to download. If your budget allows, you can also use Bacon's news release distribution services.

- *Newspapers/Radio/TV Stations.* When you need only a few of these PR contacts, you can do a search at **www.Newslink.org** to find direct links to them on the Web.

- *Syndicated columnists.* If you can get the interest of just one syndicated columnist, you may strike PR gold. There used to be a good print directory of columnists, but it's now out of print. You will, however, find a directory of leading newspaper columnists grouped by category at **http://headlinespot.com/opinion/columnists.**

- *Authors.* They are always looking for interesting people and things to write about in their freelance articles and books, so when you can approach them with a good story idea or offer a tips release containing information of value to their readers, you may be as appreciated as manna from Heaven. Check your library for the *Contemporary Authors* directory or search for individual authors on the Web. If you have an author's name and need a phone number or e-mail address, do a search at **www.Peoplespot.com** or **www.WhitePages.com** (where you will also find a handy area code and zip code finder). I also use *Reference USA,* a directory I can access online through my local library's Web site.

How to Play the Publicity Game

Product makers: When considering which publications to add to your PR list, look not only at trade magazines that directly relate to your new product and its obvious uses, but other publications that indirectly relate to it. When you find them, write a different press release that presents your product from a different viewpoint and in a way that will appeal to the new audience of readers.

Building Your E-mail PR List

The Internet has dramatically changed the way publicity is generated today. Although thousands of companies still send printed releases, businesses on the Web tend to e-mail theirs. Lesley Spencer, HBWM.com, who has a bachelor's and master's degree in PR, agrees that the Internet has greatly changed the publicity picture, both from the standpoint of how news releases are written and delivered, and how media people connect with the special contacts they need whenever they're writing articles for newspapers, magazines, or Web sites.

"The Internet has made it so much easier for media to round up potential people for stories and articles," she says, "and from my experience, most writers prefer to get news releases by e-mail or fax, rather than by mail. E-mail is often the most preferred method of delivery because it allows them to simply cut-and-paste content into their articles."

The problem, of course, is *how* to gather all the needed e-mail addresses. I asked Lisa Kanarek (HomeOfficeLife.com) if she recommended using one of the media directories to get e-mail addresses, or whether she called or faxed her old PR contacts to see how they preferred to get releases in the future. "I used to mail releases, then I faxed them, and now I e-mail them (unless I'm sending a book with them)," she told me. "For national radio or TV shows, I normally call and ask how they want the release submitted. I know I won't get the producer on the phone (although sometimes I get lucky), but their assistant will tell me. I've found that some programs have a recorded message about how to submit releases. As to what they most prefer, fax seems to win out. Of course, when my publishers send releases it has to be by mail so they can include a review copy of the book. Media directories are good sources for this information, but you still must call before you contact them since producers and editors tend to move around."

Most businesses on the Web seem to be building their e-mail PR lists one contact at a time. "I find the slow but sure methods of hand selecting sites to work with give the best results," says Deanna Ferber, eGlamKitty.com. "I don't waste my time on generic bulk e-mails or free-for-all sites. I do promote to a few targeted forums/communities and belong to several networking groups, and while this may not bring much direct sales, it has brought other more targeted connections for me to build relationships with."

Deanna has the right idea. "PR is about building a relationship with your target audiences by building a relationship with those who have influence over your target audiences," says Richard Hoy of WritersWeekly.com (one of the best sites on the Web for freelance writers and authors). "It used to be that the only way you could cost-effectively influence a large group of people was through the media. Now the Internet—with its own system of influencers independent of traditional media—offers much, if not more, impact than traditional media."

According to Hoy, the two main methods of Internet PR revolve around getting links to your site (a linking campaign I've discussed in Chapter 10), and getting stories and/or announcements about your site (a media campaign). "The first method involves registering your site with search engines and trading links with other Web site owners, while the second involves sending e-mail news releases and announcements to targeted journalists and writers on the Web," Hoy explains. "A favorable mention in a story by a few high-profile reporters can reach far more people than the PR person could reach on his or her own, and the Internet has added a whole new dynamic that is able to circumvent the power traditional media have to influence the public. A simple example of this would be our *WritersWeekly Newsletter*. Few traditional media or publications that catalogue the media have ever heard of us, yet we reach 70,000+ writers on a weekly basis."

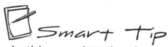

Smart Tip

"It will take time to build a good PR list, but one way to do this is to type in a keyword or phrase to turn up a list of articles containing those words," Hoy suggests. "Then you can check to see who wrote the articles and decide whether to add a particular writer to your PR list."

Helpful Information on the Web

If you're eager to learn how to get free publicity, learn insider tricks, write better copy, and reach the right media people for your special news, read a book or two on this topic. If you're on the Web, you could easily spend a whole day following up the dozens of leads you'll get by typing "free publicity," "online PR distribution services," and other related words into a major search engine. See "Other Resources" for book recommendations and a few PR Web links I found especially interesting.

I stopped seeking publicity when I closed down my book selling/publishing division to write books full time, but now that I'm on the Web with new books and services to promote, you can bet I'll be updating my old PR list to include e-mail addresses and launching a whole new publicity campaign as soon as my *Homemade Money* books are in print. Many of the homebiz/craft/smallbiz publications and organizations I used to send releases to are out of business now, and those that have survived are probably on the Web, so I'm guessing that most of my press releases in the future will be delivered electronically, and still going click . . .click . . . click as they land in some editor's e-mail inbox.

Online Distribution Services

"There are a many online distribution services that will, for a princely sum, disseminate your press release to targeted media outlets," says Patricia Kutza. "I wanted to keep that cost at a minimum yet take advantage of the power of the Web, so I chose PRWeb (**www.PRweb.com**) an online distribution service that bills itself as 'the free wire service.' PRWeb tells you up front that a small donation gets you preferred placement in its vast archives of press releases. So I took them up on it and paid a very small fee and, sure enough, my release was placed higher up in its archives. I chose a category where I wanted this release placed at their site and later I was able to pull up the release when using the Google.com search engine."

Publicity Humor

Humor is always in demand by the media, so if you can figure out how to write a humorous yet tasteful press release, you may triple your chances for publicity. For example, if you're a mother with six kids who's found a way to run a successful business at home, a humorous press release about your trials and tribulations—which also includes some solid tips on how to cope in such a situation—would surely bring results. Study the style of humorists such as Erma Bombeck for ideas.

Patricia Kutza is a wordsmith who has given her designer accessories clever names, and then written press releases that play on these names. "I consider many of my pieces 'visual puns,'" she says, "because they incorporate most of the traditional components of mens' ties in unconventional ways." Patricia promotes her WhatKnot™ business through speaking, offering such talks as "The Way We Wore," and "Fit to be Tied—Who's Who at the Zoo When Neckties Change Their Sex." When promoting her retail/wholesale line of pockets with a fusible backing, she gave her release a headline editors couldn't resist: "Pickpockets™ Are Welcome."

"There's only one thing in the world worse than being talked about, and that is *not* being talked about," said Oscar Wilde. Publicity has certainly advanced my business, just as it will advance yours. I knew I was a success when a feature story appeared on me in the newspaper published in Paxton, Illinois, the town next to my home town of Buckley, which is too small for a paper of its own. And I loved it when my sister, Mary Kaufmann, told a friend that she ought to read my book, and her friend said, "You mean to say that *you* know Barbara Brabec?"

Of course I enjoy seeing my name in print, and with all the national visibility I have received, coupled with daily messages of praise from my readers, I sometimes get a bit heady from it all. Not to worry. There's always husband Harry to keep my head on straight with his humorous putdowns. I'll never forget the day I told him there was once a saint who bore my name.

"Did you know that St. Barbara was patron saint to the artillery?" I asked in all seriousness. "No," he quipped, "but that explains why you think you're such a big shot."

To keep myself humble, I have a sign in my office that reads: "If at first you do succeed . . . try not to be insufferable."

"PANIC Button"
Package Triggers Call to Bomb Squad!

After receiving a half-page color spread in *Meetings and Conventions* magazine, Silvana Clark was astonished when the first response was an order for 3,000 of her $1 red PANIC Buttons, a novelty item she created as a promotional tool and sent to the magazine along with a news release. (It worked on any typewriter or computer keyboard, and the media ate it up.) "I'm almost embarrassed to have such a big ad for free," Silvana reported to me as she gleefully counted the profits of her aggressive publicity campaign.

Silvana's package always included a sample button and the words "Hand Stamp" because the envelope had a bulge in it. One of those releases, which promoted the PANIC Button as a stocking stuffer for computer users, generated a bizarre result that became funny sometime later. (As Woody Allen once put it, "Comedy is tragedy plus time.")

"Three days after mailing my releases," Silvana relates, "I get a message on my machine from a woman in a very shaky voice telling me to call her immediately so she can tell me what I've just put her through. The editor of a computer magazine, she was very upset by the receipt of my package. She got my envelope, saw the bump and assumed it was a bomb! She called Information, but they had no listing under my name because I'm listed under Allan and Silvana Clark. Then she gets more upset and calls Everett, the postmark on the envelope. Naturally they don't have my phone number. Next she calls the Bellingham Post Office and tells them she suspects I've sent her a bomb. They assure her that I do live at that address. Then she wants to take my package to the police but is scared to move it, so she calls an ex-police officer who tells her to fill the bathtub with water and let it soak for over an hour, then carefully slice open one corner with a razor blade. She does all this and of course finds my PANIC Button.

(Continued on Next Page)

"Needless to say, she was very upset and didn't listen when I said I'd sent out hundreds of these releases without any problem. I even told her that many marketers use 'Bumpy Mail' to get people to open their envelopes. That didn't satisfy her, and all I could do was apologize for her concern. This experience was quite upsetting to me, too, and I tried to console myself with the thought that some people have vivid imaginations. As we closed our conversation, I almost felt like saying 'Does this mean you won't use my news release in your magazine?'"

Note: You can get your own PANIC Button on Silvana's Web site at www.SilvanaClark.com.

Chapter 7

Advertising, Copywriting, and Direct Mail Strategies

If you take a chance, something good might happen or something bad might happen. But if you don't take a chance, nothing
will happen.
    —Wisdom from Dorothy, in *Golden Girls*

Where advertising is concerned, there are no guarantees. But one thing is certain: If you *don't* promote or advertise your business one way or the other, *nothing* will happen. Whereas you have little or nothing to lose by trying the free and low-cost marketing strategies discussed in earlier chapters, you must be more cautious when you begin to consider paid advertising options because here, Dorothy has it right: Something good might happen, or something bad might happen. You could get a terrific response to your ad, or you could lose the whole ad investment and get little or no business at all.

"But I expected a much greater response than I got—I don't know what went wrong," is the common lament of beginning advertisers. A *lot* of things can go wrong in advertising, and experienced marketers are as likely to encounter problems as beginners. The only difference is that the former can more easily afford mistakes than the latter. This chapter offers a crash course in advertising basics and copywriting techniques that will help you avoid a serious loss of money when placing ads in print publications or on radio or cable television. (Web-related advertising options are discussed in Chapter 10.) This chapter also includes tips on direct mail advertising, a sound and practical way to sell both products or services, *provided you use your own mailing list*. (See my cautions about renting lists later in this chapter.)

Smart Tip

Do not spend money on display advertising until you know something about graphic design and ad copywriting. If you insist on advertising this way at the beginning and don't know how to do the job right, hire a professional because this will save you money in the long run. Since ads in some of the smaller, special-interest periodicals may actually pull better than some of the national magazines, test these waters first.

Display Ads in Magazines

Large corporations live by the old rhyme, "You always buy familiar names/the ones you recognize; that's why the adman always claims/it pays to advertise." Each year, they spend millions of advertising dollars for magazine and television ads just to remind us they are in business. Because of exposure to intense media advertising, we consumers often are subconsciously persuaded to make certain buying decisions. Even on the smallest scale, homebased business owners cannot afford this kind of image advertising unless it comes in the form of publicity.

Small businesses can rarely afford the high advertising rates of most national consumer magazines either. Those who decide to risk such an ad often lose their investment because an ad can fail even when the product being advertised is salable and correctly priced. Most ads fail either because they are placed in the wrong publications or are poorly written or designed. *There is so much more to preparing an ad than just making it look good*. If the advertising copy doesn't motivate people to buy, they simply will not respond.

As you will learn in this chapter, it's important to calculate the per-inquiry cost of all your advertising efforts. In addition to comparing the costs of display advertising versus classifieds, you should also compare the pull of various sizes of display ads. For example, a one-column inch ad might draw 150 responses for a per-inquiry cost of $.75 each, while a three-inch ad might draw twice as many responses but have a per-inquiry cost of $1.10. And a full-page ad could be the least cost efficient of all, even though it might draw thousands of quick responses. That's why it's best to start with small display ads and classifieds to minimize your financial risk while you test several publications. As you increase the size of your ads, keep analyzing response and measuring actual results against the cost of each ad.

Smart Tip

If you have a mail order business, always indicate that you want the mail order ad rates of any consumer magazine you are contacting. These rates are lower than regular ad space and, for many advertisers, they actually pull better because they're placed in a special mail order section of the magazine where interested mail order buyers are most likely to look.

If you should become a serious display advertiser, ask about the availability of "remnant space," which usually is offered at highly discounted rates and available only for a short time. Sometimes a magazine will sell a particular page of an issue to an advertiser who wants distribution only to certain sections of the country, which means this particular page for the remaining sections of the country must be filled. Major consumer magazines would be a logical place to find such space.

Six Display Advertising Tips

During a seminar presented by the advertising director of a trade magazine, I gleaned these helpful tips:

1 In planning an ad campaign, make sure your strategy is consistent with your objectives. Always follow up on the leads and inquiries generated by your advertising and have a plan to evaluate the results of each ad.

2 Few readers are motivated by one ad only, so one ad in one issue of a magazine is probably a waste of money. When running an ad more than once in the same publication, figure that the response will peak somewhere between the second and third insertion of the ad, and be "worn out" by the fourth exposure.

3 Ads placed on the right-hand side of a page will get 5 to 10 percent more attention from readers, and those placed on the top corner of the right-hand page may attract as much as 25 percent greater viewing attention. (You may not get preferred positioning when you place an ad, but always ask for it.)

4 There is no right or wrong way to write an ad, but there are five basic elements of a good display ad: (1) Heading, (2) Subhead, (3) Body copy (details of offer), (4) a "call to action" (coupon, toll-free number, or anything else that motivates response), and (5) company's signature (name and address).

5 You'll increase the pull of an ad if you add a second "spot color" to it. This will cost about half again as much as a regular black-and-white ad, but much less than a four-color ad.

6 If you use a toll-free number in a display ad, you can figure you probably will be able to make a sale to at least half the people who call.

Advertising in Newspapers

Like radio, newspapers often serve local retailers best, but classified ads or one-inch display ads may be used effectively to attract prospects interested in buying a variety of personal or business services. My local paper, for example, regularly contains ads offering home-related services (masonry, carpentry, cleaning, painting, landscaping, lawn care, etc.), computer support services, financial consulting, accounting and tax services, tutoring, and child care. Most of these ads include not only a phone number, but an e-mail address and Web site, so even a tiny, inexpensive ad in the paper could be a way to draw people to your Web site where you can do a real selling job.

If you plan to advertise in your local newspaper, pay particular attention

How to Get Ad-Agency Discounts

"When I first started working for my mom, she told me I should acquaint myself with her copy of *Homemade Money*," writes Joe Wilson, Shirley Wilson's Ladybug Art Center, Springfield, Missouri. "While skimming through it I found *one* idea that, since 1986, has saved us between $25,000–30,000. And that single idea is still saving us money."

That idea? In return for bringing ad business to magazines, ad agencies always get a 15 percent commission on the ad. Sometimes you might be able to get this discount simply by asking for it, but if not, you can get it without question simply by running your ads through your own advertising agency. If you need to run display ads on a regular basis, it may pay you to set up your own ad agency. Here's how to do it:

1. Give your agency a name and address of its own, so it appears to have no connection with your home business. (You may need to rent a small P.O. box for this purpose.) Register this new business as you did your original homebased business.
2. Print business letterheads and envelopes with the new address on them. Design a professional ad-insertion order form. (I found such a form in the classic mail order guide, *How to Start and Operate a Mail-Order Business* by Julian L. Simon, available in libraries.)
3. Open a separate checking account for the agency, and consider having the numbers of the checks start with a high number to give the illusion the business has been operating for some time.
4. If one member of the family signs correspondence for the home business, use a different person's name to sign agency insertion orders and checks.

to the day your ad runs, remembering that each day's paper may include special sections targeted to specific readers. One service seller told me her newspaper ads had failed completely until she began to place them on a Friday when more men (her target market) were reading the paper to get a certain feature in that day's edition.

Many small businesses have commented to me that their ads in "penny-pincher" newspapers have yielded surprising results, perhaps because the people who like such publications tend to read them cover to cover. If your community has such a newspaper, you might want to give this type of advertising a try.

Smart Tip

With one call to Community Group International, you can place an ad that will be circulated in all the daily and weekly newspapers in a particular state and reach communities otherwise missed by the major metropolitan newspapers. These papers are delivered to homes in rural and agricultural communities. Cost varies, depending on how many papers you want to reach, but there is a package for every budget. Check ad rates on the Web at **www.CGINadvertising.com**, or get a media kit by calling 1-800-748-8249.

Two-Step Classified Ad Techniques

One thing homebased entrepreneurs can afford—and can count on to yield a fair response even when the copywriting isn't great—are classified ads designed to pull in interested prospects who can then be sold with a good follow-up mailing, e-mail promotion, or telephone call. It's called "two-step advertising," and it's a lot like going fishing. First you get the nibble . . . then you sink the hook.

This is the preferred method of advertising for all product-oriented businesses with limited budgets, but it works so well that major marketers also use it to build mailing lists of qualified customer prospects. While major companies may place expensive display ads to attract buyer prospects (manufacturers trying to interest dealers, for instance), smaller businesses are more likely to think in terms of placing classified ads in a number of magazines. And for as little as $500, you can run quite an effective campaign.

The material you send to prospects who respond to your ad has a lot to do with the number of orders you'll get. The easier you make it for people to buy, the more likely they are to respond to your offer. That's why flyers or brochures without any kind of order form do not pull as well as a brochure or catalog with an order blank. A standard direct mail package with a cover letter, brochure, separate order form, and reply envelope would be even better, but this is also more costly for the small business owner. A postage-paid reply envelope is a nice professional touch, but I never found it to be necessary in getting a good order response. In fact, the only time I ever enclosed reply envelopes (unstamped) were in mailings to expired subscribers who always needed an extra nudge. In the beginning, your goal should be to get started with the best package you can afford. To find out what works best, you'll have to test a number of different mail pieces and study the response each mailing brings.

Note that handcrafts and gifts will not sell well to consumers through inexpensively printed, black-and-white brochures or catalogs with line drawings or poor photographs. One reason is because buyers may be able to buy such items locally or see them in blazing color on the Web. Poor printed materials give buyers no visual assurance of the color, texture, or quality of such products, but the same products that will not sell this way may sell beautifully if they are featured in a full-color catalog produced by a nationally known company. The difference here, of course, is buyer confidence in the company making the offer. This is just one more key to success in selling by mail. Guarantees also go a long way in mail order, as do testimonials from satisfied customers. (Mail order pros say a money-back guarantee may increase order response by as much as 40 percent.)

Average Response from Classified Ads

The response to any classified will bring you a number of "hot prospects" (people who are obviously interested in learning the details of your offer), as opposed to the "cold prospects" you normally would reach in a direct mailing to a rental list. (The latter prospects, never having asked to receive your literature, may simply throw it in the wastebasket when it arrives.)

Since all ads attract a certain number of curiosity seekers, don't expect to sell more than 5 percent of your hot prospects with your first mailing, and be satisfied if you get a response rate of 2 to 3 percent, which most mailers consider good. Again, much depends on what you are selling, and to whom. I have received order conversion rates from 3 to 30 percent, but the book catalog I used to send to qualified propects generally brought a 10 percent order response. (Through the years, my order response increased as the quality of my printed materials improved.)

About six to eight weeks after your first mailing to a list of prospects gained from any advertising or publicity campaign, send a follow-up mailing, and *keep on mailing these prospects as long as you get back enough orders to cover all your costs.* In my experience, repeated mailings to a good prospect list will generate orders every time it's mailed, and this seems to hold true even if you mail the same people the same offer over and over again. The topic of follow-up marketing is so important I've given it a whole chapter of its own (see Chapter 9).

Figuring Per-Inquiry/Per-Order Costs

If you wonder whether a display ad or the two-step method would be best for you, try a test and evaluate the results on a per-inquiry/per-order cost basis. This is far more important than the cost of an ad or mail promotion. For example, if a classified ad costs $60 and generates 110 inquiries, your per-inquiry cost would be $.55 ($60 divided by 110).

If you were to place a small display ad in the same publication—one that cost $250 and brought in 197 inquiries—your per-inquiry cost would be $1.27 ($250 divided by 197). In this instance, then, classified ads would certainly be the most cost-effective way to generate inquiries *in this particular magazine.* (You might get an entirely different response from a different magazine.)

Your per-customer (or per-order) costs are even more important to you. As an example, take a catalog or other direct mail package that costs $.87 to print and mail first class. Using one of the examples above, let's assume that you send this mail piece to the 110 prospects who have responded to the classified ad, for a cost of $95.70. Add to this the cost of the ad itself, which was $60, or a total of $155.70. If you were to get a 4.5 percent order response (conversion of prospects to customers)—only 5 new customers—your per-customer cost would be $31.14, as illustrated below.

Depending on the cost of your product, or the size of your average order, you can easily see whether you're going to make or lose money in this kind of situation and determine whether you should be charging some kind of fee when you "fish for prospects." As you know, many classified advertisers charge from $.50 to $5 for brochures or catalogs, depending on how elaborate or expensive they are to print and mail. If you were to place the same $60 classified ad and ask $.50 cents for your catalog, you might get only 65 prospects instead of 110, but these people are likely to be more serious buyer prospects, so your order response might increase from 4.5 to 8 percent. On this basis, your actual ad investment would be $60, less the $32.50 your customer prospects send you for postage and handling, or just $27.50. To this, add $56.55 in costs to send them a catalog (65 × $.87), and you've lowered your costs to $84.05. On the basis of an 8 percent order response (5 customers), your cost per customer now drops to $16.81 instead of $31.14.

Quite a difference, isn't it, from an ad that reads, "free catalog," to one that reads, "send $.50 for catalog." Certainly you'll be money ahead whenever you can lower your advertising costs by charging for your promotional literature. These days, few sellers can afford to put anything into the mail without at least a dollar charge for postage and handling. Such a small charge will rarely deter serious prospects and only further qualifies them as likely buyers once they get your literature in hand. A popular strategy is to charge $1 to $3 for the information package and include mention in the ad that it's "refundable with first order" (which means you would have to include a credit memo or money-off coupon with your outgoing literature so prospects can get their money back if they decide to order). To illustrate the above figures:

Step One of Two-Step Advertising Method

Ad reading "Free Catalog"

Cost of ad: $60.00

Per-Inquiry cost:
$60 ÷ 110 = $.55

Ad reading "$.50 for Catalog"

Cost of ad: $60.00

Less $.50 cents sent by each of 65 prospects −$32.50

Adjusted ad cost: $27.50 $27.50

Per-Inquiry cost:
$27.50 ÷ 65 = $.42

Step Two of Two-Step Advertising Method

Cost to send catalogs to 110 prospects:		Cost to send catalogs to 65 prospects:	
110 × $.87 =	$95.70	65 × $.87 =	$56.55
Plus ad cost (above):	<u>$60.00</u>	Plus ad cost (above):	<u>$27.50</u>
Total invested in this ad promotion:	$155.70	Total invested in this ad promotion:	$84.05
If 4.5 percent response (5 customers), per-inquiry cost would be:		If 8 percent order response (5 customers), per-inquiry cost would be:	
$155.70 ÷ 5 = $31.14		$84.05 ÷ 5 = $16.81	

Instead of asking for money, some advertisers ask interested prospects to send an SASE (Self-Addressed, Stamped Envelope). In doing this, remember the importance of making it easy for people to respond to your offer. Sometimes the extra effort involved in getting an envelope and finding a stamp kills the impulse to order at all. In fact, experts say that a request for an SASE will automatically decrease by 25 to 35 percent the total number of responses you may receive. "You're cutting your own throat to save a first class stamp and an envelope," says one mail order seller.

And now I'm going to tell you what always worked best for me and many other mail order sellers. Instead of offering free information, asking for an SASE, or charging $.50 to $1 for your catalog or brochure, think about creating a special information package you could sell—a tip sheet, reference chart, resource list, sample, or special report that your prospects will perceive as being valuable to them (the same kind of promotional items discussed in the previous chapter). In my experience, prospects will gladly pay up to six bucks to get unusual or hard-to-find information targeted to their special needs. When such orders are received, you simply tuck your promotional material in with the special information ordered. To increase bounce-back orders or client business, you may wish to include a money-off coupon on one of your high-profit products or services. Surprisingly, a $3 information package may pull two or three times the response of an ad that requests $.50 for a catalog *because now you're appealing to a niche market with specific interests.*

For comparison's sake, let's say that your $60 ad will generate 200 requests for "valuable information" you have decided to offer for just $3. The figures look like this:

200 inquiries with $3 checks	$600.00
Less your cost to mail package:	
(200 × $.97—$.87 plus $.10 for the	
"info package" offered)	−194.00
Less cost of ad	− 60.00
Up-Front NET PROFIT:	$346.00

Voila! Now you've got 200 hot prospects at no cost to you. If *none* of them order, you'll still be ahead, but chances are good that your response will increase because the value of the information you've included in your package has added to your professional image and given prospects more confidence in whatever product or service you're selling.

Smart Tip

When people call to inquire or order, always ask them how they heard of you. Keep track of this information; otherwise you won't know which of your promotional or advertising methods are working.

Direct Mail Response Guidelines

In making direct mailings of any size to your growing prospect list, you must monitor results closely to gain response guidelines for future mailings. Mailings should be considered profitable any time you can get back at least 100 percent of the direct costs of your promotion. After you have made a mailing, how soon can you tell if it's going to produce a good response? Various marketing experts tell us that:

● The heaviest day's response to a mailing will come the second Monday after the first order arrives.

● Half the total response to a direct mailing will come within the first 13 days of returns.

● By the fifth or sixth day (after the first response has been received), you will have about 30 to 35 percent of the total response you are going to receive. By the end of two weeks you will have about 75 to 80 percent of the total response you're going to receive.

These helpful guidelines may also be used to project response from publicity and magazine advertisements.

Other Advertising Options

Radio and Cable TV

While advertising on radio is a great way for retailers to get business, it doesn't work well for homebased businesses. People expect a radio ad to lead them to a retail shop or store, not to someone's home (and zoning laws would surely prohibit this anyway). Certainly one cannot sell products effectively on radio without a toll-free number and merchant status, and if this is what you want to do, you don't have to pay for the privilege. As you learned in the previous chapter, news releases sent to radio and TV stations may lead to live or taped interviews, and you can also buy ad space in a magazine that reaches 4,000 producers.

Cable TV presents some interesting advertising possibilities, as Sylvia Landman learned the year she and her husband ran a 30-second commercial on their local cable station. It cost $600 to produce and generated a surprising number of clients interested not only in their consulting services, but in Sylvia's small business books and tapes (now available on the Web at Sylvias-Studio.com).

"Right there sandwiched between pizza parlors and manicure salons, viewers watched and followed our suggestions," says Sylvia. "They called. They wrote. They bought. They made consulting appointments, and the fee from our first night-owl client paid our production costs. The hardest part about doing the commercial was writing the 30-second script. We were advised to keep it to no more than 78 words since that is all one can say in thirty seconds. I wrote 325 words, then went to work editing, revising and condensing. I continued to extract words until only the most concentrated remained—92 strong, effective words survived, and I divided them into a professional script for Philip and I to share. There was no friendly 'hi' or hand waving, no dogs or kids. Just the facts, including our phone and fax numbers."

Per-Order/Per-Inquiry Advertising

Per-Order (PO) advertising is free, no-risk advertising that is offered by some special interest magazines and some radio and television stations. These opportunities are rarely publicized; to find them, contact the advertising department to see if PO (or PI) advertising opportunities are available. If so, and provided your product is deemed likely to sell to their audience, they will run your ad without charge to you, directing orders to their address and keeping half the product's retail price as their commission. You would then ship orders as they are forwarded to you, a practice known as "drop shipping."

Per-inquiry (PI) advertising is similar to PO advertising, except that in this case you would be expected to pay so much per inquiry. For example, if you were to offer your catalog or a sample of some other information product for $.50, the magazine or catalog company would keep the money sent by consumers, and charge you an additional amount (around $.50 each) for compiling and sending you address labels of the names of people who requested your information.

Remember my mention of Eileen Heifner's advertising experience in Chapter 3? Prepared to handle a thousand requests for her PI ad in a doll supply catalog, she was literally overwhelmed by the response she received. "I had researched this and still got a surprise," she says. "After they sent out their mailing, we got 300 responses per week, then 600, then 900, then 1,200, then 1,350. After that, the mail flow began to reverse itself in almost the same pattern it began. In total, we received around 17,000 requests, plus many phone calls from people who saw a copy of the catalog and just called for one."

A large response could be quite expensive and create all kinds of problems related to printed materials, inventory, and order fulfillment, so before risking this kind of promotion, you should be confident of your ability to get orders from your current catalog or other printed sales material normally sent to interested prospects.

Alternative Print Advertising Mediums

In this category are package insert programs, card deck mailings, statement stuffers, ride-alongs and co-op mailings. Companies in this field generally offer a wide selection of choices, and you can find them on the Web by searching for any of these key words. Such companies also advertise in direct marketing magazines and *Standard Rate & Data Service* (**www.SRDS.com**) publications, available in libraries.

These alternative print advertising mediums are not inexpensive advertising options, but they are exciting to consider. The right product, matched to the right audience, could really take off in this kind of promotion. Most programs of this nature must be purchased in minimum quantities of 100,000, but some companies offer interesting markets with minimum test-quantities of between 10,000 and 25,000. Two companies I've investigated in the past are

● Larry Tucker, Inc. (**www.SupermarketofSavings.com; (201)307-8888**) and

● Leon Henry, Inc. (**www.LeonHenryInc.com; (914)723-3176.**)

Larry Tucker claims to have the largest distribution program in the college market. This particular program employs people to distribute literature on college campuses throughout the United States, utilizing "take-one" posters or flyers placed under students' doors in dormitories. A division of this company also offers cooperative mailings sent to families at home addresses where a new birth has occurred within the past twelve months. An optional package, the "New Mother Hospital Sampling Program," distributes polybag packages to new mothers while they still are in the hospital. These contain product samples or inserts and coupons supplied by advertisers.

Leon Henry offers several package insert programs of possible interest to marketers of craft, hobby, and needlework products. For example, your insert could be included with the actual shipments of merchandise purchased by customers of such companies as Annie's Attic or Herrschners, Inc. Other programs enable you to reach buyers from the Brookstone catalog, which features hand and power tools, garden products, gourmet kitchenware, and unusual gifts for men and women. For more detailed information on package inserts, check this particular page on the Leon Henry Web site: **www.LeonHenryInc.com/Web/insert.htm**.

Renting Mailing Lists

In earlier editions of *Homemade Money*, I suggested that some small businesses might want to try mass mailings to rented mailing lists, but I no longer recommend this. In addition to much higher postage costs, we now have an audience of consumers who just aren't as interested in print advertising as they used to be before they got hooked on the Internet. While direct mail is a great way to communicate with prospects and customers you've attracted through other advertising methods or publicity, it's not recommended to beginners as a way to sell products or build a prospect mailing list.

I've included information on this topic only to keep novice advertisers out of financial trouble. A rented mailing list is considered a "cold mailing list" because the people on the list have never heard of you before and may have no interest in reading your material when they get it. Thus, even if you have a terrific mail piece, you might be lucky to get even a 1 percent response. That translates to only 50 orders on a 5,000-piece mailing, and you need not be a mathematician to see how easy it would be for inexperienced direct mailers to lose their shirts the first time out. Now you know why only the more expensive products are offered by major direct-mail marketers.

Although I do not recommend that you rent commercial mailing lists, I *do* suggest that you obtain copies of a couple of list rental catalogs because this is a great way to get ideas for niche markets you might reach in other ways. List houses advertise in the *Standard Rate & Data Service* publications mentioned above, and some also advertise on the Web. (Search for them using such phrases as "mailing lists to rent" or "mailing list rental.")

A study of several list catalogs will reveal hundreds of market categories you've probably never thought of before—markets you may be able to reach through (1) news releases to organizations that publish member periodicals; (2) privately published newsletters serving these niche markets, and (3) classified ads and publicity in trade or consumer publications aimed at these groups. To get you started, following is a list of niche markets I gleaned from a study of several list rental catalogs:

Boat owners
Business executives
Business opportunity seekers
Clubs, organizations, societies
Collectors (categories are endless)
Colleges and universities
Corporate gift buyers
Crafts enthusiasts
Day care facilities
Doctors
Editors
Farmers
Garden clubs
Gift shops
Gourmet cooks
Hobbyists
Homemaker groups

Meeting planners
Millionaires
Mothers-to-be
Music teachers
New mothers
Nursery schools
Photography buffs
Professionals (all fields)
Religious and ethnic groups
Self-improvement/self-help buyers
Senior citizens
Small business owners
Sports lovers (all categories)
Subscribers (various publications)
Teachers
Ultra-affluent women

The List Is Everything in Direct Mail
by Robert Bly, Bly.com

"The most important part of your direct mail campaign is not the copy, or the art work, or even the format or when you mail. *It is the mailing list.*

"A great mailing package, with superior copy and scintillating design, might pull double the response of a poorly conceived mailing. But the best list can pull a response 10 times more than the worst list for the identical mailing piece. The most common direct-mail mistake is not spending enough time and effort up-front, when you select—and then test—the right lists. The best list available to you is your "house list"—a list of customers and prospects who previously bought from you or responded to your ads, public relations campaign, or other mailings. Typically, your house list will pull double the response of an outside list. Yet, only 50 percent of business marketers I've surveyed capture and use customer and prospect names for mailing purposes.

"Remember: In direct marketing, a mailing list is not just a way of reaching your market. It *is* the market.

A Crash Course in Copywriting

Because good copywriting is so important to the overall success of your business, you should make it a point to acquire some skill in this area. You do not have to be "a writer" to do this, but you do need to acquire some of the writer's skills. Probably the best way to learn ad copywriting is to study the advertisements of other advertisers and businesses in your field. Look carefully at what you have been calling "junk mail" and pull out good examples of cover letters, flyers, and brochures you can study for style and technique. Remember that major advertisers pay a small fortune to professional copywriters, and you can get their expertise *free* simply by reading your daily mail. For continuing help, subscribe to at least one marketing magazine or ezine that includes information on how to write better advertising or sales copy. Like every other skill the homebased business owner must acquire, this one just takes a little time and effort. Meanwhile, here are a few tips to get you started on the road to better copywriting.

Smart Tip

To avoid problems with the Federal Trade Commission, acquaint yourself with the FTC rules and regulations discussed in the A-to-Z listings in Section II. The FTC is particularly concerned with truth-in-advertising, the use of endorsements and testimonials, use of the word "new," statements about warranties and guarantees, and the Thirty-Day Mail or Telephone Order Merchandise Rule.

General Copyright Guidelines

- Use everyday language. Short sentences. Short paragraphs. Don't ever try to be funny. Just be sincere and conversational.

- People like to deal with people, so establish a personality, flavor, and atmosphere by your name, concept, and what you are trying to do.

- Speak to your audience as though you were speaking to one person. Use the words "you" and "your" often. Avoid "we-centered" remarks.

- Make your offer believable by avoiding exaggerated claims and words like "astounding," "unbelievable," or "sensational." Be prepared to prove any claim you make.

- Don't use opinionated phrases such as, "You'll love it" or "It's really beautiful." Instead, stress the product's or service's benefits, such as "comfortable," "practical," "lasting." Remember that people have basic wants and needs. Among other things, they want to save time and money, worry, or discomfort. They want to be successful, healthy, informed, and attractive. They also want more money, security, confidence, and a feeling of importance. (*Note:* In a *Reader's Digest* ad test of two different headlines, the "save time" ad outpulled the "save money" ad.)

- Speak always in positive terms. Do not say, "You will not be disappointed," because this is a negative thought. Instead, say, "Satisfaction guaranteed."

- People often are motivated to buy out of greed, guilt, or fear. Whenever you can inject these elements into your advertising message, you will increase response. For *greed*, stress what people will gain from your product (money, getting ahead in business, envy of neighbors, etc.). For *guilt*, indicate what people will miss if they don't respond. For *fear*, tell people what they will lose by not responding now. (Loss of time, money, convenience? Will price soon increase? Is this the last chance to order?)

- Make a special offer. Examples: (1) Buy three, get one free, (2) Free (product) if you order within ten days, (3) Buy one at full price, get the second at half price, (4) Free freight on all orders over $100, (5) Free lesson to first ten people to respond, (6) Save 20 percent by ordering our "Early Bird Selection." And so forth.

Headline Ideas for Ads or Flyers

The headline is all important, because this often is the only thing people read. According to ad experts, five times as many people read headlines as read body copy. Try to incorporate some of the 12 most powerful words in your headline copy (see sidebar) and use action verbs for more power, such as: How to . . . *GET, BE, DO, SAVE, MAKE, STOP, WIN, HAVE, START,* etc.

Test Your Copywriting!

- The "Breath Test." Copywriter and author Bob Bly (Bly.com) suggests giving all your sentences the "Breath Test" to see if they are too long: "Without inhaling, read the sentence aloud. If you run out of breath before you get to the end, the sentence is too long. The solution? Use a dash (—) or ellipses (. . .) to break the sentence into two or more parts. Or rewrite it as two or more shorter sentences. Doing so will make your writing livelier, more conversational—and easier to read."

- The "Chicken Pox" Test. In a marketing workshop I attended, a speaker shared his "Chicken Pox Test" for good copywriting: "First circle in red all the personal pronouns (I, we, us, our, my), then change them to YOU words. Then circle all exaggerated words, such as biggest, most, best, and eliminate this diseased copy."

If you study full-page display ads, you'll note that many headlines (proven to be successful) begin with the words, "How I . . . *BECAME . . . MADE . . . STARTED . . . SUCCEEDED . . . IMPROVED*" and so on. A variation on this theme is to speak directly to the prospective customer by saying, "How *you* can . . . *BECOME . . . MAKE . . . START . . . SUCCEED . . . IMPROVE*" and so on.

Other successful headlines for ads and flyers often involve numbers, such as "10 ways to . . . ," "25 tips for . . . ," or "100 ideas on how to. . . ."

Help people read your ad more easily by using good typography in setting your headline. Avoid use of all capitals as this retards reading speed. *Never* use the kind of flowery typeface that makes readers have to look at it twice to be able to make out the letters.

Increase response to any ad or offer by giving customers the option of charging an order to a credit card. (The average mail order by credit card is said to be 20 to 40 percent higher than an order by check or money order.)

Classified Ad Copywriting Tips

● Eliminate unnecessary words.

● Write in telegraphic style. Use as many one-syllable words as possible.

● Don't try to sell two things in the same ad because the average reader can retain only one basic idea at a time.

● Don't try to sell products directly in an ad—it doesn't work. Just fish for prospects and let your mail piece do the selling job.

● Use the A-I-D-A formula in writing ads:

A= ATTRACT your reader.
I= INTEREST the reader by appealing to his or her wants or needs.
D= Stimulate DESIRE for your product by listing benefits to be derived from it.
A= Demand ACTION by closing with a phrase that gives readers something to write for or do. Examples: (1) For information write, (2) Send for free details, (3) Catalog, $1.00, (4) Order NOW! Also state your guarantee if you offer one.

Powerful Words and Persuasive Phrases
(Incorporate them into your advertising copy whenever possible)

The 12 most persuasive words in the English language:

You . . . Save . . . Money . . . New . . . Love . . . Easy . . . Health . . . Safety . . . Results . . . Discovery . . . Proven . . . Guarantee

The 10 words that spell direct mail success:

Free . . . You . . . Now . . . New . . . Win . . . Easy . . . Introducing . . . Save . . . Today . . . Guarantee

Advertising, Copywriting, and Direct Mail

Other powerful words and phrases regularly used by successful advertisers:

Bargain	Interesting	A Special Invitation
Bonus	Last chance	Buy three—Get one free
Check	Learn	Do not delay
Compare	Love	Free details
Complete	Money-back	Get started today
Confidential	guarantee	Here's news
Discover	New	It's easy
Earn	Now	Judge for yourself
Easy	Offer	Never before
End	Personalize	Proven results
Exciting	Popular	Save time and money
Facts	Profit	Send no money
Free	Profitable	There's no risk
Fun	Proven	or obligation
Gain	Quick	Three good reasons
Gift	Refundable	Trial offer
Guaranteed	Reliable	You can trust
Helpful	Safe	Tested
Here	Sale	Try
How to	Save	Wanted
Important	Secrets	Winner
Improved	Stop	Your
Informative	Success	YOU
		Act NOW

Chapter 8:
Marketing Outlets for Product Sellers

A market is a definable portion of the people in the population who are most likely to buy your goods. You must be able to identify your customers and set them aside from everyone else. When you offer your product to anyone, that's *sales*. When you select your audience, thereby narrowing the field to include the most likely prospects needing your goods or services, that's *marketing*.

> —Jeffrey Dobkin, *How to Market a Product for Under $500!* (Dobkin.com)

Every individual, every business, and every organization, institution, and government agency represents a market for someone's special products and services. This chapter includes several checklists that will serve as idea stimulators for markets that might be tapped through direct selling methods, advertising, publicity, direct mail promotions or telemarketing efforts. (For information related to selling products on the Web, see Chapter 10.)

Retail Markets to Consider

RETAILING is *direct selling* to consumers. This is personal selling, involving face-to-face meetings with buyers or the public at large through:

- [ ] *Shows/Fairs/Festivals* (art, crafts, and related products)
- [ ] *Flea Markets* (both new and used goods)
- [ ] *Home Shops and Holiday Boutiques* (generally products created by sellers)
- [ ] *Open Houses or Party-Plan Sales* (both craft and commercial product lines)
- [ ] *Person-to-Person Selling* (sales calls to prospects who have indicated interest)
- [ ] *In-Home Demonstrations* (generally by appointment to show commercial product lines)
- [ ] *State and County Fair Exhibits* (generally commercial product lines or service businesses)
- [ ] *Other Consumer Shows and Product Fairs* (all types of products and services)
- [ ] *Business Opportunity Fairs* (for general public)
- [ ] *Business Trade Shows* (for business owners)
- [ ] *Shopping Malls* (products and services—temporary leased space)
- [ ] *The Internet/World Wide Web*

● **Art/Craft Fairs/Shows/Festivals.** Professional art/craft sellers subscribe to show listing periodicals to find the best shows. See "Other Resources in Section" II to tap into print and electronic sources of information for local, regional, and national art and craft fairs, shows, festivals, and flea markets.

● **Home Shops and Holiday Boutiques.** Often set up to run on a weekend, home shops and holiday boutiques provide an interesting and profitable alternative to selling at fairs or through local shops. Twenty or thirty exhibitors may be able to ring up sales of as much as $20,000 in a couple of days, particularly if the sale has become a regular annual event noted for high-quality merchandise. Such events are usually coordinated by women,

168

and generally cause few, if any, problems with local zoning officials since they seem to be viewed in the same light as ordinary garage sales. It's always a good idea to check with authorities, however, before planning such an event.

● **Open Houses or Party-Plan Sales.** Although many artists and craftspeople successfully market through open houses and party plans, such events are commonly associated with MLM/network marketing and the sale of commercial products such as cosmetics, housewares, jewelry, lingerie, etc. While open house visitors generally take products with them when they leave, party plan selling usually involves later delivery of products. In some instances, however, zoning regulations prohibit one from using the home to transfer the sale of merchandise, so rather than let customers walk out of the door with the product, sellers may have to deliver goods later to be in strict compliance with the law.

● **In-Home Demonstrations.** This used to be called "door-to-door" selling, but the phrase has become outdated inasmuch as most sales today are generated by appointments arranged by telephone, instead of door-knocking. Many network marketers, such as cosmetics or Tupperware sellers, also come to one's home by appointment to give product demonstrations.

● **Consumer Shows and Trade Fairs.** Product sellers will find a variety of shows in which to sell their wares, from state and county fair exhibits and consumer shows to business opportunity fairs and trade shows. Such events can be found by reading related periodicals or checking events listings on the Web.

● **Shopping Malls.** Many shopping malls now offer space that can be leased on a temporary, seasonal basis—from kiosks and carts to vacant store fronts. Call malls in your area for details about plans they may offer. Artists and craftspeople might find this an excellent way to sell during the Christmas holiday season.

● **Craft Malls and Rent-a-Space Shops.** These outlets are a good way to market artwork and handcrafted merchandise at the retail level without any face-to-face selling. Sellers simply rent whatever size space they desire or can afford, fill the space with an attractive display of merchandise, maintain the sales display over a period of time, and leave the selling to those who own the individual craft mall or retail shop.

Note: Detailed information on how to sell art, crafts, and related products to all of the above markets and many others as well will be found in the author's books, *Handmade for Profit* (2002 Rev. ed.) and *Make It Profitable* (both published by M. Evans).

Selling to Canadian Consumers

If you are trying to sell a product to individuals in Canada, book publisher Leila Peltosaari (TikkaBooks.com) says your orders will increase if you give prospects both a voice mail and fax number with the option to charge their order on a credit card.

"If someone first has to go to the bank to get a money order in U.S. dollars, they may put it off until they ultimately decide they can live without whatever you're trying to sell to them," she says. "Given a choice between calling in an order to a voice mail telephone number and placing it via fax, individuals will choose the latter method of ordering. I think people hate to leave a complicated message with lots of info including peculiar spelling of names and credit card info. There is less chance of error with a faxed message."

Wholesale Markets to Explore

WHOLESALING is *indirect selling to consumers*. This is impersonal selling, involving sales through retailers, dealers, and other distribution methods. With few exceptions, the same marketing methods are used to sell on both the retail and wholesale levels. The primary difference is that, in wholesaling, the marketer has to shift mental gears because dealers and retailers do not think about merchandise in the same way as consumers do.

Whereas you must sell a consumer on his or her need for your product, you have to sell dealers and retailers on this point plus one other: why consumers will want to buy your products from them. That's one reason why wholesalers and manufacturers work so hard to make it easy for their dealers to sell, and why they offer them free or inexpensive counter display racks, finished samples (to sell kits), promotional literature they can give to consumers, camera-ready advertising copy, and so on.

If you are a small manufacturer, you may think you cannot sell at the wholesale level because of pricing or problems of limited production. Often, this is true. Other times, however, a product can be changed or redesigned in some way to permit increased production at a retail price that's high enough to allow for wholesaling, at least to some markets. By getting your feet wet in wholesaling first to small retail outlets, you will learn whether you are capable of filling larger orders or not.

If you plan to work alone and do all the work related to making and selling your products, think now about the limits to which you'll push yourself. Although we can always see the effects of overwork on other people, it's hard to recognize it when it's happening to us.

In trying to find new wholesale markets for your products, shift your thinking by looking for the wholesale counterpart of each retail market you now sell to. With few exceptions, you will find both consumer and trade shows, magazines, and organizations for each industry and each specific interest. This kind of detective work is what good marketing is all about. The sharpest marketers are those who not only dig around to find just the right distribution channels for their products, but also the most efficient and cost-effective way to use them. All types of products are purchased for resale by such buyers as:

- [ ] Retail Shops and Stores (See "Retail Outlets That Buy Products or Services")
- [ ] Mail Order Catalog Houses
- [ ] Trade Shows/Sales Reps/Merchandise Marts
- [ ] Premium Sales
- [ ] Bookstores and Libraries
- [ ] Foreign Markets

● **Mail Order Catalog Houses.** To successfully sell to this market, you will need a product that allows for at least a four-time markup; for example, you'd have to wholesale a $30 item for $7.50. The best way to sell here is to telephone the catalog company of your choice, ask for the director of merchandise or the catalog merchandise buyer. Try to determine level of interest by presenting yourself as a seller of (whatever), and say, "I just wanted to check first to see if you had any interest in this. May I send you a complete presentation package?" When you hang up, you'll know exactly what must be said in a letter, and the worst part of your selling job will be over. Follow up with a good information package that includes a glossy photo of the product. Don't send samples unless requested; they won't be returned. (See also sidebar, "Working with Catalog Companies.")

Smart Tip

You can research about 4,000 catalog companies in *The National Directory of Catalogs* published by Oxbridge Communications (available in many libraries). Better yet, do your research on the Web at **www.CatalogsFromA-Z.com.** This site lists 14,000 catalogs by category, with telephone numbers for each catalog company.

● **Trade Shows/Sales Reps/Merchandise Marts.** Although trade show exhibiting is neither simple nor inexpensive, it can often be the most important marketing move a small business can make. Find trade shows by reading *trade periodicals* in your industry (see periodical directories in your library). Because of the high cost of trade show exhibiting, many small businesses find it better to use sales representatives who not only call on certain retail outlets but regularly exhibit in certain trade shows as well. Many also have permanent exhibits in merchandise marts. Reps generally expect a commission of at least 15 percent, but on low-ticket items with limited sales potential the rate could be as high as 30 percent. Conversely, commissions may be as low as 5 percent on items with huge sales potential. You can find reps at trade shows or by reading trade magazines. Also check the Web site of Manufacturers' Agents National Association (MANA) at **www.MANAonline.org**.

Marketing Outlets for Product Sellers

- **Premium Sales.** "Premiums" are marketing tools used by companies to entice buyers into purchasing some product or service. This is a difficult market to crack, but any product or publication that can be produced in quantity may have premium appeal to buyers. You can connect with interested premium buyers by working with a marketing firm that specializes in premium offers, or by placing ads in trade publications that reach catalog buyers, premium users, and fund raisers.

  When thinking of premium sales, try to relate your product to some other product or service already on the market, then think of a way in which it might be used by that seller to increase business. Since premium sales may involve thousands of units, your discounts will vary considerably. (One of the easiest premiums for an individual to sell is a book or booklet that can be printed in quantity and sold at a deep discount for considerable profit.)

  Another kind of premium arrangement involves coupons. For instance, you might buy a sack of lawn seed and find a coupon or order form on the back of the bag that promotes a booklet on lawn care. The seed manufacturer has not gone into publishing as a sideline; it is simply working with some publisher on a premium deal. This kind of thinking can be applied to many products and services.

- **Bookstores and Libraries.** If you are a self-publisher, you may prefer not to sell directly to bookstores since their trade purchasing and payment practices aggravate even the largest publishers. Independent bookstores generally order only one or two copies of a book at a time at a 40 percent discount, then take sixty to ninety days to pay, retaining the right to return books up to a year after date of invoice if the books don't sell. Even more frustrating, the books are not always returned in resalable condition. Your best wholesaling option here is to connect with Baker & Taylor, the world's largest book wholesaler, and let them order from you and ship to the independent bookstores. For more information, check **www.BTOL.com** or call 1-800-775-2300.

  Libraries generally prefer to order from library distributors but occasionally purchase directly from publishers, desiring the same 20 percent discount they get from their distributors. ("Over the transom" purchase orders from libraries and bookstores are common if you receive a lot of national publicity for your books.)

For hundreds of other ideas on where and how to sell books, read self-publishing guides. (See "Other Resources" for some of the author's favorites.)

● **Foreign Markets.** Exporting to other countries is not something the average small business plans to do, but it is a possibility for aggressive marketers. To avoid the paperwork hassles involved in exporting, it is best to work with agent-buyers or bona fide distributors. The Department of Commerce is the place to start when you want more information on this topic. First, however, you must decide if your product has overseas sales potential. If so, you must then weigh sales opportunities against the complexities of exporting, which is both an expensive and time consuming way to market products.

Working with Catalog Companies
A Tip from Leila Peltosaari, TikkaBooks.com

"Careful! Don't count on an order from a catalog house until you have a formal purchase order in hand. I learned an expensive lesson when a major U.S. catalog house that mails 30 million catalogs expressed interest in one of my books but wanted a lower price than I originally offered. I accepted their counter offer, on phone and in writing, then reprinted the book in a larger-than-usual quantity in anticipation of their order. But when the catalog came out, my book was not listed. When I asked why, they told me that at the last minute they decided to include another book instead of mine. They said that, regardless of their correspondence exchange, their offer is never binding until the first purchase order is sent. Thus, *correspondence* is not the same as a purchase order."

Retail Outlets That Buy Products or Services

If you are wholesaling products, generally expect the retailers on the list below to ask for a discount of 50 percent off the retail price (although some may be accustomed to buying at 40 percent). You will have to do some market research to learn what is standard in each industry. For example:

Marketing Outlets for Product Sellers

● *Art galleries* rarely buy outright, preferring work that can be placed on consignment. They may sell for you, keeping from 25 to 40 percent of the retail price, and there may also be extra space rental fees involved here. Consignment selling means increased bookkeeping and paperwork for both shop and seller, and for the latter, merchandise is tied up, but not sold, which presents cash-flow problems. Common consignment hazards are shop owners' lack of concern for goods they do not own, thus losses due to shoplifting, breakage, or mishandling are the consignor's problem.

● *Craft retailers* rarely buy directly from a manufacturer, preferring instead to purchase through craft wholesalers at a 50 + 10 percent discount (see "Understanding Markups and Discounts" in this chapter). Needlework retailers, however, often buy patterns and kits from individual manufacturers, expecting only a 40 percent dealer discount.

☐ Appliance stores
☐ Art & craft galleries
☐ Baby shops
☐ Barber shops
☐ Beauty shops
☐ Bookstores
☐ Bridal shops
☐ Camera shops
☐ Candy shops
☐ Card shops
☐ Christmas shops
☐ Clothing shops
☐ Coffee shops
☐ Coffee & tea stores
☐ Computer stores
☐ Craft supply shops
☐ Department stores
☐ Fabric stores

☐ Fancy cookware stores
☐ Florists
☐ Garden centers
☐ Gas stations with food/gifts
☐ Gift shops, general
☐ Gourmet food stores
☐ Grocery stores
☐ Gun shops
☐ Handcraft shops
☐ Hardware stores
☐ Health food stores
☐ Hobby shops
☐ Home shopping centers
☐ Hospital gift shops
☐ Hotel gift shops
☐ Ice cream parlors

☐ Lawn & garden centers
☐ Magic & novelty shops
☐ Military exchanges
☐ Museum shops
☐ Needlework shops
☐ Office supply stores
☐ Pet shops
☐ Print shops
☐ Record/CD stores
☐ Religious bookstores
☐ Religious gift shops
☐ Restaurants
☐ Shoe stores
☐ Sports shops
☐ Toy stores

Establishing a Retail/Wholesale Pricing Structure

If you sell handmade products directly to consumers as well as to handcraft shops, maintain your retail prices for both markets. In other words, if you wholesale an item for $10 that will sell for $20 in a retail outlet, don't go to a crafts fair and sell the same item to consumers for $10. This is extremely unprofessional and more than likely will result in a loss of wholesale business.

"We have found that the biggest challenge to small craft and gift manufacturing businesses is the pricing structure," says Malcolm Dell, who currently represents the product lines of professional crafters to retail stores in five states. "We find that crafters are often underselling their products at retail craft shows (based on retail price), and are resistant to creating a wholesale/retail pricing structure that allows a retail store to double the wholesale cost to make a profit. Also, crafters do not seem to understand that if they sell to a store at $10, claiming this is the wholesale price, they can't go to crafts shows all over town, selling at $10 to retail customers. They really need to decide if, long-term, they are going to be in the wholesale or retail (direct marketing) business and design their business strategy and pricing accordingly. We would have many more lines to represent if crafters really understood wholesaling and associated pricing strategies. We do our best to educate them, but it's a long, slow process. Most of them are stuck in the retail craft show circuit. Some like it there, but some would rather focus on creating products and letting others sell their wares." (Visit the Dells' Web site at LewisClarkGifts.com to find a helpful online course, "Taking Your Products to Market: A Primer on Wholesale Marketing Channels.")

Understanding Markups and Discounts

Markup: The percentage a retail outlets adds to the wholesale price it pays for any item. For example, if you wholesale an item for $20, in most cases it will be marked up 100 percent to arrive at a retail price of $40. (Some stores use a higher markup, depending on what the traffic will bear.)

Marketing Outlets for Product Sellers

Discount: The percentage a retail outlet subtracts from the retail price to get the wholesale price they'll pay for merchandise. For example, if stores want a 50 percent discount off your retail price, it means they will expect to pay $20 for an item you retail for $40. Thus, in dollars and cents, a 50 percent discount is the same as a 100 percent markup.

Whether you're an importer, distributor, or manufacturer, once you decide to enter the wholesale marketplace your thoughts probably will turn to retail shops and stores, mail order catalogs, trade shows, and a variety of special markets. One point I need to stress is this: *You will find it impossible to crack certain wholesale distribution channels unless both your product and its pricing structure are right for those markets.* This requires industry research that can be obtained through books, consultation with industry experts, membership in trade organizations, and subscriptions to trade periodicals. (See "Other Resources.")

While a 100 percent markup (double the wholesale price) is standard for many retail outlets, other markets, such as chain stores or mail order catalog houses, need larger markups than this, anywhere from 150 to 400 percent. Thus, the product you make and the wholesale price you set may or may not permit selling to certain markets. If a buyer tells you he needs a three-times markup in order to accept your product, you can figure out easily enough if your wholesale price is low enough to still yield a retail price that consumers will accept. For example, let's say you offer a hobby kit with a cost of $3 in materials and labor. A general rule of thumb is that you must mark up this price five times to realize a profit, which means your wholesale price must be $15. You may be able to sell the kit in a store that marks up your price 100 percent, but will it sell for $45 or $60? The answer you get to this question will suggest your wholesale outlet possibilities.

Sometimes a buyer will tell you that a discount of 50 percent is needed. That's easy to understand—just divide the retail price by two. But you may become confused when buyers start talking about discounts of 50+10 percent, or worse, 50+10+10+5 percent. A 50+10 percent discount is standard for many distributors, but in certain industries, distributors try to get additional discounts. In fact, I've heard of some that are 50+10+10+10+5 percent. What all these figures mean is that an additional discount is taken off each adjusted amount. Here is the way to figure such discounts, so you will know what these buyers are talking about:

EXAMPLE: Suggested retail price of item is $20
Buyer wants a 50+10+10+5% discount.

1 First turn the percentage figures into decimals:
50% = .50; 10% = .10; 5% = .05

2 Multiply $20 × .50 = $10 (equivalent to a 50% discount)

3 Multiply $10 × .10 = $1
Subtract $1 from $10 to get $9 (equivalent to a 50+10% discount)

4 Multiply $9 × .10 = $ .90
Subtract $ .90 from $9.00 to get $8.10 (equivalent to a 50+10+10% discount)

5 Multiply $8.10 × .05 = $.405 (round off to $ .41)
Subtract $ .41 from $8.10 to get $7.69 (equivalent to a 50+10+10+5% discount)

Note: If you sell wholesale to a shop or store figuring your price will be marked up 100 percent, as is the normal custom in such outlets, but you later find the shop has marked up the price by 200 percent, *do not get angry.* It is none of your concern at what price the shop sells your wares. The only thing that should concern you is the fact that you are receiving a fair wholesale price for the merchandise. Some shops price items for what the traffic will bear, and they have every right to do this. However, if you notice that shops and stores in different parts of the country consistently mark up your products more than 100 percent, it probably is a sign that you are wholesaling them at too low a price. Maybe you don't know the value of what you are selling and should raise your wholesale prices.

The Importance of Tags and Labels

One of the best ways to get higher prices for handcrafted merchandise and gift packages is the inclusion of a "hang tag," a decorative and informative printed selling aid that makes all products sell better at the retail level. While hang tags cost only pennies, they send an automatic signal to consumers that a product is special, thus worth more.

A tag not only adds a professional touch to products, but is a sales tool each time it carries your message home with buyers who may later reorder. A music box seller reported that, shortly after she began attaching hang tags to her seashell music boxes, she received over $2,000 worth of business from shop owners who had spotted her boxes in other shops. Although her tag did not include her full address, they were able to track her down by phone.

 *Smart Tip*

List only your business name and logo, city, and state on merchandise tagged for resale in shops. Shops tend to remove any tag that bears a manufacturer's complete name, address, and phone number because they don't want their customers to know how to contact their suppliers.

Fabric labels are generally sewn to garments, toys, and other "soft items." Some, such as care and cleaning instructions, are required by law (see "Tags and Labels" in the A-to-Z listings in Section II) while others are optional image tools, such as a designer's name or logo. Standard labels of all kinds are available in quantities as small as fifty, and your own custom-designed label can be reproduced for a nominal set-up charge. (To find suppliers, read craft and gift industry magazines or see the author's book, *Handmade for Profit.*) Hang tags are easy to design and simple to produce. Using light-weight card stock, they can be printed on a laser or inkjet printer. (Cut costs by printing hang tags and business cards at the same time.) Children or sheltered workshop employees could be hired to punch holes, add ties, and attach to products if you lack the time to do this yourself.

The size of a hang tag and the message you put on it is up to you; options are unlimited. For starters, anything that makes you or your products unique is information that can be put on a tag, such as:

● Type and source of materials used to make the product (Georgia clay, seashells from around the world, hand-dyed yarns)

- A statement about the quality of the product ("Our woodenware is designed to give you fitness for purpose, beauty of form, and a love of old-time craftsmanship.")

- Colorful information ("It was our grandmother's idea to start this business. . . .")

- How products are made (interesting technical information about the manufacturing process)

- Consumer safety warnings ("This is not a toy—keep out of children's hands!")

- History of an old or little-known art or craft

- A whimsical note designed to tug at a buyer's heartstrings (often the most effective way to get higher prices)

The designer who shears her sheep to make handmade felt that is then turned into toys . . . the ornament maker whose wax creations are made from museum ivories . . . the rosemaler whose designs are completely authentic— all should use such information to their advantage on a hang tag because such stories give a product personality, and personality *sells.*

I'm reminded of a little handpainted picture on wood my husband and I once bought. It was just a sailor standing by a rowboat, and we never would have bought it except for the fact that beneath the picture was a "personality message" that made it the perfect gift for Harry's old school chum, a sailboat enthusiast: "Old sailors never die; they just get a little dinghy."

Chapter 9:
Follow-up Marketing Strategies

At least 20 percent of people who have purchased from you once will buy from you again *if* you follow up with them. The lifetime value of these customers is one of the greatest assets of your business. One-fifth of your customer base is just waiting for you to offer them something new, so if you're not following up with them, you're actually ignoring 80 percent of your business's profit potential.

—Corey Rudl, MarketingTips.com

Novice marketers tend to concentrate on bringing in a steady flow of new prospects through advertising or publicity while forgetting that their established customer or client base is really the heart of their business. As important as it is to regularly contact your growing list of *prospects*, it's doubly important to stay in touch with your existing *customer or client base* because it is far more expensive to make someone buy from you the first time than it is to get a response from a satisfied customer or client. In this chapter, you'll get a host of ideas on how to do follow-up marketing, from methods you can use to deliver a message to the specific kind of offers you can make to bring in the bucks.

Mining Your Mailing List

In Chapter 5, you learned how to develop and maintain your mailing list. Now you're going to learn how to *mine* it. Truly, a good mailing list is like a gold mine that just won't quit. All you have to do is grab your pick and start digging. You can do a new follow-up mailing or promotion as often as every six weeks and count on getting a response from a new segment of the list that didn't get around to responding before. (If it's a customer list, your chances of a response are even greater.)

Your own prospect lists will always outpull any you can rent, but you must keep them up to date with periodic follow-up mailings or promotions of one kind or another. If you're sitting now with a list that hasn't been mailed in a couple of years, it may be more expensive to clean it than to start all over again. If you really need to salvage a badly outdated list, however, the cheapest way to do it is to create an exciting postcard that announces some new product or service. Mail the cards first class with an "Address Correction Requested" notice to get new addresses, then update your list and remail once again. *Note:* If you elect to mail an old list without asking for address corrections and just ask people to let you know if they want to stay on your mailing list, fewer than 5 percent (of addresses that are good) are likely to respond.

Smart Tip

Although first class mail will be forwarded automatically, it won't do you any good if you don't capture a new address at the time with an "Address Correction" notice on your mail. (After only a year, at least 15 percent of your names will be out of date and, in hard times, when people move more often, the percentage could soar to 30 percent.)

Courting Your Customers

"While it's essential to bring in new customers to really grow your business, you should be 'courting' your current customers on an ongoing basis to retain their loyalty," says marketing consultant Karen Smith. She helps entrepreneurs and small businesses boost their sales revenues by showing them simple, inexpensive methods to market their products or services. She emphasizes the importance of getting to really know your customers by being genuinely interested in them as people, not just as sources of revenue.

"Ask them about their families, jot down names, ages, etc. of each member. Find out what their hobbies are, their kid's and their spouse's hobbies too. Where do they vacation? You'd be surprised how much information you will have after just a few meetings. If you don't already have one, consider getting a contact manager like Symantec's *ACT!* or Microsoft's *Outlook*. These programs will allow you to keep track of each customer's personal information, and they will also flag you every month when it's time to make the call."

Karen suggests calling customers or clients once a month just to see how they're doing. "Don't discuss business, just keep in touch," she advises. "Keep your calls short. The idea is to let the customer know you care about him or her as a person. If you come upon something that you think would be of personal interest to your customers, send it to them. If your business involves any kind of receivables, call them to let them know when their order is complete. After you have established rapport, find out why they buy from you and sincerely ask for any advice they might have to help you serve them better. After you have used these techniques for awhile, you may find that the customers with whom you have developed a close personal relationship will almost fight to keep giving you their business. They'll be resistant to the efforts of your competitors and you may find that they're even willing to put up with a few of those inevitable annual price increases." (See Karen's free articles and resources on her site at 4MarketingHelp.com.)

Planning Follow-up Promotions

In addition to the routine follow-ups you must do after placing advertisements or doing direct mail promotions, there are a host of other special follow-up strategies you can use as you continue to build your prospect and customer lists through publicity, word-of-mouth advertising, and Internet activity.

In planning your promotions, remember that even the best communication strategies are only part of the picture. We all still must cope with "consumer lethargy" and keep trying to find the right buttons to push that will get the response we are seeking. In selling books by mail, I found that 90 percent of those who responded to publicity about my books or newsletter did not place an order after receiving detailed information in my catalog, my best sales piece. Yet when I sent these prospects one of my routine follow-up postcards, self-mailers, or promotional newsletters two or three months later, I could be certain of receiving a 2 to 4 percent order response (sometimes more). And I could count on a similar response *each and every time I remailed that list over the next three years or more*. (When response dropped to a point where I could no longer make a profit on a mailing to a particular segment of my prospect list, I dumped those names.)

Smart Tip

Ask yourself what your prospects need most, then create a follow-up promotion that offers them a specific benefit for buying *now*. Once you have a prospect's interest, you need only find the right response button to get an order or close the sale. Different people respond to different buttons, but the bottom line is benefits, benefits, *BENEFITS*.

Once you've built a good customer or client base, you can spur your word-of-mouth advertising with follow-up letters, reminder postcards, self-mailers, brochures, or a print newsletter. Even when people on your list don't buy, your mailings will often be passed along to others with a word-of-mouth recommendation to 'check this out.' If your business is on the Web, figure out some kind of newsletter or ezine (electronic newsletter) you can offer to Web site visitors that will enable you to capture subscriber names for follow-up mailings, and keep mailing them until you turn them into customers or they ask to be removed from your list.

Follow-Up Marketing Strategies

"I find the best way to make 'bread and butter' is really not about product, but contact," says Deanna Ferber, eGlamKitty.com "Make sure you maintain customer lists as much as possible so that you can tell folks about new products, shows you will be at, sales or event reminders, and just notes to let them know you still exist. I focus on my customers and worry less about whether I need to keep an item in my inventory or add new ones because the loyalty factor outweighs the inventory issues."

After you've given prospects your best brochure, catalog, or direct mail piece and made the first follow-up contact, it's time to follow-up again, and again and *again*. "Don't stop with just one follow-up contact," says super-salesman Tom Stoyan. "It has been reported that of all new sales, 80 percent are made after the fifth call. Yet a survey of salespeople revealed that 48 percent gave up after one call and 25 percent after the second call."

Smart Tip

It's much easier to persuade an already-interested prospect to buy than it is to dig up brand-new prospects who have never heard of you before. If you're financially strapped, don't invest in an expensive advertising campaign until you have made a special effort to once again "touch base" with everyone currently on your in-house mailing list. Prospects who already are familiar with what you offer may need only a small nudge to buy. Satisfied customers are likely to be interested in whatever is new.

Make an Offer They Can't Refuse

When planning a follow-up promotion, the offer is important, but copywriting also comes into play here. Here are some specific offers you might make to your customer or client base:

- **Offer a Discount.** In hard economic times, it might boost your sales to offer $3 to $5 off on the first order for an advertised product or publication. In selling a service, try a 10 to 20 percent discount for using the service before a specified date (usually 15–30 days).

Doing the Two-Step
by Joe and Maria Gracia,
Give to Get Marketing newsletter,
GiveToGetMarketing.com

"Ninety-five percent of the advertising used by small business owners is based on the One-Step strategy, but it doesn't work. Most sales are accomplished in two, three, four or more steps, not one step. If you want your prospects to make a decision in your favor, then you need to be perfectly clear about what you would like them to do next. Ask them to make a decision. For example, ask them to decide to:

- meet you for an appointment
- accept a free sample
- try your product for 30 days
- attend a free presentation
- click on a link on your Web site
- request your free eBook or report
- request your free newsletter
- call your hotline or information line
- accept a free quotation.

"Let your prospects know what your offer is, and what they must do to get it, and then specifically ask them if they would like to take advantage of your offer. Marketing is no place to be subtle."

Offer a New Product or Service. Send "hot announcements" about new products or services. You might place your sales focus on a special price being offered, products appropriate for upcoming holidays or gift-giving occasions, or a service that meets a current consumer or business need. If you have a Web site, tell them what's currently being featured there.

Offer Old Products or Services in a New Way. If you have no new products, publications, or services, try offering old favorites in new, money-saving combinations, or try packaging one product with another product or service. Think about offering a "Sizzling Summer Selection," "Buy Three—Get One FREE," "Trial Sampler," "Special Introductory Offer," or "Free Consultation." Such offers could be presented in a personal e-mail message, ezine, letter, postcard, or inexpensive four-page self-mailer (folded to size 5-1/2" × 8-1/2").

● **Offer Something FREE.** The key here is to be selective, offering freebies only when their cost will be offset by an order. Remember, however, that free product samples tend to generate valuable word-of-mouth advertising even when direct sales do not result. Two things that always worked well for me in my newsletter-publishing/book-selling days were (1) Free $10 cassette tape with $40 catalog order, and (2) Subscribe Now—Get Bonus $6 Report. (Today, many Web-based businesses are offering free eBooks or reports—something I, too, plan to do in the near future.)

If your product is too big or too expensive to give away free, consider the following alternatives:

1 Create a miniature version of the item.

2 Publish a booklet with helpful information and tips.

3 Offer a free trial (like magazine publishers do: "Return invoice if not delighted").

4 Offer a free service that would attract the product buyers you want to reach (e.g., free makeup analysis for people who might then purchase cosmetics).

● **Offer a Gift Certificate.** If you've lost some special customers or clients you'd like to get back, offer them a gift certificate saying you would like to have them back, that their business is important to you.

● **Offer Personal Attention.** Telephone or send occasional reminder cards to your best customers or clients, expressing your desire to serve them better. Give them a number of choices of things they might want from you right now, such as your newest catalog, a quote on a job, or a follow-up telephone call.

Delivering Your Offer

How you deliver your special offer will vary depending on how you prefer to market, how much money you have for a promotion, or how quickly you need to get some extra cash in hand. Will you do your follow-up marketing by telephone, e-mail, or mail? All are good strategies. For best results, try a combination of all three. (While many businesses still find fax machines essential to their work with clients or customers, none that I interviewed do any kind of follow-up marketing by fax.)

Web-based businesses commonly gather only e-mail addresses and do all their advertising and follow-up marketing by e-mail, but if you are operating this way, you could be losing a lot of business by limiting your marketing to only one medium. (See Chapter 10 for tips on doing business on the Web, and note Marc Choyt's example of how he places print advertising to draw traffic to his Web site while also building a valuable in-house mailing list of prospects who prefer to shop by mail from the company's full-color catalog.) Remember that not everyone in the world is browsing the Web today, and many who are still prefer to shop by mail because they believe their credit card number has less chance of being stolen when orders are placed by mail or telephone.

Pick up the Phone

The telephone is one of our best and most affordable marketing tools, yet many business owners fail to utilize this simple technology to their advantage. In just one minute on the telephone, you can accomplish what it might take two pages of a letter to do. In the process, you not only save some of your precious time but also make a greater impression on a prospective customer, client or business associate than may be possible in a letter or e-mail message.

Repeated follow-up should convert at least 10 percent of prospects to buyers, says consultant Bob Bly. He also suggests this follow-up strategy, particularly effective in hard times: "Help existing clients or customers create new sales for you. Call existing accounts with new ideas that will benefit them while requiring them to buy more of what you're selling. They get your ideas, suggestions and solutions to problems at no charge, while you sell more of your product or service to help them implement the idea you suggested." (Bob is the author of several marketing books. Visit his Web site, Bly.com, to find an excellent collection of his marketing articles.)

The Vital Importance of Telephone Follow-ups
by Dr. Jeffrey Lant, CEO, WorldProfit.com

"If a prospect wants only information that is provided on your Web site, send an e-mail directing him or her to the particular page where that information can be found. But if a prospect has already e-mailed you in response to that information and has expressed interest in buying a product or service, don't e-mail back . . . pick up the phone!

"Just sending e-mail doesn't cut it when you want to make real money online, particularly if you're selling an item over $100. Like it or not, prospects want to talk to a real person before they plunk down their money. This is where far too many online marketers go off the rails. They simply send the prospect the information, then follow up once or twice by e-mail. When they get no response, they write off this 'prospect' as a tire-kicker. *Wrong!* Let the Internet generate prospects for you, then get on the phone to immediately qualify them and, whenever possible, go for the immediate close. Failing an immediate close, e-mail any additional information the prospect requests, scheduling a follow-up call to make the close!"

Create an Ezine

Many Web marketers send individual e-mail follow-ups to selected customers or clients, but the easiest way to stay in touch with a large list of prospects or buyers is to develop a promotional newsletter or ezine. While some ezines are offered on a subscription basis, most are informative periodicals whose primary goal is to sell the products or services of the publisher. Today, as a writer interested only in promoting her books at the bookstore level, I use an ezine to stay in touch with people who have expressed interest in my work.

What an ezine does best is keep reminding people what you have to offer. By signing up to receive your free newsletter or ezine, people are automatically giving you permission to communicate with them again. Your ezine should always link your readers back to your Web site. (Don't tell folks to bookmark your site and come back periodically to see what's new because no one has time for this, and couldn't remember all the sites they've bookmarked in any case. Instead, let your ezine regularly remind them that you're there on the Web, ready to serve their needs with this product or that service.)

Before long, your e-mail list will become your most valuable marketing tool. If you consistently deliver useful information to your subscribers, they will be attentive when you tell them about your latest product, service, or new offer. You can also use your ezine to plug affiliate programs in which you may be involved. The key to success, one marketer says, is to "pitch your sales talk softly between the lines."

Patricia Katz, PatKatz.com, writes, speaks, and consults with clients on how to get their lives organized. She stays in touch with her market through an ezine titled, *PAUSE-The Voice of Sanity In A Speed Crazed World.* "Sadly, and happily, my business has benefitted from the 'hurry up' world in which we now live," she says. "The spin-off frustration experienced by people urged to move and act faster and faster is creating a ready market for my work/life balance programs and information." Patricia's e-mail signature includes the phrase, "Make the most of time & life—Give yourself permission to pause™."

To find both free and paid ezine hosting/distribution services and related articles, use your browser to search for those words as well as "ezine publishing" and "e-mail list management and distribution," "ezine hosting services," or "e-mail list hosting services." (A few are listed in "Other Resources.)" The two most popular free e-mail hosting services are Yahoo! Groups (**www.Yahoo.com**) and Topica (**www.Topica.com**). Because of its special features for moderators, Yahoo! is best for e-mail discussion lists. Both services are free because advertisements are automatically inserted into all your outgoing messages, about which you have no choice. If you don't want advertisements in your ezine, expect to pay from $10 to $20 a month for hosting services. (For a list of both free and paid list-hosting providers, visit Email Publishing Digest (**www.EPDigest.com**).

Send Promotional Print Newsletters

Ezines are great, but print newsletters remain an effective marketing tool for product and service businesses alike. A promotional newsletter is a good communications/follow-up tool in that it enables you to do some "soft selling" to your customer or prospect lists while also updating them on what's new. As a newsletter publisher and mail order book seller, I used this strategy with great success to bring in additional book orders and new subscriptions, and it worked particularly well to recapture expired subscribers. My "newsletter" was actually a "soft-sell" self-mailer I mailed at bulk rates in quantities of 2,500 to 5,000 whenever I had some new information products to offer (or when I merely wanted to remind my word-of-mouth army to keep talking). Each newsletter included a personal message, a list of my newest reports (with an emphasis on topics under discussion in the current issue of my subscription quarterly), a collection of valuable small business tips and resources, an excerpt from one of my books, reader testimonials, and an order form for whatever information products were mentioned in that particular mailer. This was a far more effective sales tool than the old "hard sell" self-mailers I had used in prior years (and hated to write). Doing a friendly newsletter for my following of readers was not only more fun, but far more profitable.

Mail Something Extra

After checking our furnace, a company sent us a thank-you letter reminding us that routine maintenance is the best way to ensure longevity of our heating and air conditioning system. A suggestion was given on how the company could help us in the future with twice-annual checkups and cleaning. To make sure we'd remember them, a packet of Forget-Me-Not seeds was enclosed. The following week, a company promoting a business opportunity also included a packet of Money Plant seeds in their letter. Maybe it would pay you to sow a few seeds in your own thank-you mailings to customers?

Copywriter Bob Westenberg, whose unusual postcard newsletter is featured in this chapter, sends amusing cartoons or interesting clippings in personal notes and letters to people on his special contact list. "People love getting them," he says. "They put a smile in someone's business day. I put them in all my correspondence, even my invoices. If I forget, I often hear back, 'Hey Bob, where's my cartoon?' I also add a quotation at the bottom of my letters. It can be business-related, altruistic, or just-for-fun. Mine range from, 'God gives every bird its food, but He does not throw it into the nest,' to 'What's the difference between an economist and a psychic? (Sometimes a psychic is right.)'"

From time to time, Bob also uses a "blitz" marketing strategy to get new business. "I pick someone I'd like to write for and start sending them unique mailings every few days for anywhere from a few weeks to a few months," he explains. "I enclose interesting things like a deck of cards (which I get free from a client in Vegas), a million-dollar bill or a candy bar or whatever. I've found that 'lumpy' mailings get attention. And they always have a logical tie-in with my message."

Profit from Postcards

Postcards are an inexpensive marketing tool that can generate thousands of dollars of new business at minuscule cost. Send them to your prospect list to nudge them to buy now, or mail them to existing clients and customers to generate repeat business. Following are specific ideas on how to promote or market with postcards and the kind of copy to include on them.

- **Announce a New Product or Service.** A great way to bring in cash almost immediately, while also updating your mail list, is to announce a new product or service with an illustrated postcard. For the personal touch, use a line-art drawing of yourself on the front of a card with a benefit-oriented voice-box message. Include an illustration and description of your new offer on the back, asking people to do one of the following things: (1) order by returning the card with payment enclosed; (2) telephone or visit your Web site to order with a credit card; or (3) call to get more information, set up a free consultation, or request a sales presentation (if applicable to your business).

- **Invite Buyers to Upcoming Shows or Events.** Many craft sellers use postcards to promote to customers who have purchased from them at retail craft fairs. One crafter who made mailings to her customer list twice a year told me that nearly 85 percent of her show sales were from customers who had received her postcards. (To track the effectiveness of a postcard mailing, ask people to bring the card to receive a 10 percent discount on any item of their choice.) Wholesalers can also profit by sending similar postcard announcements and discount offers to buyers who have made trade show purchases in the past.

- **Offer an Exclusive Showing.** Send an invitation to your best customer or client list inviting them to an exclusive showing of your products before the general public has access to the sale. This works especially well for Christmas boutiques, open houses, and other temporary sales. Each year when she opens Village Designs at Grandma's House during the

Follow-Up Marketing Strategies

Christmas holiday season, gift wholesaler Dodie Eisenhauer sends a color postcard to all previous buyers. One of her new products is featured on the front of the card and the copy on the back explains that, on the first Sunday of the sale, only previous buyers may shop, and they will get a 10 percent discount on all purchases. "They love the idea of being able to shop before the general public comes in," says Dodie, who orders these promotional postcards a couple of thousand at a time, and uses them in place of business cards at both retail and wholesale shows.

To publicize a home studio or workshop, send special invitations to local clubs and organizations, offering them a private showing and a special discount on purchases. A potter who announced a private exhibit of her work in her home with postcard invitations to 100 customers on her mail list reported that 30 people came to see her creations, and 18 of them made purchases.

- **Do Market Research.** Contact individual buyers and prospects, asking them to check categories of interest (which you've detailed on the other side of the card) so you'll know what kind of special offers to send them in the future.

- **Enhance Your Professional Image.** Color is such a wonderful selling tool, but few small business owners can afford full-color flyers because quantity requirements are so high. Photo cards, however, can be ordered a thousand at a time at a cost of between 15 and 30 cents each. (To find such printers on the Internet, do a search for "promotional postcards.") Whether mailed alone or included with a black-and-white catalog or brochure, a photo card makes a great impression and may even make the difference between a buyer's decision to buy—or to bypass—a product or service. Such cards can be used for prepublication announcements, invitations, customer thank-you notes, and other personal customer correspondence. (For the latter, try a full-color photographic card that shows your best product or an action shot of you at work.)

- **Publicize Your Web Site.** As more and more of your customers (both retail and wholesale) move onto the Internet, it becomes all the more important for you to let them know they can order from you online and communicate by e-mail. Print a Web card with an image of your home page and use it in place of a business card. Include one with every customer's purchase or mail them to your best customers and prospects to announce special sales on your Web site. Your cards will not only be noticed, but saved for future reference.

Smart Tip

You will have more space for your message if you design and print your own postcards. While the average postcard measures 3" × 5," size can be as large as 4 ¹/₄" × 6" and still qualify for the standard first-class rate.

Two Outstanding Postcard Marketers

Photographer Jim Bradshaw and copywriter Bob Westenberg offer examples of how effective postcard marketing can be when you have properly targeted your market.

Photo Cards. Sometimes you have to reach your target market indirectly, by connecting with an intermediary that serves your customers or clients or is in a position to give you valuable word-of-mouth advertising. Jim Bradshaw specializes in wedding photography, but his marketing efforts aren't aimed directly at brides-to-be.

"Years ago when I was just getting started, I tried the traditional advertising routes to bring in brides," Jim explains. "When ads in bridal publications didn't work for me, I asked myself who brides contact first when they begin the planning of their wedding, and realized it was wedding consultants and reception site managers. (Around here, the desirable wedding sites are booked a year in advance.) I then reasoned that if I could keep my

Jim Bradshaw
PHOTOGRAPHS
3025 P STREET, S.E.
WASHINGTON, DC 20020
202-575-2223 • 202-575-2036/fax
jim@jimbradshaw.net
www.jimbradshaw.net

name in front of consultants and site managers, they would bring brides to me. I joined organizations to which these groups belong and got to know them, and this strategy worked.

Today, Jim markets exclusively through postcard mailings and word-of-mouth advertising and now has a Web site at JimBradshaw.net. Each month he designs a postcard featuring one of his most charming bridal pictures (see illustration), then prints and mails it to a select mailing list. "Every phase of production is done right here in my office, including printing of the postcards," he says. "While brides are my primary clients, all of my promotional efforts are directed to wedding professionals who can bring brides to me, so these are the people who receive my promotional postcards every month. I don't do any print advertising now—it's all word-of-mouth referrals from previous brides, wedding consultants, and other vendors in the wedding business."

A Postcard-Newsletter. Copywriter Bob Westenberg has one of the most interesting postcard strategies I've ever seen. Every month for the past thirteen years, Bob has created a monthly issue of *IMP—The World's Smallest Newsletter*, a postcard sent to people he has done business with in the past, as well as people he *wants* to do business with. (See nearby illustration.) Each card features up to fifteen interesting tidbits of information on a variety of topics, and one is always an unanswered question that generates phone calls from people who want the answer. For many years, the last tidbit on the card was a subtle reminder that Bob was available to help with clients' copywriting needs. Examples: (1) *"Most of my jobs come from referrals. If you know someone who might want to use my services, give me (or them) a call. Thanks."* (2) *"IMP is more than a keep-in-touch newsletter. It chips away at customers/prospects and gets business. It's my best-ever business-getter. Ask about your own IMP to get new sales for you, too."*

Now 68 and supposed to be semiretired, Bob no longer includes these sales nudges on his cards, but he's still working close to full-time. "*IMP* has always been my best business-getter, my primary tool for ongoing client nudging and prospect prodding," he says. "Its water-on-the-rock contacts have consistently generated new business at tiny cost, either from freelance copywriting jobs, or companies and individuals who want their own *IMP* card written by me to promote their own business. In that case, I provide the copy and they take care of printing and mailing."

Bob's postcard newsletter has never been done for profit, at least not via subscriptions. "I'm pretty stingy about adding names to my mailing list," he

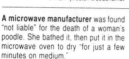

The World's Smallest Newsletter
Published on the 17th by:
BOB WESTENBERG
Copywriter/Consultant/Fund Raiser
95 Devil's Kitchen Dr. • Sedona, AZ 86351 • (928) 284-1111
e-mail: rjwesten@sedona.net

A microwave manufacturer was found "not liable" for the death of a woman's poodle. She bathed it, then put it in the microwave oven to dry "for just a few minutes on medium."

In Scotland, a new game was invented, called, "Gentlemen Only, Ladies Forbidden." And thus came the name GOLF.

"Money doesn't bring you happiness, but it enables you to look for it in more places."

About 8 to 9 minutes after liftoff, the space shuttle hits 16,867 mph. (But what kind of mileage does it get?)

Newsletter goof: "The evening will end with a toast to the new president with champagne provided by the outgoing president, drunk, as usual, at midnight."

Fastest tennis serve ever recorded was by Michael Sangster in 1963... 154 mph.

A man strapped on a pair of pontoon-like "water walking shoes" and set out for Hawaii from California (2,000 miles). He got about 10 miles before he hit some rough water and radioed for help.

WWII US fighter planes loaded a string of tracers at the end of ammo belts. Not a good idea. It's not something you wanted to announce to the enemy.

T-Shirts: "Ham and eggs: A day's work for a chicken, a lifetime commitment for a pig." "Suicidal Twin Kills Sister by Mistake."

"Zippy Chippy" is a thoroughbred race horse who holds the record for races lost (89 at last count). He was acquired by his owner in 1955 for an old van. He even lost a race to a man in a 40-yard dash.

Sign in cemetery: "Warning: Persons are prohibited from picking flowers from any but their own graves."

Ambiguous references for ex-employees: For one suspected of stealing from the company: "I'm sorry he got away." One who can't get along with others: "I'm pleased to say that he is a former colleague." For a criminal: "We found him to be a man of many convictions."

Church bulletin item for the National Prayer and Fasting conference: "Cost for attending the conference includes all meals."

A forfeited baseball game is recorded as a 9-0 score. What is it in football?

Actual resume comments: "You will find me to be extremely detail oreinted." "Objection: To utilize my skills in sales." "Served as assistant sore manager." "Reason for leaving: 'Pushed aside so VP's girlfriend could steal my job.'"

says. "I don't solicit them, but I do get publicity in business columns, newsletters, and books now and then. A small number of people do pay $10 a year to receive *IMP*, and some companies send it as Christmas gifts."

Once you start receiving Bob's impish postcard reminders, it's pretty hard to forget him. As a believer in "little things mean a lot," Bob Westenberg is an excellent example of how to come across as a real person, not an organization. "It's the little things that build strong, invisible bonds between you and customers that competitors can't break," he reminds us.

In Summary

Marketing studies have revealed that it costs the average company six times as much to get an order from a new customer as it does to get the same order from an existing customer. Whether you're selling a product or a service, your existing customers or clients will always be your most profitable source of new business, and it will pay you to go out of your way to keep them happy—with special money-saving offers, special attention to their inquiries, and personal service. In short, when you need cash in a hurry, dig in your own backyard first. Your mailing list of interested prospects and customers is a virtual gold mine just waiting to be worked!

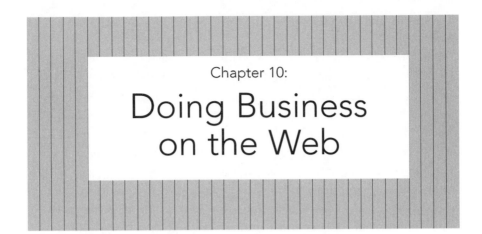

Chapter 10:

Doing Business on the Web

Any business or profession that does not seriously consider some kind of Internet business integration is deliberately and foolishly losing money.

   —Daryl Ochs, marketing consultant,
      StreetSmartBusiness.com

II **I**'ve thought about a Web site, but never got serious about it," writes Bob, a long-time home-business owner. "How does one go about putting one together? Not sure I want to, but it could be useful."

Does the Internet excite or intimidate you? Either way, you're not alone. If you're just getting started on the Web, you're only beginning to discover what long-time Web pros have known from the start: that this is a borderless world offering borderless income and opportunities never dreamed of before the mid-1990s. If the Web intimidates you—as it once did me—the only way around this problem is to educate yourself to the possibilities by reading several books on this topic. If, like Bob, you're neither excited nor intimidated by the Web, but merely curious, you also need to do some reading to see what being on the Web might do for you or your business.

This chapter doesn't attempt to explain how to design, launch, and manage a Web site—you'll need to read two or three books by Web experts to get a grip on these topics—but it does offer valuable perspective from Internet pros and home-business owners who have recently stuck their toes into Web waters. In interviewing these individuals, I asked how computer technology and the Internet have changed the way they now do business, and why they decided to open their own Web sites. I also asked whether being on the Web has enabled them to reach new markets, has helped them to move in different business directions, or has made it easier for them to "bring in the bucks." I know you will find their responses as interesting and stimulating as I did.

After you read this chapter, check "Other Resources" (in Section II) for some recommended books, ezines, and Web links that have been helpful to me and others as we've all struggled to grasp the how-tos of doing business on the Web. Also check the A-to-Z listings in Section II for some special tips and cautionary notes from me and my book contributors about registering domain names, setting up an e-commerce site, finding online merchant account providers, and protecting intellectual property on the Web.

In addition to countless print and eBooks on how to do business on the Web, the Web itself is full of how-to information, most of it free, placed there by experts who have learned that, by openly sharing what they know, they can sell more of whatever they happen to selling on the Web—books, software, Web services, consulting, etc. Thus, the easiest way to learn about doing business on the Web is to just get *on* the Web and learn how to "surf the Net." Once there, you'll learn something new every day, and before long you'll find you've developed a level of proficiency in one area or another.

P.S. Not every business needs a Web site to survive and prosper, but trying to operate a business today without e-mail and access to the store of information on the Web would be like trying to climb a mountain without any climbing tools. You might make it to the top eventually, but the journey would be fraught with peril and your risk of falling (failing) would be very high. (If you have not yet computerized your business, be sure to read the chapter, "Learning to Use the Latest Computer Technology," in this book's companion guide for home-business beginners.)

E-commerce: Still in its Infancy

As you have noticed, nearly all of the business owners quoted in this book have their own Web sites, but if I'd written this book a year ago, that would not have been the case. In fact, an SBA study on e-commerce in 2002 (see below) found that 65 percent of all businesses then on the Web had been online *for one year or less.* Some Web experts quoted in this book have been there much longer, of course, and they're the ones who are now educating the rest of us on how to do business on the Web (and raking in big profits from the sale of their how-to books, eBooks, ezines, teleseminars, software, Web tools, consulting services, and so on). As for the rest of us, there's a lot of learning and experimenting going on here! Most of the new businesses on the Web are still trying to get their act together; still working out the kinks in their Web site design, navigation, and archiving systems; optimizing graphics so pages load faster; replacing shopping carts; changing merchant account providers; and figuring out how to generate more traffic.

Lacking money to hire others to design and manage their sites, most Web entrepreneurs have spent hundreds (if not thousands) of hours figuring out how to do all this work themselves, and it's anyone's guess as to how many hours these individuals will devote to their Web activities in the future. What's interesting about the Web, however, is how quickly you can learn new things once you're actually *there.* Although many of the business owners quoted in this chapter have been online for only a year or two, what they have quickly learned from hands-on experience is amazing.

"If you're trying to build an online business, you must study hard to achieve skills necessary for success, or you must hire professionals who can deliver those results for you. Or both," says Dr. Jeffrey Lant, CEO of WorldProfit.com. "People don't want to make you rich. They want to make themselves better off. Thus, they want benefits and they want them *now.* Your job is to present your value in such a way that people easily understand just what you've got for them. These benefits must be simply, effectively presented in words and pictures. The overall design of your Web site needs to accentuate the positive and get people to look at what you've got, and stay long enough to respond."

SBA's 2002 E-Biz Report

Hundreds of companies that opened dot-com sites during the Web's "gold rush" of 2000 were out of business a year later because they jumped onto the e-commerce bandwagon before they knew what they were doing. I had an inside connection with one of those companies, and I saw how management wasted thousands upon thousands of dollars for site design services, high-tech site management software and shopping carts, outside marketing consultants, and worthless advertising—all before they had figured out who they were trying to sell to and whether this audience would even buy what they were planning to offer. One of the first things they learned was that "build it and they will come" works only for cornfields in Iowa.

Much has changed since then. The Web's gold rush is over and now businesses are going on the Web for more sensible reasons. Now the Web is being perceived as just one more way to serve an existing customer/client base and reach additional prospects. As I see it, it's like adding a patio to your home: You can live comfortably without it, but you can also do things out there that you can't do in the house.

"Unlike the so-called 'dot.coms,' 65 percent of small niche firms make a profit or cover the costs of their Web sites," says Joanne Pratt in *E-Biz.com: Strategies for Small Business Success*, her latest research report for the SBA's Office of Advocacy. "The more innovative entrepreneurs—the early adopters—see the Internet as a way to market niche products and reach distant customers in ways that were not available in the past. Their pioneering innovations foretell a structural change in industrial organization for both small and large firms. The smallest firms gain the most by reorganizing as an e-business. The power of the keyword search means that a business can target customers who need niche products without the wasteful expense of mass mailings. Instead customers find them. Finally, business owners can live in isolated locations and reach customers worldwide."

As a futurist interested in what's going to happen next, Joanne says time favors e-business growth because upcoming generations will accept technology and telecommunications as a given. "As we evolve from the Industrial Age into the Information Age we are reshaping ourselves into a more mobile, global workforce linked by technology," she observes. "Today we have teleworking, telecommuting, the virtual office, mobile workers, homebased business owners, and at-home professionals—all of which is now called E-Work in Europe."

Doing Business on the Web

E-commerce and Web Statistics

By the end of 2002, 143 million Americans (more than half the population)
were using the Internet, and new users in the United States. were coming
online at the rate of more than 2 million per month. An article on
eCommerceTimes.com stated that 39 percent of those Internet users were
making online purchases, and this percentage was expected to increase
steadily in the future.

These statistics should carry some weight in your mind as you ponder
whether to put your business on the Web. The big question is not whether
your business is successful now but whether it can *remain* successful if your
competition is on the Web and you're not. You also need to ask yourself how
many of your future customers or clients are likely to be shopping electronically in the future. "As more people flock to the Internet and grow more
comfortable with online shopping, Internet sales will continue to rise," states
Herb Wetenkamp in his article, "From Dot Bomb to Dot Boom" (*Home
Business Magazine*, October 2002). "To take advantage of the Internet
boom—and help sustain it—homebased Internet entrepreneurs need to
build a solid foundation of good business sales and marketing practices,
while staying constantly aware of ever-evolving trends and the fast-paced
nature of change on the Web."

According to the SBA, 85 percent of small businesses are already doing
business via the World Wide Web. I don't know if this statistic includes
homebased businesses or not, but what's important here is the fact that most
consumers are apt to be online in a couple of years, and these consumers—
your prospective customers or clients—are gradually being educated to the fact
that *most businesses now have a presence on the Web*. Before long, if your competitors are on the Web and you aren't, you may be perceived as being less
credible than they are, or simply too much trouble to do business with.

How Technology Changes Business Operation

Take a look at how computers, e-mail, fax technology, and the Web have changed the daily lives of some homebased business owners and entrepreneurs in my network:

● "Business life is definitely easier and much more cost-efficient because of computer technology. With each new 'tech toy' introduced to my design studio, efficiency has improved, worldwide communications have increased, professional skills and knowledge have developed, and profits have increased! Because I work in national/international markets, it's absolutely wonderful to be able to e-mail files and make direct contact with my clients without worrying that I am tying up their time on the phone at all hours." —Annie Lang, AnnieThingsPossible.com

● "The Internet has transformed our way of doing business. We're a designer jewelry studio that began as a small homebased business but now employs eight people full time. Our line includes a wide range of products from a low-end production jewelry gift line to high-end mixed metal designs, some of which retail for over $1,000. We sell wholesale (several trade shows) and retail. The Internet has allowed us to really drive our retail end, which is our most profitable part of our business, and it continues to be the strongest growth part of our business. At this time (November 2002), we're getting over 13,000 visitors per week. (Our Web sales have doubled again this year, and we're now into six figures—real money—with over 20 percent of our sales coming directly from the Web.)"—Marc Choyt, CelticJewelry.com

● "The Web made it possible for me to launch my pattern design business with a minimal investment. Whereas shipping two patterns by mail can cost up to $5 for postage and handling, I can get a new pattern up on the site and start selling it that day to people all over the world without print, packaging, and postage expenses. My patterns are designed on computer and then converted to an electronic format for delivery by e-mail. (I started with *Microsoft Publisher* for layouts, but later switched to *Adobe Pagemaker* 6.5.)" —Debbie Spaulding, PuppetPatterns.com

● "When I started my medical-legal nurse-consultant business in 1993, I had a computer, a dot matrix printer, and a fax machine shared by my computer, which meant I had to be offline when I was expecting records. In those days, nearly all my communication was handled by phone and fax. Today, about 85 percent of my communication is by e-mail, with the remaining 15 percent by fax. And my equipment has become much more sophisticated to include a laser color printer, DSL computer connections, and wonderful software for both my desk and laptop computers. I'm currently thinking about how a Palm Pilot might assist."—Susan Kilpatrick

● "The Internet has changed my approach to doing business. My ezine allows me to be so easily in touch with people on a regular basis at minimal expense—with no printing, folding, stamping or licking. When you consider the time and dollar cost of a weekly mailing to 1,000 people versus an electronic mail list, there's no comparison. Also, having that list of subscribers makes research easier. I can create a survey on my Web site, ask subscribers to respond, and have 40 surveys returned within a couple of days. I love it!"—Patricia Katz, PatKatz.com

Why You Need Fax Capabilities

Because of all the e-mailing we do now, there is a rumor that businesses no longer need fax capabilities. *Don't believe it.* It's true that old stand-alone fax machines will soon be extinct, replaced by machines that offer a combination of printing, scanning, and faxing. Most businesses, however, are using e-fax services now. None of the businesses mentioned in this book solicit business or do follow-up marketing by fax, but they need fax technology for other reasons. If you can't send and receive faxes, you may be losing sales or making it difficult for others to communicate with you. Here are some examples:

● "When someone asks if you have a fax, it would be insane to say, 'no, not yet.' Faxing is very practical and useful, both to send out info and to receive orders. I get faxed book orders from Baker & Tayler and other bookstores as well as from individuals who would rather put their credit card number in a fax than send it by e-mail." —Leila Peltosaari, TikkaBooks.com

- "I still use the fax machine because many of my clients still use the fax. I also require signatures on my work orders prior to working on a job. (Perhaps this can be done by e-mail now, but I don't know how to do it—yet.)"—Bunny DeLorie, FeFiFauxFinish.com

- "Faxing is extremely important to me. I send and receive two dozen or more faxes every day, usually proofs and forms to clients and brokerage houses. I still have my stand-alone fax, but 90 percent of my clients now use e-fax, so I use a paid version of this software. It helps keep my office paperless."—Sherry Huff Carnahan, SherryCarnahan.com

- "I find fax invaluable. I would guess that half the folks I deal with don't use the computer as much as they might, preferring to fax orders instead of e-mailing them to me. On occasion I have also faxed bills to customers who have lost their invoice. It's another option for communication that is definitely used."—Terrie Kralik, MooseCountryQuilts.com

- "I still have and use a fax to receive international correspondence/orders from overseas; to accept Visa/MC from customers who don't want to send that information over the Internet; to send and receive linework, diagrams, and idea drafts when working with clients; and to send and receive contacts."—Annie Lang, AnnieThingsPossible.com

- "Small gift shop owners often find us via the Internet, but they don't have easy access to it and they always want wholesale information faxed to them immediately. I have found that having a fax number on a separate line definitely increases the appearance of being a bigger business. (We have an extra line with two numbers—one for my husband's business and one for the fax machine. A router automatically sends the call to the fax machine if that number is dialed.)"—Karen White, NaturalImpulse.com

- "Faxing is still very much a part of our day-to-day operation. As I type this, I am in the middle of a 200+ group fax to solicit information for our 2003 event publications. We now use e-fax rather than the stand-alone machine that has served us well for the past several years. We plan to replace it soon with one of those combination machines, which will be much less expensive than a dedicated fax line."—Bill Ronay, RonayGuide.com

● "In the advertising industry, faxes are very important for transmitting contracts and agreements. I use a scanner and facsimile software with my computer. This saves not just time, but also money in paper and office expenses because I can store all my files on disks instead of hard copy."—Tammy Harrison, TheQueenofPizzazz.com

● "Granted, fax software is neater and more convenient for sending documents. If the file you're sending is on your computer, the data is already digital and this results in better resolution on the receiving end. But when you're dealing with hard copy, it makes sense to fax it using the old stand-alone fax machine rather then to scan it into your computer and fax it because then, the results would be poor because you'd be sending a picture of a picture."—Gary Maxwell, GaryMaxwell.com

Smart Tip

Check out **www.eFax.com** or search the Web for "efax" or "free efax" to turn up several places where you can download free software to send/receive faxes by e-mail.

What the Web Can Do for You

Before you invest in a Web site, make sure you know what you want the Web to do for you. Do you

● Think you need a Web site because everyone *says* you need one (or, as a friend of mine puts it, "because everyone and his dog has one")?

● Believe you can sell more of your existing products or services this way, or some new ones you've been thinking about?

● Need to be on the Web because this is where most of your customers or clients can now be found? Or because most of your *competitors* are now on the Web, stealing business from you?

- Want to be able to take orders 24 hours a day, seven days a week all year long?

- Need to make it easy for customers or clients to communicate with you, but don't want to answer common questions personally?

- Want to publish a newsletter and build an e-mail database for marketing purposes?

- Desire to write and publish eBooks or sell other products electronically?

- Need an online brochure that will enhance your professional image, or a colorful catalog that will save you printing and postage costs?

- Just *love* technology and a new challenge?

Why Some Businesses Are on the Web

I and many of my home-business acquaintances decided we needed a Web presence not because we loved technology, had the time to learn it, or needed another challenge in our already too-busy lives. Mostly, we ended up on the Web because someone or some circumstance finally convinced us we needed to be there. When I asked several others what motivated them to open a Web site, here's what they told me:

- "I've been on the Web since 1995 because I knew at its inception (circa 1993) that this would be the future, and indeed it has turned out to be so. Ninety percent of our income is now generated from the Web, and this is actually what was expected. Companies not online today are losing out on a lot of benefits, as well as millions of potential customers."—Richard Tuttle, CalliDesign.com

- "I do online information research and analysis. I opened a site because I needed an online brochure. I don't get much play directly from my Web site, but I needed to back up my real-world networking activities by having a place on the Web where potential clients could go to check my credentials and get details about the specific business services I offer."—Karl Kasca, Kasca.com

Doing Business on the Web

● "Initially, the thought of selling anything on the Web was not of interest to me. But when products I was demonstrating on television shows were not readily available in craft stores, viewers often called me, frustrated that they could not find my products. So I began selling on the Web as a convenience for viewers. That was seven years ago. Now I am pleased with the additional income the site generates every month. Clearly the number of computer-savvy consumers is growing. In 1999, 20 percent of my orders came from my order form on my Web site, with the remainder coming from phone calls, faxes, or mail inquiries. By 2002, 95 percent of my orders were coming from the printed order form on my site. Bottom line: The cost of doing business on the Internet has gone down and profits are up. I save monthly on returning phone calls, writing letters, and sending faxes. Now I just process the mailed-in order form and ship."—Bunny DeLorie, FeFiFauxFinish.com

(*Note:* See the discussion under "E-commerce Site" in the A-to-Z listings in Section II for how Bunny and others operate successfully on the Web without the extra expense of merchant status.)

● "Since the development of my product was so expensive, and so is carrying inventory, I choose the Web as a way to keep overhead costs down. Compared to a brick-and-mortar shop, Internet stores are inexpensive. I can still show my products, like a catalog, without the print and mailing costs, plus I can reach an audience larger than what I'd find in my hometown. Ninety-five percent of my sales of cosmetics and skin care products are now made on the Web."—Deanna Ferber, eGlamKitty.com

● "Initially, I wanted to be on the Web because it provided an opportunity to reach more women in business through my writing. Today, I'm on the Web because it's a necessity for the serious business owner and because it offers the opportunity to expand my market base. In the last year or so, I've fallen in love with the technology behind the Internet. As a direct result of my Web experience, I decided to return to school to update my Web development skills."—Donna Snow, SnowWrite.com

● "I use the Web mainly as an online brochure. It saves me time and money on postage, paper, etc. I can't think of a better method for dealing with clients when they ask 'Where can I get more information?' Having a Web presence puts all businesses on a level playing field. It makes your business look as professional as any Fortune 500 company and suggests to clients that you're techno-savvy and ready to service them with the most up-to-date methods and technology."—Gary Maxwell, GaryMaxwell.com

- "I am on the Web because it is the future. I do believe you have to assess your current marketing strategies and know when to test new techniques. The Web is a new technique for me and my current clients find it very useful when wondering if I am experienced in certain areas. All they have to do is click on my Web site and all my information is available."—Pam Hunter, CreativeOfficeService.com.

- "I initially created a Web site in 1997 so I could reach clients nationwide. Within three months I had my first out-of-state client. Now, 90 percent of my customers are all over the United States. If I didn't have a Web site they never would have known about me. I believe the Web will soon replace (or almost replace) the hard copy Yellow Pages for how customers locate and learn about a company or its products."—Sherry Huff Carnahan, SherryCarnahan.com

Because of all the new and constantly changing technology affecting the way businesses operate and sell products or services, there is no longer any guarantee that what works today will work tomorrow. And the fact that you may have been a success for years doesn't mean you can continue to operate successfully if you don't pay attention to what's happening on the Web. For example, I've been a leader in my field for nearly three decades, but how much credibility would I have *today* as a home-business expert and author if I didn't have my own Web site and a showcase for my books like other authors in my field? When I opened my site in 2000, it was because I wanted this kind of image advertising, and because I figured a Web presence would help promote the sale of my books at the bookstore level. Now I see the Web as a place where I can also sell information electronically and offer my editing and writing services to beginning writers and self-publishers.

As your business and personal goals change, you need to constantly rethink how you might use the Internet to your advantage, even if you perceive the transition to be painful. After so many years of doing things the old-fashioned way, making the leap to the Web in my senior years was not easy for me. It hasn't been easy for most of my home-business friends, either, but we all agree it has been well worth our time and effort. This kind of business move is rather like diving into an icy pool of water—initially shocking to your system but not so bad once you're fully immersed in it.

Smart Tip

If you decide you need a Web site and you're already drowning in work, the only sensible thing to do is hire someone to design it for you. (See "Other Resources.") As time allows, however, you should learn how to manage it yourself. Relying on others to make changes or do site updates on *their* time schedule will ultimately prove more frustrating (and costly) than simply learning how to do it yourself.

Protecting Your Name on the Web

Do you know for sure what you will be doing a year or two from now, or how all the new technology may affect your business or personal life? If you are currently selling on the Web through ad space or free pages provided by your Web host, that may be the only Web presence you'll ever need or want. But considering how quickly things are changing these days, can you be absolutely sure? In 1998, I was absolutely sure I did not need a Web site at all. A year later, I was just as sure that the space I had then on someone else's site was all I'd ever need or want. But I was wrong.

In January 2000, when a friend told me that businesses were then registering 20,000 new Web site names every day, I finally got off my duff and registered the domain name of BarbaraBrabec.com. At that time, I had no idea what I was going to do with that name, but I was finally moved to action when I suddenly recalled the four other Barbara Brabecs I had encountered through the years. I knew one was a professional writer, too, and what if she decided she wanted this name for a Web site? I figured I'd better grab my own name while the grabbing was good! A couple of months later, my professional life turned on a dime when I was invited to write content for a new e-commerce site, and I suddenly needed my own domain. Fortunately, I already had the name.

How important is your personal or business name to you? Would you want someone else using it on the Web? I'll never forget the sad e-mail I received from a woman who had registered her personal name and then decided she didn't want a Web site. Once abandoned, her domain name was picked up by someone else who turned it into a porn site. If you haven't already registered your personal and business name, perhaps you should do it now, if only to keep others from using it on the Web. For example, when I finally got online, I was upset to discover that the dot-com names of my two best-selling books, *Creative Cash* and *Homemade Money*, had been registered by others. Because different legal rules apply to the Internet, names that I thought were protected by common law trademark had been legally stolen right out from under my nose.

Remember that the home-business industry and your opportunities in it are going to continue to change in the future right along with your personal goals and dreams. Who knows when you might decide you need a new business site or simply want an electronic playpen bearing your own name? By registering your personal or business name now—perhaps with several extensions—you will be protecting it from use by others while ensuring that you'll have a great Web address if and when you need it. (For more information on this topic, see "Domain Name Registration" in the A-to-Z listings in Section II.)

Special Benefits of Being on the Web

"People make purchasing decisions based on all sorts of questions and anxieties, either real or otherwise," notes Peter Simmons, editor of Dynamiq Ezine (*Dynamiq.co.uk*). "A Web site provides a place where they can help themselves to find out more and answer those questions and anxieties or take any other action. That's an often overlooked Internet benefit that wasn't really possible previously: easy self-service. If they can't find what they want, they can simply send you a message from your Web site and await the tailored response. Another benefit: rapid and personal communication."

Of entrepreneurs on the Web, Joanne Pratt's research revealed that 67 percent gained new customers; 62 percent improved their competitive position; 56 percent increased total sales; and 56 percent attracted new types of customers. Clearly, the benefits of selling on the Internet are many and varied. In addition to being able to communicate and sell to a worldwide audience at any time of day or night without actually being on the computer (thanks to automatic systems that can be set in place), each business owner usually discovers some special benefit he or she hadn't anticipated prior to actually getting on the Web. For example:

Doing Business on the Web

- **Increased Credibility/Visibility.** "As a futurist, certainly credibility is the key reason I have a Web site. But there are other reasons as well. In contrast to the hard copy brochures I used to send out, I now have an up-to-date presentation of my business. It reaches the potential client instantly and the Web site allows me to offer in-depth coverage on many topics. Although I'm not selling a product or service directly from the site, it does generate calls from reporters and potential clients, and those calls generate business."—Joanne Pratt, JoannePratt.com

- **Lower Expenses and Increased Revenue.** "My Web site has given me name recognition beyond immediate borders and opened the door to a worldwide audience. In the last five years, I've actively worked to lower expenses and increase revenue potential, and I have found electronic products such as books, patterns, and workshops to be extremely cost effective. Soft products that sell while I'm off doing something else are of primary interest to me. While I am creating a piece of art, my Web site is selling books and patterns for me, and my online students are busily working away with me checking on them regularly. It's a wonderful way to do business!"— Myrna Giesbrecht, Press4Success.com

- **Manufacturer Connections.** "The Internet has provided us with the ability to contact manufactures in other countries, enabling us to import directly rather than going through a middle person. Although our company is American craft, we do purchase gemstones and jewelry components (silver chain, for example) made in other countries. This has saved us tens of thousands of dollars."—Marc Choyt, CelticJewelry.com

- **Reinforcement of Other Sales Efforts.** "Children's clothes are hard to sell on the Web, so I don't get a lot of orders from my site. But I find people are using it for reference before they see me at a show or to learn what fabric options I have if they want to make an exchange. Being on the Web has also given me the opportunity to sell my work on other crafter-based Web sites. Recently my work was accepted by a company who doesn't keep an inventory of my work but orders as it gets orders. I find this to be a benefit because many of these companies put more money into advertising their sites than I do, and this, in turn, generates additional wholesale inquiries to my Web site."—Pamela Burns, Injeanious.org

● **A New Way to Sell Specialized Knowledge.** "The Internet opened a way for me to sell my knowledge of dogs to people trying to decide what type of dog breed to buy. Then I help them figure out how to care for their new pet. On my site and also on eBay, I sell a manual on starting and running a pet-sitting business. It's packaged in a three-ring binder along with a CD-ROM of templates and forms for pet sitters. Being on the Web beats the hassles and high cost of dog breeding!"—Louise Louis, ToyBreeds.com

● **A New Way to Reach Old Customers.** "The Internet is expanding so rapidly that, whatever the individual's business might be, the Web can be used to overcome changes in economic situations, equaling or surpassing what was lost. Michaels stores were a good five-figure source of income for us for many years, but when we found it necessary to cease doing business with this account, instead of losing all that money we found that many of their customers readily located our Web URL and became instant retail buyers. (So far, we estimate that nearly 75 percent of those who purchased our craft event publications at Michaels stores have gone online or contacted us via the Internet for direct sales.)"—Bill Ronay, Events2000.com

● **A New Way to Work with Clients.** "As a virtual administrative assistant (VA) with clients spread across the nation, the software program, *GoToMyPC,* has enabled me to be right there in their offices, working on *their* computers, without ever needing to leave my own office. *GoToMyPC* is a Web-based program that allows you to enter another person's computer (host computer) via user ID and password. Now I can log on to a client's computer, view my tasks for the day, schedule their appointments, update their databases, client files and so on without having to keep two separate files or our having to e-mail updates every day or week to one another. An extra benefit is that I can log on to a host computer from any location as long as I have an Internet connection. I also use *Paperport Deluxe*, a program that allows me to have a paperless office and also scan and digitally file documents on a client's computer or private Intranet Web site. This eliminates their need to hire someone to come in and do their filing."—Sherry Huff Carnahan, SherryCarnahan.com

Note: The above-mentioned software programs can be purchased from various providers on the Web, such as **www.cnet.com.**

Smart Tip

"*GoToMyPC* software can also be used to access your own computer when you're away from your office," says Joanne Pratt. "Because the service is available on a monthly basis, I sign up just before I leave the country, which I do frequently for speaking and consulting contracts, then drop the subscription when I return. Although I pay more than the monthly charge of an annual subscription, the service gives me the assurance that I can get into any of my files from an Internet cafe, no matter where I am."

Extra Income from Affiliate Programs

According to Forrester Research, by 2003, 21 percent of all online sales will be driven by affiliate sites promoting affiliate products. *Affiliates* earn small sales commissions by linking their customers to other Web sites offering compatible but noncompetitive products or services. If your site draws a lot of traffic, adding a few selected affiliate programs could add a nice chunk of change to the mix with no effort on your part once the original setup is made. The how-tos of this topic are too complex for lengthy discussion here, but a search on the Web will turn up countless links to companies offering affiliate programs and many articles explaining how to make them work for you. (See "Other Resources" for a few of them.)

Because it is so easy to set up an affiliate program, everyone is doing this with little regard for whether a particular program is actually going to be profitable or not. The only way an affiliate program is going to work for you is if the products or services you select fit the audience served by your own Web site. For example, I enjoy nice commissions from Amazon.com because I sell my books online, and the people who visit my site to learn about my books are apt to pop over to Amazon to order one of them or buy some other book. Amazon doesn't pay much unless someone buys on the first click, but some affiliate programs pay from 20 to 50 percent of the sale.

The key to success here is to form relationships only with companies related to your own products or services. For example, Louise Louis, who markets her knowledge of toy dog breed selection and caring at ToyBreeds.com, is an affiliate of PetsMart and Amazon.com. She spotlights

Should a Crafter Have a Web Site?

Is selling on the Internet the wave of the future for marketing crafts, or do buyers need that hands-on visual look-see where the purchase of handcrafts is concerned? As I see it, both statements are true. There are some crafts that will never sell well on the Internet because people cannot touch them, but such products will sell well at fairs or in shops. What makes the Internet so wonderful is that if you sell at craft fairs or other retail outlets and *also* have a Web site, you can use it to get follow-up orders by mail. Your Web site can provide interested shoppers with the kind of color catalog you can't afford to print and enable them to order online or by phone or fax. You can also use the Web site to build a database of e-mail addresses you can use for a promotional ezine or regular follow-up mailings.

On a home-business discussion list, a crafter was debating about whether she ought to have a Web site to sell her handcrafted jewelry and, if so, how much business could she expect to receive from it. Her query was answered by Donna Snow, who said: "There are more than three million Web sites in cyberspace, so it's a mistake to start with the assumption that you will do the bulk of your sales on the Web. Web sites are simply another marketing tool, much like a brochure or business card. Although Web sites are now a mainstay of small business, they rarely constitute the majority of a company's sales. Developing relationships and networking will sell your products, not your Web site. Those who tell you they were able to build their business exclusively on the Web have neglected to inform you that they also advertised extensively offline and promoted their site via business cards and brochures, networking, and cold calling to build a client base."

If you're trying to sell arts, crafts, needlework, or related products and services, read my completely revised new edition of *Handmade for Profit* (M. Evans, 2002). It features a dozen success stories of crafters on the Web, with detailed information on how they got started on the proverbial shoestring.

some neat products on her site along with dog training books people can order online.

Author Diana Ratliff, BusinessCardDesign.com, says 10 to 15 percent of her Web income now comes from affiliate programs. "I've found my ezine subscribers to be quite responsive to offers," she says.

"Affiliate programs work for us," says Coleen Sykora, WorkersonWheels.com and RVLifeandTravel.com. "People come to our Web sites to learn about RVing. In addition to offering interesting articles, we link our site visitors to many other resources, including affiliate programs. Although we don't consistently make hundreds of dollars a month from any one product or even from one affiliate program, we do well with them as a whole because we also promote them in our electronic newsletters. Many of our readers are looking specifically for information on how they can earn a living while RVing, so we are affiliates for informational products that offer job and career advice and home business help. Magazines, hard copy books, and eBooks are the best affiliate products we've found."

Let Autoresponders Do the Work for You

Check to see if your Web site host offers an autoresponder service. If so, you can set up a variety of single e-mail messages that can be sent automatically on command. For example, you can tailor a standard e-mail order confirmation message or thank-you note that will be sent to everyone who places an order on your Web site. You can set up a message that will be sent every time someone mails a particular e-mail address. People who can't answer e-mail messages immediately upon receipt often send a short message that acknowledges receipt of the message and promises a reply at a later date (particularly useful when you're ill or plan to be out of your office for an extended period of time).

Autoresponders can also be used to offer a free report or article that isn't posted on your Web site. People simply click a link to get the requested information by return e-mail. For follow-up marketing, autoresponders can be used to send a series of messages to a particular e-mail address. For example, you might confirm a customer's order, then follow up periodically with a series of messages, each making a new offer that might appeal to the customer. For this, you'll need a program such as MailLoop (under $400). This software enables one to send up to 50,000 e-mails per hour, with each being personalized so customers are greeted by name. You can download a demo of this software from **www.Tornadopromotions.com/mailer.html**.

For an article on this topic, go to: **www.marketingtips.com/mailloop**. A series of articles on how to use autoresponders will also be found at **www.GaryNorth.com.**

The Changing Needs of Web Site Owners

In 1999, Susan Scheid reasoned that the Internet was a great place for home-based businesses to sell their products and services, providing their customers could find them. "I found many online malls, directories, and shopping services on the Web," she says, "but most were either too expensive for a new business to afford, or too vast to enable a small company to stand out from the mega malls and superstores. I decided to form SmallBizCommunity.com so small businesses could network with one another and list the availability of their products and services inexpensively."

As Susan brainstormed for things she could add to her site to generate additional income, she began to pay attention to questions being asked on user groups she frequented. "I discovered that most home businesses either needed a shopping system on their site, or they wanted to make it easier for their customers to use. Most who already had a system in place were using Mals-E cart, so I took all those questions and created Option-Cart Catalog (OptionCart.com) to address these issues. This program lets stores with a Mals-E cart account easily plug in a few details about their site and instantly have a searchable shopping cart catalog on their Web site without the need for programming or detailed coding. I found it had to be easy enough for the average person to use, yet be filled with great features they really need. It also had to be something low in cost because the average home business owner doesn't have the budget for a lot of extras. People don't want all the technical details; they just want something that fixes a problem they have, and they want that fix to be easy and inexpensive."

During the 2002 recession, Susan noticed how things were changing. "A year ago, clients were happy with just a simple shopping cart on their site," she says. "Customers were spending, and businesses weren't desperate for sales, so they could afford to just focus on the basics. But now, with 10,000 other sites vying for a customer's money, these clients need to do more, provide more services for their customers. So I'm seeing an increase in extra features like searchable products, newsletter systems, wish lists, inventory tracking systems, and so on. In short, today's Web site owners are no longer satisfied with just a simple site—they want to compete with the big names. And they all want affiliate programs so they can market to other home businesses and make money by having others refer people to them—a very smart move! If online stores don't try to compete with other sites that have a lot of extra features, they'll never make it. That's because today's customers are picky and will go to the competitor in a heartbeat."

Integrating Print and Web Marketing Strategies

Bringing over twenty years of business marketing and management experience, Daryl Ochs recently escaped the corporate world to set up his own brand of small business consulting on the Web at StreetSmartBusiness.com. Through his eBook, *Re-Engineering Your Business*, and ezine, *The Profit Zone*, he is helping the professional practice and small business owner attract new clients and customers through the integration of print and Web marketing strategies.

"From being on the street talking to small business owners and professionals, I'm seeing a definite interest in that sector for effective Web integration," he says. "Many already have a Web site, but it isn't doing much of anything for them, and the trend is toward looking for solutions to make Web integration work. I've observed that people who spend considerable money to get a Web site that doesn't contribute to their bottom line are feeling negative and frustrated. Due to their experience, they are more difficult to approach, but they don't have any idea as to what will make a difference. At the same time, the word is spreading and the perception is gaining ground that *not* having an effective Web site may be a terminal situation for the future. So the expectations are rising along with frustrations."

Display Ads Do Double Duty. "The thing about the Web is that it takes time and a lot of expertise," says Marc Choyt, who has been on the Web since 1997. "We've learned you have to look at the Internet like any other business. It takes years to get a site going and it requires a lot of attention to make it work. A site can be 95 percent right and not make money. On the other hand, a small business can create a Web site that competes with big companies. According to an independent Web site rating service, our site rates as well as Tiffany's and Zales."

Marc offers a good example of how to integrate print and Web marketing strategies. To draw visitors to CelticJewelry.com, he runs $300 to $400 spot ads in Irish and Scottish magazines throughout the country. In full-color ads featuring outstanding jewelry products, he promotes the site and offers a free four-page color catalog to interested mail order shoppers. In the first year of running such display ads, Marc grew their in-house mail list from 3,200 to 6,000 and doubled their Web site sales. To increase mail order sales, he began to send a four-color catalog to this growing mailing list in the fall of 2002. By doing photography and layout in-house, the cost of 10,000 catalogs was kept to just 37 cents each and could be mailed at the one-ounce rate.

"Because many who get our print catalog ultimately order through the Web site, it's impossible to know the percentage of orders that have come directly from the catalog mailings," says Marc. "All we know for sure is that our strategy of using print ads to advertise a catalog and draw traffic to the Web site has proven to be an affordable and profitable way to grow the business."

Note: If you're just starting out on the Web, Marc suggests looking for a high school student who is responsible and willing to develop your Web site for a percentage of the income it generates. "I pay my Webmaster 15 percent of sales, which motivates him and gives him more reason to be invested in the site than if he were just an hourly worker," says Marc. "He's a computer science graduate who formerly made less than $10 an hour. But we have a long-term contract and he's now making excellent money."

Classifieds Reach Targeted Markets. Sculptor Robert Houghtaling, who enjoys Web site design, shares this little story about the marketing power of a simple classified ad: "I designed and built a Web site for some friends of mine who have a lodge and cottage in northern California. Of course I submitted their site to the search engines, but do you know how they get most of their business? From a two-line classified ad in the San Francisco paper under 'Vacation rentals.' It contains just the name of their business and their Web address. *They targeted their customer base*—in this case, the nearest large metropolitan area."

Branding Yourself Online

When you begin to sell online, you need to have a plan for how you're going to position yourself and your business. You're in control of determining who you are and how you want to be portrayed to your potential customers and fans. You must decide what specific messages are sent out into the world and through what avenues those messages will travel. The key to establishing a personal brand identity in the cyber world is focusing on who you are and what you stand for, and then getting the word out through a variety of Internet channels that are frequented by the people most likely to be interested in your message.

As people start seeing your name and the benefits you offer, an impression begins to form. At first, ten people will be attracted to you and what you do, then 50, and then 100. Before you know it, thousands of people will not only know who you are, but will come to view you as the resource of choice on your particular subject. As your circle of online influence grows, a multiplying effect takes place and your notoriety suddenly starts growing in bursts. A critical mass occurs, and before long, you find yourself in the enviable position of being an online celebrity of sorts—or at least a well-known expert among people who are immersed in the topic, craft, industry, or idea you represent.

—An excerpt from *Poor Richard's Branding Yourself Online— How to Use the Internet to Become a Celebrity or Expert in Your Field* by Bob Baker (Top Floor Publishing). Get more of Bob's self-promotion tips at **www.BrandingYourselfOnline.com**.

Generating Web Traffic

Setting up a Web site is only part of the secret to success in marketing electronically. You must constantly promote the existence of your Internet domain and look for new ways to draw people to it. In a chat with PR expert Alan Caruba (AlanCaruba.com) about the benefits of having a Web site, he confirmed something I've heard from many other consultants and service sellers: "A Web site alone doesn't generate the inquiry or the business; it merely serves as a brochure or media kit that helps convince a prospective client to work with you. You still have to generate interested clients on your own, through direct mail, phone contact, or news releases."

In addition to generating traffic through all the basic marketing strategies discussed to this point in the book, the Internet itself must be used as a traffic generator. Here, the most common low-cost strategies include networking and linking to other sites on the Web, seeking publicity on and off the Web, publishing a promotional ezine (see next chapter), registering with search engines, and placing selected paid ads on the Web.

The same basic marketing strategies that work for an offline business also work on the Web. For example, when Martha Oskvig decided to get involved selling BeautiControl products, she told me how she planned to generate traffic to her new Web page at Beautipage.com/here4u. She planned to

- List her Web page address in all ads and press releases, and on all return-address labels and literature she distributed.

- Write/send press releases about self-improvement and fashion forecasts.

- Follow-up corporate mailings to customers with an initial phone call and survey about color trends, likes/dislikes, suggestions for the company and personal needs. ("The phone calls add the personal-service aspect that print catalogs don't have. I'll ask if they wish to continue to receive the free subscription but will remove individual addresses after a year of mailings without an order.")

- Outreach to people she hasn't yet met in areas far from her home. ("I'll use insert programs, image presentations, or literature tables at conventions, business how-to seminars, and wherever else I may travel)."

- Welcome business partners to join her group. ("In addition to corporate-sponsored training, I'll offer them my own training tips via regular and personalized e-mails.')

Doing Business on the Web

Search Engines

"You've got to register with the search engines!" Ever since I got on the Web, I've been reading about the importance of submitting my site to search engines, and everyone seems to believe that Yahoo.com is the most important place to be listed. But is it? (See sidebar, "A Study of Web Site Traffic.")

What puzzles me is that I've never submitted my site to any search engine because I just haven't had time. Yet, anyone who types "Barbara Brabec" into any of the leading search engines will find "Barbara Brabec's World" and my BarbaraBrabec.com URL at the top of the list. In fact, the last time I searched for my name at Yahoo and Google, they both turned up nearly 4,000 pages with my name on them. Obviously, the Web robots have done all this work for me.

At least one Web expert thinks that repeatedly resubmitting your site to the search engines is probably a waste of time. On the WebProNews.com site, I found an interesting article about search engine registration by Dan Thies, who suggests it is no longer necessary to submit sites to the search engines because their robots regularly find and crawl Web sites that have enough external links pointing to them. The more people linking to your site, the quicker the search engines are going to crawl your site, he maintains, which suggests that our time may be better spent by getting people to link to our sites. (Reference: "Resubmission Tactics: Follow-Up" at **www.webpronews.com/2002/1017.html**)

Of course you need to educate yourself on this topic. For a quick lesson in search engine submission essentials, and a list of the top ten search engines, go to **http://searchenginewatch.com/links/major.html** or just type "search engines" in your browser window to turn up a host of sites offering information on this topic.

Using Freebies and Interactive Media

To attract readers, Donna Snow, owner of an Internet production company, has tried both banner ads and ezine classifieds (discussed below). "Over time, I've found that the 1 percent response one normally attracts with the comparable offline direct mail campaigns is significantly lower on the Web," she says. "Banner ads and ezine ads may be appropriate for nonrevenue generating events and freebie offers, but I've found it more effective to draw readers to my site with a freebie or interactive media."

Donna's examples of freebies site owners might offer include wallpaper, e-greetings, screensavers, free reports or eBooks, coupons, online workshop, and so on. "Interactive media" include such things as games and cartoons-of-the-day, bulletin boards and chat rooms, calculators (a pregnancy site might have an estimated due date calendar, while a nutrition site offers a Body Mass Index), and instant quotes on the site (so visitors don't have to e-mail for that information, but can immediately learn whether a price is affordable to them or not).

A Study of Web Site Traffic

When Dennis Gaskill analyzed how 464,157 unique visitors to his Boogiejack.com Web site had found his site, he learned that 36.45 percent of his traffic was coming from search engines, 32.37 percent from links, and 31.18 percent from bookmarks and other means. "This shows I've had a very well-balanced strategy of promoting my site," he says. "Those who say 90 percent of your traffic will come from search engines just aren't promoting successfully in any other way."

Dennis then identified the top ten search engines and directories that were sending traffic to his site. He found that Google was bringing in 45.21 percent, followed by MSN (8.43 percent), AOL NetFind (8.43 percent), and Yahoo (6.52 percent). The rest of the traffic came from AltaVista, Google Canada, CompuServe, Dogpile, HotBot, and Direct Hit. "Bear in mind that traffic from search engines depends on your ranking at that search engine," Dennis adds. "Google updates its database frequently, whereas Yahoo is very slow. I enjoy a #1 listing at Yahoo for some keywords, but they don't even know there are HTML tutorials on my site, and I've had them there for years. Am I impressed with Yahoo? Not exactly."

Trading Links

Inbound links to your Web site will increase your chances of rising in the search engine ranks. To increase links, increase your networking activities online to develop new business relationships with site owners whose products and services *complement* but do not *compete* with your own. To identify other sites, type in keywords related to your products and services to pull up a list of the high-traffic sites (the first ten that come up in your search), and then contact those site owners about a link exchange.

Although most Web entrepreneurs believe links are the best way to build traffic to a Web site, some hold to the theory that, once you get someone on your site, you should try to keep him or her there. Much depends on what you're selling, of course. While you shouldn't send visitors to another site that's selling the same thing you're selling, you can provide a real service to your customers or clients and build customer loyalty by helping them obtain related products and services—especially if you happen to have an affiliate relationship with them.

This strategy has worked well for Coleen Sykora at WorkersonWheels.com. Her site offers a wealth of information about RVing, including articles and links to many other sites and resources on the Web. "We don't claim to give everyone all the information they could possibly want about RVing, but we do try to provide links that will lead them to more information than they can possibly absorb," says Coleen. "This flies backwards to the theory that once you get someone to your Web site you should keep him there, but our income has significantly increased since we've stepped up sending our site visitors away. Some links are to affiliates, but many are reciprocal links to network friends. This kind of linking helps our site visitors, helps our friends increase their Web traffic, and helps us by increasing our traffic and improving our search engine placements."

For more information on linking strategies, read "How to Get a Flood of Traffic from Linking Partners" by Kevin Bidwell at: **www.WebProNews.com/articles/1024kb.html**.

Smart Tip

Find out how many sites have linked to yours by using a search engine such as Google.com and type "link: http://www.[your Web address]" Example: link: http://www.BarbaraBrabec.com

Some sites charge a modest annual fee to link to your site, but if you plan to go this route, select your referral sites with care. "The bottom line is to hand select your promotional partners as well as your link partners," says Deanna Ferber. "A bunch of links isn't the point, nor is a bunch of ads. Free or not, if they are not targeted, you lose. You may even miss a perfect opportunity to reach your ideal target market while you are busy with some generic free ones. Take your time and think, 'If I were my customer, would I be here to see this?' If the answer is no, then pass. If it's 'maybe,' then base your choice upon the funds and time involved and see if it's worth it."

Advertising Options on the Web

Space does not allow for a detailed discussion of this topic, but if you have advertising dollars to part with, you won't find it difficult to spend them on the Web. Search engines offer pay-per-click ads where you pay every time someone clicks over to your Web site. Most commercial Web sites offer banner ads and many ezines published on a regular basis offer classified ads. (See "Other Resources" to find such newsletters.)

For this book, I couldn't do a major survey of Web entrepreneurs to see how effective such ads are, or which ones might work best for the average business owner, but the responses I got from a few of my book contributors will give you some perspective on this topic.

Deanna Ferber, who sells cosmetics and skin care products, has tried all of the above ad options with mixed results. "I do try to arrange swaps for most of these now," she says. "This works best when you have hand-selected the sites/companies you are approaching. Then there is a better fit for both my products to their subscribers/customers, and their site/product line is likely to appeal to my customer. This means we both have a chance to profit from the exchange.

"Banner ads are, to me, a necessary part of a Web presence," Deanna continues. "Many will argue that the low or virtually non-existenct rate of clicks means they are dead, but I disagree. Any time you can get your name seen, and perhaps remembered, is a good thing. No one puts potato chip commercials on television and expects the program viewer to get up and go buy a bag, but they hope through repetition the viewer will be so familiar with the product name they will purchase a bag the next time they are shopping. That's how I use banners—to build the company name and perhaps build credibility, since the more they see it, the more they believe the company is not only 'here to stay' but even popular."

Personally, I never click on a banner ad because I'm simply too busy. I prefer to do keyword searches on Google or Yahoo when I'm looking for a particular product or service. Deanna may have a point, however. Even if you don't click on banner ads, the fact that you see a particular banner ad on many sites will eventually register in your mind, and someday, your decision to buy a particular product or service may be influenced by this kind of advertising.

Doing Business on the Web

"Banner ads were highly successful for me until the Web became inundated with them," says Richard Tuttle, a Web designer who has been online since 1995. "Now people easily ignore them. New methods are needed beyond the visual spam that now permeates the Web."

Ezine classified ads are a popular form of Web advertising now because they are affordable and can be targeted to specific niche markets. For example, Sue Krei advertises her rubber stamps and special Web site sales on rubber stamping e-mail lists. "These lists all pertain to how people are using rubber stamps, covering new techniques, products, and so forth. There are classes given online, as well as card contests, exchanges, secret sister exchanges, and all kinds of fun things. I am on about 25 of these lists and advertise regularly. Some are quite small (about 30 subscribers) but most have 200 to 300 subscribers. One I am on has over 2,000 members, so this gives me a large audience of buyers to tap. I have my own e-mail list as well that I use to advertise new designs and specials on my site at WoodCellarGraphics.com."

The same principles that apply to advertising in print also apply to advertising on the Web. Ads have to be well written and targeted to the specific audience you're trying to reach, and you need to track the results of each ad to see if they're worth repeating. (To do this, you'll need special "ad tracking software." Just type those three keywords into any search engine to turn up a number of inexpensive or free programs available.)

"I use tracking to see the results of my promotions," says Deanna Ferber. "It tells me who is coming from where, how long they stay on my site, and so on. I can see if my traffic has increased from an ad, and if my subscriptions or sales increase, I know it was well targeted. Unless you use a coupon or sales code, however, you cannot really be certain a sale was from that promotion. And since it takes seven to twelve visits to a site to convert a visitor into a buyer, your first time ads are not likely to result in a sale. That's where you hope they subscribe to your newsletter!"

• • •

Building a presence on the Internet with a Web site of your own is the ultimate small business diversification strategy of the twenty-first century. But if you decide to pass on this opportunity, there are other ways to diversify an offline business and multiply sales and profits, as the next chapter proves.

I would like to continue my research on how Web site owners are building their online businesses and perhaps do an eBook on this topic. If you'd like to be interviewed for this book, please e-mail Barbara@BarbaraBrabec.com with a subject line of "Add me to your eBook interview list." When you write, tell me something about your growing Web business since I may be able to give it some visibility in my other writing.

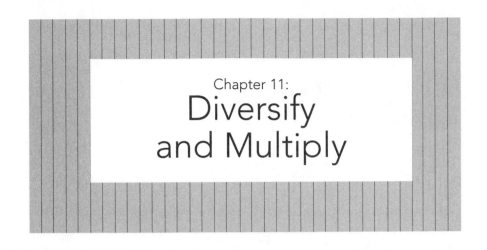

Chapter 11

Diversify
and Multiply

Once you have struck gold from one profitable product or service, you can extract more gold from the same mine shaft, so to speak, by diversifying and expanding around the product and services that have made you successful.

—Richard Albert, from an article in *Home Business Magazine* (February 2001)

This chapter presents a broad overview of the many different ways you can diversify an existing business, and it's one you should return to from time to time as your business grows and you continue to develop expertise in new areas of endeavor. In time, you may find that your lifetime of experience and know-how has positioned you nicely to start a sideline business based around one or more of the "big five" diversification strategies that fall under the "advice business" umbrella—writing, publishing, speaking, teaching, and consulting. I've discussed these topics and more in this chapter and you can continue your research by exploring the books and Web links I've included in "Other Resources." (You may also wish to read Chapter 6,

"Profiting from Special Expertise and Know-How," in this book's companion guide, *HOMEMADE MONEY: Starting Smart!*)

Why You *Must* Diversify Your Business

You may never make a million dollars from your homebased business, but once you get going, you certainly can increase your income through diversification. This is very important to the small business owner because often only a certain amount of profit can be realized from a particular endeavor, no matter how hard one works. Yet if that endeavor is tied to one or more closely related activities, profits may increase dramatically while overhead costs stay virtually the same.

An interesting mix of activities not only adds spice to one's home-business life, but may be crucial to some businesses, such as mail order and seasonal operations that die down in certain months of the year. Clearly, something else must be done if income is to roll in regularly. It's never too early to start thinking about an "understudy" product or service—one that could go onstage should your star performer suddenly fall ill. In fact, if you're still in the stages of trying to decide what business to start, the deciding factor in whether it's going to be profitable may lie in whether your idea has good diversification possibilities.

If you're the key individual in a business that is labor intensive, the real trick to growth and increased profits has to lie not in working harder, but in working smarter. By getting a handle on how you're spending your time (refer back to Chapter 2), you can see what you must do to get more productivity from the same hours you've always worked. (Example: computerizing your business to save time in one area that can more profitably be used in another.) "I agree that the best way to make money doing what you love to do is to leverage your time," says crafts publisher, author, and designer Karen Booy, KarenBooy.com. "I do many things—speak, write, publish, design, manufacture, demonstrate at trade shows, etc. In that way, I maximize each and every minute I spend on my business. I can turn one meeting or contact into several income streams."

Growth may also be achieved by getting control of business costs (refer back to Chapter 3) by making sure you're really charging enough for your products and services, and seeking markets that might pay you more for the same work you've always done—topics discussed at length in earlier chapters. In addition to being important to the financial success of a business, diversification is often the antidote to business boredom or burnout, a serious topic discussed in the next chapter.

▷ Smart Tip

The more ways you can think of to diversify, and the more products or services you can offer, the more dollars you're likely to generate. Remember this simple formula for business success: *Diversification of Business = Multiplication of Dollars.*

In brainstorming for ideas on how to diversify your business, try this "recipe": Take your primary product or service and add to it a list of other products and services related to it. Stir in your knowledge about all of these things and mix well with the experience you have in all areas related to them. Add any business, professional, or marketing contacts you may have, and season with such intangible things as your personality and long-range business goals. The resulting mixture is sure to lead you to an interesting discovery about what you might do to "diversify and multiply."

Service Business Diversification Strategies

In brainstorming for additional services you might offer, try thinking backwards by first considering your market possibilities. Who needs what? What special problems are your clients having now? If your service is directed to consumers, could you modify it in some way to make it salable to the business community, or vice versa? For example, an organizational specialist might help families organize a home while also helping companies battle office chaos. A dressmaker might specialize in bridal gowns while also designing uniforms or dressing gowns for the medical community. (See sidebar, "From Sculpting to Programming.")

It's important to pay attention to what your clients need. When Susan Scheid opened her business and Web site, SmallBizCommunity.com, it was with the idea that she would design Web sites for new business owners. Merely by being on the Web for awhile and paying attention to what people really *needed* (as opposed to what she planned to offer when she started her business), Susan came up with a business concept that has led to the development of several inexpensive programs for home business owners. It has generated a considerable amount of new business, thanks to word-of-mouth advertising from satisfied clients. "I have diversified my business simply by staying alert to what the average home business site wants, not what I think they need," she says, "and I keep users' suggestions in mind when creating each feature."

In response to a need she recognized, Nina Feldman, NinaFeldman.com, expanded her word processing business not by subcontracting work, but by developing a network of over 150 other word processors, desktop publishers, and computer support services who wanted business. She refers jobs to these businesses who, in turn, pay her a referral fee of 15 percent of the first job they do for each client, or 15 percent of all work done for them in the first 90 days, whichever is greater. In addition, they pay an annual membership fee of $85. "My referral income now represents about 95 percent of my gross," says Nina, "and I add new service providers as needed."

Smart Tip

"Going mobile can be an excellent way to diversify a business," notes Sandy Larson in an article about mobile businesses in *Home Business Magazine* (December 2001). "If you are operating a service business from your home, look at ways you can take your services on the road, and provide that service to a local client base."

Adding Products to the Mix

Service businesses often diversify by adding a retail product line. For instance, a calligrapher who does diplomas or scrolls might create a calendar, print quotes on parchment paper suitable for framing, or design a line of greeting cards. A wedding consultant might commission local artisans to create handmade garters or embroidered handkerchiefs to serve the "something blue" needs of brides, or perhaps offer handmade cake ornaments. Commercial items such as bride's books or paper products (napkins, nut cups, etc.) could also be purchased wholesale for resale to clients. A teacher might elect to sell books; a hairdresser, related hair care products; a computer consultant, software; and so on.

Diversify and Multiply

Service providers who become skilled in a particular area often diversify by creating their own information or software products (see sidebars in this chapter), which in turn leads them into marketing by mail or through a Web site. As they become known as an expert in their field, they are often asked to speak or consult, and may even be invited to write a book.

After teaching himself how to design Web graphics and build a Web site, Dennis Gaskill opened Boogiejack.com and quickly gained a reputation for delivering helpful how-to advice to Web beginners. His visibility on the Web soon brought him to the attention of Morton Publishing, who asked him to write a book he titled *Web Design Made Easy*. Today, that book and other income from related products on his informative site supports the Gaskill family.

From Sculpting to Programming— How the Brainstorming Process Works

Many people have diversified their businesses simply by working day after day on work that just naturally leads them into new areas and enables them to diversify with new products or services. Michael Harvey is an artist/metal sculptor by trade who started out with the idea of setting up a Web page to show his artwork, and ended up totally involved in programming and selling programs and modules that would enable others to design and manage their own sites. He explains the brainstorming process he used to get from one place to another:

"Initially, I was helping others by getting them set up on the Web and then maintaining their sites for them. But I found I hated doing the same thing over and over, which is what you have to do if a client has a lot of product. Every time a client needed a change in a price, or a new picture, they had to contact me to make the change for them, and if I was busy, I couldn't do this right away. And then there was the dilemma of 'Do I charge for a five-minute update?' and 'What if there are several five-minute updates in a month?' etc.

"Then I thought, 'What if the client could do these minor updates on their own, without having to know HTML?' I started to work on such a program and Visual Energy Studio Hosting was born. While writing this program I started coming up with many features and 'toys' that would be useful. But not all of them would be useful to everybody, I thought. Too much in an administration area could be just as confusing to a client as the code itself. So I started to make the program more modular so clients could use just the features they wanted.

"Then it occurred to me that the small client couldn't really afford a high-end program, especially if they were only using a few basic features. It just wouldn't be worth it. Yet people who need all the features would think a higher price would be worth it. Then it occurred to me that not everyone would want this program at all, but would want some of the features or tools. So IBiz-Tools.com was born. I began creating modules for my other program and then started adding things that businesspeople (myself included) need every day. I began shopping around the Net for Open Source PHP programs that I could adapt/modify to fit my needs and found many. Most only needed to be adapted to the multi-user environment that I wanted to create."

Today, Michael offers several programs and modules clients can buy on a subscription basis. He adjusts the price according to how many tools a person wishes to use.

Product Business Diversification Strategies

People who make their own products for sale often diversify by adding compatible products made by other small business owners. Joann and Bob Olstrom started Joann's Honey in 1981 and the business is still going strong today, thanks to their smart diversification strategies. To their own line of honey, the Olstroms first added a variety of honey-related food products such as ice cream toppings and Honey Stix®, then began to carry the honey of other beekeepers as well. Later, they added beeswax candles, ornaments, honey cookbooks, and a line of supplies for other beekeepers. A recognized expert in her field, Joann has been speaking on the subject of bees for many years. "We've always had more business than we can handle," says Joann. (I found a listing for Joann's Honey on the FarmWorld.com Web site, but the Olstroms have no plans to set up a Web site of their own.)

Product manufacturers who reach their limits in terms of what they can produce often begin to sell the finished products of others, sometimes buying them outright or, more commonly, taking them on consignment or setting up drop-ship arrangements. (See "Drop-Ship Programs" below.) Other product sellers diversify by carrying supplies and raw materials, sometimes importing hard-to-find products for a niche market they've identified.

Some product businesses expand their operation merely by changing their method of selling to open up new markets. For example, they may move from retailing to consumers to wholesaling to retail shops and stores. They may also establish a mail order division by placing ads, opening a Web site, or creating a catalog for distribution at retail shows and fairs.

Smart Tips

To automatically increase product sales, offer your customers an 800 number and credit card privileges. If you can publicize your business on radio or television, your ability to sell this way will make all the difference in whether such appearances are profitable or merely ego-boosting.

Drop-Ship Programs

As discussed in the previous chapter, affiliate programs on the Web make it easy to earn small commissions for linking your Web site visitors to the sites of other companies who sell related products or services. Another way to diversify a product line and increase income (both on or off the Web) is by adding the related products of other companies that are available on a drop-ship basis. Here, instead of sending people to another place to buy the merchandise, you directly solicit orders in return for a commission on any sales made.

Selling Books. When I first began to sell books, I didn't have many products to sell, so I created a catalog featuring books from several other publishers and took orders for them along with my own titles. I deposited customers' checks and then sent my book orders with payment to the appropriate publishers, retaining my 40 percent commission on each sale, but including the previously agreed-upon postage and handling charges I had tacked onto the price of each book.

Ideas for Sideline Art/Craft Products

- **Note Cards**. Consider creating note cards that feature a line drawing or photograph of one of your most outstanding works of art or craft, or perhaps a colorful collection of products. (Examples: Dolls, teddy bears, needlework, quilts, flower arrangements, sculpture, stained glass, marquetry, and decoupage.)

- **Pattern Packages.** Turn one or more of your products into a pattern package. Print pattern instructions on standard-size paper, fold in half and package in a plastic zipper-lock bag with a color photo of the finished item and an appropriate header with your business name or logo and price. Create a line of at least six designs, and you'll have a product you can wholesale to craft or needlework shops. (Visit such shops for ideas on how to package patterns professionally.)

- **Craft or Needlework Kits.** People who won't buy your finished products might be interested in buying a kit containing a pattern and necessary supplies and materials to make it themselves. Don't duplicate your best-sellers as kit products, but create different designs and/or make your kit items smaller than something you make for sale. Price them lower than the finished product, yet high enough to make a good profit.

For more specific how-to information on all of the above, see the author's book, *Creative Cash*, 6th ed. (Prima Pub.)

Publishers then shipped my orders using the typed shipping labels I provided, giving my customers the impression that I had personally inventoried and shipped that book myself. Trade publishers don't promote drop-shipping services today, but many still offer them. Self-publishers, however, are usually delighted to work with mail order booksellers on a drop-ship basis. If you sell to a niche market and have found some specific book titles you think you could easily sell, just call the publisher and ask if you can sell their books on a drop-ship basis.

Selling Other Products. There are thousands of other products you can sell on a drop-ship basis. To find companies who work this way, do a search on the Web for "drop ship programs." The nice thing about drop shipping is that you can build a product line without ever laying out a dime for inventory. I caution you, however, to be sure that the company you're working with is reliable and will actually ship promptly as soon as you've forwarded orders to them. Make sure you know how the company will handle lost orders or merchandise that may be damaged in shipment. Since you're the one who will be soliciting orders and collecting the money, you're the one customers will complain to if there are any problems.

Licensing

Some artists and craftspeople who design and sell their own handmade products become so skilled in designing that they are able to move into the lucrative field of licensing designs to manufacturers. Annie Lang, Annie Things Possible, was once a waitress who earned extra money by painting signs on trucks. She began to sell her art in the early 1980s, then went on to self-publish a line of design books. Membership in the Society of Craft Designers (CraftDesigners.org) enhanced her professional image and helped her move into licensing relationships with several craft, giftware, and textile manufacturers. Her whimsical frogs, turtles, ladybugs, bumble bees, and elves have appeared on rubber stamps, giftware, resin castings and painted wood items, iron-on/rub-on transfers, scrapbooking papers, suncatcher ornaments, a line of fabrics, and machine embroidery software.

How does Annie turn up so many licensing opportunities? "My designer name and published works have provided visibility in the marketplace, which has made it easier to sell designs to licensees who are seeking out high profile designers to help them sell their product lines. I also attend numerous trade shows each year, and networking opportunities from contacts at those shows have certainly played a leading role in helping me find potential licensees."

"It's hard to get out of the crafts production train of thought to consider licensing," says Annie. "To explore the possibilities in this field, you have to rethink what you're doing. To get an idea of the market potential for your designs or products, walk through a department store and look carefully at all the gift items and decorative accessories. Consider whether your designs would work on similar products and whether they would be adaptable to different surfaces. You have to think in terms of cross-marketing. The trend today is toward designs that can be used on a wide variety of products. In the near future, I expect to have my designs on other product lines such as buttons, rugs, towels, sheets, and curtains."

(For more on this topic, also see "Licensing" in the A-to-Z Business Management section of this book.)

Couple Builds Business on a Line of Inventions

In the process of designing and making their own products for sale, creative people often stumble on ways to improve construction methods and design tools or related products for sale. In 1987, then in their sixties with no retirement income, Emma Graham and her husband, Don, invested everything they had in a new business. It was built around Emma's sewing skills and Don's invention of a sewing tool that enabled sewers to turn fabric tubes from wrong to right-side out. Called Fasturn®, it quickly found a ready market in sewing and craft stores nationwide. Soon the Grahams had to build a building on their property so they could hire employees to make this and other products Don was inventing. He modified his original invention to enable rug makers to make tubes of fabric for use in braided rugs, a smart move that automatically positioned the company in a parallel industry and a new niche market. Further diversification of the business came with the publication of a complete line of patterns showing sewers and rug makers how to use fabric tubes to make a variety of products from jewelry to decorative accessories. Don later followed with yet another companion tool and a unique sewing machine foot called Fastube®. Don and Emma finally retired in 2002 after selling the business to their son, David. It's now on the Web at FasturnJunction.com.

Consulting As a Sideline Business

Do people often approach you, asking questions about how you did this or that? If so, it's time to add a consulting sideline to your existing business. The more successful you become in your business, the more you will be asked for help and advice from others who would follow in your footsteps. It's one thing to network with other businesspeople, and quite another to freely give to a curious beginner (who may become a competitor in short order) all the information it has taken you years to acquire on your own. At least charge that person for the privilege of picking your brain because every hour you give to someone else is one hour you cannot devote to your own business.

Consulting is not a regulated business, and anyone can sell advice in any form (except for advice in some regulated or licensed professions). Even in those fields, one is free to sell general advice to the public at large because it is then considered "information." Or, as explained by the late Herman Holtz in this book's companion guide, *HOMEMADE MONEY: Starting Smart:*

> Any layperson is free to write, lecture, and otherwise render advice in general for fees as long as the advice or information is general and not offered to an individual. For example, you may write or lecture about legal matters in the abstract, but unless you are a licensed attorney, you may not counsel a person in legal matters for a fee. Anyone with a marketable skill of any kind is in a position to become a consultant, teaching others to do what he or she does, solving others' problems, and/or doing work for others on a temporary, permanent, or semi-permanent basis.

Extra Profits from Writing and Publishing

When you know something other people might want to know, or you have gathered hard-to-find information that others might pay to receive, you should think about putting it in written form. (Ideally, you already will have access to the market most likely to buy it.) Following is a brief introduction to your writing/publishing diversification options.

Books

Many people who have acquired special expertise or knowledge about a particular topic could profit by writing a book about it and publishing it themselves if they can't find an interested trade publisher. Books are among the easiest things to sell by mail, and even easier to sell if you also teach classes or present workshops or seminars on the book's topic. There are several good guides for writers and book publishers (both print and eBooks) to help you succeed in this area, and I've listed my favorites in the "Other Resources" section of this book.

Unless you're a professional writer or an English major, your self-published book will probably benefit greatly from an editor's assistance. As series editor of Prima Publishing's line of For Fun & Profit books, I found that many of the authors knew their topic inside and out but had difficulty in presenting material in an orderly fashion (often putting the cart before the horse, so to speak). In addition to needing help with grammar and punctuation, most of the authors also had occasional difficulty with sentence or paragraph construction or the creation of interesting chapter titles, subtitles, and sidebars. If you're lucky enough to find an interested trade publisher, your book will receive this kind of content and copyediting as it moves through the production line. As a self-publisher, however, you must assume this responsibility. At the very least, hiring a freelance editor to check your book manuscript prior to publication may save you personal embarrassment, keep you out of legal trouble (copyright law, permissions, etc.), and help ensure better reviews. (Check my Web site, BarbaraBrabec.com, for the editing services I now offer writers and self-publishers.)

Booklets

Booklets come in different sizes, depending on content. An artist I know has found an appreciative audience for her little $5^1/_2" \times 8^1/_2"$ booklets of drawings and poetry, and a crafts designer is successfully selling a nostalgic booklet of her stories and poems. Booklets that can be mailed in a #10 business envelope are the most practical size if you're selling business information, however, and thousands of such booklets are now being offered on the Internet for around $6 each. Some booklet sellers print booklets on demand and send them by mail while others sell them in electronic form only. It's hard to know how many of these booklets are actually selling, but as discussed in the publicity chapter, their use as a promotional tool may far outweigh any money that might be generated by selling them. Although I haven't turned up anyone who is doing this with success, I understand that the real money in booklets lies in finding premium buyers who will buy them in bulk (a thousand or more at a time) for their own promotional purposes. (Refer back to Chapter 8 for more information on this topic.)

Newsletters/Ezines

In previous years, a natural diversification strategy for an ongoing business was to launch a subscription newsletter to share the knowledge and research one had gained from years of hands-on experience in a particular field. But the Internet has had a dramatic effect on periodical publishing. Since few people will pay for something they can get for free, you should think twice before launching a subscription newsletter. NEPA (Newsletter and Electronic Publishers Association, on the Web at Newsletters.org) reports that the industry's sales are getting socked hard by online competition, and direct mail and renewal results have been in a continuous downward spiral since 1995. The best information I've found on this topic is in Howard Penn Hudson's book, *Publishing Newsletters* (**www.newsletter-clearinghse**).

The safest bet is to publish a promotional ezine that allows you to share your expertise while also promoting and selling products or services advertised on your Web site. (To find how-to articles on the Web, use your browser to search for such phrases as "ezine publishing," "email-list management and distribution", and "ezine hosting services." Also see "Other Resources" for some specific Web links on these topics.)

Freelance Writing

If you have the desire to write, but not self-publish, you might be able to add to your income through the sale of articles to consumer or trade magazines. Professionals in all fields are well paid for articles that share inside information while also promoting themselves or their businesses through promotional blurbs tacked on to the end of articles. Authors, consultants, business service providers, attorneys, and accountants are only a few of the many self-employed individuals who fall into this category. Craftspeople and designers can profit by selling how-to projects to craft consumer magazines and other business owners may find they can sell a column to newspapers or magazines.

Diversify with an Information Product
by Joan Stewart, PublicityHound.com

"Info-products help establish you as an expert in your field. They include everything from traditional things such as tips booklets and audiotapes to an array of electronic items like eBooks and special reports that cost next to nothing to produce. If you can find your niche audience, identify its problems and provide the solutions, you're more than halfway down the road to creating lots of info-products that will put you among those who like to work once and get paid over and over again. Info-products attract media attention and create publicity for your business. They help you cross-sell and up-sell other more expensive products and services such as consulting projects. Best of all, they can add a huge, dependable revenue stream for your business."

Profiting from "The Gift of Gab"

If you have special knowledge or experience, plus the "gift of gab," you can earn extra income by presenting the occasional speech, workshop, or seminar. Speaking can be financially profitable all by itself, but it's doubly so when you have a product line to sell—books, tapes, patterns, newsletter, kits, supplies, etc. In my twenty years as a speaker and workshop presenter, I usually traveled five or six times a year to deliver a keynote address and/or a home-business workshop or seminar for one group or another, and the extra books and newsletter subscriptions I sold as a result made each trip very profitable. You may not be able to command the high fees full-time professional speakers usually get, but speaker fees of from $500 to $1,000 (plus expenses) are common in the home-business industry, and much higher fees are possible if you can break into the corporate marketplace and do the major business conferences.

Traveling for Free. Being able to speak in public can also open the door to traveling to places you might not be able to afford to visit otherwise. Silvana Clark (SilvanaClark.com), a recreation specialist who presents innovative business presentations in many locations in the

Diversify and Multiply

United States and Canada, was delighted when she received an invitation to speak in Germany and learned that the sponsor would pay the airfare for her daughter and husband to go along. An entertaining speaker, Silvana's gimmicks include costumes, various products and props, and small gifts taped under everyone's chair. "I also pass around a hat during my speeches," she says, "asking everyone to put in their business card. Then I hold a drawing and award several door prizes such as flowers or gourmet coffee—a small price to pay for getting the names and addresses of everyone in the room." Like most speakers, Silvana has diversified by publishing books.

Cruising for Fun and Profit. Would you like a free cruise? Many home-business owners can't afford a vacation, but savvy business owners with knowledge that can be shared through speaking or teaching may be able to trade a program for a cruise and get an extra ticket for a spouse or friend. (For more information on how to cruise for free, as well as professional speaking in general, subscribe to Dottie Walter's *Sharing Ideas Magazine* for professional paid speakers (**www.Walters-Intl.com**).

To give you an example of how profitable cruising can be, consider Kaye Wood's story. Now the most renowned quilt designer in the country, Kaye began her homebased business in 1978 by traveling throughout northern Michigan teaching machine embroidery and selling supplies. In 1981, after teaching a class on how to make strip-pieced vests, Kaye developed a line of handmade quilted vests she wholesaled for awhile. But it was her special knowledge of "strip quilting" that enabled her to broadly diversify her little sewing business into a major corporation. After teaching on a few cruises, Kaye began to sponsor her own trips, taking other quilters on cruises sixteen times. (I've never forgotten the brochure she sent me for one of her classes, which she still teaches today: It read: "Come Cruise With Kaye and Learn to Strip Like a Pro!")

"Now, instead of running our own cruises—which is very time consuming—I just get hired to be one of the teachers on the cruise," says Kaye, who has taught and lectured throughout the United States. as well as in Mexico, Canada, Denmark, Germany and Holland. At all speaking engagements, she profits from the sale of her extensive line of books, videos, patterns, and tools, which are also sold by mail, on the Web at KayeWood.com, and on her popular television show on PBS. (See also sidebar, "Profits from Books, Videos, and TV Shows.")

Profits from Books, Videos, and TV Shows

Kaye Wood, who has made a lot of money teaching quilters how to "strip like a pro," has written 28 books on quilting and is currently working on five more at the present time. She has also diversified her product line by producing her own videotapes for quilters and selling videos, books, and quilting supplies from other companies as well.

Although costly to produce, Kaye has found videotapes to be great profit generators. At the time she introduced her first videos back in the 1980s, Kaye told me it cost $6,000 to produce the first three, all of which were done in one day. They were each one-hour long and retailed for $29.95 (wholesale, $19.50). Each tape cost Kaye $9.25, netting her more than $20 apiece (far more profitable than her self-published books), and she quickly sold 1,400 of them.

"Videos are a strange game," says Kaye today. "I have taped videos of my own to accompany the last five books I've written, and these videos are ordered in quantities of 250. We've been able to cut production costs because we now tape at the same time we tape our TV show. We also distribute (wholesale and retail) every video from the last ten TV series—130 videos altogether. The masters are kept at the production company we use and we don't stock these but simply special-order them as we get orders."

To date, Kaye has produced thirty-two 13-week series of "Kaye's Quilting Friends" (over 400 individual shows), and this is now the #1 rated quilting show on PBS. No wonder Kaye plans to keep doing this show for awhile! "TV continues to be expensive, at approximately $65–80,000 for each thirteen-week series," she says. "But thanks to our sponsors we are able to continue. And thanks to the local PBS stations we continue to be shown. We also distribute all the books, patterns, and tools that we show on TV. On the TV show, I show my techniques on five or six programs in each series. On the other seven or eight programs, I have a guest teacher. Then we offer his/her book or pattern for sale at the end of the show. Our complete catalog is online at KayeWood.com, but we still print 50,000 catalogs at a time."

Teaching Others What You Know

Many home-business owners diversify and promote their businesses by offering adult-education classes related to what they do. For example, Lori Seaborg, TreasuresPlanted.com, grows and sells herbal plants, dried loose herbs, and herbal products. She also teaches landscaping and gardening courses at her local junior college. As a result of having sold plants locally for several years, she has also been asked to guest lecture at women's events.

Although some teaching/speaking jobs pay little or nothing, they could give your business extra visibility while also enabling you to sell your products or service to students for an optional fee. Always clarify this point prior to taking a job, however. If product sales aren't possible, you still have the option of getting a list of student names you can add to your mailing list for later follow-up promotions.

With just a little effort, artists and craftspeople may be able to find profitable teaching opportunities in local craft supply or sewing stores. I've often emphasized how one thing always leads to another, and quilter Terrie Kralik, MooseCountryQuilts.com, has certainly found this to be true. After teaching in various shops and working with the patterns of other designers, she decided she could improve on what was available. "If not for teaching, I might not have been led to design and publish my own line of patterns in 1997," she says. "And, thanks to teaching classes in shops where the atmosphere is comfortable and relaxing, I've gained confidence in my speaking ability and am now being hired to speak to a growing number of groups about quilting and publishing patterns."

Electronic Teaching/Coaching. If teaching for extra income is of interest to you, be sure to explore your opportunities for online teaching. Opportunities exist on sites that offer a variety of classes. Here, teachers split class fees with the site owner. In addition to maintaining her own Web site at Press4Success.com, professional quilter and author Myrna Giesbrecht teaches quilting online through the QuiltUniversity.com Web site. "They organize and collect, and I get 80 percent of student fees," she says. "It works like a charm without the stress of managing and credit cards."

Even greater profits are possible if you offer a class from your own Web site. For example, Karen Booy publishes *Craftlink* Magazine and owns Ewe and Me pattern company. On her site at Craftlink.net, she offers a six-week online course on how to start a successful craft business. Each weekly lesson includes instructional materials along with guide sheets to help beginners direct and organize their thoughts and ideas into a workable plan.

Like online classes, business coaching also seems to be growing in popularity and can pay very well. Take a look at what others are doing here by searching Google.com for "professional business coaching" and "online classes."

Telephone Seminars (Teleseminars). I have noticed that many ezines published by business experts are now promoting telephone seminars they and other business pros are offering. If you have inside information others are dying to get and willing to pay for, consider offering monthly or weekly telephone seminars. You'll need merchant status (see discussion in the A-to-Z listings) and a way to attract people interested in hearing your ideas and answers to questions (newsletter, promotional ezine, Web site, flyers in every package you send out, etc.).

Dottie Walters, guru to professional speakers the world over and publisher of *Sharing Ideas Magazine* (mentioned earlier in this chapter), explains how she offers her phone seminars on how to vastly increase speakers' incomes in many ways, including how to *do* phone seminars. "Each individual pays his or her own phone bill, as well as my fee ($150 for the two-hour session, which includes instruction sheets and various forms, enabling them to use the ideas right away). I offer my phone seminars on Saturday mornings, usually with twenty attendees at a time. The cost of my own phone line runs about $80, so my gross is $3,000 for the two hours, less the $80 for my phone."

Often, people decide they want more help and sign up for Dottie's one-on-one consulting service ($200/hour, two-hour minimum). Some business experts sell memberships and include as part of the package the ability to join their phone discussion once a week—"a round table sort of thing," she says. "If you've got special knowledge and a market for it, this kind of consulting will provide a steady continual income stream for you while enabling many people to get good seminar material right in their own home."

To present your own teleseminars, you'll need a teleconferencing service. (A search for "teleconferencing services" on Google.com turned up several sites. Free quotes from multiple vendors are available at **www.Buyerzone.com** (click "Telecom services"). Also check Maria Marsala's Web site at **www.CoachMaria.com**, as she rents her teleconference phone line (called a bridge line) for just $15 an hour. "Our teleconference service uses the latest bridgeline technology to connect from two to thirty callers who live anywhere in the world," she says. "Your callers pay only their usual long distance rates. The moderator of the call pays an hourly teleconference fee (to connect everyone), but there are no other 'per caller' fees involved."

Shannon Seek also offers a similar service from her site at **www.Rentabridge.com**, but she can serve up to sixty callers for about the same price.

Franchising Your Business

Although franchising is a good diversification option for large businesses, in my opinion, few—if any—homebased business owners should consider it. Although the following information is discouraging, it may prevent you from making an expensive mistake—always an important goal of my books. Franchising is a time-consuming and expensive process that could cost as much as $100,000 to launch if you use a franchising consultant. While you might be able to save a small fortune by doing all the work yourself (including the complicated franchising documentation), some important questions to be answered here are:

1 Does your business have a profitable track record?

2 Have you found a good market niche?

3 Will your service idea work anywhere?

4 How much competition is there?

5 Do you really have the time to devote to this separate business enterprise? and,

6 Are your marketing skills such that you could successfully market your franchise once it is ready to roll?

In all my years of communicating with homebased entrepreneurs, I have encountered only one individual who opted to franchise her service business. While she appeared to be a sharp businessperson, had an impressive franchise package, and got a fair amount of publicity in business magazines, she didn't make it. I was going to use her as a success story for my book, but when I called to interview her, the phone had been disconnected.

I learned more about franchise pitfalls from Bob Johansmeyer, a former franchise consultant who switched to tax consulting when he became disenchanted with the industry as a whole. "Few small business owners have enough cash to do the job right," he told me. "If your goal is to franchise on a shoestring, you're doomed to failure. A franchise operation is a long-term investment with a payoff far down the road—probably five years or more. Most people don't realize that starting a franchise means starting a whole new business, and anyone who is already busy is going to find it almost impossible to do the job right.

"Even if you do get the franchise up and running before you run out of money, you will be heavily restricted by federal and state laws on what you can say to prospective franchisees," Bob adds. "Because of these laws, most franchisors now skirt claims about how much money one might make, which only makes it more difficult to sell a franchise. While franchisees are protected by these laws, there is no protection for the prospective franchisor. Most of the 'franchising sharks' have been caged now, but the ones making the most money in this industry are often the ones who are selling franchise consulting services to would-be franchisors."

Smart Tip

Always question who's giving you advice. Trust least the advice of those who stand to profit most from giving you their advice.

An Outstanding Diversification Example

Sandra Manning is a perfect example of how the business diversification process works, and how naturally it often occurs as people go about their day-to-day business activities. In 1990, Sandra started Kaleidoscope Connections, Inc., a home day care and preschool operation geared towards encouraging the development of children's creativity. "I was able to utilize an educational background, set up my own educational 'system,' and venture into the business world while also being at home with my three children," she says.

When she began, Sandra had no idea how each of her new ideas would blossom and flower into other business activities. Networking led her to begin speaking on the importance of encouraging the imaginative process in young children. Special Saturday classes for creative children soon led Sandra to offer her service to local resorts and businesses. When she approached a local resort complex with a proposal to offer services to families vacationing in the summer, they described a need for a children's program that would free parents to attend seminars, golf, or shop. Later, she added another resort to her client list, one in need of a summer camp. "I also set up the adult entertainment and children's activities for their Family Nights," she said. "Two other resorts then asked me to write recreational programs for them and provide training programs for their in-house staff."

All of the above led Sandra to begin producing monthly displays at a local educational supply store to promote creative activities for teachers. The response from teachers in need of more ideas led Sandra to offer yet another service: that of developing hands-on activities around any subject area needed, to be shared with educators.

In 1996 when I checked with Sandra, she was in the process of pursuing funding for a new "reachout program" she wanted to develop, one that would provide more support and networking for those in the child care field, as well as incentive towards recruitment of individuals interested in child care as a profession. She had also just begun a weekly radio program on child-related issues. When I touched base with her again in mid-2002, she confirmed she was still going strong: "KC is currently staffing and managing a child care center at a ski resort, managing a summer Kid's Camp for a City Parks and Recreation program, and providing a summer camp three mornings a week in the summer for a small private resort."

Sandra's only advertising is word-of-mouth and networking. "We have answered calls to do many interesting new things as they have come to us," she says. "A benefit race called us to assist with children's events for their fundraiser; we have filled children's gift bags with locally produced souvenirs; we have found baby-sitters, cribs, and videos for corporate executives; have helped with anniversary parties, reunions, and company picnics all over northern Michigan. As my children have grown older, I have been able to become more involved in our church again, and my ideas are even filtering over into this area. I've found that when you incorporate this way of thinking into your lifestyle, the creative thinking process and willingness to try new things becomes an enjoyable pattern, and you find yourself looking for new challenges and creating new systems wherever you go."

Many people have expressed interest in buying a book of Sandra's ideas, which as yet does not exist. "But I have kept a mailing list of their names," says Sandra, "and plan to start my writing career soon." There she goes . . . diversifying once again! As Sandra's story proves, the same four-step concept I've urged people to use when brainstorming for a new business idea works equally well when you're trying to expand an existing business:

1 Read, listen, and observe.

2 Find a need and fill it.

3 Do what you love.

4 Build on what you know and do best.

Keeping up with Consumers' Changing Interests

If your particular business does not lend itself to diversification into related products or services or simply has limited income potential to begin with, you may need to start two or three separate businesses to bring in the dollars you desire. (See this book's companion guide, *HOMEMADE MONEY: Starting Smart!* for hundreds of ideas for new businesses you might start.)

Deanna Ferber, eGlamKitty.com, deals in rare and out-of-print books and other collectibles, and also has a cosmetic company and a small crafting business. "When you juggle more than one business, there is so much timing involved," she says. "Organizing by each business's cycles, cash flow, time involved in buying inventory (or supplies to create inventory), marketing each by its cycles and needs. . . . it takes a bit of managing. But

Diversify and Multiply

I am involved in different businesses because it generates cash during changing markets—very similar to diversifying one's stock portfolio. My businesses are very different, and while they each prosper during the winter holidays, the other surges are unique to each field."

Above all, don't overlook the economy, which can be a fierce foe or a staunch ally, depending on your particular business. Certain products and services may be in greater demand when the economy fluctuates, or not needed at all. "During difficult economic times, it's important to diversify as much as possible," confirms Marc Choyt, CelticJewelry.com. "Then if one of your income streams doesn't come through, you'll have others that will continue to flow." Marcia Yudkin, Yudkin.com, has diversified by writing books, consulting, presenting seminars and producing and selling audiotapes and videos. "The odds that all of those enterprises will fall apart at once are very small," she says.

If you happen to be in manufacturing or sales, strive for diversification in your product line. If you make or sell only one type of product, your business might not survive if the bottom were suddenly to fall out of that product's market. Especially in product-related businesses, remember that consumer interests change constantly and you may have to keep changing your product line—possibly your marketing methods as well—to keep up with their fickle buying habits.

Take Leila Peltosaari, TikkaBooks.com, for example. For sixteen years, she has had an extremely successful publishing business selling sewing books of all kinds. But her market is changing and this is forcing her to take her business in new publishing directions. "I have ideas for many new sewing books, but it is getting difficult to find the people who sew," she says. "Fabric stores have closed all over the place and only a few big ones have survived. Sewing columns have been discontinued in many papers and there aren't many sewing publications around. Most of my friends who still have a sewing machine keep it hidden in their closets and hardly ever use it. Mothers are not teaching sewing to their kids anymore."

Leila's challenge now is to find new niche markets for books she can write. She accidentally found a good one the day she was helping her son prepare to live on his own. They sat down to calculate how his little budget would stretch for everything, including food. "What you need is a poor student's cookbook," Leila said, instantly realizing she had just discovered the idea for a new book. Now in its second edition, *College Cuisine* is selling well to mail order catalogs and grocery chains and Leila is currently trying to tap a premium market now. But what bothers her is that she read recently that people don't want to cook anymore. "They just want to eat out or take something home on their way from the store," she says. "So I must make money from my cookbook while I can. Now that people do not have time to sew and perhaps soon may have no time to cook either, I have to look ahead and get going on some new book ideas!"

Meanwhile, Leila is focusing on new publicity angles to get reviews of her books as she pats herself on the back for finally getting them into Costco stores and UNICEF boutiques. "It took a couple of years to crack these markets," she says, "but it was worth it because the sales potential here is gigantic."

• • •

Changing . . . changing . . .things are always changing and we must change, too, or be left behind. "Diversification doesn't necessarily mean loading up your business with a lot of diverse items and overwhelming your customers," says sculptor Robert Houghtaling, Frogart.com, "but you do have to realize that times, tastes, and trends change. If you don't pay attention, your products will be outdated and passé and you'll be wondering why you aren't selling. Then you will start blaming the economy or complaining that the products of others are selling, and yours aren't. Keep your ear to the ground and don't fall in love with your stuff and always be willing to change."

Smart Tip

Nothing stays the same. Remain flexible. Go with the flow.

Chapter 12:
Reviewing the Situation

Take any decision that's troubling you and frame it as a yes or no alternative. Yes, you should do it. No, you shouldn't. Make one alternative heads; the other tails. Then flip the coin. Your instant gut reaction to what the coin comes up with will reveal your intuitive call.

> —a smart tip from *Sixth Sense—A Whole-Brain Guide to Intuition, Hunches, Gut Feelings and Their Place in Your Everyday Life* by Lawrie Nadel (Prentice Hall)

The longer you're in business, the harder it will be to keep things "status quo." The day will come when you have to face reality and ask some hard questions that will force you to make tough decisions:

● Are you really happy doing what you're doing?

● Would you be happier if you made some changes? Reinvented yourself?

- Will you have to hire employees to keep growing?

- Will growth force you to move the business out of the home?

- Are you feeling stressed beyond your ability to cope? Totally burned out?

- Are complications in your personal life forcing a change you didn't anticipate?

- Is it time to throw in the towel?

This chapter explores situations related to the above questions and offers examples of how I and other homebased entrepreneurs have addressed them.

Thinking It Out Again

Whether you plan to keep your business small and controlled or are shooting for the moon—and ready to handle all the stress that comes your way—you need to sit back and carefully rethink your grand plan from time to time. You may have to make certain modifications—perhaps even decide if you are on the right track after all. Or, as Fagin sang in the Broadway musical, *Oliver*:

I'm reviewing the situation . . .
I think I'd better think it out again.

The harder you work on your business, the more likely you are to have ambivalent feelings like these, expressed by one of my readers: "I've run into so many problems that I wonder if it is as worthwhile as I once thought. I feel I'm at a crossroads. I can choose to continue to work extremely hard and possibly overcome my problems, or let my fears get the best of me and stop the ball from rolling any farther. One part of me wants to scream and say, 'Hang in there, your rewards are coming,' while the other part argues back, You're only deceiving yourself."

As a home business owner, you must expect feelings like these and learn to cope with them. *They come with the territory.* One day you can be on a terrific "high" because of some new achievement, a big order, or some publicity that boosts your business; the next day you may feel totally overwhelmed by the weight of too many responsibilities, too little time, and not enough money. An argument with a loved one or even a minor family problem often can seem like the last straw. At times like these, you may feel like a salmon swimming upstream. Although you feel compelled to keep going, you are no longer sure you can make it. What seemed like a little swim at first has now become a fierce struggle to survive. In retrospect, you may discover, like so many others before you, that beginning was easy. It's *continuing* that is hard.

Although each new upstream swim gets easier, the decisions to be made only get harder. To grow, or not to grow? To take a risk, or not to take a risk? To stay at home, or move the business out? Is this the right business after all? What's all this doing to the family?

I think I'd better think it out again.

After reviewing the situation, some people slow down while others throw in the towel. Some change direction completely while others forge ahead in the original direction, pushing all the harder. Driven by some force even they do not understand, they work with unceasing fervor, supremely confident that the success they dream of one day will be theirs.

Like salmon, some home business owners make it, some don't. There are no sure bets in this game, but one thing is certain: It *is* a game worth playing. Even those who fail as businesspeople will succeed as individuals. It takes gumption and guts to start and operate a business of any kind, and anyone who does it, even for a little while, is a winner in my book.

Evaluating the Need for Change

Extremely stressed after five tough years in business as a designer, writer, teacher, and speaker, Myrna Giesbrecht decided it was time to reassess her business and the direction in which she was going. "I spent about six months destressing myself while asking myself why I was designing patterns in the first place, was I having fun, was the profit worth the pain, and so on," she recalls. "When I realized that the direction I was heading in was not focused correctly, I began to change things. After applying similar questions to every area of my life, I eliminated many of the things that were causing me stress. In the end, I decided I wanted to use my skills to encourage other women to treasure their families, use their skills and gifts, and open businesses of their own, remembering always to keep things in balance. In the end it's relationships that count. I'm balancing wife, mother, money making, and art. You can have it all but not all at once!"

Today, Myrna enjoys all the work she does, particular its variety. "In the past twelve years, my business has evolved through many painful turns where at times I questioned my sanity," she says. "But I am finally at peace now with my goals and directions and increasingly satisfied with the payoffs. I've learned it is much easier to make decisions based on what you know you *don't* want to do than on what you think you *might* want to do."

Change Brings Its Own Rewards

Have you ever wondered how your customers or clients would respond if you suddenly made a dramatic change in your business? If so, you might be worrying for nothing. I've learned that change—always hard to make and painful to one degree or another—also brings its own rewards.

Early in 1994, I finally admitted to myself that I was burned out on publishing a 28-page quarterly periodical. With each passing calendar quarter, I had found it more difficult to find the 80-hour block of time I needed to create each new issue. After doing this four times a year for ten years, I simply couldn't bring myself to do it anymore. Rather than stop publishing at that point, however, I renamed my newsletter for the third time and went back to the 8-page format and bimonthly publishing schedule I originally began with in 1981. Although it now took me less time to create each issue, the deadlines were closer together and, by mid-1995, I felt burned out again. And now I had a contract for a new book whose deadline seemed too close for comfort.

Just before Christmas, an inner voice said, "If you're ever going to find time to write all those books you're dreaming about, you must cease publication of your newsletter *now*. On the spur of the moment, I picked up the phone and negotiated a deal with a fellow publisher to fulfill my subscriber obligations. My last issue in the Spring of 1996 marked the end of my fifteenth year of newsletter publishing, and when it was done,

I collapsed like a house of cards. As my chiropractor later joked, until then, tension was the only thing holding me together.

Of special concern to me was how my subscribers would react when I told them I was throwing in the towel. I expected a rash of refund requests and complaints, particularly from newer readers. Instead, I received nothing but letters of thanks for past efforts and congratulations for having the courage to make changes. One woman spoke of a problem common to many small business owners: "I find I have difficulty disappointing someone else, which means I do not say no very well. I need to practice that more. Reading your words is going to make it easier for me to make some changes." Another note that warmed my heart said, "When our leaders make difficult decisions and follow their hearts, it gives us all permission to do the same thing."

Within a month of getting this elephant off my back, my blood pressure dropped thirty points, proving to me the direct relationship between stress and ill health. Quitting, however, was both emotionally difficult and financially painful. Suddenly, after fifteen years of speaking to a devoted following of readers through my newsletter, I no longer had an active network or a soapbox from which to deliver information, opinions, and advice. The newsletter had generated about 30 percent of my income, so I also lost needed income I couldn't quickly replace. It took a year or so to get back on track financially, but making this change turned out to be the smartest move I'd made in years. Since then, I've had time to write new books and new editions of old books, time to learn new computer technology and Web site design, and time to explore a host of new income opportunities on the Web that may ultimately prove more profitable than anything else I've done to date. Thanks to the Internet, my home-business network is even larger than before, and I have my soapbox back in the form of an e-mail newsletter called *The Brabec Bulletin*. I'm still doing my favorite things (writing, publishing, and teaching), but now I'm doing them in a totally new way that is more satisfying and invigorating, yet less stressful.

The hard thing about making a big change in your business life is that you can't be sure you've done the right thing until after you've made the change. All you can do is *think it out again*. Carefully consider all your options, weigh the pros and cons of each, and, above all, *trust your instincts*.

Fish or Cut Bait

After suffering a case of burnout from the organizing work she had been doing for twelve years, Lisa Kanarek solved her problem by repositioning her business.

She changed her company name from Everything's Organized to Home Office Life (HomeOfficeLife.com), and began to focus exclusively on work-from-home topics, from setting up a home office to furnishing it to making a home office run more smoothly.

"I've learned that one's level of belief in a product or service will not always determine the success of one's business," she says. "You have to know when to cut your losses and move on. If your business no longer meets your financial expectations, your client list has dwindled or interest in your product has diminished, you'll have to follow the old axiom, 'fish or cut bait.' Resign yourself to the fact that you need to make major changes in your product or service, close your business and open another one, or work for someone in a similar business to gain additional knowledge and experience."

Managing Stress

Running a homebased business and trying to have a personal life, too, is stressful by itself. But when you are suddenly faced with having to make an important change in your life, your stress level is going to rise. Since the way you deal with stress has everything to do with how healthy and happy you will be in both your personal and home-business life, it's important to put some emphasis here on stress management strategies.

We all have stress, but not all stress is harmful. While *distress* (negative stress) can play havoc with your mind and body, *eustress* (positive stress) is energizing. For example, if you challenge yourself by setting a worthwhile goal and then work very hard to achieve that goal, this can be healthful stress—especially if you enjoy what you're doing. I agree with the stress experts who say the dangers of overwork and excessive striving are exaggerated, and only arouse unnecessary anxiety. Each of us gradually develops an instinctive feel that tells us whether we are running above or below the stress level that suits us best. A good antidote to the stress of ordinary life is first to decide if you are a racehorse or a turtle (do you want to run fast or slow?), then choose your own goals (don't let others impose their goals on you). Since nothing in life is as stressful as a feeling of purposelessness, you would be wise to practice "altruistic egoism"—which is looking out for yourself by being necessary to others.

Making a New Plan

The last edition of *Homemade Money* featured Judy's Maternity Rental business. When I contacted owner Judy Schramm for an update for this edition of the book, she told me how her whole business life had changed, and why.

"While I was running Judy's Maternity Rental, I kept having questions about running the business and I thought if I had an MBA I would have the answers. I didn't have time for an MBA so instead I signed up for a year-long course through AWED (American Women's Economic Development—since disbanded). Each month a group of female entrepreneurs would get together and hear a lecture about one aspect of running a business—accounting, sales, marketing, etc. At the end of the year, we had to present our business plans.

"It was a fantastic experience. The process of writing the plan made me look at all aspects of my business and I saw things I had never seen before. One of the things I realized was that the business wouldn't scale well. Although I had grown it to be the biggest business of its kind in the country, it would be very difficult to make the kind of money I wanted to make with it.

"It was a difficult decision to make, but I decided to get out of the business. I didn't do it immediately, though. I spent about a year examining my life, reading extensively and doing lots of analysis of what I was good at, what I loved to do, and what I could make money at. In the end I decided to go back to software and marketing, but in a different way than I had done before. So I started the business I have now, JMR Consulting. It took about a year to get off the ground and it has been very successful since then. In fact, I have been turning away clients for more than five years because I can't handle the volume. There are no slow periods. I have about five people working for me part time and I'm getting ready to expand more."

> ### Whoops!
> "You know you're pushing too hard when you put the raw corn on the table and microwave the salad," says one of my readers, adding that a friend of hers actually did this . . . the same day she dropped her bank deposit in the mailbox instead of at the bank.

Stress-Busting Strategies

Many have told me they find it a constant struggle to find ways to build in some downtime to relieve stress and just have a life. In fact, the more creative you are, the harder this will be to do. When I asked a group of creative people in my home-business network to tell me what they did to gear down or lower their stress level, many commented on the rewards of reconnecting with nature by walking, sitting outdoors, feeding the ducks on the lake, sitting on a pier, going to a park, or watching the birds—things that suggest our natural need to reconnect with God and everything He has made. General relaxation strategies used by others included swimming, aerobic exercise, gardening, a picnic, a bubble bath, or an enjoyable hobby activity in the evening.

Personally, nothing relaxes me more than an evening of good music as I cross-stitch another Bengal Tiger or work a jigsaw puzzle. I can also dump a lot of stress by burrowing into a good mystery by one of my favorite authors, but even here my subconscious mind must be on business because I keep finding great quotes to use in my writing. For example, in Lawrence Sanders's *Timothy's Game*, I found this little gem: "Always expect calamity. Then when a mere misfortune arrives, it's good news." (I know a lot of home-business owners who can relate to that one.)

Smart Tip

Lower your stress during the day by taking little five-minute breaks every half hour or so to stretch your muscles and rest your eyes. This is especially important if you do detail work or spend your day in front of a computer screen.

Many home-business owners say they never take a vacation because they don't have the time or money, but sometimes just getting away for two or three days can make all the difference. As Beverly Neuer Feldman once commented, "The great advantage of a hotel is that it's a refuge from a

Reviewing the Situation

home-based business." Harry and I used this strategy for years whenever we needed to get away from the demands of our mail order/publishing business. We'd find a comfortable motel in a nearby city with a good pool and hot tub and stay for three or four days, trying out new restaurants and exploring local museums or other spots of interest.

Some of my readers have told me that an exercise program has been very helpful to them in relieving stress. I keep telling myself I'm going to start an exercise program soon . . . as soon as I find time. I really hate to stop doing something I love—which is working—to do something I hate—which is exercising—and am I ever good at finding reasons not to exercise. Actually, I get a lot of exercise every day in my homebased business. The only trouble is it doesn't burn enough calories. I'm talking about:

Stretching to reach new heights . . .
Leaping to grasp opportunity. . .
Running to meet deadlines . . .
Hopping from one project to another . . .
Struggling with responsibility. . .
Beating the bushes for new business . . .
Jumping to conclusions . . .
Flying off the handle . . .
Pulling myself together, and
Pushing my luck!

Schedule a "Play Day"

Artist/designer Annie Lang has a great stress-busting suggestion. "You know stress is coming, so you need to prepare to cope with it in advance," she says. "I try to schedule at least one Play Day a month. This day can include a trip to the mall, lunch with a friend, or just taking a day to work on pet projects for myself. I post my Play Day Possibilities on a bulletin board near my work area in clear view where I'll notice it every day. I recently came off a strenuous three-week project. To help me get through it mentally, I could look at my posted possibilities and choose my reward when the project was completed."
—a tip from *Make It Profitable* by Barbara Brabec (M. Evans)

Fighting Burnout

"Burnout," says one stress expert, is the "total depletion of one's physical and mental resources, caused either by trying to reach unattainable goals, or as a result of things that get in your way over which you have no control."

Symptoms of burnout include irritability, insomnia, mental or physical exhaustion, and feelings of inadequacy or hopelessness. In the home-business community, burnout can occur in times both good and bad. Having more business than one can handle can be as stressful as too little business to pay the bills. What finally puts many entrepreneurs over the edge is one personal problem too many on top of the normal stress of doing business. An illness or disability may slow or stop business altogether, while a death in the family, a divorce, or some other family situation will put an individual on overload.

Because home-business beginners often lack clear-cut goals, or are not monitoring their progress in the right way, they begin to feel their expectations are not being met and, before long, they may begin to feel like a failure. In addition, many people receive absolutely no positive feedback from family or friends, and one cannot long work in such a vacuum without a mental or emotional collapse.

"People who work at home successfully learn to crack their own whips and to pat their own backs, sometimes all in one day," said one entrepreneur in an interview. She's right. As a self-employed individual, you may be the only person from whom you can draw the strength you need on any given day, and you may also be the only one around who's going to pat you on the back, and say "Well done!"

Burnout affects men and women alike, but if my reader mail is any indication, more women than men working at home suffer its consequences. If any one theme runs rampant through the mail I receive from mothers who run businesses at home, it's guilt. "Guilt is an easy trap, especially for the self-employed," says a psychology professor in an article I read. "It is anger turned inward; it produces a growing sense of failure, dwindling self-esteem, and a gnawing questioning of our ability."

In reaching for their dreams, most women have to sacrifice something, whether it's time with their family or attention to homemaking details such as housecleaning, laundry, meal planning, and grocery shopping. While they're busily succeeding in business, they secretly begin to see themselves as failures in other areas of life, simply because they can't figure out how to do it all, like some kind of superwoman.

If such women do not take steps to control the way they are spending their lives—trying to mix too many activities at once—they may eventually suffer burnout symptoms. Sometimes the cure is as simple as taking a vacation. Other times, they must cease something altogether in order to avoid serious health problems or destructive influences on their personal life. Sometimes it's the marriage, rather than the business, that ends up on the chopping block.

Being a superwoman was never one of my goals, and being perfect isn't important either. *Doing the best job I can under the circumstances is what matters most to me.* I think that if more women would look at their lives from this viewpoint, there would be less guilt and lower blood pressure readings all around.

The psychologist I mentioned earlier says it's dangerous for anyone to compare himself or herself to others, because everyone brings to a career or business a unique set of personality variables, family, financial and health factors—not to mention a differing ability to cope with stress. Therefore, it's impossible for one person to tell another how to successfully balance his or her life. Each of us must learn to do this ourselves—the hard way—trying first one strategy, then another, until we find one that we and our loved ones can live with.

Moving the Business out of the Home

The challenge for most home-business owners is how to constantly increase business income and profits while keeping the volume of work at a level that can be handled alone, by family members, or perhaps outside contractors. That's precisely why some business owners—particularly mothers who work at home because they want to be there for their family—set a limit on the number of hours they will work and the level of income they wish to make. When they reach their income goal, they simply quit striving for more because to grow would only create problems they don't want to face. Many others, however—particularly those individuals who originally entered the home-business field with total self-employment in mind—look at their growing business and decide to keep growing, even if it means hiring employees. But this is a disturbing thought to many.

"Small business owners know their trade, but few of them are ready to take on the responsibility of leading and developing people," notes one business owner. "The hardest part of growth is letting go, delegating responsibilities," groans another. "You get so used to doing it all yourself for so long, and then when you have to let someone else do it, it's hard."

The trouble with hiring employees is that it usually necessitates moving the business outside the home. Zoning laws in most areas limit employees to family members only or just one outside employee, but even when zoning laws don't interfere, limited space in one's home often forces a move. "Now that the business has begun to grow so quickly, I'm feeling overwhelmed about how much space it occupies," says one homebased entrepreneur. "There's a delicate line as to when it's ideal to be home and when it's time to move out."

After several years of working at home, Susan Krei's rubber stamp business, WoodCellarGraphics.com, suddenly took an upwards turn. "My husband had to quit his job and join me to keep up with all the orders," Susan told me. "We continued at home for another year and just about lost our minds. We continued to grow and grow, and pretty soon we had the house full, and also a two-car garage. We were overflowing the space we had with nowhere to turn. We needed to hire help, but had nowhere to have them work. After muddling our way through the summer months with our kids helping us fill orders, we made the decision to move our business into a shop/warehouse.

With three employees and a completely organized business, Susan could finally heave a sigh of relief. "What a boost for the old self-esteem—to create something, work your buns off for it, and then see it succeed," she says. "There's nothing better!"

Bursting at the Seams

It was the great success of their Web site, CelticJewelry.com, that finally forced Marc Choyt and his wife, Helen Chantler, to move. "Five years into our business, we were employing eight people and sales were over half a million dollars—way too big to be working out of our house," he says. "Sales from the Web site alone were approaching $200,000 a year by the end of 2002."

Reviewing the Situation

This business—the sale of designer Celtic jewelry—was begun by Helen in a 400-square-ft. studio in the home. Initially, she was assisted by one production person who worked in her own home. As the business grew, the studio space was turned into an office and the business was moved into a rental apartment in the back of their house that had previously been rented to someone else. A temporary heated shed in the back housed additional employees.

"We kept a low profile to avoid problems with zoning officials," says Marc. "Although we lived off a long hidden driveway and didn't have a sign, people kept tracking us down after having seen our product on the Internet. We finally bought a commercial building to house our growing business. It had to be completely gutted and rebuilt in order to create an efficient space, and this was when we learned there is a law in New Mexico that says anyone who even lifts a paint brush must have a general contractor supervising the job. Other state laws favoring contractors automatically increase the costs of this kind of work by about 30 percent.

"Going public has been a boon to the business, of course," Marc continues. "We're growing at over 100 percent so far this year, and getting walk-ins into our retail showroom nearly every day. I think having a public space helps the imagery of a business. People respond to what's out there on the airwaves, and if you're legit, they feel it on an unconscious level and react more positively. In spite of all the difficulties we had in making this move, I'm glad we did it."

Opening a Shop on the Highway

After selling their soaps in a homebased shop for two years, Tim Tyndall and wife Karen Wylie took the leap to opening their own retail shop along the Blue Ridge Parkway. "What a difference a few miles makes!" Karen exclaims. "It took only ten days to see the difference between having a shop in your home versus a retail shop separate from your production area. Our new shop is right off Milepost 334 in Little Switzerland, North Carolina, and our home shop/production area/showroom is located six tenths of a mile off Milepost 331 in Spruce Pine."

With the help of three part-time employees leased through Manpower, Tim and Karen run both shops—Tim up on the highway, Karen managing production at home. They currently produce about 60,000 bars of soap a year, but have recently streamlined production to the point where they can now make up to 2,500 bars a day, "thanks to my scientist-husband who knows the tricks of the trade," quips Karen. "Knowing how different oils interact with certain ingredients is our trade secret and the thing that makes mass production and competitive pricing possible."

Although the home shop draws fewer visitors, Karen says they are serious customers who either love handmade soap or have a specific skin need for which they are seeking help. "Others come out of curiosity to see how we make soap, some because they remember making lye soap with their grandmother. Since we're off the main road, such visitors have to seek us out by obtaining a rack card or getting directions, and the dollars spent once they get here are about three times that of the average customer in Little Switzerland. Visitors who come to the home shop also require a different level of service in that they are looking for more personal attention, want more information about our craft, and also stay longer with us—about 30 to 45 minutes."

The new Parkway shop is benefitting from the large number of Parkway travelers who tour the Blue Ridge and get off the Little Switzerland exit looking for meals, something to do, or someplace to stay. "But we get a much a different kind of customer there," says Karen. "They're the kind who stumble upon us and may come in, as compared to customers who are specifically looking for a craftsperson or handmade crafts, or soap in particular. Our retail shop customers buy less than our home shop customers, but the sheer volume of people and sales makes up for that."

Moving in New Directions

Someone once observed that getting on the wrong streetcar didn't mean you had to stay on to the end of the line. A year after she had separated from her husband, a woman who prefers anonymity spoke of how this move had impacted both her personal and home-business life. Her spouse had played an integral role in the writing/publishing business she ran out of her home, so it was necessary that both of them retain a piece of the business. But this meant she had to assume her maiden name and begin operation under a different business name, which cost her a lot of marketing momentum.

"My husband continues with our original company while I am trying to develop a second company I started earlier," she told me. "This is splitting the energy, efforts, income, and momentum in so many ways. Right now, things are slow as I am torn in so many directions. Recuperating from this kind of lifestyle change is difficult at any age—emotionally, physically, and financially—but it is especially difficult when you're past fifty. At this point, I am trying to understand and comprehend that this is now my life and I can do anything I want (if only I knew what it was). Increasingly, I am learning to think of my own needs, which is exciting and wonderfully energizing. I am growing and changing dramatically, learning finally to like myself as I am and what a feeling that is! I had to leave to grow up in so many ways. I can even enjoy the pain of sadness, regrets, anger, bitterness, and self-pity since I recognize it as an essential part of growing up. Sometimes I sit in wonder at the courage and reckless sense of adventure it took for me to actually do what I had contemplated for so long. I hope to be like a phoenix and rise again."

Cutting Back, Closing Down

Pat and Ed Endicott were partners in their incorporated crafts business and things were going just fine until Ed had a stroke that completely disabled him, leaving Pat not only with all the business responsibilities but heavy caregiving responsibilities. I heard from her again after she had taken a job.

"For the past eight years, there has been little or no income," she said. "We kept the corporation going because it was paying Ed's high medical expenses, but with no income, we couldn't pay salaries, and soon found ourselves in a very uncomfortable tax position. After returning from my last wholesale market show, I finally admitted things had to change. I have tried so hard for the past eight years to make the business support us, but Ed's medicines are high, and all the out-of-pocket expenses are killing us. So I decided to downsize the business to where it was eight years ago, servicing my existing accounts and letting my sales rep go. No more shows. No more have-to-get-new-items-ready deadlines. I've felt so much better since I made this decision! I do believe this was meant to be and the Lord had a lot to do with it. If only we could trust Him more, we would be much better off."

Interestingly, Pat's new job is related to textiles, the field in which she has been involved as a self-employed individual. "I'm now a Textile Specialist for Consumer Testing Labs, which does all the garment testings for Wal-Mart," she says. "I didn't think there was such a position, but it's right up my alley. The pay is very good, there are many perks, and I'll be saving bundles on medical insurance even as I build my social security account. Once I get my feet wet in the corporate world, I may decide to close shop completely."

When You Get Too Old to Work

Many people in their sixties and seventies who are still working at their businesses are certainly thinking about the day when they'll have to close up shop. Such people may continue to work not only because they like the extra income, but because life without some kind of meaningful work would simply be unimaginable. As a writer, I fall into that category, and if I struck oil tomorrow and never needed another dime of income, I'd have to keep writing because writing is as essential to me as eating or sleeping. But that doesn't mean I plan to write about business for the rest of my life.

As seventy-year-old Yvonne Conway (mobile beauty services) puts it, "My work and my clients give me a rewarding purpose in life. The majority of my clients are elderly (some as old as 102), and several have told me I can't retire until they die. I like making people feel good about themselves, but when the time comes to quit, I will be challenged to find something else for the rest of my life just like I did at fifty when an earlier business died. I believe that if we are accountable, if we have integrity and self-discipline, and if we can see our life as an adventure, it will be."

Etiquette for Going out of Business

"Any damn fool can start a love affair, but ending one successfully takes a real genius," said George Bernard Shaw. That applies to starting and ending a business, too.

As one who may be on the brink of success with many exciting years of good business ahead, it may seem ridiculous to think now about how you're going to get out of the business you're currently working so hard to build. But take it from one who's been there: it's a kind of insurance to know where the exit is. Remember my business motto: "Hope for the best . . . prepare for the worst . . . and always leave yourself an escape route."

There will always be new people ready to jump on the home-business bandwagon, but many who merely anticipate an exciting ride will get off quickly when they learn they have to do the driving and it isn't as easy as they thought. You may have heard the joke about the pig and the chicken who were discussing the fact that they're the most popular items on the breakfast table. "Yeah," says the pig. "But you're only *involved* in breakfast. Me? I'm *committed*." The day may come when you may find yourself asking if you're really committed to the idea of business, or just taking an interesting side trip on the road of life.

Home businesses come and home businesses go. I once surveyed a group of my expired subscribers to see why they had let their subscriptions lapse. Most said they simply weren't in business any longer. Some readers told me they had found it necessary to take outside jobs. "My homebased business could not provide the money that working for others can," said one. "The economy of our small town is in considerable distress," said another, "and I must apply to the basic needs." Still others said their activities were more hobby than business. A mother who recently had her third child said the children had "cramped her style for home business." A widow said she now had other interests to occupy her remaining years.

Being able to make yourself work when you'd rather not is, in my opinion, a determining factor in whether you will succeed as a self-employed individual. It is no easy job to stay motivated when you are tired from overwork, challenged by marketing problems, concerned about your cash-flow situation, or pressured because of time restraints or family responsibilities. During those fifteen years when I was publishing a print newsletter, the hardest time of the year for me was December. While other women were baking cookies, decorating their homes and trees for Christmas, and shopping for gifts, I was always struggling to get my January newsletter to the printer before the holiday.

I think the second law of thermodynamics applies to homebased business owners at year's end. It holds that "all organized systems tend to slide slowly into chaos and disorder, while energy tends to run down, and the Universe heads into darkness." (Would you believe I found this tidbit in a John MacDonald novel?)

Tips for Publishers and Mail Order Sellers

A sole proprietorship is a double-edged sword in that one usually has little money with which to start, and even less if the business must cease because of lack of profit. Two kinds of businesses suffer most: publishing and mail order. That's because the mail never stops coming, especially if you've done a good job with your advertising and publicity. People will continue to send you money for your products and publications for years after you've ceased business. There will also be letters of inquiry from people who still want your brochure, catalog, or whatever else you may have been advertising. You have a professional obligation to respond in some way.

Some people who want to escape a business and its obligations will simply move or close their post office box without leaving a forwarding address. This, at least, will get the mail returned to senders. It's also the coward's way out, and it doesn't work if you've been using your street address as your business address. If you have nothing else to sell, and can't afford to respond to your mail, order a rubber stamp that says, "Refused/Out of Business—Return to Sender." You will incur no extra postage costs, and interested people who send you money will get their checks back or know why you aren't sending the information they requested.

Don't be like the publisher who was listed in an earlier edition of this book and continued to accept checks for sample issues of his periodical long after it had ceased publication. When a reader brought this situation to my attention, I contacted the publisher, who told me, "Don't worry, we're not cashing the checks. Just tell people to look at their bank statement." How unprofessional! Besides, it's not my job to tell people that some of the businesses I've publicized in earlier editions of my book or periodical are no longer in business.

If you should ever find yourself on the verge of bankruptcy, or just ready to quit, try to exit gracefully, professionally. Remember, you might want to start a new business someday, and if you ruin your reputation the first time around, few will give you a second chance.

Smart Tip

In closing down a business, look for other businesses like yours who might be able to fulfill your orders or inquiries with substitute products or publications. If you have a PR list you've promoted to in the past, send a news release stating you're closing the business and no longer want publicity.

Looking on the Bright Side

Dreams die hard for some. For others, giving up a home business is easy when boredom sets in or major lifestyle changes necessitate the ending of a business. Every year, a certain number of home-business owners also disband their business simply to preserve their sanity or to keep peace in the family. If and when your business does cease, do not for a minute let yourself feel that you have failed. What you will have learned from your entrepreneurial experience will benefit you for the rest of your life, in ways you cannot yet imagine.

As I've documented in other books, ex-home-business owners often find that their years of experience as a self-employed individual have beautifully positioned them for other work that proves even more profitable and interesting to them than their business. Darlene Graczyk, whose Errands and More business was featured in the last edition of *Homemade Money*, had to close her business when she broke her leg. After months of surgeries and therapy, she knew she could never "run" a business again. Needing a desk job, she went back to work for State Farm Insurance Company where she had previously worked for twenty years. Not long afterwards, Darlene's husband died.

"I've learned that when a door slams shut, a window opens," she says. "Now when I look back at my broken leg, I see it as a gift from God because it got me back to my State Farm 'family' and gave me the benefits and financial security that are now a necessity. I've learned that when your life changes, you have to change with it whether you choose to or not. I've also learned to enjoy every day for what it offers and to 'not sweat the small stuff.'"

Interesting to me was the fact that Darlene originally started her home business because she was burned out after twenty years as a graphic designer for State Farm. But after seven years away from it, she found she was ready to go back to the company in a different capacity and now says she has a dream job that's perfect for her at this stage of life.

As the stories in this chapter prove, nothing stays the same, and as things and circumstances in our personal life or business change, we must be prepared to change in response to them. It's a smart tip at any stage of life: Remain flexible. Go with the flow.

Found by Barbara:

A New Source of Strength

When my mother—my greatest motivator—died in mid-1992, I felt as though a part of me had died, too. The following summer, I learned I had breast cancer. Caught early, I took it in stride, but the experience (which I viewed as a wake-up call from God) took a lot out of me. I made some changes to reduce my business stress, but my spirits continued to sag until the fall of 1994 when I finally admitted for the first time in my life that I lacked confidence and a sense of direction. I was tired, restless, insecure, and totally burned out, a woman whose previous ambition and spirit had fled.

What do you do when you realize you've used the last ounce of your personal strength resources and don't know how to replenish them? In discussing this with a good friend, she said, "Have you tried praying? To get help, you must *ask* for it."

In thinking about this, I saw that I had always taken great pride in the fact that I could "do it myself." I had always been so self-sufficient that I never asked anyone for help, even when I needed it. Certainly I'd never thought of asking God for help for He was surely too busy with the important things of the world to be concerned about my little problems.

One night, however, unable to sleep because of all my cares and worries, I got down on my knees and ardently prayed for the first time in thirty years. I said, "Lord, I really need some help here!" Then I told Him in detail what was bothering me and asked Him to give me strength, courage, and guidance.

My prayer was answered the next night in a way that to me was both miraculous and glorious. Since this is a business book, I'll spare you the details, but you can find them on my personal Web site if you're interested. I'll say this, however: my whole life began to change in exciting ways as soon as I plugged myself into God's power.

It's now clear to me that we can go a long way under our own steam and much farther when others are behind us offering motivational support and encouragement. But sooner or later, with or without emotional and motivational support, we're all going to run out of ourselves someday. The problem today is that there are so many books and so many humanists out there saying, "You can do it! All you have to do is believe in yourself."

As many before me have learned, that's not enough. There is a limit to the number of times you can pull yourself up by the bootstraps. Unless you plug into a source of power greater than yourself, one day you may discover, as I did, that without God, you're as dead and useless as a lightbulb without electricity.

So remember to thank God for the special skills, talents, and abilities He has given you, and don't hesitate to lean on the LORD when you need help or encouragement in either your personal or home-business life. From experience I have learned that if we will simply put our faith in God and give Him an opportunity to work in our lives, He will lead us in surprising new directions and reveal wondrous things we never could have discovered on our own. As the Bible confirms, "Commit to the LORD whatever you do, and your plans will succeed" (Proverbs 16:3 NIV).

• • •

P.S. Drop by my Web site at **www.BarbaraBrabec.com** to sign up for my free newsletter and get additional information and motivational support as you continue to work to make your present business—or any new endeavors you may start in the future—more efficient, more satisfying, and more profitable! If this book has been helpful to you, I'd love to hear from you by e-mail at Barbara@BarbaraBrabec.com.

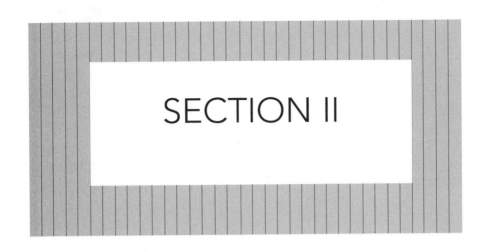

SECTION II

Some of the material in this section is in such "professional service" categories as legalities, taxes, and accounting. While this information has been carefully researched and is accurate to the best of the author's knowledge as this book goes to press, it is not the business of either the author or publisher to render such professional services. Readers are therefore asked to exercise normal good judgment in determining when the services of a lawyer or other professional would be appropriate to their needs.

An A-to-Z "Crash Course" in Home-Business Management

This section of the book offers answers to hundreds of questions related to home-business management. It incorporates tax, legal, and financial information from several experts in my network along with the shared experiences of my readers and lessons I've learned from a lifetime of self-employment. In particular, I would like to thank the following individuals for their help in double-checking the accuracy of my information on accounting, taxes, copyrights and trademarks:

● Bernard Kamoroff is a CPA and the author of *Small-Time Operator— How to Start Your Own Business, Keep Your Books, Pay Your Taxes, and Stay Out of Trouble* (Bell Springs Pub.). This small business classic is now in its 27th edition with over 640,000 copies in print. Kamoroff's publishing company, Bell Springs Publishing, is located in Willits, California, and is on the Web at **www.BellSprings.com**.

● Mary Helen Sears has been in private law practice in Washington, D.C., since 1961. The M. H. Sears Law Firm is mainly devoted to patents, copyrights, trademarks, and related matters.

Note: Information in this section is presented alphabetically in logical topic categories, but since different aspects of some of these topics are also discussed in the text, check the index to make sure you have all the information needed on any given subject.

Table of Contents

Table of Contents

Accountant

(See also *Business Records; Cottage Industries; Employees, Family; Employees, Nonfamily; Independent Contractors; Partnership Pitfalls*)

It has been humorously said that an accountant is someone who solves a problem you didn't know you had in a way you don't understand. Many business novices hire accountants when they actually need bookkeepers. Although accountants know how to do bookkeeping, they are not book-keepers. Their primary function is to analyze your books and prepare tax returns based on the figures in them. In the process, however, they often perform other important jobs as well. In truth, a good accountant can be something of a management consultant for you, helping you to understand your total financial picture and make wise decisions in all areas of your business.

For instance, an accountant or CPA can give you advice on whether or not to purchase equipment, hire employees versus independent contractors, take on a partner, or incorporate your business. If you need a business loan, an accountant can prepare the necessary financial reports in a way that will show your business in the most favorable light. He or she can also help you plan strategic financial moves that will save or defer taxes each year, and represent you should the IRS audit your return. And when you do reach the point of hiring employees, even if it's just your spouse or children, an accountant will take the hassle out of all those aggravating government tax forms and quarterly reports and perhaps save you tax dollars as well. (See "Employees, Family" in this section.)

Enrolled Agents

When selecting a professional to help you with your tax return, consider the services of an enrolled agent. Generally, their fees are higher than those of a tax preparer (not recommended for business owners), but less than those of a CPA. Enrolled agents are approved by the IRS to represent taxpayers before the IRS, and such agents have completed a comprehensive IRS-administered examination in federal taxation and related subjects. To find an enrolled agent near you, call the National Association of Enrolled Agents, 1-800-424-4339; **www.NAEA.org**. (On the Web site, you'll find answers to frequently asked questions [FAQs] and live chats where taxpayers can get questions answered on the spot.)

Do You Have the Right Legal Form of Business? A good accountant will always help you save tax dollars, either through better documentation of expenses or through use of different financial strategies. Bill and Camille Ronay own A Step Ahead, Ltd., a publishing company in Buckhead, Georgia. "Our company has been incorporated since 1984," says Bill. "Pleading ignorance in the beginning, Camille and I chose to be incorporated because neither a Sole Proprietorship nor a Partnership fit our needs at that time. In our first meeting with a new CPA, he immediately asked why we were paying taxes twice, and suggested that a Sub-Chapter S Corporation was the most practical solution for us. We had to change our fiscal year calculations and a couple extra monthly accounting procedures, but the bottom line was that we no longer were paying *two taxes*—taxes on income from the corporation and then the actual taxes on the corporation itself.

"Make sure your CPA or tax adviser is aware of the variables for your particular tax needs," Bill advises. "If not, shop around until you find one who does understand them." I would add that, when selecting an accountant or CPA, avoid those professionals who handle corporate work only. You want someone who understands *small business*. (Ask for references of other home-based entrepreneurs served by the firm.)

Attorney/Lawyer

(See also *Contracts; Intellectual Property, Protection of; Trademarks*)

In shopping for a lawyer, ask for recommendations from business acquaintances or other professionals you know and whose advice you trust. When you think you've found an affordable attorney with some experience in business law, ask if a free initial consultation is offered. In discussing fees, ask if a retainer arrangement is available. Many attorneys will agree to meet with a client a couple of times a year, answer quick questions on the telephone throughout the year, and even throw in the preparation of a short legal document.

Note: Artists and craftspeople who need advice, but cannot afford it, should contact Volunteer Lawyers for the Arts at (212) 319-ARTS, ext. 1; **www.vlany.org**. This organization provides free legal assistance to artists and arts organizations in all creative fields and has branches in many states.

Smart Tip

Time is money in a lawyer's office, so you'll save a lot of both if you go prepared. First check available legal self-help guides to gain a better understanding of your situation or problem. Then, in the shortest time possible, you'll be able to clearly explain it to your lawyer and get answers you couldn't find on your own.

Prepaid Legal Services

If you think you're going to need the services of a lawyer from time to time in your business, the most affordable way to go is to sign up for a prepaid legal services plan. Search the Internet for such companies, or join a small business organization (see "Other Resources") that offers its members prepaid legal services as part of its membership package. Depending on whether you select a family plan or business plan, annual cost may run between $200 and $600 a year. The most affordable plans are family packages that generally include a review of legal documents, unlimited calls about personal or business matters, and either a letter or phone call per topic discussed.

Bad Checks

(See also *Collection Techniques*)

Checks may bounce because of nonsufficient funds (NSF), a closed account, or no account (evidence of fraud). Often, NSF checks are caused by people's inability to balance a checkbook. When this happens, their embarrassment causes them to quickly make good on the check. In more than thirty years of doing business by mail, I never had more than two or three bad checks a year, and all of them were for very small amounts. Bunny DeLorie, owner of Fe Fi Faux Finish, confirms that most mail order shoppers are honest people. "Only twice in eight years have I had to collect on bad checks for mail order products," she says. "Each time I gave the bad-check writer four days to send me a money order or I said I would turn them over to my local sheriff's bad check department. Both times I received the money order promptly."

Most checks returned because of insufficient funds in an account will clear the second time you deposit them. A check can be redeposited only once, however, so if it's for a large amount, you may want to telephone the person who wrote it to make sure there will be sufficient funds to cover it the second time around. If the check bounces again, you have a couple of options. For a small fee, your bank will try to collect it for you. Normally, the bank sends the bounced check back to the originating bank with instructions to pay you as soon as funds have been deposited to the account. However, if a deposit isn't made during this holding period—usually a month—you're out of luck. Your next option is to send a *certified letter* notifying the recipient that you intend to put the matter into the hands of an attorney if payment has not been received within the time you specify. (You may not have an attorney, but the recipient of your letter won't know this. A well-typed letter on good stationery will add considerable strength to your demand for payment.)

Smart Tip

Check to see if your state has a "Bad Check Law." In my state of Illinois, for example, any person who writes an NSF check can be sued in small claims court for three times the amount of the check plus the face value of the check. Being able to quote your state's law to a delinquent account will add weight to your demands for payment.

Always hang onto a bad check as proof of one's indebtedness to you. If the bad check is from an out-of-state individual, your police department may be able to work with the police in your customer's city to get action. They can't actually collect the money, but since it's a crime to write a bad check, police intervention might give your bad check writer a good scare.

To prevent bad check problems in the first place, learn how to spot bad checks and establish guidelines for the kind of identification you will require when accepting a check. (This topic is discussed at greater length in *HOME-MADE MONEY: Starting Smart!*) If you believe there has been intent to defraud, and the check is for a substantial amount, you may wish to send a copy of the returned check, along with notes about your efforts to collect the money, to the attorney general's office in your state. You can find a listing of all the attorney generals at: **www.co.eaton.mi.us/ecpa/proslist.htm**

Checks and Balances. Network marketer Martha Oskvig, in business for more than thirty years, has had few bad check problems, perhaps because she has certain guidelines for accepting checks. "I accept checks from local banks in the first year with a customer," she says, "but I verify the account if the customer is new and the amount exceeds $75. I accept checks from other areas after I've known the mail order client at least a year. I deposit all checks the same day they are received. In some situations with my direct-sales businesses, I have scheduled product deliveries and open-house events on the afternoon, evening, or day after a group of customers receive their paychecks."

Bar Codes

A bar code, or UPC (Universal Product Code), is a set of numbers that identifies a company and a product it sells. The first six digits (assigned by the Uniform Code Council) identify the company, while the next five digits (assigned by the manufacturer) indicate the product. A last "check digit" provides additional identity information. Bar codes can be computer-generated through special software programs readily available on the Web. For more information on such software, as well as a primer on bar codes, go to **www.barcodehq.com/primer.html**.

Bar coding is not necessary if you are selling handmade products to gift and craft shops, but it may be required on products wholesaled to large retailers, chain stores, bookstores, and other outlets who use a computerized inventory system. You're talking "expense" here, however, as the *minimum* one-time UPC registration is currently $750. The only way to get the exact fee, however, is to complete a UPC registration form. These forms are available from the UCC's Operations Center in Dayton, Ohio at (937) 435-3870 or on their Web site at **www.UC-Council.org**. Once you've indicated your annual sales revenue and the numbering capabilities you need, you will be given a quote. (Filling out a registration form does not obligate you to any expense unless you agree to pay the fee you've been quoted.)

Bartering

If you trade services or products for personal use, the IRS code requires that the value of that trade be declared as taxable income. Check with an accountant if you have questions about this.

The Benefits of Bartering. "Barter exchanges have come a long way," says Patricia Kutza, who uses barter exchanges on the Internet to publicize her products (Whatknot™ neckwear, pressed flower cards, pressed flower prints) and services (press release and online media kit creation). She also gets rid of unwanted inventory this way. "The old mode of barter required one-to-one exchanges—the person whose goods or services you wanted needed to want your goods or services in return," she explains. "Now the mode is many-to-many, and anyone can trade with anyone else in their exchange (which is typically a network of exchanges) so long as they have the 'barter' or trade dollars (vernacular) to do so."

Examples of Patricia's barter exchanges include hot air balloon rides, restaurant certificates, condo rentals at Lake Tahoe, perfume, prepaid phone cards, and massages. "A barter exchange is only as good as its members' offerings," she says. "Sometime you encounter 'dilution,' meaning that members overcharge for their services. I shun these members' offerings just as I would any overpriced goods or services. Barter needs to be evaluated just like any other item in a person's business strategy. Study the return on investment (since bartering has transaction and membership costs) and weigh the constraints and benefits to your overall business plan."

(To find barter exchanges on the Internet, type these words into your browser's search engine.)

Better Business Bureau

You can give your business added credibility by registering it with your local Better Business Bureau. (*Registration* is not the same as *membership*, which is neither important nor practical for the average homebased business.) Although the BBB will not offer to register your business (because they want you as a paying member), an official of the BBB told me that, as long as you have a license for your business, they will be happy to register your company *upon request*. All that's involved is the completion of a simple questionnaire, to which you may wish to attach copies of customer testimonials, your promotional literature, and any favorable publicity you've received. Then, if people should inquire about you, the BBB can say, "Yes, they're registered; we've had no complaints about them." A good reference, indeed. However, be advised that there are *no* tangible benefits to be derived from registration with your local BBB, and even members receive only a plaque for their office wall and occasional written reports on companies they might want to deal with.

In fact, the BBB seems paranoid about anyone even *mentioning* its name, and *no one* can legally say, to promote their business or give it added credibility, that they are a member, or even registered. The BBB symbol and name are registered trademarks owned solely by the Council of Better Business Bureaus, Inc., and no one can legally use its name in promotional or printed materials. To quote the BBB, they "cannot lend credibility to an individual firm as they neither recommend nor deprecate any product, service, or company."

So, although customers who call the BBB for information about your business may *think* you more credible by the mere fact that you are registered, the BBB denies that such registration adds to your credibility. Although a consumer may get a favorable reply about you from the BBB (meaning no complaints on file), the BBB denies that this is any kind of "reference" or "recommendation." Therefore, even if home-business owners would be accepted for membership, they would derive questionable benefits at best. But since it costs nothing to *register* with your local BBB, and may result in favorable information being passed on to customers in your area, do consider this action. *Just don't tell anyone you've done it.*

BBBonline Reliability Program Seal

Members of the Better Business Bureau who have been in business for at least one year may apply for the BBBonline Reliability Program Seal, which can be displayed on a Web site to assure consumers of a company's reliability. More information will be found at **www.BBBonline.org**. This site has a search area where you can type in the name of a company or other information you may have about it, and turn up any bad reports people may have filed on this site. You are also encouraged to file your own scam reports here.

Business Expenses, Tax Deductible

(See *Business Deductions Checklist for Home-Business Owners* below; *see also Business Records; Home Office Deduction*)

Business Deductions Checklist for Home-Business Owners

Generally speaking, all money spent in connection with the operation of your business is tax deductible. Following is a checklist of business deductions that may be applicable to your homebased business. Note that these deductions are *in addition* to the other tax deductions listed under Home Office Deduction. Since tax laws are constantly changing, always verify the legality of a questionable business deduction with your accountant or other tax authority.

____ Accounting or bookkeeping services
____ Advertising and promotional expenses
____ Bad debts/bounced checks[1]
____ Bank charges
____ Books and periodicals (business related)
____ Briefcase or samples case
____ Business development expenses[2]
____ Business gifts
____ Business seminars
____ Christmas cards (for business associates)
____ Cleaning services (office, business, uniforms, equipment)

Business Deductions Checklist

____ Collection agency fees

____ Computer software

____ Consulting fees

____ Conventions and trade show expense

____ Copyright fees[6]

____ Delivery charges

____ Donations

____ Dues/membership fees, professional

____ Educational expense[7]

____ Entertainment expenses[3]

____ Equipment lease/rental costs

____ Equipment purchases[2]

____ Freight and shipping charges

____ Insurance premiums[8]

____ Interest on business loans or late tax payments

____ IRA or Keogh account deposits[4]

____ Labor costs (independent contractors)

____ Legal and professional fees[2]

____ Licenses and permits

____ Mail list development/maintenance

____ Maintenance contracts (office equipment) and repairs

____ Office supplies

____ Postage

____ Product displays, exhibiting expenses

____ Professional services (artists, designers, copywriters, Web services, etc.)

____ Refunds to customers

____ Research and development (R&D) expense[2]

____ Safe deposit box[9]

____ Sales commissions

____ Sales and use tax

____ Start-up/organizational expenses[2]

____ Stationery and printing

____ Subscriptions to business periodicals

____ Supplies and materials

____ Tax preparation fees

____ Telephone, fax, modem expense

____ Tools of your trade

____ Trademark expenses[6]

___ Travel expenses[5]
___ Uniforms or special costumes used only in trade or profession
___ Union dues (related to homebased business or profession)
___ Wages to employees, including those paid to spouse or children

Footnotes

1 If you use the accrual method to report income, you are entitled to a deduction for bad debts (bounced checks and other uncollectible accounts) because they were previously counted as reportable income. If you use the cash method, however, you cannot deduct an uncollectible account because the payment was not previously counted as reportable income.

2 Start-up expenses are deductible only when one is already in business. As a general rule, you are not entitled to a deduction for legal and accounting advice you obtain before you start a business. This is considered an organizational expense. Therefore, it would be tax-advantageous if you were to legally establish your business before you hired any legal or accounting advice. (The same rule applies to start-up expenses and research and development costs.)

3 Deductions for entertainment are a touchy area; ask an accountant for help in taking such deductions because they could trigger an audit.

4 Under current law, deductions for IRAs are primarily limited to those who do not participate in the pension plans of their employers.

5 Travel expenses (meals and lodging, airfare, train, bus, taxi, auto expenses, tips, tolls, etc. are fully deductible, but deductions for business-related meals and travel expenses are currently limited to 50 percent. Spousal travel deductions are allowed only when the spouse is an employee of the company.

6 Previously nondeductible until they were sold, trademarks, as well as copyrights and patents, can now be deducted over a fifteen-year period.

7 If your business is established, the cost of business education (seminars, conferences, workshops, book purchases, etc.) is fully deductible. Such expenditures prior to business start-up would not be deductible. (See point 2 above.)

8 Most insurance premiums related to your business—product liability, home-office policy or special rider on homeowner's policy, computer insurance, etc.—are fully deductible. Premiums on your house insurance and car are deductible in part, as explained under the Home Office Deduction listing.

9 Safe deposit box rental is deductible only if the box holds documents related to production of income or business documents, computer backup disks/tapes, etc.

Business Loans and Other Money Sources

(See also *Financial Reports*)

Bank Loans

If you ever expect to get a bank loan, you have to know how to speak the language of bankers and write a proper loan proposal. "Collateral" is an asset that can back up a loan. Generally it means property, stocks, bonds, savings accounts, life insurance, and current business assets—any or all of which may be held or assumed to ensure repayment of a loan. In addition to collateral, banks will also consider the overall health of your home business—how much money it's generating—or can be expected to generate—and your ability to repay the loan. Your character, credit history, and net worth are also of great importance.

It's important to know the kinds of loans a bank normally offers. While most banks offer only "conventional loans," some specialize in making loans to people who are into art or oil, while others might invest in a chicken farm or a race horse. In short, each bank has to feel comfortable in its ability to sell the kinds of things it accepts as collateral on a loan. If a bank isn't into art, oil, chickens, or horses as an investment, it wouldn't know what to do with this kind of collateral if it had it. But every banker knows what to do with stocks, bonds, and other securities, thus their preference for them as collateral. Bankers also like to deal with people who have accounts in their bank, not to mention excellent financial reports.

Smart Tip

Although banks rarely lend money on purchase orders (because they are always subject to cancellation), *unpaid invoices* for goods and services already rendered are collateral that could be assigned to a bank for a loan.

Business Line of Credit

Once your business is well established and showing a profit, talk to your banker about the possibility of obtaining a business line of credit instead of a loan. There are both secured and unsecured lines of credit. If your total net worth is between $50,000 and $100,000, you can generally get a $5,000 to $10,000 line of credit against which you can borrow whenever you need it. A line of credit normally has an expiration date of a year, but it may be renewed if you've had a profitable year. Although payable on demand, few banks would call in this kind of loan unless they were unduly concerned about a borrower's ability to repay it.

It seems laughable, but the best time to apply for a line of credit is when you don't need the money. But take it anyhow, because the day may come when you will be grateful to have something to fall back on. The best time to apply is when your personal finances are in tip-top shape, all your business bills are paid up, and you're showing a nice monthly profit from your business. By establishing a line of credit before you actually need the money, you'll have added peace of mind that you'll be able to handle unexpected business expenses in low cash-flow months, take advantage of special sales on supplies or equipment, or make major business purchases earlier than you might otherwise have been able to do.

What's Your Collateral? When applying for a regular line-of-credit loan, your banker will tell you that collateral is needed. I learned from experience that such credit is also available on one's signature only, particularly if the business is profitable and one has a good credit rating and an account in good standing with the bank. When I started shopping for a line of credit after four years in business, I visited two local banks, explaining my needs and presenting each of them with what I felt was an impressive package of business credentials and financial information. I was surprised when both banks indicated an interest in loaning money. I selected the bank I wanted to do business with and went in for a visit. When the banker asked what collateral I was offering, I said with a smile, "You're looking at it: me." He pointed out (with a smile) that the bank's depositors aren't too thrilled with this kind of collateral and said that if I were truly serious about building my business, I ought to be willing to risk a second mortgage on the house or give up access to the family savings account.

I said no—it was a matter of principle at this point—that I was tired of having to use personal funds to advance my business, adding, "I've proven myself, shown what I could do with an initial investment of just $1,000— and besides, I have it on good authority that business loans do not have to be secured in this way, particularly when one's credit is excellent."

Grinning, he took another look at my papers. In the end, my ploy worked. I walked out of the bank with an unsecured line of credit (signature only) for $10,000—more than enough to meet my needs at any given time. All it took to get it was the right paperwork and a little moxie.

SBA Loans

The U.S. Small Business Administration has a Microloan Program that offers loans from $200 to $35,000 through selected private nonprofit lenders. To get an SBA loan, you will need a good credit rating and a business/financial plan with figures for the past year and projections for the coming year. Guaranty Loans are available to certain new/young businesses when a local bank will not provide a loan without additional backing. Some Direct Loans are also available to disabled individuals. More information can be obtained from an SBA or SCORE office near you or from this toll-free number: 1-800-827-5722.

An SBA Loan Example. "The SBA was easy to work with when we wanted a loan to set up a shop in our home," reports a couple in my network. "We learned the SBA will offer up to $10,000, basically unsecured, except they will not loan money for intellectual property, nor will they underwrite a computer programming business. There is a monthly judging process where the plans are reviewed by a committee of ten or so who decide who's worthy of a loan. The interest rate is comparable to what banks would give, and we were offered a repayment schedule from one to six years. We paid a loan closing fee of $300."

Credit Card Loans

A study in 1999 by the SBA revealed that almost half of all small business owners with ten or fewer employees used credit cards as a financing source. In unskilled hands, charge cards are a dangerous thing. Used properly, however, they can be an effective business tool. In addition to helping you build a good credit rating, credit card receipts provide an excellent tax record of business transactions. A special feature of a credit card is that it gives you access to emergency cash at any time, especially useful when traveling. Simply present your card to any bank and receive an immediate cash advance determined by your account's balance and credit limit.

Many small business owners also use charge cards to obtain short-term loans to cover business expenses. Although interest rates are high, it seems a small price to pay if one has a great and immediate need for a certain sum of cash. If a couple were to have two credit cards with high credit limits, there might be access to as much as $20,000 overnight—a comforting thought, indeed.

Prepublication Offers

The "prepublication offer" used mostly by self-publishers has also worked well for other product makers, and it's a good way to use your customers' money to finance a new project. A few weeks before a new product is scheduled for release, the publisher or manufacturer may offer its best customers a special prepublication price (usually 20 percent off the retail price) in order to bring in a surge of orders to cover up-front production costs. If you try this, keep your customers happy and avoid problems with the Federal Trade Commission by meeting the shipping date promised in your offer. (See "Federal Trade Commission/Mail or Telephone Order Merchandise Rule.")

Business Records

(See also *Accountant; Financial Reports*)

"Records are at the heart of controlling your business destiny," states a Department of Labor booklet, "and all businesses must deal with a variety of them." Records that should be retained permanently include business ledgers, financial statements, check registers, all legal papers (including contracts, patents, trademarks, copyrights, etc.), depreciation schedules and inventory records, executive correspondence, copies of office forms used, systems and procedures records, and tax returns.

Since the IRS can bring assessment or collection proceedings for a given taxable year for up to three years after a return is due or filed, you should keep all records relating to income and expenses for at least this long in case of an audit. These records should include accounts payable invoices, bank deposits and statements, payroll registers and petty cash records, sales commission reports, general correspondence, and manufacturing records. Some accountants advise that you keep income and expense records for at least six years. "There is no time limit on when the IRS can begin an audit if you fail to file a return or you file one that is considered fraudulent," says tax attorney Julian Block. "The tax for that year can be assessed at any time."

Protecting Vital Records

As important as the business records themselves is the way in which you protect them once they're established. Many sad stories have been reported about loss of irreplaceable records and other papers—everything from damage caused by pipes that burst in the winter to flooded basements where such items are stored, to total destruction by a fire, tornado, hurricane, or earthquakes. Until you imagine the results of such a loss, you cannot begin to take steps to protect against it. Ask yourself which of your business documents, mailing lists, correspondence, customer files, artwork, printed materials, etc. are *absolutely vital* to the continuation of your business, then take immediate steps to protect this material.

If your printed materials were not generated on your computer, create a master file of samples of all printed materials. (If the original art is damaged, at least you'll have an image to work from and all your valuable copywriting won't have been lost.) All vital documents, contracts, information and artwork that can't be computerized should be stored in a safe deposit box along with computer backup disks or tapes. (Until you can make transfers to your safe deposit box, keep computer backups and other important files in a small fireproof box in your office you can quickly grab in an emergency.)

Chamber of Commerce

Chambers of commerce are supportive of businesses in their area. Membership in your local chamber is an indication that you're a stable part of the business community, and it generally provides special opportunities for networking with other businesspeople in the area that can lead to invaluable word-of-mouth advertising and opportunities to develop local business relationships. Often, membership can lead directly to sales (see story below). Depending on the size of your community, dues may vary from $25 to $300 a year.

Some chambers publish directories of licensed homebased business owners to help others in the community use their products and services. They also sponsor community events that provide members with additional opportunities to distribute free literature, network, and donate products and services for higher visibility in the community.

Smart Tip

If you are looking for affordable hospitalization/major medical insurance, call your local chamber and inquire about the United Chambers group insurance program available to its members.

Get Free Publicity from Chamber Membership. "I can't stress enough how helpful I believe chamber memberships can be for publicity purposes," says Karen Wylie, who moved her business out of the home and into The Blue Ridge Soap Shed in Little Switzerland, North Carolina. "We have done craft shows for years and sometimes customers couldn't remember our business name, only our town. Or maybe only our business name (and not our personal names) in the days before we had a Yellow Pages listing. These customers could call our chamber of commerce and get our number, and we would then get their order. Most chamber annual memberships for entrepreneurs are in the neighborhood of $100 to $150 a year, and that only comes to $.27 to $.40 cents a day. Every time I get a referral, a customer call, or a customer arriving at our shop who's been given directions to us, I know it's worth it.

"We belong to two local chambers of commerce, and two regional tourism groups, and have product displays and brochures available at each building. We've found them to be very effective. I think craft sellers could have quite an advantage in their community if they took advantage of chamber memberships and opportunities for display. Since most chamber members tend to be manufacturing or service industries, with either boring display items or lack of interest in doing a display, craft items are usually quite visually entertaining and catch attention from visitors. Our products are also sold at one chamber and one regional tourism association. Visitors don't usually buy the products at the chamber, but seeing them causes them to plan a visit to our shop."

Collection Techniques

(See also *Bad Checks; Credit Bureaus; Small Claims Court*)

As discussed in Chapter 3, it's one thing to sell your products or services; it's another to collect payment for them. In addition to dealing with the problem of bad checks or credit cards, you must keep a sharp eye on your receivables and take whatever steps are necessary to collect overdue accounts. If you haven't done this already, establish a firm policy about how payment must be made for orders or services rendered. (See *Terms of Sale*.)

Unpaid Invoices

It used to be that the greatest business excuse was "The check's in the mail." That has now been replaced with "The computer is down." If your invoices (or monthly statements) are not paid on time, send a friendly reminder. If payment isn't forthcoming, you can either drag out the collection procedure with a series of ever-stronger reminders, or simply pick up the phone and find out what the trouble is. If the collection process drags on, try to work out a payment arrangement. "Few people want to be hounded by a bill collector and may pay just to avoid this hassle," says a wholesaler in my network.

Some business owners don't have the problem of unpaid invoices because they have established a cash-up-front policy at the beginning. If you're wholesaling products, most of your customers will expect to be invoiced, but that doesn't mean you have to *keep on invoicing them* when they order a second or third time but haven't paid their first invoice yet. As one seller puts it, "Extending credit is like giving a loan, and I'm not a bank."

When All Else Fails, Try Humor. Dodie Eisenhauer, owner of Village Designs in Daisy, Missouri, shares this amusing story: "I sell to a company that has ordered from me for several years. They eventually pay but are often several months behind. In an effort to be favorable and not lose their business, I have not charged interest on their past due accounts until recently. One summer, while operating on a loan, I felt the need to pass on the interest charges. After they had ignored several statements, I decided to try a little humor. On the statement, I wrote a personal note saying, 'A check would be preferred but chickens and produce would be accepted.' They responded immediately by sending me a packet of checks to cash at regular intervals, which will clear their account, including the interest."

Collection Agencies

If you decide to use a collection agency, realize that it could take up to a year for an agency to collect even half the unpaid accounts you send them, so anticipate at the beginning that you'll probably have to write off the balance. Dodie Eisenhauer, mentioned above, uses a collection agency to collect accounts she simply can't collect herself. "They will send a ten-day demand letter for free and not charge if they collect," she says. "If they can't, they proceed with collections and keep a percentage depending on your history with them and time lapse from payment due date. The caution is to be sure of the collection agency. One agency that solicited me collected on a very late customer. I was impressed and gave them several more accounts. Although they did collect them, they never paid me—they just kept the money—and all my efforts to collect from the collection agency itself failed."

To avoid this problem, note that all the better credit agencies belong to the American Collector's Association (also known as ACA International—the Association of Credit and Collection Professionals). Before signing with an agency, ask if they are a member, or check the membership area of the ACA Web site at **www.collector.com** to see if the agency you plan to use is a member.

An agency will try to collect accounts locally, but when you need to collect from someone out of state, they will pass along your account to a member collection agency in the appropriate state. All member agencies trade accounts this way, making regular ninety-day reports back to the originating agency. Agencies normally take 40 percent of a local account or 50 percent if the collection is made by a member agency. Since half is better than none, a collection agency is at least an alternative bill collection technique you may wish to try at some point in your business.

Contracts

(See also *Licensing*)

A "contract" can be any written agreement that is dated and signed by the parties involved, and it will be considered a legal document whether legal language is used or not. Note that electronic signatures now have the same legal weight as a signature written in pen and ink, so contracts and other legal documents bearing an electronic signature have the same legal force as a contract written on paper. (The text of this law is available online at **www.ecommerce.gov/ecomnews/ElectronicSignatures_s761.pdf**.

Amending Standard Contracts

Unless you understand "legalese," various contract clauses (or lack of them) could cost you a great deal of money or grief. Thus it is always prudent to seek legal advice before signing any contract, particularly complicated agreements, involving partnerships, cooperative arrangements, exclusive dealer or distributor agreements, franchise agreements, licensing arrangements or royalty contracts. When offering a contract, most companies will offer their "boilerplate" contract containing clauses heavily weighted to their financial advantage. While beginners often sign such contracts without question (because they're thrilled to have the work or job), business pros will always try to get certain clauses amended. Although you can do this yourself once you've gained some experience in your industry, an agent or attorney with good negotiating skills is likely to give you greater power in making contractual changes while also increasing your profits from the deal.

Electronic Rights Issues

If your contract involves the sale of intellectual property of any kind, pay particular attention to contract clauses related to the electronic use of the material in question. (On my BarbaraBrabec.com Web site in the Writing/Publishing department, you'll find a personal experience article documenting the electronic rights pitfall I encountered when I agreed to provide content for an e-commerce site. My inexperience in this area at the time cost me a magazine column I had been writing for twenty years.)

Freelance writers should note that magazine publishers typically expect writers to include the electronic rights to their articles or columns so they can be published on the magazine's Web site. Don't give these rights away without getting something in return. Book publishers also expect authors to give them electronic rights to books they plan to publish, even when they have no plans to publish such information electronically. Authors may be able to retain (or get back) electronic rights if they can prove their electronic use of the material will not impact the publisher's trade book sales.

Due to the ease with which images can now be scanned into a computer or onto a Web site, graphic artists who sell their work to publishers, manufacturers, art agencies or other buyers should include a contract clause that outlines or limits the electronic use of their illustrations or art. In the case of unauthorized use, whether you've registered a copyright or not, you would at least be able to sue for breach of contract. (See also *Electronic Publishing* and *Intellectual Property, Protection of.*)

Copyrights

(See also *Electronic Publishing; Intellectual Property, Protection of; Patents; Slogans; Trademarks*)

For basic information on what copyrights protect, how to do copyright searches, or how to file a copyright application, call the Copyright Office's automated message system at (212) 707-3000, or get the same information online at **www.loc.gov/copyright**. This book's companion guide, *HOMEMADE MONEY: Starting Smart!* also includes this basic information and a discussion of how to avoid infringing on the rights of other copyright holders.

Cottage Industries

(See also *Employees, Nonfamily; Independent Contractors; Industrial Homework Laws*)

Some people call any kind of home business a "cottage industry," but in actuality, a cottage industry is one that is based on a central marketing and management operation with craft production done by individuals working at home. For example, you might start a small manufacturing company, then hire other individuals in your community to do the actual labor involved in the production process, allowing them to perform this work in their own homes for a per-piece price.

For years, acting on the advice of accountants and attorneys, small business owners have hired such labor on an independent contractor basis (instead of an employee basis) because they were told this would avoid all the usual tax and paperwork problems associated with the hiring of employees. *This is now a dangerous practice.* In recent years, many cottage industries have fallen under the scrutiny of the IRS or Department of Labor and been sued for thousands of dollars in back taxes and related penalties.

Manufacturing of Women's and Children's Apparel

You will be particularly at risk if you use homeworkers to make women's and children's apparel. This problem dates back to the 1980s when some Vermont home knitters protested the 1943 Fair Labor Standards Act that imposed a nationwide ban on home knitting and other homebased production industries. The Vermont knitters received considerable media attention and, despite extreme opposition from labor unions, eventually won exemption. By 1984, the federal ban had been lifted from home production of knitted outerwear, jewelry, gloves and mittens, buttons and buckles, handkerchiefs and embroideries. However, thanks to the power of labor unions—particularly the International Ladies Garment Workers Union—*hiring homeworkers to make women's and children's apparel is still illegal.* (The bitter irony is that if you were to manufacture *men's* clothing, you would have no problem.) Adding to the problem is the fact that several states have enacted their own laws prohibiting homeworkers from knitting outerwear or manufacturing common items such as toys, dolls, purses, men's clothing, pipes, and jewelry. (For a list of those states, see *Industrial Homework Laws* below.)

What all this means is that homebased garment designers or sewers cannot expand a business beyond their capability to make women's and children's apparel for sale because the hiring of homeworkers to produce such garments is prohibited by federal law, and possibly state law as well. To do this legally, one would have to move the business outside the home and hire regular employees.

Smart Tip

In seeking legal advice on any matter relating to the formation or operation of a cottage industry that will employ homeworkers or independent contractors of any kind, *you need an attorney who is fully versed in labor law.* In this instance, you can no longer rely merely on the advice of an accountant or business attorney. The small business press has published many horrifying articles about small business people who have been caught in this trap, thanks to poor legal advice.

Credit Bureaus

(See also *Better Business Bureau; Collection Techniques; Trade References*)

While businesses can use credit bureaus to get credit information on individuals, individuals cannot use them to get credit information on businesses. For example, if you're an individual craft seller who wants to check the credit of a small shop across the country who asks you to ship and invoice, there's not much you can do to verify the credit worthiness of the shop itself. However, if you know the name of the individual who owns the shop (information you should always have in your files), you might be able to get a credit report on that individual by calling a credit bureau. According to Associated Credit Bureaus in Washington, D.C., you can get a credit report if you have "a permissible purpose that includes a financial relationship with the individual or other party."

For information on companies large enough to be rated, check *Dun & Bradstreet* directories in your library, or the D&B Web site at **www.DNB.com**. To get a free D&B listing, or to look up the phone number and address of any U.S. company in the D&B search engine, visit this page: **http://sbs.dnb.com/default.asp.** Once you find a company in their files, you may then elect to purchase a detailed credit report on them.

Smart Tip

If you're trying to check the credit of someone in your area, an alternative to trying to get credit information from a credit bureau is to go online to your local court house and see if the individual or business has any judgments against them. Prior to accepting a new client, a CPA who did this kind of check found that her prospective new client had five judgments against him for nonpayment of bills.

Domain Name Registration

There is a lot of confusion about domain name registration. In the early days of the Internet, Network Solutions was appointed by the U.S. government to be the sole domain name registrar. In time, they were forced to give up their monopoly, at which time many other entrepreneurs began to offer the service of registering domain names. (For the official list of ICANN accredited registrars go to **www.icann.org/registrars/accredited-list.html**.) Since Network Solutions retains ownership of the database that contains all the dot-com names (called the SRS database), all the accredited registrars are actually doing for Web site owners is placing their domain name into the SRS database. It costs them only $6 to do this, so anything over this amount becomes their profit. That's why you see so many different prices for domain name registration.

"There are now more than a hundred companies that are allowed to enter names into the SRS database," says Chris Maher, my technical Web site adviser (ArtWebWorks.com). "Each registrar will give you certain specific rights when you sign a contract with them. Because domain names are not considered property, however, it's important that you read and understand the contract you sign. If someone should steal your name, for example, you will find that you have no property rights to your domain name beyond what the contract says."

Since domain name registrars may come and go, it's wise to know who you're dealing with. If you register a domain name with one registrar, you can transfer to another at renewal time. But when you get a renewal notice, be sure it has come from the registrar you originally signed up with, since anyone can look at the SRS database and see who's coming up for renewal, get their e-mail address and send them a renewal notice.

If you have decided who's going to host your Web site, there is no reason not to let them register your domain name for you. "But be absolutely sure," says Chris, "that the registration is in your name and not that of your Web hosting company because this can cause many problems if you later decide to move your Web site to another server."

Every domain name record has three contacts: administrative, technical, and billing. To have complete control over your domain name, you must be registered both as the owner and the "administrative contact." It's fine to have another party listed as the technical or billing contact, however. "The administrative contact is considered to have authority over the name," Chris explains. "Whoever hosts your site will be the technical contact, but if you are not shown as having authority over the name, you could have great difficulty in getting the registrar to update your domain name record, making it very difficult to move your site to a new server."

Researching a New Domain Name

I believe many Web beginners are being lured into buying domain names or renting the use of them when all they have to do is a little research on the Web. A friend of mine found someone had taken the name she wanted for her domain and he "kindly" offered to let her use the domain name for "only" $25 a month if she hired him to build the site and administer its content for two years. At the end of that period he guaranteed to renew the agreement, but the domain name would still be his. *What a deal for this scam artist!*

To get the same name this fellow wanted to rent to her, all my friend had to do was register it with a different extension (see *New Top Level Domain Extensions* below). Or, better yet, she could have registered the name with a hyphen or period between the two words she wanted instead of running them together.

If you're trying to come up with a good name for your new Web site, visit **www.e-gineer.com/domainator**. Here, you can type in a couple of key words and the software on this site will give you combinations with dashes or different extensions that are still available. In checking one of my book titles on this site, I found that while CreativeCash.com and dot-net had been taken, Creative-Cash.com (with a hyphen) and five other combinations were still available if I wanted them. On the above site, you can also learn whether a name you want has been trademarked or not and, just for fun, if you're looking for words that rhyme with a certain word, this site provides a big list of them for any word you type in—some good, but many unusable. When I typed in "creative," for example, I got "administrative," "stimulative," and "authoritative," in addition to "frustrative," "corporative," and "presuppurative (the root word of which means to discharge pus!)."

To do a trademark search for a domain name you have in mind, go to **http://tess.USPTO.gov/bin/gate.exe** and enter the words into the search box. You'll then get a list of all trademarks, live or dead, containing those words. Also check out the Web site of the U.S. Patent and Trademark Office at **www.USPTO.com**.

Smart Tip

To find out if the domain name you'd like is still available, go to **www.whois.net** to do a name search and find answers to common questions about domain name registration. Also check out **www.betterwhois.com**, which offers the same search service but provides a list of active domain name registrars if you want to compare costs and services.

Multiple Domain Name Registrations

How valuable is your personal name or URL to the success of your business? It costs so little to register a name that it's foolish not to do so if you are serious about your business. After registering a name, you can "park" it for up to two years at no additional cost. (Depending on which service you use, you can register and park a domain name for between $15 and $35 a year.) This will give you time to ponder your future plans while preventing someone else from using your good name. Remember the "cybersquatters," people who buy domain names, hoping to sell them at a hefty profit. Worse are people who take a person's good dot-com name, register it with another extension, and then publish objectionable material on that site while making people think it's connected to the dot-com site bearing the same name. (Lots of unethical stuff going on here that is hard to stop once it begins.)

Smart Tip

Domain name registration scams are now common. If you get a notice that you must renew your domain name or lose it, make sure it's the company you originally signed with, because many companies are now sending such e-mails in an attempt to steal accounts from other companies (much like the companies that try to steal your long-distance service). Any notice from an unknown company should be discarded. In particular, *never* click on an imbedded URL in the e-mail that will supposedly take you to a site for more information. Such clicking will automatically transfer your name to the e-mail sender, and they will then claim that you have requested this transfer.

New Top Level Domain (TLD) Extensions

Whether you're applying for a new domain name or trying to cover all bases to keep others from using the business name you've trademarked or are otherwise trying to protect, you need to familiarize yourself with the seven new TLDs now available—the first to be introduced to the Internet since 1988. They include dot-biz, dot-info, dot-name, dot-museum, dot-coop, dot-aero, and dot-pro. You will find more information about all of them at **www.icann.org/tlds** and **www.internic.net/faqs/new-tlds.html**. (It has been estimated that 15 million dot-biz names will be registered by 2005, making this extension even more popular than dot-com.

Domain Name Registration

Domain Name Theft. "Something I learned the hard way was the importance of registering my URL in all forms," says Bunny DeLorie. "For example, I own www.fefifaux.com and .net as well as www.fefifauxfinish.com and .net. I have also registered my own name as both .com and .net, and I'm currently checking out the new TLD domain names to see which ones I need to register as well. It's amazing the people out there who try to extort money for a URL they have registered with your name! I've had many others start up a business and even sell product with my business name, but because I have a trademark for my FeFiFaux business name, I've been able, with the help of my attorney, to prevent other businesses from using this name or any variation on it. In fact, one company ended up having to pay me for selling product nationwide using my business name."

Domain Name Disputes

All of the new names are subject to ICANN's *Uniform Domain Name Dispute Resolution Policy*, referred to as UDRP (**www.icann.org/udrp/udrp.htm**). Under this policy, most types of trademark-based domain name disputes must be resolved by agreement, court action, or arbitration before a registrar will cancel, suspend, or transfer a domain name. For an article that spells out the details of when someone else's use of your domain name is clearly "use in bad faith," link to **www.icann.org/udrp/udrp-policy-29sept99.htm**.

"Because the .biz TLD is limited to use by businesses, it is likely that any infringement of a trademark owner's rights will come from this TLD," says attorney Ivan Hoffman. For suggested remedies to this problem, read his article, "Domain Names and Trademarks: An Update" at **www.IvanHoffman.com/domain2.html**. Also see the article, "Cybersquatting: What It Is, and What Can Be Done About It" in the article archives at **www.Nolo.com**.

E-commerce Site

(See also *Merchant Account Providers*)

To fully understand how to do business on the Web, you'll need much more information than this book can deliver. Fortunately, there is a wealth of free information on the Web that focuses on this topic, plus books (both print and electronic) to help you work through all the details and avoid the many pitfalls that await novice sellers. (See "Other Resources" for some helpful Web links to get you started.) The standard method of operation is to first select a merchant account provider, a shopping cart system, and a secure server, but it is possible to do business on the Web without any of these things (see *Doing Business on the Web Without Merchant Status* below).

Shopping Carts and Secure Servers

Many sellers elect to have a specially designed shopping cart system set up by their Web site designer or other freelance service provider. Simple shopping carts are offered with most electronic credit card programs, but don't sign any contract with a merchant account provider until you've read all the fine print and know exactly what is offered. One of my readers told me about the surprise she had when she set up her e-commerce site. When she signed the credit card contract she *thought* it covered a shopping cart on her site, but it didn't, so she had to pay someone $362 to design one for her.

Most people on the Internet are concerned about privacy protection, authentication, and security. "Credit card processors are going to eventually require that Web sellers have a secure web site, using an Internet-software based program that verifies a transaction online as it happens," says Barbara Arena of the National Craft Association (1-800-715-9594; **www.CraftAssoc.com**). "Once you're on the Internet, you have to do a little surfing to find the companies that offer secure site services."

If you already have merchant status when you go on the Web, it's just a matter of getting secure server status for your site. You probably won't find anything for less than $25 a month, plus all the other usual fees associated with a merchant account. "Your ISP where you rent space on a server can provide you with a secure site," says Barbara, "but you need merchant status before you can use it. Some ISPs say they can get that for you, too, but you can assume they will be getting a percentage of sales for doing this for you."

Smart Tip

If you have your own merchant account and just need a way to take orders through your Web site, check out Mal's Free E-Commerce Service, **www.mals-e.com**. When customers click on a "Buy Now Button" on your Web site, you get an e-mail saying you have an order. You then go to Mal's administration area to retrieve the secure credit card information stored there and complete the process. This service is free to start with, and you can upgrade to a premium account later if you want to do online payment processing.

Doing Business on the Web Without Merchant Status

A professional-looking Web site with a shopping cart, real-time credit card processing, hosting fees, and business phone lines can really add up, and not every small business can afford to start this way. Make sure you really need this service before you assume the costs that go with it. Many artists and craft sellers, for example, simply include an order form on their site that customers can print out and mail with a check. You might think this unprofessional, but Barbara Arena of the National Crafts Association says she gets at least 30 percent of her orders this way because a certain percentage of the population still prefers to order by mail with a check.

Other online retailers in my network have confirmed they do not have to take credit cards to get sales. Bunny DeLorie (FeFiFauxFinish.com) says she's very happy with her "checks and balances" system. "I offer a few tools on my site that regularly bring in from $400 to $600 a month," she says. "So far, only a handful of people have wished I took charge cards and that was only during the holidays when they waited too long to order gifts and needed the order in a hurry."

Publisher Bill Ronay agrees. "Unless you expect to do hundreds of dollars' worth of business a week off the Internet, you probably don't need an online merchant account and shopping cart, particularly if you have a toll-free number or fax. We do nearly half our business via the telephone. Much of it is off the Web, but many of our customers are of the 'old school' and do not want to have credit card information relayed via the Internet."

Electronic Publishing

(See also *Contracts/Electronic Rights Issues; Intellectual Property, Protection of; Merchant Account Providers*)

Electronic publishing is currently the hottest thing going on the Web as thousands of individuals enter this field with their own electronic patterns, booklets, reports, or eBooks. A growing number of books on how to succeed in this field are now available (both print and eBooks), so the information here merely touches on some of the more important issues involved in this kind of publishing, now both a business in itself as well as a popular diversification strategy for entrepreneurs of all kinds.

To sell information electronically, you must have a merchant account or some kind of ordering system that accepts credit cards and a means of delivering the electronic material to buyers. Some companies, such as DigiBuy (**www.digibuy.com**) and Kagi (**www.kagi.com**) offer publishers both a merchant account program and download system. Although ClickBank (**www.clickbank.com**) has no delivery system, many eBook publishers work through this company because it offers an affiliate program that enables them to sign up dealers for their books.

PayPal (**www.paypall.com**) remains the simplest and easiest method for beginning Web retailers. They accept all credit cards and offer shopping cart tools and a "payment gateway" that will connect purchasers to your Web site to download your eBook or other electronic offering. Some publishers simply e-mail the product to customers after being alerted by PayPal that they have paid for the item.

How to Copyright eBooks and Other Electronic Property
To register a work transmitted online, send the following three items together in the same envelope or package to Register of Copyrights, Library of Congress, Washington, D.C. 20559:

1 A completed and signed application form;

2 Appropriate deposit material;

3 A filing fee of $30 payable to Register of Copyrights.

Use the form that corresponds to the type of authorship being registered. Example: *Form TX* (text) for literary work of any kind (including computer programs); *Form VA* (visual arts) for pictorial, graphic, or sculptural works, including photographs, charts, technical drawings, diagrams, or models; or *Form PA* (performing arts) for audiovisual material, music, or lyrics. If the work contains more than one type of authorship, use the form that corresponds to the predominant material. The "deposit material" may be either a computer disk or a reproduction of the entire work:

- **Computer Disk Deposit.** Clearly label the disk with the title and author's name, and include a print-out of five pages representative of the authorship being registered, including the title and author, and copyright notice, if any. (If the entire work can be printed out in fewer than five pages, send a printout of the entire work and confirm this fact.) Also, if your claim to copyright specifically includes a sound recording (sounds without any accompanying pictorial images), send an audiocassette containing the sounds; for audiovisual material, send a videotape.

- **Reproduction of the Entire Work.** This might include a printout, audiocassette, or videotape. Send the format appropriate for the authorship being registered. No computer disk is required.

For more specific information on registering eBooks (which the Copyright Office calls "Online Books"), check this page: **www.loc.gov/copyright/circs/circ66.html**.

Digital Rights Management (DRM)

Everyone who sells information electronically has the same concern: How to prevent buyers from copying the copyrighted downloaded material and e-mailing it to others. Currently, to keep files totally protected, they must be encrypted and sent through Adobe Content Server, whose $5,000 to $50,000 annual licensing cost is too high for all but the largest electronic publishers. A less costly option is to try to find a DRM company who has this license, and let them deliver the downloaded content in return for a percentage of sales. Such companies seem to come and go, however. "I have used two DRM companies in the past, but both have folded," says Debbie Spaulding, who sells her patterns electronically from PuppetPatterns.com.

Currently, Debbie is sending her electronic patterns in PDF format (see *PDF File Conversion* below), using the settings in *Adobe Acrobat 5* software to password-protect each document. "Limited encryption is available with this software in that its security features can prevent anyone from changing, deleting, or copying the work," she says. "It also can prevent someone from printing it, but this is not recommended because most people prefer to print out documents rather than read them online. What the software cannot do, however, is prevent buyers from forwarding the material to others by e-mail."

Here are some strategies being used by other electronic publishers to deter theft of their electronic reports, books, and patterns:

- **Using PDF encryption software.** James Dillehay, author of *Your Guide to EBook Publishing Success* (**www.00ebooks.com**) recommends PDFEverywhere ($199). "The software encrypts the PDF file with a password that allows only the user of the downloading computer to unlock it," he says. "The file can't be passed on. This discourages all but the most serious of hackers from pirating your material."

- **Placing downloads on a separate server and using a weird page name rather than an easily guessed name.** This is the strategy used by Louise Louis, ToyBreeds.com. Normally, a buyer gets the URL to download an eBook only after they have paid for it, but if someone can figure out the download page, they can bypass the payment page entirely and download the book. "You'd be surprised how many people cruise Web sites, trying to guess download pages for popular eBooks or special reports," says Louise, who suggests making it difficult for them by giving your download page an obscure title. For example, if you're selling a book on beads, don't use a page title such as "eBook on beads," but create a unique name such as "xyn432d.htm."

- **Adding copyright information to all e-documents.** Include a strong copyright notice that specifically states the document may not be forwarded electronically, and include a note about penalties for copyright infringement. Add your e-mail address and URL and hope for the best. As Louise Louis puts it, "If someone does buy my eBook and sends it to friends, at least I'm getting some free advertising. And perhaps people who obtain the eBook illegally will visit my site and buy something from me."

PDF File Conversion

There are free PDF file converters on the Web (search for "PDF file conversion"), but if your document includes hyperlinks, they will not be clickable when using such programs. The same thing is true with some versions of word processing software. For example, *WordPerfect 9* lets you convert files to PDF format, but only *WordPerfect 10* activates the hyperlinks in a document. Serious electronic publishers are using *Adobe Acrobat* software (mentioned above), but beginning publishers can find less expensive programs. (Begin your search at **www.zdnet.com** and type "PDF conversion" in the site's search engine to turn up a list of them.)

Note: To merely read PDF files, all you need is *Adobe Acrobat Reader* software, which can be downloaded free from **www.adobe.com**.

Employees, Family

(See also *Employees, Nonfamily; Employer's Identification Number; Independent Contractors; Medical Reimbursement Plan*)

There are numerous tax advantages to hiring your spouse or child/children. Many couples go into business as a partnership, each taking owner draw from the business instead of wages (which would not be a deductible expense to the partnership). In most cases, however, it makes better tax sense to put the business in the name of one spouse and put the other on the payroll, just to get the legal tax deduction and help cut self-employment taxes. As a sole proprietor, wages paid to your spouse become a business deduction that automatically lowers the amount of self-employment taxes you must pay on your Schedule C profits.

Once your spouse is on your payroll, you may get additional tax benefits by electing to set up an employee benefit plan that will enable you to deduct 100 percent of your family's health insurance premiums and out-of-pocket medical, vision, and dental expenses not covered by insurance. Although your spouse must pay social security taxes on his or her earnings, and state and federal income tax must also be withheld from such income, the tax benefits of this plan are obvious. (See *Medical Reimbursement Plan* for details.)

Hiring Your Children

An often-overlooked tax break is that it may be possible for you to employ one or more of your children, which can result in sizable tax savings. Wages paid to a child under the age of eighteen are exempt from social security (FICA) taxes and, as Julian Block, a former IRS agent and tax columnist explains: "Putting your youngster on your payroll can be a savvy way to take care of his or her allowance at the expense of the Internal Revenue Service. Significant tax savings can result merely by moving the money from one family pocket to another."

The Tax Court has upheld the deduction of reasonable salaries for children as young as seven years old, even for simple jobs such as cleaning your workshop. Check with an accountant about the amount you can pay a child employee without having to pay taxes. (This amount would be a deduction for your business that would lower taxes on your business profits.)

Smart Tip

Since the IRS may scrutinize the tax aspects of transactions involving family employees, be sure they are performing "meaningful work," and keep careful records of the hours they are employed and the manner in which you've calculated wages.

Tax Forms and Paperwork

As an employer of nonfamily employees, you must comply with certain labor laws discussed under *Labor Laws* in this section. As an employer of your own family members, however, your concern will largely be one of taxes and corresponding paperwork. You will want the help of an accountant when you hire an employee, even one in your own family, because there are a number of tax forms to be completed and filed. They include:

● An SS-4 form to get your Employer's Identification Number (EIN);

● A form 940, which will exempt you from paying unemployment taxes on wages paid to family members;

● A W-4 tax registration application for withholding tax, similar to the form you must complete when you file for a tax identification number to collect sales tax;

● An Employer's Quarterly Federal Tax Return (Form 941), which indicates wages paid to family employees, and taxes withheld—your accountant will give you a handy chart for this.

At year's end, you will also need to complete W-2 forms stating income paid to each employee for the year, plus a W-3 Transmittal form to accompany the W-2 forms you must send to the appropriate Social Security Administration office and your state's Department of Revenue.

This sounds a lot worse than it is. Let an accountant help you get set up. After that it's nothing more than repetitive paperwork.

Employees, Nonfamily

(See also *Cottage Industries; Employer's Identification Number; Independent Contractors; Industrial Homework Laws; Labor Laws*)

There are four types of nonfamily workers: regular employees, statutory employees, leased employees, and independent contractors (a topic discussed separately in this section). For general guidelines on tax forms and paperwork involved in hiring employees, see above listing. Since each state has different laws about workers who perform duties in your place of business or in their own homes, you must contact your nearest Department of Labor for more information on this topic. An accountant or tax adviser can also explain the tax implications of hiring outside help.

Workers' Compensation Insurance. If you hire even one employee, your state probably requires that you carry workers' compensation for that individual. Such insurance is available through individual agents, and the amount you pay will vary depending on the number of employees you have and the kind of work they do for you.

Smart Tip

Don't let an employee use your personal vehicle to run business errands for you. If he or she should have an accident that seriously injures someone, you could be held accountable since the employee was "acting in behalf of the employer." To avoid this legal problem, ask your insurance agent about "non-ownership contingent liability protection" (which can be included as part of your overall liability insurance policy or obtained separately), or consider having your vehicle rated for business.

Statutory Employees

An employee solution used by many small craft manufacturing companies is to hire statutory employees. Although it costs a business more to hire statutory employees than independent contractors (because you must pay social security and Medicare taxes), such employees are less expensive to hire than regular employees because there are no unemployment taxes to be paid. (Like independent contractors, statutory employees can deduct their trade or business expenses from their W-2 earnings).

According to the IRS's *Tax Guide for Small Businesses*, "If an individual who works for you is not an employee under the common law rules, you do not have to withhold federal income tax from that individual's pay." However, for social security and Medicare taxes, the term *employee* includes any individual who works for you for pay in one of the following two categories (two additional categories are excluded here because they are not applicable to this book's readers):

Employees, Nonfamily

1 An individual who works at home on materials or goods you supply and that must be returned to you or to a person you name, if you also furnish specifications for the work to be done;

2 A full-time traveling or city salesperson who works on your behalf and turns in orders to you from wholesalers, retailers, contractors, etc. The goods sold must be merchandise for resale or supplies for use in the buyers' business operations. (If you were to hire a sales rep who worked only for you and no other companies, that person could be considered a statutory employee for tax purposes but could not legally be called an independent contractor.)

Switching from Independent Contractors to Employees. Dodie Eisenhauer, VillageDesigns.com, uses a combination of regular employees who work in her workshop and statutory employees who work for her out of their own homes. She says it was a big step for her to switch over from independent contractors to employees but it wasn't as painful a process as she had been led to believe and the benefits have been enormous.

"I encourage people who are still using independent contractors to reclassify their workers as soon as possible," says Dodie. "You immediately gain peace of mind from knowing you're operating on a 100 percent legal basis and you no longer have to worry about the IRS or Department of Labor putting you out of business."

—an excerpt from *The Crafts Business Answer* Book by Barbara Brabec (M. Evans)

Leasing Employees

Here's another employee option you should explore. A jewelry manufacturer who once had nine employees told me that *leasing* employees was the smartest thing he ever did because it enabled him to fire people without getting emotionally involved, and took all the tax and paperwork problems off his back. Check your local telephone pages for employee leasing services such as Manpower. The way it works is that you would hire the employees you want and use the service to manage them. In return for 20 percent of the employee's gross wages, the employee service will do a drug test, offer the employee medical insurance, and take care of workers' compensation and FICA.

Employer's Identification Number (EIN)

This federal taxpayer number is required by the government at the point when one becomes an employer. Partnerships, corporations, and non-profit organizations also need an EIN (or FEIN, as it is also called). Sole proprietors without employees may also obtain and use an EIN instead of their social security number on all business forms that ask for a "taxpayer identification number." This number is obtained by filing IRS Form SS-4, available wherever tax forms are found. Only one EIN is needed, even when you own several businesses, and if you should change your business name or relocate to another part of the country, your EIN goes with you.

Federal Trade Commission (FTC)

(See also *Tags and Labels Required by Law; Trade Practice Rules and Regulations*)

In addition to matters related to consumer safety, the labeling of certain products, and scams and frauds against consumers and small business owners (all of which are discussed at length in *Homemade Money: Starting Smart!*), the FTC is especially concerned with truth-in-advertising, the use of endorsements and testimonials, warranties and guarantees, and the Thirty-Day Mail or Telephone Order Merchandise Rule, all of which are discussed below. Detailed information about all FTC rules and regulations can be obtained by calling 1-877-FTC-HELP, or by checking the FTC Web site at **www.FTC.gov**.

Truth in Advertising

It is not what you say in actual words that counts, but what people believe after they have read your ad. In evaluating whether an advertisement has the tendency or capacity to deceive, law enforcement officials and the courts apply certain standards involving (1) the message as a whole (the impression left by the total advertisement), (2) the "average person" standard (ads must be viewed from the perspective of the "average" person, not the sophisticated or skeptical person), and (3) deceptive nondisclosure (giving selected information or omitting facts the average person would need to know to make an intelligent purchasing decision).

"An advertisement must not fool even gullible or ordinarily trusting people," warns mail order expert Julian L. Simon, author of *How to Start and Operate a Mail Order Business* (out of print). "If you fool any substantial portion of your public, you are in the wrong. And what counts is not your actual words, but what people believe after they have read your ad." In short, customers must get exactly what they *expect* to receive, and must not feel they have been gypped. (Note, however, that a customer can feel dissatisfied without feeling gypped. Being unhappy isn't the same as feeling cheated.)

What you do about unhappy customers depends on what you have *promised* to do. If you offer a guarantee of satisfaction or money back (like most successful mail order companies), you have little choice but to issue a refund when a customer returns your product, even when the item is returned in unsalable condition. (Throughout the twenty-five-year life of my mail order book-selling business, I rarely received more than one or two refund requests a year, and I'm sure my personal guarantee of satisfaction was often the determining factor in whether a new customer ordered from me or not.)

Use of the Word "New"

As a general rule, a "new" product can be advertised as new for a period of only six months. An older product, although new and unknown to a particular market, may not be advertised as "new" insofar as it gives the impression it has just recently been discovered, developed, or invented. It can, however, be advertised as being new to a specific market area.

Use of Endorsements and Testimonials

These must be based on actual use of the product and the endorser's informed knowledge of the field. Statements of opinion should be so identified to avoid the impression that they have a scientific or other authoritative basis. If you publish a periodical, note that you cannot use testimonials from readers whose subscriptions have expired. Endorsers must actually use the advertised product. Also, never use people's names without written permission.

Warranties and Guarantees

Warranties inform buyers that the products they are buying will perform in a certain way under normal conditions. An *implied* warranty means that a product will perform as similar products of its kind under normal conditions, while an *express* warranty states a specific fact about how the product will perform. Claims made in advertisements may constitute an *express* warranty that imposes legal obligations on the advertiser.

Guarantees must clearly disclose the terms, conditions, and extent of the guarantee, plus the manner in which the company will perform the guarantee. FTC standards require not just a statement, such as "Satisfaction guaranteed, or money back," but a detailed explanation, such as "If not completely satisfied with the merchandise, return it in good condition within ten days to receive a complete refund of the purchase price."

Mail or Telephone Order Merchandise Rule

It is extremely important to comply with this rule—also called the "30-Day Mail Order Rule"—because it is strictly enforced with penalties up to $10,000 for each violation. The FTC says it is unfair or deceptive to solicit any order through the mail unless you believe you can fulfill the order within the time you specify. Or, if no time is specified, then you must ship the order within thirty days after receipt of a customer's paid order. *You are not affected by the thirty-day rule if you invoice orders after shipment, or if you specify a particular length of time for delivery*, such as "Allow six weeks for delivery." If you are unable to ship within the specified time, or within thirty days if no time has been specified, then the FTC ruling demands that you notify the buyer of the additional delay, *and enclose a postage-paid reply card or envelope*. You must give the buyer the option either to cancel the order for a full and prompt refund, or extend the time for shipment. If the buyer does not respond, the FTC ruling states that you automatically get the delay, as silence is construed as acceptance.

This rule, once applicable only to mail orders, now applies to all orders placed over the phone, by fax, and on the Web. In such cases, the thirty-day period begins with the actual charging of a customer's account.

Trade Practice Rules and Regulations

When requesting information from the Federal Trade Commission, mention your type of business and specifically ask for information about rules relating to it. For instance, there are certain rules for industries such as jewelry making, leather, ladies' handbags, feathers and down, the catalog jewelry and giftware industry, millinery, photography, furniture making, and mail order. When an FTC rule has been violated, it is customary for the Federal Trade Commission to order the violator to cease the illegal practice. No penalty is attached to most cease-and-desist orders, but violation of such an order may result in a fine.

Financial Reports

If you ever hope to get a bank loan, you will need well-prepared financial reports such as Income Statements, Profit and Loss Statements, Balance Sheets, and Cash Flow projections. Refer to a book on financial accounting to learn how to prepare these various statements, such as *Small Time Operator* (**www.BellSprings.com**). Many computer software accounting packages will also generate these reports for you once you enter your income and expense figures.

Even if you don't want a bank loan, you should prepare quarterly and annual reports because this is the best way for you to monitor your business growth. At times, it may seem as though your business is unprofitable because there is so little money left at the end of a month, quarter, or calendar year, but a study of previous years' financial reports may reveal surprising growth or advancement in terms of lower cost-of-goods figures, higher gross or net profit margins, lower administrative costs, and so on. In short, financial reports can be highly informative and very comforting at times when you're not sure if you're just treading water or actually making gains.

Home Office Deduction

(See also *Business Expenses, Tax Deductible*)

Many homebased entrepreneurs are so frightened of the IRS and the possibility of an audit that they do not take home office deductions to which they are legally entitled. But this is ridiculous! If you're not cheating on your taxes, and can defend all your regular tax deductions, adding legitimate home office deductions to your Schedule C report could save you thousands of dollars in the years ahead. Don't let a nervous accountant rob you of this deduction with warnings of possible audits, because the IRS insists that you will *not* be audited simply because you take a deduction for your home office, studio, workshop, etc.

Obviously, the higher your home office deductions, the lower your self-employment taxes will be. Is there a limit to the percentage of your home you can use and write off as a business expense? In some areas, zoning laws may stipulate that business use of a residence must be limited to a certain percentage, but local zoning officials don't go around checking this sort of thing unless a neighbor complains, and they also do not report such space usage to the IRS, so most business owners simply take deductions for what they actually need and use. For example, an Ohio couple who runs a photography business writes off 40 percent of their home expenses for business. Their home is divided so that half of it is used entirely for business and they have separate business insurance coverage for that part of the house. They even had a separate furnace put in for the business side.

To take a tax deduction for using a part of your home in business, that part must be used exclusively and regularly as:

1 The principal place of business for any trade or business in which you engage; or

2 A place to meet or deal with your clients or customers in the normal course of your trade or business; or

3 A structure that is not attached to your house or residence and that is used in connection with your trade or business (examples: garage, studio, barn).

Home Office Deduction

Calculating Deductions

To deduct expenses for your home, you must be able to show the part of your home that you use for business (take photographs). To calculate the part of your home used for business, figure the total square footage of your home, then the square footage used in your business. This will give you a percentage figure you can use to apply to all the expenses related to the maintenance of your home. Another acceptable way of figuring the percentage is to count the rooms of your home—provided they are all about the same size—and divide the number of rooms used for business by the number of rooms in the home. *Examples:*

> 2,500 square feet in home, with 500 sq. ft. used for business = 20 percent
> 10 rooms in home, with 2 used for business = 2/10, 1/5, or 20 percent

Then, to determine applicable home office deductions, you would total your expenses (see lists below) and take the percentage figure that applies to your business or, in this case, 20 percent of each amount. Although this is the basic principle on which home deductions are calculated, there are some exceptions plus a number of special guidelines for each type of expense. Currently, the deduction is limited to the gross income from the business use minus the sum of (1) the business percentage of the mortgage interest, real estate taxes, and casualty losses; and (2) the business expenses other than those related to the business use of a home. *Translation: Deductions for the business use of a home cannot create a business loss or increase a net loss from a business.* Deductions in excess of the limit, however, may be carried forward to later years, subject to the income limits in those years.

Indirect Expenses

The business part of expenses that benefit both the business and personal parts of your home are deductible as a business expense on Form 8829, "Expenses for Business Use of Your Home"—known as the "Home Office Deduction." These expenses include:

● Rent (on percentage of home used for business)

- Mortgage interest (percentage related to use of home for business; balance of interest is currently deductible on the personal portion of your tax return)

- Insurance premiums on home

- Utilities (gas, electric, oil, water)

- Services (trash removal, snow removal, yard maintenance). The latter two may be questionable unless clients or customers normally visit your home.

- Home repairs, plus related labor and suppliers (furnace, roof, etc.)

- Depreciation of home (not the land, however). Ask your accountant to explain the tax problem that can occur if you take a deduction for depreciation of your home, and then sell it at a profit.

Direct Expenses

In addition to the *indirect expenses* above, home-business owners are also entitled to deduct all costs of *direct expenses* that benefit only the business part of the home, including:

- Decorating or remodeling costs/expenses (that do not result in capital improvements); painting or repairs made to the specific area or room used exclusively for business; or repairs done to change an ordinary room into a place of business, such as rewiring, plumbing changes, walls or flooring, etc.

- Certain room furnishings. Larger purchases, such as office furniture and equipment, are generally depreciated (or expensed) while inexpensive items (such as an office bulletin board) can be deducted under office supplies and materials.

Other Expenses

If the use of your computer, telephone, or family automobile is partly personal and partly business, you'll need to keep a record or time log so you can calculate a percentage related to business that may be used to figure your business deduction.

- Personal Computer. You may depreciate the business percentage of the computer's cost and also deduct related supplies and materials.

- Personal Telephone. Fully deductible are all business-related long distance telephone calls and all extra charges for business extensions or services, such as call forwarding, call holding, Internet, etc. However, homebased business owners may not deduct a percentage of the basic monthly charge for the first phone line coming into the home.

- Family Vehicle. All business-related mileage or actual operating expenses related to business use is deductible, provided you document such expenses for the IRS with some kind of log or diary. Note the odometer reading at the beginning and end of each year and log each business-related trip you make.

You may find your deductions for business use of your vehicle will be larger if you calculate on the basis of total operating costs. In this case, you would add all expenses for the year, including gas, oil, supplies, repairs, maintenance, parking and tolls, towing, washing, tires, garage expenses, license tags, inspection fees, taxes, insurance, depreciation, even Motor Club memberships. Take total miles driven for business and divide by total miles driven for the year to get a percentage of business use. Multiply total car costs by this percentage figure to get your business-related, tax-deductible automobile expenses for the year.

Identity Theft

According to the Privacy Rights Clearinghouse, half a million people are victims of identify theft each year, and the FTC says this is the number one scam today. You can help protect your financial identity by never giving your credit card number to anyone on the phone unless you initiate the call, and *never* put your social security number anywhere on the Web, or even in an e-mail. For more information on this topic, check **www.FTC.gov** or the government's Web site on identity theft at **www.consumer.gov/idtheft/index.html**.

Theft of your Mail. In some parts of the country, mail theft has become epidemic. Some thieves target mail drop boxes while others case the homes of individuals and steal mail left for pickup. To lower risk of the latter, know when your mail person regularly delivers mail and don't put your letters and bills out for pickup until near that time.

Lost or Stolen Wallet or Credit Cards. If you lost your wallet or credit cards or they were stolen, you would naturally notify your credit card companies to let them know about this loss. But in addition to canceling any credit cards that have been lost or stolen, you should also call the Social Security Administration and the three major credit reporting organizations listed below to place a fraud alert on your name and social security number to prevent someone from making application for credit over the Internet in your name. This alert will ensure that any company that checks your credit will immediately know that your information has been stolen. Here are the fraud-alert numbers you need to call:

- Equifax: 1-800-525-6285

- Experian: 1-888-397-3742

- Trans Union: 1-800-680-7289

- Social Security Administration fraud line: 1-800-269-0271

Independent Contractors

(See also *Cottage Industries; Employees, Nonfamily; Industrial Homework Laws; Labor Laws*)

As a self-employed individual, you will have many occasions to work for others as a freelancer or independent contractor. Payment for such work is made with the understanding that you will be responsible for all taxes related to this work, and at year's end, you will receive a 1099 Miscellaneous Income tax form representing total wages paid by your clients or employers.

Independent Contractors

If you routinely perform work in the homes or offices of customers of clients, you may wish to obtain liability insurance to protect you from such risks as damaging another's property, possessions, or equipment. (See *Insurance/Liability Insurance*.) Note, too, that some corporate clients may require evidence of liability insurance before they hire you—and perhaps workers' compensation insurance as well. They will not want to be held liable in the event you injure yourself while in their plant or office. By the same token, any independent contractor you hire—such as a neighborhood handyman who climbs a ladder to remove the leaves from your gutters—ought to have liability insurance, too. Without insurance, if he fell and injured himself while on your property, his medical bills could be your problem.

Independent Contractors vs. Employees

Small business owners prefer to use independent contractors whenever possible because it cuts paperwork in half and eliminates tax withholding. If you hire independent contractors, all you have to do at year's end is complete a 1099 form (Statement for Recipients of Non-Employee Compensation) for each individual to whom you have paid $600 or more. One copy goes to the IRS and the other to the contractor. Just make sure that the people you hire are truly independent contractors, and not employees.

These days, however, the use of independent contractors is risky because the stand taken today by both the IRS and Department of Labor seems increasingly to be that all workers should be considered employees or employers—period. State tax collection agencies have also gotten into the act. In the early 1990s, the IRS systematically began to identify employers who were misclassifying employees as independent contractors. In their first purging, they reclassified 76,000 workers as employees and socked 16,000 employers with $93.8 million in back taxes and penalties. Before long, the IRS had assessed more than $500 million in penalties and back taxes and forced numerous companies to reclassify over 400,000 independent contractors as employees. But this was only the tip of the iceberg. At that time, the IRS estimated there were 5 million independent contractors in the United States, and they thought 3.4 million of them should be reclassified as employees.

What this means to a business who needs outside help is that it doesn't matter how many "agreements" you may have stating that you have an employer/independent contractor relationship instead of employer/employee; *the bottom line is that, if questioned, you'll have to prove the legitimacy of the relationship. If you can't prove independent contractor status, you may find yourself faced with a huge back-taxes/penalties bill that will bankrupt your business.*

You may think that it would be difficult for anyone to find out that you're using independent contractors, but many companies have been caught when an independent contractor is let go for some reason, or is injured, then files for unemployment insurance or employee benefits under workers' compensation. This kind of action from one of your independent contractors would bring your company under the kind of scrutiny that could prove financially disastrous.

The problem comes when you, as a business owner, hire an individual to work for you in some capacity when that individual, in truth, is not a self-employed businessperson. Thus, the only safe independent contractor relationship these days seems to be when one business or self-employed individual buys the products or services of another business or self-employed individual.

For a good article that explains the difference between an independent contractor and employee, visit this Web site:

http://employment-law.freeadvice.com/independent_employee.htm

Smart Tip

Be careful about hiring your spouse as an independent contractor since the IRS and Labor Department could reclassify him or her as an employee and stick you with tax penalties and payment of back taxes. Actually, the independent contractor relationship works best if both spouses have businesses of their own and occasionally use the services of the other. Be sure to discuss this point with your accountant.

To quote the IRS: "If an employer-employee relationship exists, it does not matter what it is called." In short, an employee is an employee if the IRS (or the Department of Labor) says so. In general, an "employee" is one who "follows the usual path of an employee" and is dependent on the business he or she serves.

Independent Contractors

Supreme Court Guidelines

The Supreme Court has offered the following guidelines, which are considered "significant" in the determination of whether a person is an employee or independent contractor:

1 The extent to which the services in question are an integral part of the employer's business. (The more integral they are to the employer's business, the more it will tend to show an employee-employer relationship.)

2 The permanency of the relationship. (The more permanent the relationship, the more it tends to show an employee-employer relationship.)

3 The amount of the alleged contractor's investment in facilities and equipment. (The more substantial the investment, the more it will evidence an independent contractor relationship.)

4 The nature and degree of control by the principal. (The more control exercised by the principal over the person, the more it will evidence an employee-employer relationship.)

5 The alleged contractor's opportunities for profit and loss. (The more opportunity he has to make a profit, or sustain a loss, the more it will evidence an independent contractor relationship.)

6 The amount of initiative, judgment, or foresight in open market competition with others required for the success of the claimed independent enterprise. (The more initiative, judgment, and foresight that is required, the more it will show an independent contractor relationship.)

IRS Guidelines

The IRS also has its own list of twenty factors that are now used to determine proper classification of an independent contractor.

1 **Instructions.** An employee must comply with instructions about when, where, and how to work. Even if no instructions are given, the control factor is present if the employer has the right to give instructions.

2 **Training.** An employee is trained to perform services in a particular manner. Independent contractors ordinarily use their own methods and receive no training from the purchasers of their services.

3 **Integration.** An employee's services are integrated into the business operations because the services are important to the success or continuation of the business. This shows that the employee is subject to direction and control.

4 **Services rendered personally.** An employee renders services personally. This shows that the employer is interested in the methods as well as the results.

5 **Hiring assistants.** An employee works for an employer who hires, supervises, and pays assistants. An independent contractor hires, supervises, and pays assistants under a contract that requires him or her to provide materials and labor and to be responsible for only the result.

6 **Continuing relationship.** An employee has a continuing relationship with an employer. A continuing relationship may exist where work is performed at frequently recurring although irregular intervals.

7 **Set hours of work.** An employee has set hours of work established by an employer. An independent contractor is the master of his or her own time.

8 **Full-time work.** An employee normally works full time for an employer. An independent contractor can work when and for whom he or she chooses.

9 **Work done on premises.** An employee works on the premises of an employer, or works on a route or at a location designated by an employer.

Independent Contractors

10 **Order or sequence set.** An employee must perform services in the order or sequence set by an employer. This shows that the employee is subject to direction and control.

11 **Reports.** An employee submits reports to an employer. This shows that the employee must account to the employer for his or her actions.

12 **Payments.** An employee is paid by the hour, week, or month. An independent contractor is paid by the job or on a straight commission.

13 **Expenses.** An employee's business and travel expenses are paid by an employer. This shows that the employee is subject to regulation and control.

14 **Tools and materials.** An employee is furnished significant tools, materials, and other equipment by an employer.

15 **Investment.** An independent contractor has a significant investment in the facilities he or she uses in performing services for someone else.

16 **Profit or loss.** An independent contractor can make a profit or suffer a loss.

17 **Works for more than one person or firm.** An independent contractor gives his or her services to two or more unrelated persons or firms at the same time.

18 **Offers services to the general public.** An independent contractor makes his or her services available to the general public.

19 **Right to fire.** An employee can be fired by an employer. An independent contractor cannot be fired so long as he or she produces a result that meets the specifications of the contract.

20 **Right to quit.** An employee can quit his or her job at any time without incurring liability. An independent contractor usually agrees to complete a specific job and is responsible for its satisfactory completion, or is legally obligated to make good for failure to complete it.

The IRS also offers a mouthful-of-a-form that may be helpful (or possibly more confusing): "Information for Use in Determining Whether a Worker is an Employee for Purposes of Federal Employment Taxes and Income Tax Withholding." (Form SS-8, available at local tax offices, on the Internet, or by mail from the IRS.)

Industrial Homework Laws

(See also *Cottage Industries; Labor Laws*)

The state laws discussed here may surprise you as much as they did me when I first learned about them back in the early 1980s. Until I brought them to the attention of my readers, state homework laws had never been discussed in home-business books except in passing, such as ". . . be sure to check on any state laws that may apply to you." They came to my attention only because of their similarity to the Labor Department's "sweatshop law," which attracted wide attention in the national media in early 1983 because of the Vermont Knitters dispute (discussed earlier in the "Cottage Industries" section). Most of the state homework laws were meant to reinforce federal law, and they have been on the books since 1937 when the legislature became aware of homework abuses and passed a federal Industrial Homework Law.

In addition to Labor Department regulations against the manufacture of women's and children's garments by homeworkers, the following states reportedly have industrial homework laws that specifically prohibit the manufacturing of other products at home, including food and drink, wearing apparel, toys and dolls, cosmetics, and jewelry. In some cases manufacturing may be allowed if a special homeworker certificate or permit is obtained. Contact your state's Department of Labor for more information.

Smart Tip

To avoid problems with the Department of Labor, do not use homeworkers to manufacture goods of any kind until you've checked the legality of this with an attorney who specializes in labor law. To be safe, you should obtain a legal opinion about any homework laws that may exist in your state.

Industrial Homework Laws

A labor attorney in my network sent the following list of states known to have a homework law on the books:

California	Massachusetts	Rhode Island
Connecticut	Michigan	Tennessee
District of Columbia	Missouri	Texas
Hawaii	New Jersey	Virginia
Illinois	New York	Wisconsin
Indiana	Ohio	Puerto Rico
Maryland	Pennsylvania	

Insurance

(See also *Medical Reimbursement Plan*)

Hospitalization/Major Medical Insurance
Nearly 3 million self-employed Americans are currently uninsured. Some people have preexisting conditions that make them uninsurable or severely limit their ability to get adequate coverage, while others simply can't afford today's high insurance premiums. Until recently, the fact that only a small amount of one's health insurance costs could be deducted made it difficult for many self-employed individuals to justify this kind of expenditure. Soon, however, health insurance premiums will be deductible in full.

Group Insurance Programs. Many home-business owners work a part-time job just to get into an affordable group insurance plan, but you may be able to buy comparable coverage by joining one of the home-business/home-office organizations that now offer HMO insurance programs. (See "Organizations" in "Other Resources.") Also check out the cost of membership in your local chamber of commerce and ask about its United Chambers group insurance program.

If you are presently insured, take a moment to double-check the cancellation/conversion clauses in your policy. My husband and I learned the hard way that a group insurance policy can be canceled at any time, particularly if a small group of insured individuals is entering too many claims. In the mid-1980s, we were both insured through my membership in a small writer's organization. With only thirty days' notice of cancellation of our major medical policy, Harry decided he'd better have that angiogram the doctor had been advising. Good thing, too, for it revealed an immediate need for quadruple bypass surgery. With only days to spare, the old policy covered all expenses, but a month's delay here would have wiped us out.

Smart Tip

If you can employ your spouse in your business, you will qualify for membership in the AgriPlan/BizPlan program, which allows self-employed individuals to deduct not only all of their insurance premiums, but 100 percent of their entire family's health insurance premiums, prescription costs, and other out-of-pocket costs for medical, vision, and dental expenses. For details on this program, call 1-800-422-4661 or check the Web site at **www.TASConline.com.**

I participated in the AgriPlan/BizPlan program for several years. Being able to deduct up to $12,000 for my "employee reimbursement program" on my Schedule C report greatly lowered the amount of self-employment taxes I had to pay every year as well as the stress I felt every time I paid my high (though fully deductible) insurance premium. (You never saw a woman so happy to finally be 65 years old because going on Medicare translated to an immediate annual insurance savings of $7,000.)

Homeowner's or Renter's Insurance Policies

In a 1999 survey of more than 900 home-business owners, Terri Lonier (WorkingSolo.com) learned that 60 percent of those surveyed had no business insurance at all. This is *not* a good business management policy. In the event of a tragedy, you stand to lose twice as much as the average homeowner or renter—both your home and business. If you are uninsured, take immediate steps to protect the investment you've already made in your business.

Would your business survive if a thief stole your computer? (Are all your files regularly backed up and stored off site, such as in a safe deposit box?) If your home were to be destroyed by fire, flood, tornado, hurricane, or earthquake, would you have the money to refurnish your office, studio, or workshop, not to mention all the product inventory and other supplies that may be stored in it? You probably have homeowner's or renter's insurance, but this kind of policy does *not* cover business equipment, supplies, or inventory, or, in all probability, any losses due to fires that may be caused by such things. Note that "goods for sale" are considered business property that must be separately insured, either with an individual policy or a special rider.

Home Office Policies. Many of the major insurance companies, including Aetna, Liberty Mutual, and Firemen Insurance Co., now offer home office policies for as little as $150 a year. Such policies typically offer up to $50,000 all-risk protection, $5,000 per person medical payments, and a million dollars in general liability insurance (both product and professional). Many home-business/home-office organizations also offer this kind of insurance to their members.

Liability Insurance

Business owners need to be concerned both with personal and product liability insurance. *Personal liability insurance* protects you against claims made by people who have suffered bodily injury while on your premises, while *product liability insurance* protects you against lawsuits by consumers who have been injured while using your product.

If clients or customers regularly come to your home for business reasons, you will need personal liability coverage beyond what is normally included in your homeowner's policy. (*Why* people are on your property will determine the coverage your insurance policy provides.)

A rider to your homeowner's policy, called a Business Pursuits Endorsement, is an inexpensive answer for many small businesses since it offers coverage for furnishings, business equipment, supplies and products you may be storing, as well as some liability coverage for people who may come to your home for business purposes. (If you have more than $3,000 of inventory, however, you should obtain a separate fire, vandalism, and theft policy.)

If you make and sell garments or products for children, you may find that product liability insurance is critical to the sale of merchandise, especially if you're trying to sell to national mail order catalog houses or large retailers. Some craft shows require it, too. However, sometimes you may be asked to provide product liability insurance when it's not needed.

"In selling one of my books to a large retail outlet, I was asked for huge product liability coverage," reports book publisher Leila Peltosaari. "But when I explained that this is not applicable to my book since there is a disclaimer in it already, they agreed and waived the need for insurance. To date I have not lost a sale because I didn't have this insurance."

Product liability insurance rates vary greatly from state to state, depending on your annual gross sales (or anticipated sales), the number of products you sell, and the possible risks associated with each of them. If your income is low, or your product line small, you may be able to buy an affordable policy.

Smart Tip

The least expensive way ($150–$250/year) to get some product liability insurance is to buy a home office policy that offers protection for your whole business while also giving you a minimum of $1 million in liability insurance (both product and professional). An often-recommended company in this field is RLI Insurance Company (1-800-221-7917; **www.RLICorp.com**). Also check the group insurance programs offered by home-business/small-business organizations listed in "Other Resources."

Other Insurance You May Need

- **Business Interruption Insurance.** Here's a "for instance": Your home is destroyed by a fire, flood or tornado, and your business stops until you can piece it together again. Business interruption insurance could make a big difference, and it may not be as expensive as you think. Talk to an insurance agent about it or investigate group plans offered by professional organizations.

- **Computer Insurance.** Personal computers used for business will not be covered by your homeowner's or renter's policy, except possibly against loss by fire or theft. But that still leaves you at risk for damage caused by water, high humidity, or power surges not contained by your surge suppressor. If you have made a substantial investment in your computer system and software, the only practical thing to do is buy a home office policy that covers all your office furniture and equipment, or buy separate insurance for your computer system. (Check out the policy offered by Safeware, The Insurance Agency, Inc. [1-800-848-3469; www.Safeware.com].

- **Disability or Income Replacement Insurance.** If you are the major breadwinner in your family, what would happen if you could not work for an extended period of time . . . or ever again? To keep premium costs as low as possible on this type of insurance, consider a waiting period of three to six months before benefits would begin.

Intellectual Property, Protection of

(See also *Copyrights; Domain Name Registration; Electronic Publishing; Licensing; Patents; Slogans; Trademarks*)

All forms of intellectual property are real and valuable assets to any business. Even if you don't have a patentable invention, you may still have intellectual property that can be protected by copyright, trademark, patent, and trade secret laws. For instance, distinctive company and product names are protectable with a registered trademark. Copyrights ensure that publications, logos, art, and computer software are protected from copying. Patents protect new and useful inventions from literal or even substantial copying. And trade secrets protect all kinds of business know-how as long as they do not become a matter of public knowledge.

How to Handle Copyright Infringements

There will always be people who will use copyrighted works, either innocently or deliberately. If you become aware of an infringement of one of your copyrights (whether officially registered or not), immediately send a cease-and-desist letter. Because infringers have no way of knowing whether you have registered the copyright or not, they will probably stop using your work to avoid any legal problems. Naturally, it helps if your letter is written with authority on impressive stationery, and it will carry more weight if an attorney writes it for you.

Innocent Infringers. If you are dealing with an individual who has innocently infringed your copyright, a friendly, yet strongly worded letter from you may be all it takes to resolve the matter. Simply explain that, as the legal copyright owner, you alone have the right to profit from the work in question and that you will take any legal steps necessary to protect your rights. Ask for a reply by return mail confirming that the infringement will cease at once. Often, this will do the trick.

Corporate Ripoffs. If you've been ripped off by a large corporation, skip the friendly letter and contact a copyright attorney at once. It won't cost much to have an attorney write a letter for you, but to proceed further than this may be more costly than you can afford. In the end, you must ask yourself how valuable your work is to you and how much time and money you are willing to invest to protect it. An important consideration here is whether you have filed a formal copyright registration of the work in question. Under present law, if you decide you want to sue, you can file the registration after you discover the infringer—although such late registration will limit the kind of damages you can sue for.

Note: In the past, there has been a movement in Congress to abolish the requirement that one must register a copyright in order to be able to sue for infringement. Though much discussed, this had not become law as of November 2002, and whether Congress will succumb remains to be seen. If this does become law, it will become almost impossible for anyone to investigate the copyright status of a work, and we will all have to presume everything is protected by copyright.

Illegal Use of Your Freelance Articles. Many major publications have previously committed copyright infringement by posting articles to their Web sites without asking permission or making extra payment to the original authors. A press release discussing the Supreme Court's ruling in favor of freelancers will be found at:
 www.writenews.com/2001/062501_freelancers_supreme_court.htm.

How One Designer Handled Copyright Infringement. While conducting one of her "Designer Sweatshirts" classes at a shop, Mary Mulari (MaryMulari.com) noticed a packet of information and designs for sale on the topic of decorating sweatshirts, also the subject of her first book, *Designer Sweatshirts*. Since Mary keeps a close eye on what her competition is doing, she purchased the packet.

"It was a shock to recognize my own diagrams, illustrations, and designs, as well as my text only slightly reworded," she wrote. "This was clearly an infringement of my copyright; my information and drawings had been stolen and now were being offered by another company at a price much lower than my own book."

Mary found an attorney who informed the company publishing the packet that the designer was aware of their unlawful use of her materials, and that they had to cease selling their packet or face a trial. "The first response from the company was to pay me royalties," said Mary. "From that point, we were able to work out an agreement which includes royalties, their payment of my attorney's fees, and written information in each packet crediting me for the information and listing my name and address. A court trial was avoided."

This experience taught Mary the importance of keeping in touch with the marketplace and with other publications, as well as the value of registering a copyright. Her story also illustrates how infringements are discovered, and why it can be costly to steal the creative work of another individual.

Protecting Your Trademarks

Trademarks prevent one company from trading on the good name and reputation of another, but trademark infringements are common, particularly on the Web (see one example below). Like copyrights and patents, trademarks can be expensive to protect, and small business entrepreneurs don't have the money to battle aggressive and/or much larger companies in court. A good example of this is the number of home-business owners who have been unable to defend their use of the word "entrepreneur" in their domain name or business name.

For some time now, Entrepreneur Media (publisher of *Entrepreneur* magazine) has taken a hostile stance toward the entrepreneurial community by trying to monopolize the word "entrepreneur." Lacking money for a court battle, many small business owners have simply backed down. One company that won its case in court is EntrepreneurPR, a Sacramento, California, firm that provides public relations services to small businesses. Initially, Entrepreneur Media's aggressive legal efforts forced Scott Smith, president of EntrepreneurPR, to change his business name. In February 2002, however, the 9th U.S. Circuit Court of Appeals unanimously ruled that Entrepreneur

Media's trademark is "weak" and that it does *not* have exclusive rights to the word "entrepreneur."

An article by Sherri Cruz in the *Star Tribune* (one of the top twenty largest newspapers in the United States), reported on this case, explaining how trademark rights arise out of use. "If the general population associates a name with a thing, then it is trademarked," she wrote. "What Entrepreneur Media might be doing is using its muscle (attorneys and money) to be the last one standing. If Entrepreneur Media gets enough companies to stop using 'entrepreneur,' then Entrepreneur Media will have won trademark rights."

As things now stand, the courts have ruled that Entrepreneur Media can't use the word "entrepreneur" for its exclusive use but that it does have the right to use "entrepreneur" to identify the products described in its registered trademark. But what small business owner is going to risk using this word now if it means they have to go to court to defend it? "The average cost to litigate a trademark dispute is $25,000," says Scott Smith. "Large companies definitely have an unfair advantage over small businesses when it comes to intellectual property disputes."

For more information on this topic, visit **www.entrepreneurs.com** (owned by WebMagic, Inc.), which has also successfully defended its right to use the word "entrepreneur").

Example of a Common Trademark Problem. If someone tells you you're infringing on their trademark, what can you do about it? Maybe more than you think. Here's an example. Pamela Burns wholesales a line of handmade clothing for children under the state-registered name of *Injeanious*. She also registered the domain name of Injeanious.org (as .com and .net had already been taken). In mid-2002, she was challenged by a mall shop named *Injeanius* that sells a commercial line of adult clothing. Pam received a letter from the mall's lawyer asking her to change her name. After referring Pam to my attorney, Mary Helen Sears, she sent this report:

"Initially, Ms. Sears said that since Injeanius had the name first, I had a 50-50 chance if it went to court. As it turned out, they had not trademarked their name, either. They do not have their own label as I do, but simply use Injeanius as their store name, which currently is only at one location, and they sell other labels in their store. Their lawyer did express surprise that the state approved the name for me since they are so similar. He also tried to convince me it would not be hard to change my name, although I strongly disagreed. (In addition to the expense and letters and phone calls, I would have had to re-sew labels in 2,000 pieces of clothing at that point.)

"After speaking with Ms. Sears, and my finally mentioning that I always use the same typeface, as well as always adding 'by Pamela Burns' along with my Injeanious name, she said that definitely clarified the fact that I was different from the store, Injeanius. The fact that we also serve different markets, and my products are handmade and theirs are not, gave added weight to my continued use of the unregistered mark."

In speaking with Ms. Sears about this, she said she would be surprised if Pamela hears from the other lawyer again. "*Injeanious* by Pamela Burns" as a business name is different from *Injeanius* and isn't likely to cause confusion as to source," she explained. "But *Injeanious* alone and *Injeanius* are so close in sight, sound, and apparent meaning that the best advice I could have given if that were the situation was that whichever one was the *second* one to use their variant of that name should change it as soon as possible.

"On the trademark registration point, I would also clarify that through use in trade and commerce of "Injeanious by Pamela Burns," Pam is building up common law trademark rights that will accrue to her advantage if she later seeks a registration. Meanwhile, however, a person who designs and personally makes her own line of children's clothing and sells mostly through trade shows has far too many places for the money that her business brings in and doesn't need the expense of getting a registered trademark as a first, second, or even third step. I always like to give those practicalities consideration when advising small business owners."

Protecting a Patent

The smaller you are, the less you can afford the high cost of litigation. If you get a patent and it's contested by a company with clout, it will be child's play for them to prove that it resembles some item already patented by them, which in turn will automatically void any patent you may hold. "If you're a small person suing a large company, they can outspend you in court and impose so many tasks on you that it becomes difficult to stay the course," says patent attorney Mary Helen Sears. She adds, however, that many patents litigated today are being held valid, and because judgments are often quite large, a few lawyers now take patent cases on contingency.

Since patent cases may take years to resolve, costing a law firm as much as $300,000, the only cases likely to be taken on contingency are those that have the potential of generating at least a million dollars in damages. "A patent is nothing more than a license to sue," says Houston patent attorney James H. Riley II. "It gives you the right to go to court, but if you don't sue to enforce your patent, it's just a piece of paper. The test of a patent is how it stands up in court, not how it's written."

Protecting a Trade Secret

A trade secret is anything that gives your business a competitive advantage over others who do not know it. It might be a confidential formula, recipe, pattern, process, device, information or compilation of information, used in your business. For example, a soap manufacturer working out of her home told me she can produce up to 2,500 bars of soap a day because her scientist-husband knows how to blend oils and ingredients to speed up the production process. These soap formulas—a valuable trade secret—gives her company an important edge on the competition.

The best way to protect a trade secret is not to tell anyone about it. If someone should steal it, however, you should know that common law trade secret protection exists and you might have grounds for a lawsuit if you discover the theft.

Labor Laws

(See also *Cottage Industries; Employees, Nonfamily; Independent Contractors; Industrial Homework Laws*)

The U.S. Department of Labor administers several laws that affect the operations of businesses both large and small. *The sole proprietor, however, need not be concerned with any of them (save minimum-wage laws) until nonfamily members are hired as employees.* At that point, the following laws apply to one's business:

Labor Laws

● *The Fair Labor Standards Act of 1938, as Amended.* This law establishes minimum wages, overtime pay, record keeping, and child labor standards for employees individually engaged in or producing goods for interstate commerce, and for all employees employed in certain enterprises described in the act, unless a specific exemption applies. Employers are required to meet the standards established under the Act, regardless of the number of their employees and whether they work full or part-time. A complete copy of this act, and additional information about the hiring of employees, can be obtained from your nearest Wage & Hour Division of the Department of Labor. (See "U.S. Government" in your telephone book.)

● *Occupational Safety and Health Act* (OSHA) of 1970. If you have even one employee, you need to know about OSHA, which is allowed to inspect or investigate any workplace in response to an employee complaint and issue citations and assess penalties for violations. This statute is concerned with safe and healthful conditions in the workplace, and it covers all employers engaged in business affecting interstate commerce. Employers must comply with standards and with applicable record keeping and reporting requirements specified in regulations issued by OSHA.

OSHA regulations also extend to employees' use of your vehicle. If one of them were to be hurt in an automobile accident, you could be held responsible, particularly if they were injured because they weren't wearing a seatbelt. Details about OSHA regulations are available from area offices of the United States Department of Labor.

● *Social Security Act of 1935, as Amended.* This act is concerned with employment insurance laws, and each state requires employers who come under its employment insurance law to pay taxes based on their payroll. For more information, contact your local Employment Security or Job Service Office, or talk to an accountant.

● Other laws administered by the U.S. Department of Labor. You need not be concerned with these laws unless you are involved in situations that concern (1) garnishment of an employee's wages, (2) hiring of disadvantaged workers, (3) federal service contracts using laborers and mechanics, (4) federal contracts for work on public buildings or public works, (5) employee pension and welfare benefit plans, (6) government contracts, and other special situations.

Libel/Defamation of Character

You can be held liable for defamation of character if you disparage a person's business reputation or character with statements that are untrue. "When talking about a competitor, be careful not to disparage that person's reputation, unless of course the negative comments are *true*," says attorney Leonard D. Duboff. "If the matter should wind up in litigation, the burden of establishing truth will be imposed on the person making the disparaging remarks."

Duboff emphasizes there is a big difference between promoting your work and reputation and undermining another's, so be careful about intentionally undermining a competitor's product or integrity when talking to strangers. "You can say your products are first-rate, but it would be risky to say that your work is better than another's unless that fact can be established," he adds. (Source: *The Crafts Report.*)

Licensing

(See also *Contracts; Copyrights; Patents/Working with a Manufacturer*)

A license grants specific rights to someone to do something that could not legally be done without the license. Creators of ideas or products may grant licenses for such things as the use of a name, a graphic image or design, a cartoon character, or an invention or unique product. Sometime during the life of your business, you may either wish to obtain a license from someone to sell a certain product (see *Obtaining a License* below) or, more likely, you may find yourself in a position to license your own designs or property to others (see *Granting a License*).

It can cost thousands of dollars to package and market a product nationally, and the average designer, artist, or small business owner simply doesn't have this kind of time, energy, or financial resources. Through licensing, however, it's possible to get an unlimited number of products into the marketplace without any up-front costs to you. To get a better handle on this

Licensing

market, you might want to attend one of the annual licensing shows held in New York City each year, sponsored by Int'l. Licensing Merchandisers' Association (LIMA). Call (212) 244-1944 or check **www.Licensing.org**.

Although it may take up to a year or more to get a product manufactured and on the market, you might earn royalties for many years thereafter. Some artists and designers are earning thousands of dollars a year from royalties on products or designs they have licensed to manufacturers. But this is an industry fraught with pitfalls and frustration for those who don't do their homework on this topic, so here are some tips to get you started.

Granting a License

Let's assume you have some artwork or product concept you'd like to sell in the form of a license. Your first task is to identify a manufacturer, publisher, or company whose products or services match what you have to offer. If you're thinking about offering artwork or photography, check the latest annual edition of *Artist's Market* to identify potential prospects for calendars, greeting cards, posters, etc.

When you're ready to begin negotiating, do so with the understanding that there are no standards in the licensing industry. Because each licensing agency and manufacturer operates differently, no two licensing deals are going to be alike.

Agents and Attorneys. Some designers have agents who represent them to major manufacturers, but they are hard to find and may take as much as 50 percent of one's royalties. Thus, licensing newbies often negotiate their own contracts. This is not easy, however, and it can be disastrous if you don't seek the advice of an attorney. "If you don't know what you are doing, there are a lot of 'gotcha's' in this kind of arrangement," says one craftsman who made a bad licensing deal to have his handcrafted clocks reproduced. While you may be able to draft your own legal licensing agreement, there are so many points to be covered that you could easily overlook something important.

"An attorney can negotiate a contract for you, but lawyers tend to scare off small manufacturers," says Terrie Floyd, Laughing Moon LLC (Toymakers Collection). Over the years, she has licensed over a thousand designs to a dozen companies for jumping jacks, clocks, lamps, textiles, dinnerware, dolls, and Christmas ornaments. "I've had more than my share of problems related to those sales," she says. "I've learned it is sometimes better to negotiate contracts yourself, using an attorney only as a consultant. In this case, what an attorney may do best is give you maximum protection while someone else is preparing to profit from your creativity or intellectual property."

Contracts and Royalties. A licensing arrangement can be made for a period of one to five years, but most contracts are set up for two years with renewal options. If an agent or representative helps you sell your idea or product, expect to pay that person either a flat fee or a commission of between 10 and 15 percent of your total royalties. Such royalties can vary from 2 to 10 percent but 5 to 7 percent is most common. (The lower the retail price of the item, the lower the percentage is likely to be.) "You must understand the market potential for a product before you can successfully negotiate the terms of a contract and the percent of royalties that will be paid," says Annie Lang, author of numerous design books for crafters. Many of her designs have been sold to manufacturers for reproduction as rubber stamps, textile items, and paper products. (Four of Annie's active licensing contracts have come as a direct result of the decorative painting books she self-publishes through Eas'l Publications, **www.easlpublications.com**). "These books are the means by which I introduce characters to consumers and industry manufacturers," she says.

While an advance on royalties is common, the amount of both royalties and the size of an advance has much to do with the industry, your reputation as a designer, and the market for the products in question. "Established designers may be able to command an upfront designer fee," says Annie, "but beginners will be lucky to get a small advance of $250 to $500 against royalties that won't begin to materialize for a year or more. Once they start, however, payments are made monthly or quarterly, depending on the manufacturer's policy."

Be particularly careful when establishing royalty arrangements of any kind. There is a big difference between being paid a percentage of the retail price, net receipts, or net profit. You can't bank on the last one, and net receipts may be less than half the retail price due to discounts given to wholesalers.

Licensing

Savvy Licensing Tips

The following tips, gleaned from interviews with designers Annie Lang and Terrie Floyd, will help you negotiate a good licensing agreement with a manufacturer:

- Only license a certain image for a certain use for a certain period of time. When a contract comes up for renewal (and most have renew clauses), you will then have the option of renegotiating a new contract or letting it expire if you choose. Short-term contracts also allow you to explore other licensing opportunities for those designs, perhaps with a larger company or one with more marketing potential and better royalty terms.

- Don't leave the contract open as to the products the designs will be used on.

- List everything individually on which a particular design will be used. Contracts can always be amended at a later date to increase the line.

- Don't budge on copyright ownership. Insist on a clause that states the work is your own creation and intellectual property, and the manufacturing, advertising, distribution, and sale of the work in no way infringes upon the rights of any third parties who may also wish to license the same design for a different use. (Although the copyright will be yours, you probably won't get designer credit on the manufactured product unless you are a 'name' designer. Fabric manufacturers may be an exception, however. Annie Lang had no trouble getting designer credit—a copyright notation—on the selvage of the fabrics she designed for Erlanger Group, Ltd.)

- Specify what kind of changes can be made (colors, design details, etc.), and ask for final approval on the product's design and quality of the samples.

- Include a clause that states you cannot be held liable if there is a consumer lawsuit against the manufacturer.

- Understand the company's policy regarding derivative uses of a design and always ask for an approval clause that gives you the right to refuse to allow the design to be used in a way you don't like. ("Artists should decide if they want creative approval of the work," advises Terrie Floyd. "They usually can do a deal where they can have their name removed from the product without affecting royalty payments. I usually work with companies that actually care and want my input before the work is marketed, but not all companies operate that way.")

- Pay close attention to the clause about international sales since many contracts include a stipulation about lower royalties for sales to Canada and other countries. (Because Terrie Floyd did not hire an attorney to check one of the first contracts she got, she overlooked the clause that stated no royalties would be paid on products sold in Canada or overseas. She later learned that, in order to give American companies a cheap manufacturing price, overseas manufacturers make many more than they expect to sell to the American buyers, so they just sell the excess themselves on the open market without regard to licensing or copyright laws. "Thousands and thousands of my designs were sold internationally with no royalties paid," she says, adding that she learned of the copies after seeing ads for her work on television and in newspapers. After realizing the enormity of her loss, Terrie hired an attorney who managed to get at least some money for international sales under this contract.

- Before entering into a licensing arrangement, be sure to register appropriate copyrights, trademarks, or patents, and establish quality-control standards for the manufacturer of your product or designs. Never send an unsolicited design or craft sample to any manufacturer since this constitutes "public exposure" (according to the patent and copyright laws), and automatically gives a company the right to steal from you. Instead, ask the company to sign a nondisclosure agreement (NDA) or "proprietary rights agreement" stating they will merely look at your designs and not copy them. Nondisclosure agreements vary, but should contain a definition of what is and what isn't confidential information as well as the obligations of the receiving party, and time periods.

If a manufacturer expresses interest in your products or designs, check out the company carefully. "You have to be able to trust the manufacturer because there is no way you can check how many products they make and sell using your designs," says Terrie Floyd, who learned this fact the hard way. "Since contact people change regularly, try to deal with the owner or someone high up on the ladder," she urges.

Obtaining a License

Few homebased entrepreneurs can afford to make a licensing arrangement with a major company or institution because they cannot produce items in sufficient quantity to have enough profit margin available to cover the costs involved in any licensing arrangement. Sports team logos are one exception, however. Since sports organizations like publicity for their teams, their licensing rules and regulations are relatively easy for small business owners to comply with. Of course, one must pay a licensing fee and percentage of sales for the use of any logo, and the bigger the organization, the higher the licensing fee. Begin this process by contacting the team's home office by phone, asking to speak to the Licensing Agent. (Your librarian can get these telephone numbers for you if you can't find them yourself.)

Licensing Agreements Between Individuals. Small business owners may also find it easy and profitable to work with other small business owners or individual designers, as the following story illustrates. Two needlework designers made a profitable arrangement with an artist whose work they admired. They sold him on the deal simply by stitching one of his paintings and explaining how they would market an entire line of his designs in cross-stitch and needlepoint. Working with an attorney, they came to an agreement on royalties and term of contract (which included renewal options and a termination clause). Here are three of their special tips:

1 You or the licensor may want to branch out into other related fields, so you need a "Right of First Refusal" clause that will give you first chance at the opportunity to expand into a different area of business. If you decline, the opportunity may then be offered to others.

2 Be sure to work out what will happen in the event of death of either licensor or licensee.

3 Specify the territory in which you plan to sell and don't limit yourself to a small area.

Mailing List Maintenance

Keeping a mailing list up to date is a real challenge, given the way people move around these days. If you're trying to salvage an old but important mailing list containing out-of-date addresses or phone numbers, here are three ways to update the list:

1 Using your browser's search engine, type in the names of individuals or businesses to see if they have a presence on the Web.

2 If you don't have a viable mail address and need to track down an individual or business, try your library e-resources. In my city, for example, I can access my library's *Reference USA* directory and other information resources on the Internet simply by entering my library card number on the library's Web page. (Having this resource enabled me to quickly reconnect with many individuals and companies I had quoted in earlier editions of this book but had lost touch with over the years.)

3 If you have a phone number that's bad, often you may need only a new area code number. In this case, go to **www.Americom.com** and click its "Area Decoder" to look up area codes from all over the world.

Medical Reimbursement Plan

(See also *Employees*)

While many people believe you must be incorporated to be able to write off 100 percent of your health insurance and medical expenses, even sole proprietors can do this—without incorporating, without buying a new insurance policy, and with a minimum of paperwork. This tax-saving strategy—AgriPlan/BizPlan—has been available for years, but few home business owners seem to be familiar with it. If you are a sole proprietor, C Corporation, LLC, or partnership, this plan will allow you to deduct 100 percent of your family's health insurance premiums and out-of-pocket medical, vision, and dental expenses not covered by insurance.

By establishing a fair annual salary for the kind and amount of work being done, you can legally pay your spouse with a combination compensation package of salary and medical reimbursement for all family out-of-pocket costs. Thus, a salary of $8,000 for part-time work being done by the spouse might break down into $2,000 of W-2 wages and $6,000 in medical reimbursement. Your spouse would then pay *from the family checking account* all insurance premiums and other unreimbursed expenses not covered by your insurance and you, as employer, would reimburse your spouse for these expenditures *from the business account*. (This is nothing more than taking money out of one family pocket and putting it in another, but it's a perfectly legal tax strategy.)

This tax strategy can easily cut self-employment taxes by a thousand dollars or more, and the really good news is that your spouse does not have to pay any state or federal taxes on the medical reimbursement portion (the $6,000 mentioned above)—only on the W-2 wages. For complete details, call 1-800-422-4661 or check **www.TASConline.com**.

Merchant Account Providers (MAPS)

(See also *E-commerce Site*)

If most of your selling will be done on the Web, you'll find many merchant account options simply by surfing the Internet. Unless you expect to sell $1,200 a month or more from your Web site, however, forget about going the traditional route of getting merchant status from your bank or one of the many online merchant account providers because the costs are just too high. For example, one business owner reported that, in addition to her basic monthly fee, she was also paying a monthly batch header fee of $3.30, a statement fee of $10, a minimum processing fee of $9.98 plus a .30 cent transaction fee for every sale.

Rather than getting stuck for the high fixed monthly charges of a regular account (and penalty charges when sales fall below a certain amount per month), most beginning sellers on the Web use a merchant account provider that merely takes a percentage of each sale (see list below). Although such services are still costly, at least you know going in what your selling costs will be.

- **www.PayPal.com.** Now allied with eBay, this service provider is often the choice of beginners who have no sales track record yet. Fees occur only when sales are actually made. Currently, the cost is thirty cents per transaction for sales under $15; for items $15 and more, the cost is thirty cents plus 2.2 percent of the sale. The downside of PayPal is that some shoppers who aren't already registered with PayPal may not take the time to open their own account there (which is necessary before they can buy on a PayPal site).

- **www.ProPay.com.** Similar to PayPal, except that shoppers do not have to register before making a purchase. This service provider claims to be 55 percent less expensive than other merchant account providers and is easy to set up. Currently, the fee is 3.5 percent of the sale, plus thirty-five cents per transaction.

- **www.CCnow.com.** This quick-and-easy shopping cart solution for new Web site owners offers secure transaction processing for all major credit cards with no extra charge for international orders. No startup costs or monthly fees; just a straight 9 percent commission on sales.

- **www.GoEmerchant.com.** Another e-commerce solution, but the $49.95 monthly fee makes this service too costly for most beginners. Probably best for established/growing Web sites with sales of $1,000 a month or more.

- **www.ClickBank.com.** This company will handle the processing of credit card orders but only one item can be purchased at a time, which is why it is often used by electronic publishers selling reports or books. Currently, the charge is $1 per transaction, plus 7.5 percent of the sale. This program also includes an affiliate program, in case you want to sell your publications through other dealers on the Web.

Note: By listing the above MAPS for your convenience, please understand that I am not personally recommending any of them. In the Web's here-today-gone-tomorrow atmosphere, nothing is certain. Know who you're dealing with before you sign on the dotted line. One seller told me she lost a couple of thousand dollars when her Web-based merchant account provider went out of business without paying her for sales that had cleared. That's what prompted her to bite the bullet and get a regular merchant account locally.

Smart Tip

Avoid companies that offer a credit card service and throw in free Web hosting. The average cost for this type of credit card service/Web hosting seems to be around $50 a month, but the annoying pop-up ads included with this kind of service could kill your business.

"One thing not everyone knows about are chargebacks," says Eileen Heifner, owner of Create An Heirloom. "If a customer says they never received your merchandise, and you cannot prove they did, you get a chargeback—which means the credit card company won't pay. If you are selling at a show, it's very important to make an imprint of the card and have the customer sign the slip. You also need to get an authorization number to put on the slip. If you do not do this, the credit card company may not pay. You may also be responsible for taking someone's card if the credit company suspects it is lost or stolen. When you sign up to be a credit card merchant, make sure you understand all the rules and regulations related to authorizations and chargebacks and know how to handle sales to a card that has been reported lost or stolen."

In various articles on his invaluable business site, **www.WilsonWeb.com** (see "Other Resources"), Dr. Ralph Wilson discusses the problem of credit card fraud and ways merchants can minimize their risk. Those selling downloadable software and other high-ticket items are at greatest risk, he says, but all merchants will get hit by credit card fraud at one time or another. Although this is just a cost of doing business that you must accept. Dr. Wilson suggests that online merchants can add a layer of protection by looking carefully at purchases made from a free e-mail address, those with different shipping and billing addresses, and bounced e-mail order confirmations. When in doubt, telephone the buyer before shipping a high-ticket item.

Partnership Pitfalls

Although many small business owners have formed profitable partnerships, through the years I've heard far more sad tales about them than happy ones. "Partnerships can be very tricky," says one small business owner. "I would suggest that people think long and hard before forming one." Adds another, who once formed an informal partnership with a friend, "Ours was a craft production type business, and our partnership ultimately ruined our friendship and set my business back. I've learned that if something is worth doing, or if I have a good idea, I should do it by myself or with my husband. If the idea works, the glory and profit will be all mine and I'll have no resentment about who is doing the most work."

Buying Out a Partner. One reader who bought out her partner told me how difficult it was to determine a fair net worth figure based on inventory totals, raw materials, accounts payable, and accounts receivable. An accountant helped in that regard. The partners worked out an agreement whereby payments would be made over a three-year period, and the buyer took out declining term insurance to cover the contract in case anything happened to her before the balance was paid in full. "Dissolving a partnership is somewhat like a divorce in that neither person wants to get shafted by the other," she says. "I suggest that anyone looking for a business partner think ahead, asking 'What would I do if . . . ?' A partner may die or want out of the business, or you may simply want to buy out your partner as I did."

Or, as newsletter editor Shep Robinson once said, "Just because you get on the wrong streetcar, nothing says you have to stay on it to the end of the line."

Three Strikes and You're Out! "I think three words can fairly sum up my partnership experience," says business consultant Daryl Ochs (StreetSmartBusiness.com). "I've had three business partnerships over the years, with the most recent ending in December 2001. In general (realizing there are exceptions), my advice is very simple: *Don't go there*. Partnerships are deeply fraught with danger. If you're working with a friend, the most likely scenario is that you lose a friend. More likely you lose a friend *and* gain an enemy! There is just too much assuming that goes on in partnerships, and you know the old saying about 'assume.' From my own disastrous experience with three attempts at partnership, I will never do another."

Patents

(See also *Intellectual Property, Protection of*)

A patent, which now lasts for twenty years from date of filing (with some complex qualifications you need to discuss with a patent attorney), is a grant issued by the U.S. government giving an inventor the right to exclude all others from making, using, or selling his invention within the United States and its territories and possessions.

Patents may be granted to anyone who invents a new and useful product, process, or any new and useful improvement of either. You cannot patent anything in the public domain, or anything that would be obvious to anyone skilled in the process or field. Essentially, to be patentable, an invention must add to the pool of knowledge, not take from it. In other words, you can't reinvent the wheel.

All this sounds simple enough, but in truth, patents are a very complicated and expensive way of protecting intellectual property. Actually, all a patent really does is give the inventor the right to exclude anyone else from making, using, or selling the invention. It is possible to get a patent on something, yet not be able to use it if someone has a more encompassing, earlier patent.

You can do a U.S. patent search in one of four ways: (1) by visiting the public search room of the Patent and Trademark Office in Arlington, Virginia; (2) by providing the Patent office with specific information to enable them to do a search for you, (3) through a search of one of the patent databases now available in some libraries; or (4) by searching the Patent Office's Web site at **www.USPTO.gov/patft/index.html**. (Includes only patents dating back to 1976 or so, however; for info on older patents you must visit a patent and trademark depository library.) Also see the book, *Patent Searching Made Easy by David Hitchcock* (Nolo Press).

Smart Tip

Because there are many requirements of disclosure and conduct in the patent statute that the average person is not going to know about, it would be foolhardy to file for a patent without an attorney's help. When you try to do your own patent, you create more opportunity for someone to defeat your patent based on some legal rule or pitfall you've overlooked. An attorney will be more knowledgeable about these pitfalls and help you avoid them.

An important consideration when trying to decide whether to patent something or not is whether you can afford to maintain a patent and protect it in the event someone tries to steal it from you. High maintenance fees ($440–$1550 for a small entity) must now be paid at 3-1/2 , 6-1/2 and 11-1/2 year intervals, or the patent will lapse. Since a patent gotten with the help of a patent attorney can cost from $3,000 to $20,000 (depending on attorney's fees) and can take up to ten years to acquire, many inventors would be better off selling their ideas to manufacturers for a flat fee up front, or on a royalty basis if possible. But as patent attorney Mary Helen Sears stresses, "It is dangerous to submit a patentable item to a manufacturer before filing a patent application unless the manufacturer, in advance of hearing the invention, commits itself that you are the owner. Don't do this without competent legal help or you will lose all."

Finally, the fact that you might be able to get a patent is meaningless unless you know how to market the product itself. As one patent expert points out, "Less than one percent of the over seven million products that have been patented in the United States have ever been marketed, and less than one percent of the products on the market have a patent." If you decide to manufacture a patented product yourself, get it on the market *fast* to beat the crowd, says an experienced marketer, because a good idea will be stolen the moment you display it at a trade show. "And," adds Ms. Sears, "if you decide to manufacture, that is the time the patent usually is worth the investment and effort involved—in part because it deters others from suing you on their patents, and in part because it does deter some copiers as well."

Patents

Prepatent Considerations

In his thirty-five years of experience in getting new products and ideas into the marketplace, inventor Jeremy Gorman in Wilmington, Vermont learned a lot about the patent process and the value of its protection. Sales of products of his inventions exceed $500 million annually and, prior to his retirement, he counseled inventors individually and through seminars. "Ninety-seven percent of the U.S. patents issued never earn enough money to pay the patenting fee," he told me. "They just go on a plaque on the wall or in a desk drawer to impress the grandchildren fifty years later. Except for your ego, nothing is helped by having a patent on an unsalable idea, no matter how creative it is." Jeremy offers these tips for beginning inventors:

1 Before considering patenting an idea, first determine if there is a market for the product. If so, consider whether you will make the product yourself or have it made under license.

2 Don't spend money to get a patent unless a market study tells you how much money you can expect to make on the product. Be sure a patent is worth the cost, and *be sure it will protect you.* For example, if you have a simple invention like the paper clip, all a patent would do for you is give you about a two-year head start. There are ripoff companies whose business is to copy simple things, and they don't give a hoot for patents. They will make a hundred million of your paper clips in three months and flood the market with them. By the time you even know they exist, they will have scrapped the mold, moved to a new address, and be making thumbtacks under another name.

3 If you decide a patent is worth the expense, don't apply by yourself. Get a patent attorney. This will cost between $2,500 and $8,000 or more, but if the attorney is good, you'll have a good patent that legitimate outfits will have difficulty getting around.

4 You can write much of the patent yourself. Go to a store and find a similar product that is patented. You'll find a patent number on the package. For a $1.50, you can get a copy of the patent from the U.S. Patent Office in Washington, D.C., or print the patent directly from the Patent Office's Web site (listed above). Using this as a guide, you can write a similar patent for your invention. Take that to your attorney and tell him or her to make it legal and as broad as possible. That will give you the biggest bang for the buck.

Design Patents

Design Patents are primarily for manufacturers who want to protect new and ornamental designs on two- and three-dimensional objects. This might include anything from the design of a garment to the motif on a belt buckle, to the shape of a coffee mug. Fabric designs are often protected this way, too. Like copyrights, design patents are hard to police and just as expensive to defend in court. Unless you're a commercial manufacturer, they're probably not for you. To qualify, a design must be new or novel, original, ornamental, and inventive in character. These patents can be obtained for different terms of years, depending on the fee paid.

Working with a Manufacturer

Are you trying to sell a product to a company who will manufacture and market a product for you in return for a royalty fee, or are you just looking for a company who will manufacture the product for you to patent and market yourself? Either way, make sure you get competent legal advice as the financial risks are high either way. Never submit any product idea to a manufacturer until you have a signed nondisclosure agreement (NDA) from them (preferably your own agreement since a manufacturer's NDA is likely to favor their interests instead of yours). Also, when entering any kind of manufacturing agreement, ask your attorney to build clauses into the contract to ensure that you get your goods on schedule.

Getting a Product on the Market. After reading Woodie Hall's book, *Your Ideas May Be Worth a Fortune*, lifelong entrepreneur Yvonne Conway, owner of My Line (mobile beauty services), decided to let someone else go through the patent process and do the manufacturing and marketing of a specially- designed, inflatable shampoo tray she invented for use in giving shampoos and permanents to people who were bedridden. But it took seven years to get the product on the market, and her royalties (10 percent of retail—a little over a dollar per unit sold) didn't begin to pick up until four years after the product was on the market. To give you an idea of how long this kind of process takes, here is a brief history of Yvonne's experience.

August, 1991:	Yvonne receives a favorable response from the Maddak Company. ("I learned it took months for my idea to creep from one desk to another, including their patent attorneys.")
February, 1992:	Yvonne is told that her tray has passed the four required steps, but cannot be manufactured for at least four years because the company has just replaced new dies for their existing product.
December, 1994:	Yvonne's idea is officially accepted for manufacture.
April, 1995:	She signs the royalty agreement.
June, 1996:	She receives notice the product is being manufactured.
August, 1996:	Yvonne signs the patent over to Maddak.
January, 1997:	Her shampoo tray is placed *not* in the company's catalog but only on an insert sheet. ("I was very disappointed and let them know it.")
April, 1998:	Maddak's lawyers file a U.S. Patent Application for the tray.
January, 1999:	The product finally shows up in the regular catalog, generating a royalty check a year later in the amount of $384.00.

"The first check I received after all those years of waiting was for only $17.64," says Yvonne. "I promptly framed it and hung it on the wall even though my husband wanted me to hang a copy and cash the real thing. Since 1999, my royalty checks have been averaging about $300 twice a year. I'm pleased and hopeful of better sales in the future."

Slogans

(See also *Trademarks*)

A slogan is a word or phrase used to express a characteristic position, stand, or goal of endeavor (refer back to Chapter 4 for slogan examples and how to use them as an advertising or marketing tool). If a slogan can pass the originality test required by the copyright law, and it is not intended to be used as a trademark, it may be possible to protect it via copyright. For more information on this topic, check attorney Ivan Hoffman's Web site, specifically his page, **www.IvanHoffman.com/slogans.html**.

Slogans may be trademarked if they meet the Patent & Trademark Office's strict requirements for same, says Hoffman. To qualify for trademark status, a slogan must be used as a source identifier. It cannot be merely informational. That is, upon hearing the slogan, buyers must relate it to the particular product or service being advertised.

Small Claims Court

Small claims courts are designed to resolve small monetary disputes, and many small business owners have had success in collecting money owed to them by individuals or companies who have passed bad checks or refused to pay an invoice. Generally speaking, small claims court procedures are simple, inexpensive, quick, informal, and effective. Or, as one of my readers put it, "It's cheap, quite direct, and painless." Each state has a statute of limitation (usually at least one year) that limits the time you can wait to sue after an event occurs. The amount of the dispute and the maximum amount that can be claimed varies from state to state, but in some states, you can sue for $5,000 or more. Small claims court offices are listed in your local telephone book under municipal, county, or state government headings.

If you decide to sue, first check to see whether you can sue the defendant in your state; that is, do your state courts have jurisdiction over the defendant? If the defendant does not reside in your state or do business there, you might have to sue in the defendant's home state, which might require assistance from an attorney and be more trouble than the bad check or unpaid invoice is worth. Also find out if you can file a claim by mail, or whether you must appear in person to present your case.

Sometimes the mere threat of a suit in small claims court will convince a person to pay up; others may hold out until a judgment has been entered against them and finally pay when they learn that the sheriff can walk into the place of business, make a list of property advertised for sale, and sell enough of it at auction to pay their debt. Many losers do ignore a judgment altogether, however; in fact, one source I found said that in 79 percent of the cases, the winner of a judgment never sees a dime. Of course there are legal methods you can use to collect a judgment, such as garnishing wages (if you can find the individual's employer), seizing money from a bank account (if you can trace his/her bank assets), or filing a lien against real estate the individual may own. But gathering all this information is difficult for the average person to do and knowing what to do with it once it is in hand is the next big challenge. Remember that the court does not require a loser to pay you, nor will it help you collect any judgment you may be awarded.

After winning a case in small claims court but being unable to collect payment, writer and business coach Sherry Huff Carnahan began to ask for and make a copy of a client's driver's license and social security number, as well as making copies of clients' checks (for their bank account information) before she would extend credit. "Taking steps like this doesn't guarantee you'll get your money if you win in small claims court," she says, "but having this information will help you garnish wages, file credit reports, and more. If you do go this route, be prepared to spend *a lot* of time preparing for court, sitting in court, and trying to get your money."

(*Note:* You can *ask* for a person's social security number, but I personally would *never* give my number to anyone unless they had a legal need for it. Of course, if the government ultimately has its way and forces states to put our social security number on our driver's license, my point is moot, and we'll all be more at risk than ever for identify theft.)

For more information on this collection method, see the book, *Everybody's Guide to Small Claims Court* by Ralph Warner (Nolo Press).

Small Claims Court Doesn't Work for Everyone. "As a freelance writer, I had an experience with Small Claims Court," writes Martha Oskvig. "A newspaper's check to me bounced twice, so I went to the office in person to seek cash. I received some of the total due that day by walking to the bank with the owner. However, the promised remainder never arrived, so I filed with the county's small claims court to get my due. It was the first time I'd ever done such a thing. I later decided that my filing with small claims court was a mistake: it cost me money to file, the court ruled in my favor (no newspaper representative came to the hearing), the sheriff's department didn't get any funds for me after two attempts, and I was simply placed on a list with several larger creditors when the newspaper owner later filed bankruptcy. When the same newspaper owner started a successful new venture after several years, I wasn't in a position to work with him. Since anyone can misjudge their business projections and expenses, I now wouldn't file with the court system. Instead I'd attempt to arrange a private installment plan (even a few dollars per week) just to encourage my debtor and maintain a relationship."

Tags and Labels Required by Law

If you make and sell any of the handcrafted products named below, you are required by law to affix certain labels or hang tags to them even if they are one-of-a-kind creations sold at retail. This topic is discussed at greater length in *HOMEMADE MONEY: Starting Smart!* but you can easily obtain the same information by calling the FTC or checking the Web sites indicated below. Craft sellers may also wish to refer to the author's book, *The Crafts Business Answer Book & Resource Guide* (M. Evans) for additional insight and information on this topic plus a variety of other laws and regulations related to the sale of craft products.

- *The Textile Fiber Products Identification Act*, monitored by both the Bureau of Consumer Protection (**www.FTC.gov/ftc/consumer.htm**) and the FTC (1-877-FTC-HELP; **www.FTC.gov**), requires a label or hang tag on all textile wearing apparel and household furnishings that includes the name of the manufacturer and the generic names and percentages of all fibers in the product in amounts of 5 percent or more. *Examples:* "100 percent combed cotton" or "92 percent cotton, 8 percent other fibers." ("Textiles" include all fibers, yarns, and fabrics; "textile household furnishings" would include such items as quilts, pillows, placemats, stuffed toys, and rugs.)

- *The Wool Products Labeling Act* (regulated by the FTC) requires that all wool or textile products bear a label that clearly indicates where the product has been made, and when imported ingredients are used. *Examples:* "Made in the USA," or "Made in the USA from imported products."

- *The Fur Products Labeling Act* (regulated by the FTC) requires the addition of a very specifically worded and sized label to wearing apparel that contains any kind of fur.

- *The Fabric Care Labeling Rule* (regulated by the FTC) requires a permanently affixed care label on all textile wearing apparel and household furnishings that indicates exactly how an item is to be cared for. *Examples:* "Wash in warm water; use cool iron" or "Dry clean only."

Terms of Sale

Establishing firm guidelines on how payment must be made before you sell your products or services will help you avoid collection problems later on. Include your "terms of sale" on your printed materials (order forms, brochure, Web site, etc.). If you plan to invoice all customers, give them a choice of "Net 10 days," "Net 30 days," or "2%/10/30" (which is the same as "2% 10 days, net 30"). Either of the latter two terms indicates to a buyer that you will give a 2 percent discount if payment is made within ten days, and full payment is expected within thirty days.

Offering customers a choice of payment options may be the smartest move you can make since many will elect to pay up front. *Example:* Gift wholesaler Dodie Eisenhauer, VillageDesigns.com offers her customers four payment options: (1) Net 30 days (with three credit references), (2) prepayment by check, (3) COD (extra cost is passed on to customer), and (4) credit card.

Writer/speaker/coach Sherry Huff Carnahan (SherryCarnahan.com) never hands over finished work without payment by credit card. For new clients, she asks for a nonrefundable deposit at the time a client signs a contract. "It's good toward so many hours of work and establishes them as a retainer client," she says.

Toll-Free Numbers

The total number of 800 numbers was 9,999,999. Although the supply of new numbers ran out some time ago, old 800 numbers are still available. But it could be a mistake to take one of them because when you do, you automatically assume the liability for calls coming into the old 800 number. Old vanity numbers (777-DIET) are even more likely to keep generating calls after the number has been assigned to someone else.

You may have wondered about the difference in getting an 800 number through AT&T or one of the other major service providers, as opposed to working with an independent provider. The primary difference is that when you use an independent voice mail service, *the phone rings at their end, not yours, and many calls can be handled at one time.* When you get an 800 number installed directly to your office, however, you get all the noise of the phone ringing and have to answer it yourself. Putting your 800 line in your basement on an answering machine is not a good solution if you expect to draw many calls, since only one call can get through at a time. What happens when you get a surge of publicity or response to an ad that brings in dozens of calls in a matter of days? Not only will these calls tie up your phone, but callers will get a constant busy signal (just as you have so many times when you've dialed an 800 number). The result? *Lost business.* With voice mail, however, many calls can be answered simultaneously.

Trademarks

(See also *Intellectual Property, Protection of; Slogans*)

The best way to protect your business name on the national level is to design a logo that incorporates both your business name and a related graphic. This will prevent another business or company from trading on your good name and reputation.

To establish a trademark, first decide which mark you want to use, then do some research to be reasonably sure no one else is using that mark. You can do a preliminary search on the Web at **http://tess.USPTO.gov** to see if the name you've chosen has been trademarked. This is no guarantee that the name is clear, but it's a good starting place. In large city libraries, also look for the annual *Trademark Register of the United States*, which includes all registered trademarks in use. An attorney can also order a trademark search for you at reasonable cost. And this is a wise thing to do now because of the thousands upon thousands of new trademarks that have been—and are still being—generated for use on the Web. A simple word you believe to be common or generic may now be claimed by another. (Under *Intellectual Property*, Protection of, see discussion about recent court battles over the use of the word "entrepreneur.")

To prevent others from using the mark you've selected on the same or related goods, you must file an application for trademark with the Patent and Trademark Office in Washington. (Get more information about this online at **www.USPTO.gov** or by calling 1-800-786-9199.) *Note that you cannot register a trademark until you've used the mark in interstate or foreign commerce.* One way to do this is to place a display ad in a national magazine or include it on direct mail materials that result in out-of-state orders (which constitutes "interstate sales" and thus "use in commerce"). Sales and promotions from the United States. to Canada, Mexico, or any other foreign country also qualify as "use in commerce."

Note: Foreign commerce of the United States—for example, with Canada and/or Mexico—has become important since NAFTA, even for home businesses. Also note that "interstate commerce" is involved if one shows goods or advertises services in a region where there is a lot of interstate or cross-border traffic, even when sales don't reflect this.

Use of Trademark Symbol. Inexperienced businesspeople sometimes believe they have legal protection for their designs, logos, and other creative works when in fact they don't. For example, when one business owner asked me to refer her to a lawyer who could help her defend her mark after someone stole it, I learned that, although she had placed the trademark sign (®—an *R* in a circle) on the logo she was using for her business, she hadn't actually registered the trademark because she didn't have the money for it. She was heartbroken when I told her she had lost the name as a result because the company that was now using it *had* trade-marked it.

"But I've been using this business name for ten years," she moaned. "Doesn't that give me the common-law trademark protection you spoke about in your *Homemade Money* book?" I said only an attorney could answer that question, but in my opinion, the answer was no. Once someone trademarks your good business name and logo design, you won't have much (if any) legal power to get it back.

After reading this story, Mary Helen Sears commented, "Using the trade-mark sign as this woman did was a false representation that jeopardized the validity of her use of the mark. Had she *not* done this, she could have obtained cancellation of the other party's mark if she could *prove* that she had used the mark first." (See below for a discussion of how one can build up common law trademark rights.)

 **Smart Tip**

You may not legally use the trademark symbol ® until your trademark registration has been confirmed. You can, however, apply a superscripted ™ to any mark you wish to protect. (Use ℠ if you sell a service instead of a product.) Although this gives you no legal protection and does not obligate you to file a formal trademark application, it does give notice to others that you've claimed the mark, and it may discourage its use by others as well.

Common Law Trademarks. Your constant use of an unregistered mark gains trademark status through the years. I had an interesting trademark case a few years back when someone stole my *Homemade Money* book title and applied it to a sleazy MLM (multi-level-marketing) magazine. The publisher hadn't yet applied for a trademark, so my attorney, Mary Helen Sears, was able to stop him from using this name. Because it has been so closely identified with my name since 1984, she was able to prove that my personal reputation would have been damaged if someone had seen this name on their magazine. Ms. Sears sent a powerfully worded series of letters that convinced the publisher he had to stop using my book's title—or else.

As Ms. Sears explained, "Because it is strongly associated with Barbara Brabec in the minds of persons engaged in, or interested in engaging in, home-based business enterprises, the term 'Homemade Money' has acquired a secondary meaning, not only as the identification of a book that has the reputation of being the handbook and primer in how to start, maintain and conduct a home-based business, but as the trademark and service mark for educational materials relating to home-based business, and for educational and informational activity of all types in regard to such business." Thus, anyone using this phrase for their own profit would be in direct violation of trademark law 15 U.S.C. 1125(a), and I could take appropriate legal action against them.

Trade References

(See also *Credit Bureaus*)

Always ask for credit references when you're opening an account for one of your customers. Get two trade references (other businesses your customer deals with on credit) plus the name of a bank. Also make sure you have the owner's name, phone, fax, and e-mail address in file. Some unpaid accounts go uncollected simply because the owner can't be tracked down.

You will be asked to provide similar references whenever you open supplier accounts, and having good credit with your suppliers can be one of the smartest business moves you'll ever make. For example, if you can get net 30 day terms from your printer, it means you can order printing, get it in the mail, and start bringing in business before you ever have to pay the printing bill. If you are an especially good customer, a supplier might agree to wait up to 90 days for payment if it means that such terms would guarantee a large order from you.

Web Site Design Codes

Many types of code are used to design a Web site, including HTML (Hypertext Markup Language), JavaScript, CGI (Common Gateway Interface) scripts, Cascading Style Sheets, and others, I'm sure, that I don't know about. Web site developers commonly steal design ideas from other Web sites, and you can do this, too, provided you know the difference between what's legal to do and what's outright theft of someone else's creativity. (The Copyright Law prohibits the use of someone else's Web content, graphics, photos, etc. without their express written permission.)

While you're making an effort to learn HTML (use your browser to search for free "HTML tutorials" on the Web), you can also learn design tricks by studying other Web sites. Once you can read the code on a Web site, you will be able to find and grab HTML codes, JavaScript, or CGI scripts for your own use. Unless a site has locked their code to prevent copying, you can right-click on any Web page to bring up a menu that enables you to "View Source Code" on that page. And this code is what you can legally "lift" for use on your own Web site, *provided you change all text, links, and graphics.*

While it would show a great lack of creativity to steal *all* the design elements of any one Web site, it can be very helpful to lift small pieces of code when you're trying to get a certain effect on your own site.

Zoning

Many homebased businesses are operating illegally as far as zoning laws are concerned. If you're just getting started in business and need more information on common zoning law restrictions and how other home-business owners are dealing with them, see *Homemade Money: Starting Smart!* You'll also find a great collection of zoning articles at **www.Entrepreneur.com** by typing "zoning" in the site's search engine.

If outdated zoning laws are restricting the growth of your business, you might want to organize a group of homebased business owners in your community and try to get them changed. Start now to build a list of all known homebased business owners who can give support or testimony when the time is right. In some areas, groups of home-business owners have formed networking groups or official organizations, done all the work involved in writing proposed zoning amendments, and then presented this information to city officials for consideration. After further discussion, sometimes in a town meeting, such efforts have resulted in changes in the law.

If, in the end, you choose to operate illegally until things change, you do need to plan on the possibility that you might someday be caught and forced to cease business operations. Although there have been exceptions, people are rarely fined for zoning violations unless they persist in the operation of a business after they've been warned to stop.

Zoning

A Group Effort May Bring Results. When her town tried to outlaw home-based businesses on a technicality in the law, a reader in Andover, Massachusetts, sent this report: "Several local homebased people, including myself, met with the building inspector and the Board of Selectmen. We reached this unofficial agreement: so long as the business did not disrupt the *general* residential area (one neighbor's complaint might be ignored), the business would be allowed to continue. Current law is vague in some areas and quite specific in others, so it was agreed that if a specific area of the law was violated, then the business would be asked to 'cease and desist' that particular part of the law."

What to Do If You Get Caught

"When you find your homebased business is in violation, you have one of three options," says Christopher L. Hansen, in an article on Entrepreneur.com. "You can shut down, go undercover, or attempt to have the law changed. If you are challenged, you can:

- Deny it. Require that they get a search warrant and proceed with legal action. They'll either back off, or a very expensive lawsuit—which you'll likely lose—will ensue.

- Admit it. Cease operation until you can obtain a variance. But be aware, variances are costly and seldom given.

- Bring media attention to your plight. Since the media love stories on the government abuse of average citizens, you might just wiggle your way out of it.

"Note that if you do challenge a zoning ruling, you may still have to pay a fee for the board to even consider your request, regardless of the outcome. Check with your state and local zoning officer.

Notice

This book, addressed to established business owners, does not include the basic home-business start-up information some readers may need. If you're just getting started in business, you may want to add *Homemade Money: Starting Smart!* to your reference bookshelf to get the important business management information contained in its A-to-Z section and resource chapter. (*Note:* Some of the A-to-Z headings below also appear in *Starting Smart*, but the information is different.)

Accountant

Accounting Methods

Attorney/Lawyer

Bonded Service

Business Checking Account

Business Expenses/Tax Deductions

Business Forms and Terms

Business Loans and Other Money Sources

Business or Trade Name

Checks and Money Orders

Consignment Laws

Consumer Safety Laws

Contracts

Copyrights

Credit/Credit Cards

Environmental Protection Laws

Federal Trade Commission

Government Agencies

Hobby Business

Insurance

Invoicing Terms

Legal Forms of Business

Licenses and Permits

Mail Order Laws

Merchant Account Providers

Occupational and Health Hazards

Post Office Box Address

Resale Tax Number

Scams and Frauds

State Bedding Laws

State Laws

Taxes Businesses Must Pay

Telephone

Trademarks

Trade Secret

United Parcel Service

Zoning Laws

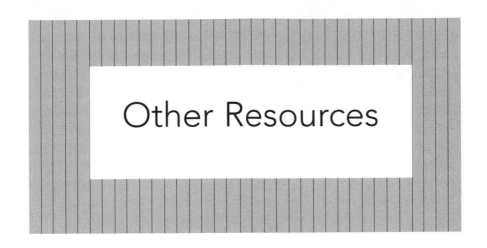

Other Resources

Only resources deemed useful to established business owners are included in this section. Check the index to locate additional resources mentioned in the text that are not repeated here. If mail addresses are required, telephone for same, or check the Web site. If you need recommendations for resources related to home-business startup, general management, planning, tax and legal issues, see the resource chapter of *HOMEMADE MONEY: Starting Smart!* this book's companion guide for home-business beginners.

Table of Contents

Recommended Books

The books listed below are merely a representative sampling, most of them by authors in my network. For a complete guide to all books in print, as well as those about to be published, check your library for *Books In Print* and *Guide to Forthcoming Books* (R. R. Bowker), or browse online bookstores for titles in a specific category.

Business Management
The Crafts Business Answer Book and Resource Guide by Barbara Brabec (M. Evans)

Home Office Know-How by Jeffrey D. Zbar (Upstart)

Home Office Life: Making a Space to Work at Home by Lisa Kanarek (Rockport)

Inc Yourself—How to Profit by Setting Up Your Own Corporation, 9th ed., by Judith H. McQuown
  (Bantam)

Make It Profitable—How to Make Your Art, Craft, Design, Writing, or Publishing Business More Efficient, More Satisfying, and More Profitable by Barbara Brabec (M. Evans)

Net Strategy: Charting the Digital Course for Your Company's Growth by Rob Spiegel (Dearborn)

101 Home Office Secrets by Lisa Kanarck (Career Press)

Organizing Your Home Business by Lisa Kanarek (Made E-Z)

Working Solo–The Real Guide to Freedom and Financial Success With Your Own Business by Terrie Lonier (John Wiley & Sons)

Business Diversification
The Complete Guide to Self Publishing—Everything You Need to Know to Write, Publish, Promote, and Sell Your Own Book, 4th ed., by Marilyn and Tom Ross (F&W Pub.).

How to Get Happily Published, 5th ed., by Judith Appelbaum (HarperPerennial)

How to Make at Least $100,000 Every Year As a Successful Consultant in Your Own Field, by Jeffrey Lant (Jeffrey Lant Associates)

Money Talks: The Complete Guide to Creating a Profitable Workshop or Seminar in Any Field by Jeffrey Lant (Jeffrey Lant Associates)

Homemade Money

Profitable Email Publishing: How to Publish a Profitable Emag by Angela Adair-Hoy, an eBook available from **www.WritersWeekly.com**

Publishing Newsletters—A Complete Guide to Markets, Editorial Content, Subscriptions, Management, Design and Ancillary Products, 3rd ed., by Howard Penn Hudson (Newsletter Clearinghouse)

The Self-Publishing Manual—How to Write, Print and Sell Your Own Book, 13 ed., by Dan Poynter, (Para Publishing)

Speak and Grow Rich by Lily Walters (Prentice Hall)

Teach Yourself Grammar and Style in 24 Hours by Dennis Hensley (Macmillan)

Your Guide to EBook Publishing Success by James Dillehay, an eBook available from **www.00ebooks.com**

Marketing and Publicity

The Basic Guide to Selling Crafts on the Internet by James Dillehay (Warm Snow Publishers)

The Complete Idiot's Guide to Direct Marketing by Bob Bly (Agora Pub.)

Creative Cash—How to Profit from your Special Artistry, Creativity, Hand Skills, and Related Know-How, 6th ed. by Barbara Brabec (Prima Pub.)

EVEolution: The Eight Truths of Marketing to Women by Faith Popcorn (Hyperion)

Getting Business to Come to You: A Complete Do-It-Yourself Guide to Attracting All the Business You Can Enjoy by Paul and Sarah Edwards, 2nd ed., (J. P. Tarcher)

Getting Everything You Can Out of All You've Got by Jay Abraham (St. Martin's)

Guerrilla Marketing–Secrets for Making Big Profits from Your Small Business by Jay Conrad Levinson (Mariner Books)

Guerrilla PR Wired: Waging A Successful Publicity Campaign On-Line, Offline, And Everywhere In Between by Michael Levine and George Gendron (McGraw-Hill)

Handmade for Profit!—Hundreds of Secrets to Success in Selling Arts & Crafts, 2nd ed., by Barbara Brabec (M. Evans)

How to Design Logos, Symbols & Icons by Gregory Thomas and Earl A. Powell (How Design Books)

How to Market a Product for Under $500 by Jeffrey Dobkin (Danielle Adams Pub. Co.)

Internet Marketing for Less Than $500 a Year by Marcia Yudkin (Independent Pub. Group)

Recommended Books

Licensing Art and Design by Caryn R. Leland (Allworth Press)

Make Your Web Site Work for You: How to Convert Your Online Content Into Profits by Jeff Cannon and Geoffrey Ramsey (McGraw-Hill)

Online Promotions: Winning Strategies and Tactics by Bill Carmody (John Wiley)

Poor Richard's Branding Yourself Online—How to Use the Internet to Become a Celebrity or Expert in Your Field by Bob Baker (Top Floor Pub.)

Poor Richard's Web Site Marketing Makeover by Marcia Yudkin (Top Floor Pub.).

Publicity on the Internet: Creating Successful Publicity Campaigns on the Internet and the Commercial Online Services by Steve O'Keefe (John Wiley & Sons)

Self-Promotion Online: Marketing Your Creative Services Using Web Sites, E-Mail and Digital Portfolios by Ilise Benun (North Light Books)

Shameless Marketing for Brazen Hussies by Marilyn Ross (Communication Creativity)

Six Steps to Free Publicity, 2nd ed., by Marcia Yudkin (Career Press)

Smart Services: Competitive Information Strategies, Solutions, and Success Stories for Service Businesses by Deborah C. Sawyer (CyberAge Books)

The Unabashed Self-Promoter's Guide, 2nd. ed., by Jeffrey Lant (Jeffrey Lant Associates)

Money and Taxes

422 Tax Deductions for Businesses and Self-Employed Individuals by Bernard Kamoroff (Bell Springs Pub.)

Money-Saving Tax Strategies for Homebased Entrepreneurs by Barbara Brabec, an eBook available from **www.BarbaraBrabec.com**

Online Operator: Business, Legal, and Tax Guide to the Internet by Bernard Kamoroff, CPA (Bell Springs Pub.)

The Small Business Money Guide: How to Get It, Use It, Keep It by Terri Lonier (John Wiley & Sons)

Small Time Operator—How to Start Your Own Business, Keep Your Books, Pay Your Taxes, and Stay Out of Trouble by Bernard Kamoroff, CPA. Revised annually. (Bell Springs Pub.)

Organizations

American Craft Council (ACC). Publishes *American Craft Magazine*.
Membership: 1-800-724-0859; ACC trade shows 1-800-836-3470;
www.CraftCouncil.org
Association of Business Support Services, Inc. (ABSSI). 1-714-695-9398;
www.abssi.org
Home Business Institute, Inc. 1-888-DIAL HBI; **www.HBIweb.com**
National Association for the Self-Employed (NASE). Publishes *Self-Employed
America*. 1-800-232-NASE; **www.NASE.org**
National Craft Association (NCA). 1-800-715-9594; **www.craftassoc.com**
National Mail Order Association. 1-612-788-1673; **www.NMOA.org**
Small Business Service Bureau. 1-800-222-5678; **www.SBSB.com**
Small Publishers Association of North America (SPAN). 1-719-395-4790;
www.SPANnet.org
Society of Craft Designers (SCD). 1-740-452-4541; **www.CraftDesigners.org**
Support Services Alliance. 1-800-322-3920; **www.SSAinfo.com**
Volunteer Lawyers for the Arts. 1-212-319-ARTS, ext. 1; **www.vlany.org**

Government Agencies

(Check your telephone book for local offices.)

Bureau of Consumer Protection, **www.FTC.gov/ftc/consumer.htm**
Census Bureau, **www.Census.gov**
Consumer Product Safety Commission, 1-800-638-2772; **www.CPSC.gov**
Cooperative Extension Service, **www.reeusda.gov**
The Copyright Office, 1-202-707-3000; **www.loc.gov/copyright**
Department of Commerce, **www.DOC.gov**
Department of the Interior, **www.FWS.gov**
Department of Labor, **www.DOL.gov**
Environmental Protection Agency, **www.EPA.gov**
Fish and Wildlife Service, **www.FWS.gov**
Federal Trade Commission, 1-877-FTC-HELP; **www.FTC.gov**
Food and Drug Administration,1-888-INFO-FDA; **www.FDA.gov**
Internal Revenue Service, 1-800-829-1040; **www.IRS.gov**
Patent & Trademark Office, 1-703-308-9000; **www.USPTO.gov**

Small Business Association (SBA), 1-800-827-5722; **www.SBA.gov**
Service Corps of Retired Executives (SCORE), 1-800-634-0245;
  www.SCORE.org
Social Security Administration, **www.SSA.gov**
United States Postal Service, **www.USPS.com**
  Postal Inspection Service, **www.USPS.gov/postalinspectors**
  Identity Theft, **www.consumer.gov/idtheft/index.html**

Media and Periodical Directories

(Available in Libraries)

Bacon's Directories (**www.Bacons.com**). *Bacon's Publicity Checker; Bacon's Newspaper-Magazine Directory* and *Bacon's Radio-TV-Cable Directory.*
Encyclopedia of Associations (Gale Research Co.).
Gale Directory of Publications and Broadcast Media (Gale Research Co.). Newspapers, magazines and periodicals in the United States and Canada.
Gebbie Directories (**www.GebbieInc.com**). Three directories list daily and weekly newspapers, radio and TV stations, and consumer and trade magazines.
Hudson's Subscription Newsletter Directory (**www.newsletter-clearinghse.com**; 1-800-572-3451). Lists about 5,000 subscription newsletters.
Literary Market Place (R. R. Bowker). Lists trade book publishers, wholesalers, and distributors; book reviewers and more.
Oxbridge Directory of Newsletters (Oxbridge Communications).
Radio-TV Interview Report (Bradley Communications; **www.RTIR.com**; 1-800-989-1400). Reaches over 4,000 radio/TV producers across the United States and Canada. Other publicity products available from this source include *Bradley's Guide to the Top National TV Talk & Interview Shows* and *Book Marketing Update.*
The Standard Periodical Directory (Oxbridge Communications). The largest annual guide to United States and Canadian periodicals of all types.
Thomas Register of American Manufacturers (**www.ThomasRegister**). A multivolume directory (searchable online) that lists company names, products manufactured, brand names, and trademarks.
Writer's Market (**www.WritersMarket.com**). An affordable and useful annual directory for compiling a PR list of selected magazines and syndicates.

Note: For information on other periodical directories not listed here, also check **www.MediaFinder.com**.

Business Periodicals & Other Marketing Resources

Book Publisher's Resources (**www.BookMarket.com**). Author John Kremer offers assistance to independent book publishers with reports on wholesalers, distributors, bookstores, catalogs.

The Crafts Report—The Business Journal for the Crafts Industry (**www.CraftsReport.com**; 1-800-777-7098).

Entrepreneur Magazine (**www.Entrepreneur.com**; 1-800-274-6229).

Gifts & Decorative Accessories Magazine and annual *Gifts & Decorative Accessory Buyer's Guide* (**www.Gifts&Dec.com**; 1-800-309-3332). Includes sources for manufacturing and assembling materials, show and shop display cases, listings of trade shows, and more.

Home Business Magazine (**www.HomeBusinessMagazine.com**; 1-714-968-0331).

National Directory of Catalogs (Oxbridge Communications). Describes products carried by over 4,000 U.S. and Canadian catalogs, with contact names and list rental data.

Small Press Record of Books in Print (**www.dustbooks.com**; 1-800-477-6110). List your self-published book here to be found by libraries, bookstores, and teachers.

Writer's Digest Market Directories (**www.WritersDigest.com**; 1-800-754-2912). Publishes several annual directories for writers, graphic designers, artists, photographers, and poets.

Show Listing Periodicals for Artists/Crafters

The ABC Art & Craft Event Directory. National show listings. 1-800-678-3566; **www.theABCDirectory.com**.

Art & Craft Show Yellow Pages. Listings for CT, MA, NJ, NY, PA, and VT. 1-888-918-1313; **www.CraftShowYellowPages.com**.

Arts & Crafts Show Business. Listings for FL, GA, NC, and SC. 1-904-757-

3913; **www.ArtsCraftsShowBusiness.com**.
Craftmaster News. West Coast shows. 1-562-869-5882;
   www.CraftMasternews.com.
The Crafts Fair Guide. West Coast shows. 1-800-871-2341.
Mid-Atlantic Craft Show List. Shows in PA, NJ, NY, MD, DE, and VA. 1-
   610-264-5325; **www.CraftShowList.com**
Midwest Art Fairs. Shows in MN, WI, IA, ND, and SD. 1-800-871-0813;
   www.MidwestArtFairs.com
SAC Newsmonthly. National show listings. 1-800-825-3722;
   www.SACnewsmonthly.com
The Ronay Guides. Three volumes list shows in GA, NC, SC, and VA. 1-800-
   337-8329; **www.Events2000.com.**

Selected Trade Shows

George Little Management. 1-800-272-SHOW; **www.GLMshows.com**.
The National Needlework Associaton (TNNA shows). 1-740-452-4541;
   www.offinger.com
Quilts Inc., International Quilt Market. 1-713-781-6864; **www.quilts.com**
Super Floral Show. 1-480-998-3992; **www.SuperFloralShow.com**
Toy Industry Association (American International Toy Fair). 1-212-675-
   1141; **www.Toy-TIA.org**

Recommended Web Sites

In addition to the many Web sites listed in this book's text and included with
other listings above, the following sites are those the author has personally visited in connection with research for this and other books. A brief description of
content or a reason why you may want to investigate the site has been included
with some links if the site name alone is not self-explanatory. Web sites come and
go every day, so if some of the following links go bad, simply use your browser
and search for related keywords to turn up additional sites.

Affiliate and Drop Ship Programs

- www.AffiliateWinners.com

- www.AssociatePrograms.com

- www.CJ.com (Commission Junction)

- www.LifetimeCommissions.com

- www.MyDSSD.com (The Drop Ship Source Directory)

- www.ReferIt.com

Computer/Web Technology

- **www.BigNoseBird.com**. Over 300 pages of tutorials, reference materials, and other free resources located on this site—everything you need to built a great Web site, including HTML tricks, free graphics, scripts, software tools, and more.

- **www.Boogiejack.com**. Author Dennis Gaskill (*Web Design Made Easy*) has a wealth of how-to information and articles on his site.

- **www.CNET.com**. When looking for free/inexpensive software to do a particular job, visit this link to find specific programs you can download. (To turn up other free programs on the Web, type "free computer software" in your browser's search box.)

- **www.Doctor-HTML.com**. This is a remarkable tool. Enter any URL and you'll get an immediate report on all the HTML errors on that page.

- **www.e-Comprofits.com**. This "Online Marketing Center" includes articles, tutorials, Webmaster resources, merchant accounts, marketing software, affiliate marketing resources, and more.

Recommended Web Sites

- **www.HTMLgoodies.com**. Free stuff to help you design a Web site; HTML tutorials, style sheets, image maps, Java Scripting, CGI scripts, and more.

- **www.HTMLhelp.org**. The Web Design Group offers a valuable reference site on HTML-related topics. Web site authoring tools, HTML- validator, HTML FAQs, and more.

- **www.Ibiz-Tools.com**. A collection of business management, Web site, and promotional tools for small and big business alike designed by Michael R. Harvey. Some programs are free, including a site statistics package and site-mapper software that allows you to list all links in your Web site so you can find the broken ones.

- **www.ShortCourses.com**. Information and articles on buying and using digital cameras.

- **www.SmallBizCommunity.com**. Promote your Web business here and check the collection of marketing/PR articles, Web design links, biz tools, and Susan Scheid's inexpensive Web site design services.

- **www.SmallBizTechtalk.com/index.html**. Computer technical info and support.

- **www.Steve.Maurer.net**. Free online e-mail and software tutorials, computer tips, ezine, and *Email Primer*, a free eBook you can download in your choice of formats.

- **www.WebMonkey.com**. Excellent Web developer's resource, with a library of how-to articles, a JavaScript library, "HTML Cheatsheet," color codes, and much more.

- **www.WorldProfit.com**. Web site hosting, custom design services, and traffic generation tools.

Ezine Directories

- www.eMailResults.com

- www.eZineAdAuction.com

- www.Ezinehub.com

- www.Ezine-Universe.com

- www.EzineUniversity.com

General Home Business

- **www.BarbaraBrabec.com**. Barbara Brabec's World features details of all her books with a table of contents, reviews, and reader feedback for each title, plus a variety of articles on homebased business, "Computertalk," writing and publishing. Previously published issues of *The Brabec Bulletin*, the author's free e-mail newsletter, are also archived here.

- **www.Entrepreneur.com**. Site includes a large archive of articles on all business topics, plus several free ezines.

- **www.HBWM.com** (Home-Based Working Moms). Founded by Lesley Spencer. Offers support, networking, information, PR and work opportunities, a monthly print newsletter, and a weekly ezine.

- **www.HomeOfficeLife**. Lisa Kanarek's site offers a collection of home office organizational tips, Q&A pages, and online seminars.

- **www.PatKatz.com**. Offers a collection of articles on time management, encouragement, motivation, and more.

- **www.VirtualAssistantsNetwork.com**. Founded by Sherry Huff Carnahan. Motivational support and resources for VAs, free e-mail newsletters, and a networking forum.

Recommended Web Sites

Industry Research and Business Trends

- **www.Bizjournals.com**. From this site, you can track what is going on in your business in your neck of the woods. As a registered user, you would have access to a searchable archive of a half-million local business articles from across the nation, the ability to set up your own personalized Industry Journal (with over 45 industries to choose from), and access to industry-specific updates by email. You can also track your customers, prospects, and competitors and receive an e-mail whenever they are mentioned in an article.

- **www.BrainReserve.com**. The Web site of trendmaster Faith Popcorn includes a collection of fascinating articles on current trends relative to business and marketing.

- **www.Business.com**. A directory of business industries, with dozens of subindustries, all linking to articles and related Web sites. (A good place to research an industry you're trying to break in to.)

- **www.FutureSpeak.com**. Check the archives for trend forecasts contributed by a number of experts.

- **www.HermanGroup.com**. Strategic business futurists Roger Herman and Joyce Gioia issue an e-mail "Trend Alert" every week and their site includes a collection of their articles.

- **www.JoannePratt.com**. This site contains several reports by Joanne Pratt of interest to home-business researchers that can be downloaded free of charge in PDF format.

Legal Resources

- **www.ContingentLaw.com**. Independent Contractor Law On Line.

- **www.FreeAdvice.com**. You'll find answers to many of your legal questions here, including information about your state's laws, business law questions, and answers to questions about the use of employees and independent contractors.

- **www.IvanHoffman.com**. The Web site of attorney Ivan Hoffman contains many articles related to law for writers and publishers, entrepreneurs, Web site designers and owners, trademarks and domain names, Internet and electronic rights.

- **www.LawGuru.com.** A network of over 2,000 attorneys and law firms in over 35 countries. Various attorneys answer questions online free of charge, and the Web site's database now includes answers to 35,000 FAQs in 45 legal categories.

Marketing and Publicity

- **www.BrandingYourselfOnline**. Author Bob Baker offers an ezine and free online e-mail workshop.

- **www.Caruba.com**. Site features an archive of articles by Alan Caruba on how to get publicity.

- **www.Dobkin.com**. Good collection of marketing articles by author Jeffrey Dobkin.

- **www.eBookBroadcast.com**. Press releases on new eBooks will be posted on this site (eventually) without charge; $19.95 buys "priority service" and faster posting.

- **www.eReleases.com**. A press release submission service.

- **www.GaryNorth.com**. Site contains good collection of articles on how to market with autoresponders.

- **www.GivetoGetMarketing.com**. Web site of Joe and Maria Gracia. Free marketing tutorial articles, articles on Internet marketing, case studies, resources, free *Give to Get Marketing* newsletter and Marketing Idea-Kit.

- **www.iMediaFax.com**. Send your release to this site, and they will fax it to appropriate media for $.25 a page.

Recommended Web Sites

- **www.InternetNewsBureau.com.** Offers press release writing/editing/delivery services, and journalists may sign up here to get news releases on topics of interest or e-mail newsletters of latest releases.

- **www.iSquare.com**. Web site of Robert Sullivan, author, small business and e-commerce expert. General business advice for small business owners, tax advice, info on how to sell to the government, FAQs, source for mailing list of Small Business Development Centers, and free SmallBiz newsletter.

- **www.MarketingTips.com**. This site is jam-packed with the information you need to start, build, and grow your Internet business.

- **www.SendFree.com**. Information about free autoresponder service.

- **www.Yudkin.com**. The Net's best collection of fresh, effective strategies for attracting clients and customers.

- **www.WebProNews.com/archive.html**. Dozens of links to e-commerce articles and free business and marketing newsletters.

- **www.WilsonWeb.com**. The Web's largest source of key information about doing business on the Net, with hundreds of articles and thousands of links to resources on e-commerce and Web marketing. This site also offers three free e-mail newsletters on Web marketing, eBiz, and eCommerce.

- **www.WorldProfit.com/ezines**. Worldprofit's free newsletters include the daily "Marketing Hot Tips" newsletter and several weekly newsletters containing marketing and business development information.

Marketing Resources for Art/Craft Businesses

- **www.ColorMarketing.org**. The Web site of the Color Marketing Organization. Click "Press Releases" to read about the latest color and design trends.

- **www.CraftAssoc.com**. Maintained by the National Craft Association, this site is a primary information and resource center for the professional crafter, offering insurance programs, merchant card/Web site design/hosting services, Internet business tools, links to craft and trade show information and wholesale suppliers, an e-mail discussion list, a newsletter, and more.

- **www.Craftmarketer.com**. This site features the books of crafts author James Dillehay and includes many valuable business resources, articles, and links. A special "Toolbox" department also lists free software programs and business aids James has personally checked out.

- **www.CraftsReport.com**. Check this site's archives of crafts business articles from back issues of the magazine, and use the search engine on the site to turn up several articles by Barbara Brabec.

- **www.Procrafter.com**. This site contains business articles, crafting tips, and a bulletin board for professional crafters.

- **www.WWAR.com**. At the World Wide Arts Resources site, artists without a Web site can set up an online portfolio here for just $36 a year. A "Premier" portfolio is available for $75/year and a one-time jury fee. No commissions are taken on sales made through the site.

Web Site Designers

The following individuals can be trusted to do a good job in designing a Web site for you at a reasonable price. Or, if you are trying to do your own Web site and merely need some extra technical assistance or guidance with this job, one of these professionals can help you. Explain your needs by e-mail and ask for a quote, mentioning Barbara's name in your message.

- John Dilbeck, Dilbeck Consulting, www.JohnDilbeck.com. This expert programmer offers computer consulting and Web site development services. Art/craft sites a specialty.

Recommended Web Sites

- Chris Maher, **www.ArtWebWorks.com**. Chris and his partner, Larry Berman, offer expert Web site design services.

- Susan Scheid, **www.SmallBizCommunity.com**. Offers professional Web development specifically designed for home businesses on a limited budget.

- Richard Tuttle, **www.CalliDesign.com**. Designs personal, business, and educational sites, specializing in artist sites.

Writing, Publishing, and Speaking

- **www.BarbaraBrabec.com**. The author's Web site includes articles on her experiences in writing and publishing.

- **www.Freelancewrite.about.com**. Includes links to hundreds of other sites of interest to writers.

- **www.HappilyPublished.com**. Web site of Judith Applebaum, author of *How to Get Happily Published*. Contains a wealth of articles on this topic.

- **www.ParaPublishing.com**. The Web site of publishing guru, Dan Poynter. Includes hundreds of pages of information and free documents on self-publishing, with links to many self-publishing resources.

- **www.VoicePower.com**. June Johnson's site contains a collection of articles and guidelines to help you develop a winning voice.

- **www.Walters-Intl.com**. Dottie Walters's site will connect you to valuable resources for professional speakers, including the newsletter *Sharing Ideas*—the largest newsmagazine in the world for professional speakers, meeting planners, agents, bureaus, consultants, trainers, and seminar leaders.

- **www.WritersWeekly.com**. A wealth of info for freelance writers from Angela Hoy, with links to paying markets and an excellent collection of articles by Angela and other pros in her network. Free ezine.

● **www.WritersWrite.com**. A good one-stop resource for information about books, writing, and publishing.

Book Contributors

(Home Business Owners, Web Entrepreneurs, Authors, and Other Professionals)

Barbara Arena, **www.CraftAssoc.com**
Bob Baker, **www.BrandingYourselfOnline.com**
Robert Bly, **www.Bly.com**
Karen Booy, **www.KarenBooy.com**
Barbara Brabec, **www.BarbaraBrabec.com**
Jim Bradshaw, **www.JimBradshaw.net**
Pamela Burns, **www.Injeanious.org**
Sherry Huff Carnahan, **www.SherryCarnahan.com**
Alan Caruba, **www.Caruba.com**
Marc Choyt and Helen Chantler, **www.CelticJewelry.com**
Silvana Clark, **www.SilvanaClark.com**
Malcolm and Sandy Dell, **www.LewisClarkGifts.com**
Bunny DeLorie, **www.FeFiFauxFinish.com**
James Dillehay, **www.00ebooks.com**
Dodie Eisenhauer, **www.VillageDesigns.com**
Nina Feldman, **www.NinaFeldman.com**
Deanna Ferber, **www.eGlamKitty.com**
Terry Floyd, **www.ToymakersCollection.com**
Dennis Gaskill, **www.Boogiejack.com**
Myrna Giesbrecht, **www.Press4Success.com**
Joe and Maria Gracia, **GiveToGetMarketing.com**
Don and Emma Graham, **www.FasturnJunction.com**
Donna L. Gunter, **www.SohoBizSolutions.com**
Steve Harrison, **www.RTIR.com**
Tammy Harrison, **www.TheQueenofPizzazz.com**
Michael Harvey, **www.Ibiz-Tools.com**
Eileen Heifner, **www.CreateanHeirloom.com**
Robert Houghtaling, **www.Frogart.com**

Book Contributors

Richard Hoy, **www.WritersWeekly.com**
Pam Hunter, **www.CreativeOfficeService.com**
June Johnson, **www.VoicePowerOnline.com**
Bernard Kamoroff, **www.BellSprings.com**
Lisa Kanarek, **www.HomeOfficeLife.com**
Karl Kasca, **www.Kasca.com**
Patricia Katz, **www.PatKatz.com**
Kate Kelly, **www.KateKelly.com**
Terrie Kralik, **www.MooseCountryQuilts.com**
Sue Krei, **www.WoodCellarGraphics.com**
Patricia Kutza (e-mail only: **pkutza@pacbell.net**)
Phillipa Lack, www.PKLdesigns.com
Sylvia Landman, **www.Sylvias-Studio.com**
Annie Lang, **www.AnnieThingsPossible.com**
Jeffrey Lant, **www.WorldProfit.com**
Louise Louis, **www.ToyBreeds.com**
Chris Maher, **www.ArtWebWorks.com**
Maria Marsala, **www.CoachMaria.com**
Steve Maurer, **www.Steve.Maurer.net**
Gary Maxwell, **www.GaryMaxwell.com**
Mary Mulari, **www.MaryMulari.com**
Daryl Ochs, **www.StreetSmartBusiness.com**
Martha Oskvig, **www.Beautipage.com/here4u**
Leila Peltosaari, **www.TikkaBooks.com**
Cathryn Peters, **www.WickerWoman.com**
Joanne Pratt, **www.JoannePratt.com**
Diana Ratliff, **www.BusinessCardDesign.com**
Sharon Richwine, **www.JerryAnthonyPhoto.com**
Bill Ronay, **www.Events2000.com**
Susan Scheid, **www.SmallBizCommunity.com**
John Schulte, **www.NMOA.org**
Russ Schultz, **www.WriteandReap.com**
Tim Selberg, **www.SelbergStudios.com**
Karen Smith, **www.4MarketingHelp.com**
Donna M. Snow, **www.SnowWrite.com**
Debbie Spaulding, **www.PuppetPatterns.com**
Lesley Spencer, **www.HBWM.com**
Joan Stewart, **www.PublicityHound.com**

Homemade Money

Tom Stoyan, **www.CanadasSalesCoach.com**
Coleen Sykora, **www.WorkersonWheels.com**
Jim Turner, **www.YourProfitStation.com**
Richard Tuttle, **www.CalliDesign.com**
Dottie Walters, **www.Walters-Intl.com**
Karen White, **www.NaturalImpulse.com**
Michelle Winterhalter, **www.AtHome.com/Shelle**
Kaye Wood, **www.KayeWood.com**
Karen Wylie, **www.Soapshed.com**
Marcia Yudkin, **www.Yudkin.com**
Jeff Zbar, **www.ChiefHomeOfficer.com**

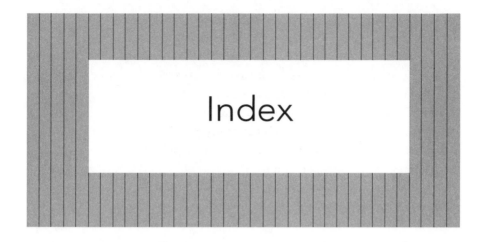

Index

Index

Index

Index

Index

Index

More great advice from Barbara and her readers!

If you're just getting started in a home business, be sure to read this book's companion guide for home-business beginners, *HOMEMADE MONEY: Starting Smart!*—the ultimate idea book and home-business generator for people who want to learn how to turn existing talents, experience, and know-how into a profitable business at home. Topics include:

- Home-business idea charts and checklists
- Business brainstorming ideas
- Business selection guidelines
- Warnings about scams, schemes, and unprofitable ideas
- Business name selection tips
- Outlines for business, financial, and marketing plans
- Pricing guidelines for business beginners
- Tips for learning and applying computer technology to your business
- Time and stress management techniques
- Blending business into your personal life
- Hundreds of print and online resources to help your business grow

Like this book, Starting Smart! also features a comprehensive A-to-Z "Crash Course" on topics related to business start-up and management, including:

- Laws and regulations affecting new businesses
- Licenses and permits
- Tips on accounting and taxes
- Money management tips and banking
- Business forms and terms
- Business loans and other money sources
- Insurance needed by home-business owners
- Legal forms of business
- Copyright and trademark basics
- Getting merchant status for your business

. . . and much more!

Published by M. Evans and Company, Inc.
Available in bookstores everywhere, as well as on the Internet.